TITANIC
SCANDAL

Captain Henry James Moore of the *Mount Temple*.

TITANIC
SCANDAL

THE TRIAL OF THE *MOUNT TEMPLE*

SENAN MOLONY

AMBERLEY

*To W.H. Baker and all the brave
who attempt to save life at sea*

By the same author:
The Irish Aboard *Titanic*
Lusitania: An Irish Tragedy
Titanic and the Mystery Ship
The Phoenix Park Murders
Titanic: Victims and Villains

THE AUTHOR

Senan Molony is Deputy Political Editor of the *Irish Independent*, the largest-selling daily newspaper in Ireland. Born in 1963, he has over twenty-five years' experience in journalism. An uncle was a Merchant Marine Captain in the Second World War whose vessels were twice sunk by enemy action. Another uncle became Flag Officer of the Irish Naval Service. Mr Molony lives in Dublin with wife Brigid and their beloved children Pippa, Millie and Mossie.

APPEAL

There is always the prospect of new information becoming available. In this case, the author would like to be apprised of it at sennbrig@indigo.ie, or in care of the publishers.

Cover painting of *Mount Temple* by Stuart Williamson (stuartw158@hotmail.co.uk)

First published 2009
Amberley Publishing
Cirencester Road, Chalford,
Stroud, Gloucestershire, GL6 8PE

www.amberley-books.com

British Library Cataloguing in Publication Data.
A catalogue record for this book is available from the British Library.

ISBN 978 1 84868 699 1

Typesetting and origination by FonthillMedia
Printed in Great Britain

Contents

PROLOGUE

ONE. 1am. The bowl of midnight is inverted, and all existence and everything that matters poured into this solitary hour. An elemental peace imbues the marrow-arrowing cold. An age has passed since silence nipped the banshee-shriek of steam blowing off.

The water waits the succumbing ship.

The pity is in the minds of men. Crowds of men, agitated, murmuring their funerary orisons, moving here and there. The creaking ropes pay out the drop while fear, raw as frost, escapes every mouth. Those stars that wish to watch, and listen, glisten.

Intermittent splashes. Individual hearts hurtling through space – flailing shadows flung up against the night, and down. Seeming desperate tokens from the huddled masses that shrink the threatening liquid. Still the numbing swell comes on.

Feverish activity bathes the centre of this perfect composition, as if the boundless backdrop were but glacial witness. And now the ship's orchestra saws and plucks – but full the while the boards must gradually melt beneath their feet, and all lights extinguish.

There is a light – a ruby tinge – within the horizon. The ember-warmth of a ship that came and sharply ceased to care, she lies there now, studiedly unsympathetic. More than that to the mordant hordes, she taunts their very word: *Titanic*.

> *Knowing by wireless the Titanic's predicament, the Officers were exceedingly anxious to go to her assistance, and their feeling against the Master of the ship because he would not do so <u>at once</u> was very strong …*

Letter from Charles P. Grylls, General Secretary of the Mercantile Marine Services Association, to the Marine Department of the British Board of Trade, August 27, 1912. (Document M25699 from file M9/920F).

From the Wireless Log (PV) compiled by the Marconi operator of the *Mount Temple* –

10.25pm New York Time – *Titanic* sending CQD ['Come Quickly, Danger' – forerunner of the SOS]. Says requires assistance. Gives position. Cannot hear me. Advise my Captain.

(Ten minutes go by …)

10.35. MGY (*Titanic*) says "Come to our assistance at once."

(Five more minutes go by …)

10.40. MGY still calling CQD.

10.40. Our Captain reverses ship.

It took Captain Moore of the *Mount Temple* a quarter of an hour to turn around from the time he was first told of the emergency, according to his own vessel's wireless log. Was his ship a reluctant rescuer from the beginning?

EXPOSITION

A plea of Not Guilty is entered on behalf of Captain James Henry Moore, Master of the *Mount Temple*, and hereby duly noted.

The indictment presented is an altogether more complex matter, because it is laid before the bar of History, which is inherently a most unusual jurisprudence. But first let it be said that, of course, there is no statute of limitations when it comes to mankind's self-conceived chronology of the unfolding ages. Such a thing would be absurd, especially when history itself might be compared to a limitless statute of all our tidings from one age to another.

Therefore a charge, or a challenge, even in the case of real events, may be brought at any time, even if all actual participants have long since passed away. The concept must be one of an ever-flexible narrative that does justice to our continually changing times, which not always change as they unfold forward, but backward as well, in the light of new discoveries.

The men and women who consciously contribute their minds to consideration of fresh questions, or new evidence as to old events, are themselves the arbiters of history. Yours are the scales in which all considerations, not just those provided in bygone courts of inquiry, must be weighed. Because mere common opinion, no matter how broadly held, does not form history – it is instead hewn of the actual truth of whatever happened, however much the truth may be hidden from our eyes; and for however long.

For that reason, the more facts that are brought to bear, the better. As to this case at issue, it happens to touch on one of history's most celebrated, yet mythologised, disasters. It shall therefore comprise as much relative importance as whatever weight should devolve, now or in the future, on the fate of 1,500 human beings on the freezing North Atlantic on the night of April 14/15, 1912.

The charges that will be made by individuals in this case are various. It may be that Captain Moore is guilty of some, but not others. It may be that he is Not Guilty of them all, as his spirit would insist. But the matters to be aired, set out in the pages hereafter – with, one hopes, somewhat less pomposity than these opening remarks – are issues which you alone will decide.

The very notion of guilt is itself a value judgement. It is formed of moral interpretation, while history is instead interested predominantly in the facts, and surpassingly, the truth. Therefore, if a preliminary set of circumstances is established – the facts of a situation, as it were – the next judgement, as to the actions of an individual found within those facts, and who may be in a moral dilemma, is to be a keenly-felt thing. It properly resides with jurors.

We cannot know all the facts, let alone all the truth, of any situation. For this reason, leaving aside moral consideration of 'guilt' – and, then, in the matter of *degree* – it is surely obvious that the standard of proof in historical cases need not be that applying in a contemporaneous criminal trial on indictment.

Such a standard, as on a murder charge, for example, stands as one of proof beyond reasonable doubt. But in this instance, relating to events in 1912, grim death has claimed all those from whom we might be interested in hearing further. They have taken that exacting standard with them, and dissolved it in the void.

Here, before the bar of History, there must therefore be allowed a more intuitive insight – whereby what would be excluded as hearsay in a court of law may be accepted in retrospect as 'grey evidence,' and given its proper gravity, wherever that might lie in the scale between black and white.

The balance of probabilities is therefore the proper test in a 'cold case' such as this, allowing for all the information we may find, for testing that evidence, placing it in the whole, and then considering the totality.

Only thereafter may we talk about possible conviction. Not conviction in its criminal sense, but historical conviction – a convinced acceptance, born of rational assessment of the evidence, that any charge laid before the bar is true. That is, that such a charge is the likely actual occurrence, based on all the facts at present disclosed.

Some of the assertions to be uncovered purport that Captain Moore, metaphorically before you, was the Master of a vessel that became known as the Mystery Ship. This vessel was in close proximity to the RMS *Titanic* as the latter was sinking. It did not arrive as a blessed saviour, but instead stood off, unreachable and apparently impervious.

It will be contended that Captain Moore had full knowledge and awareness that the *Titanic* was sinking, and indeed had learned it from the very earliest. It will be vouchsafed that he could not have been where he said he was, which was out of range of reaching the stricken vessel before she sank. But the specimen charge in the indictment is that he committed perjury, covering up the full truth, rather than that he wilfully ignored the plight of a mass of suffering humanity such that one thousand and a half people went to bone-chilling deaths.

Counsel for Captain Moore will also appear in this case, as witnesses are examined, to draw out the facts as he sees them, and to contend to the contrary, that the Master of the *Mount Temple* is guilty of no wrong whatever. If you accept that, and the evidence provided on his behalf, you may discharge the indictment – in effect, tear it up – and the prosecution will have failed in its case, which, naturally, is no concern of yours. In such an eventuality, you will at least, one hopes, emerge much better informed.

There is no particular law here. What happens at sea has always been a law unto itself, in any event, and so there is no need for independent direction as to the conduct of this trial. All will be allowable, for the reader must be both judge and jury, and may freely reject any matter they feel extraneous to the equation. Nonetheless, questions will be unapologetically raised as to the motivation of individuals, their character, past behaviour – in short, anything which may touch upon the credibility of what they have to say. Thereafter, all the matters adduced are for your own appraisal.

It is proposed to begin with a short exposition of the circumstances in which the RMS *Titanic* came to grief in the Grand Banks off Canada. The speed of the vessel, having regard to the prevailing weather conditions and the natural and expressed expectation of ice, is not a matter that need concern this tribunal. It has already been very fully canvassed by both the British and American Inquiries in 1912, albeit that they came to very different determinations.

The American Inquiry, under Senator William Alden Smith of Michigan, found it impossible to escape the conclusion that Captain Edward John Smith, Master of the *Titanic*, had not recklessly endangered the lives of everyone aboard his vessel – indeed, found that he had so done. This may have wounded Senator Smith, who had personally crossed with Captain Smith, or 'E.J.' as he was commonly known, but it did not cause him to shirk his duty as he saw it.

The British Inquiry, under Sir John Bigham, Lord Mersey of Toxteth, stipulated to the contrary that Captain Smith may have erred grievously, but that it was a mistake born of sixty years of largely accident-free navigation of the North Atlantic, and hence there was no negligence on his part whatsoever. It was all a most unlucky mischance.

These divergent reckonings are a useful indicator that the same set of facts may be open to very different interpretation. Indeed, the divinings might have been even more different again, had the Americans been more forgiving of British frailty, or the British been more determined to make an example of the most powerful for the common good. But all that is by the by. Captain Smith, who went down with his ship, was not made amenable to any court other than the highest seat of judgement, and he is not before you now.

No-one is being charged with bringing about the death of 1,500 people, although the evidence in the case at hand turns on the duty of care one might owe to one's fellow creatures whose immediate plight is no cause of one's own.

Certainly the British Board of Trade, which equipped the *Titanic* with fourteen standard size lifeboats (each capable of holding 65 persons), two cutters (40 apiece), and four collapsible rafts, of indeterminate efficiency, is not on trial here – albeit that its case has already been pronounced on by history.

Captain Edward John Smith, Master of
the *Titanic*, went down with the ship.

Nor will any case be made out against the White Star Line, which rejected suggestions that it should prepare for coming changes in regulation by having more lifeboats under davits, and therefore be capable of saving more lives. Nor will there be any questioning of the owners, designers and builders who availed of legislative encouragement to offset structural integrity against lifesaving devices, and then failed to meet the wishes of official inspectors in relation to the desired height of a forward bulkhead.

You must put all these matters out of your mind when it comes to the specific indictment. It is not to be supposed for one moment that, in the absence of satisfactory redress against any other parties, a form of compensatory punishment is to be exacted for the directly-occasioned loss of life against any person named in these proceedings. We have already seen, and in this very episode of the *Titanic*, where such tendencies have taken us.

But enough digression. To return to the point, there will be a short recapitulation of the facts in relation to the casualty, an explanation thereafter of the importance of the mystery ship and of her bearing on the loss of life, and a setting-out of the circumstances whereby an English shipmaster was wrongly accused of being the Captain of that vessel, an accusation that the prosecution here accepts was wholly flawed and wrong-headed from the start. Indeed we offer our apologies on behalf of both the American and British Inquiries …

Thereafter we will proceed to call witnesses from the *Titanic* as to the nature of the mystery ship they saw, together with technical evidence as to the scene. It is only then that the case proper against the *Mount Temple* will begin, with the calling of witnesses, both passengers and crew, who were aboard that vessel on the night of April 14/15, 1912.

The RMS *Titanic* did not depart from Southampton on Wednesday April 10 with any much pomp or ceremony. No brass band saw her off on her maiden voyage. Most morning newspapers accorded her leave taking but a paragraph or two – for she was not the first ship in her class, a distinction that belonged instead to her sister. All the adulation had been expended on her, the *Olympic*, one year earlier, as the harbinger of a new era in ocean travel, with New York tugs and fireboats, hoses pluming, piping her past the Statue of Liberty.

The *Titanic* was not even the first shipwreck of 1912, nor the first British vessel victim. So many craft went down that on January 1, New Year's Day itself, a Lloyd's message from Constantinople to the *Daily Express*, reported in the next day's paper, spoke of disaster to the *Titan* ...

The steamer *Titan*, of a puny 3,013 gross tonnage, built in 1894, had been on a voyage from Braila to Hull. Formerly the *Craigearn*, she foundered 20 miles from the nearest point of land, leading to the death of four of her crew. Fortunately those who remained of her complement were picked up by the British steamer *Empress*. Ships had always to look out for one another.

The *Titanic*, leaving Southampton in modest circumstances – although luxuriously appointed and of truly stupendous proportions (more than fifteen times the size of the unlamented *Titan*) – might even have done well to look out for a nearby ship that was moored firmly to her berth.

Not firmly enough – the displacement caused by the passing leviathan caused the steamer *New York* to snap her moorings and drift dangerously towards the new White Star liner. The breaking of cables had sounded like 'pistol shots', just as some think the snapping of steel funnel-stays a few days later might have caused those already afloat to hear further gunfire above that already accompanying the *Titanic*'s demise ...

But here busy tugs fussed about the *New York* in the nick of time, shepherding her away from the intending transatlantic voyager, and the 2,200 flesh-and-blood voyagers aboard her, two-thirds of whom would see this much of New York and no more.

Nonetheless, the *Titanic* steadied herself and paused. Those on the quayside, never packed in crowds deep, whatever was later represented, could survey her and take stock. A four-funnel liner, her stacks a buff yellow, she was 882½ feet long (three times the height of Big Ben, or the length of four city blocks), and had two masts that stretched like steeples. She was peppered overall with portholes and studded with rivets.

Most imposing was the white superstructure, more than one-and-a-half times the length of a football pitch, that climbed above the black cliff of her hull, and rose fully 65ft to the boat deck – where a few boats dangled, decorations to give the name.

She had reputedly two miles of corridors within her passenger spaces, with the ship's tonnage – over 46,000 – being a measurement, somewhat paradoxically, of volume rather than weight. On this inaugural voyage, however, there were hardly enough passengers to populate the place. A recent coal strike had paralysed shipping and sent bookings tumbling. The vast vessel was certified to carry 3,500 in all, yet this April day saw but 1,316 paying passengers aboard to bother an 892-strong crew.

It was still an enormous consignment of souls. They included many immigrants, some transferred from cancelled sailings, and a smattering of the well-heeled who had either stayed overnight at the plush South Western Hotel, or journeyed commodiously down by train from Waterloo that morning.

There were men of large affairs, Captains of Industry and Presidents of banks and railroad concerns. The mystery writer Jacques Futrelle, whose 'thinking machine' character pondered how anyone could escape a locked cell, was for now enjoying the freedom of the decks. He may have rubbed shoulders with the rambunctious journalist William Stead, jailed in the previous century for purchasing a girl from her mother as proof in a groundbreaking piece on the exploitation of children. It had been entitled 'The Maiden Tribute of Modern Babylon,' and here was Stead now on the maiden trip of another modern Babylon, though he had no idea how soon it would claim its own gigantic tribute.

The Irish seminarian, Francis Browne, leaned over the rail with his box Brownie camera and captured immortal images. He was taking the *Titanic* home to Queenstown, Ireland, where his uncle was the Roman Catholic Bishop. Another man of the cloth, Rev Thomas Roussel Byles, was intending to preside at the marriage of his brother in Manhattan, but would end up ministering to the damned a few nights later.

The steerage was a collection of flat caps, gathered shawls, and swaddled bundles. Many a small family was on its way to the American Midwest or to fruit farms in Canada, all they had previously eked out converted into a small clutch of sovereigns or a bank promissory note pinned inside their shirts. With nothing left to lose, or so they thought, they had opted to up sticks and move *en masse* to a better life. There was no doubting their gumption.

From here, in the harbour confluence of the rivers Test and Itchen, they would nose slowly out into Southampton Water, heading for the open sea of the Solent, where the Isle of Wight stood four-square in front of them as England's last sentry against the French.

Down she came at length, stately and resplendent, gliding into sight of Cowes atop the island, then choosing to make rudder so that she turned to port, rather than the narrower passage by the Needles. Breathing an idle smoke, she swooped past Gosport and the naval yards, ran on beyond the perched terraces of Ryde on the island side, and steadied herself for the gate to the open sea framed by Selsey Bill and the Bembridge foreland.

Off she raced in the afternoon sun, and the cloud of seagulls about her reared back at seeing her sense of purpose. Away she steamed in the glitter, ever dwindling, the speck of ship becoming a hallucination, until she was lost to England for all time.

It was still light, but descending dusk, when the liner had mastered the Channel and lay in what were now the shallows of La Manche, between the Grande and Petite rades, or breakwaters, of Cherbourg harbour. The tenders *Traffic* and *Nomadic* preened like pilot fish against her sides, disgorging passengers from the whole of continental Europe into her cavernous interiors, including those from as far away as the Middle East. Thereafter they received but a handful of disembarkations, including one Mr Meanwell and his caged canary.

Now the *Titanic* had vastly extra inhabitants, from swarthy Syrians and thick-tongued Bulgars to pale Finns and pipe-clamping Germans. In addition, they had the parasol brigade – proclaiming Americans returning from the Grand Tour for the summer season in the States; the men in blazers and slacks, worn beneath top coats to ward off the evening chill, the ladies wrapped in furs and discreetly carrying canines, as if further fur were warranted.

Titanic clanked her giant anchor, forged at the Netherton Bingley works, with whole teams of horses having been required to drag it to the railhead; then paused as if for a last look at the low land of Europe, with a snail-track of glint along the headlands. Reluctantly she moved, gathering resolve, until steaming towards those waters last touched by the dying lake of fire that was the western sun.

All night she carved her way, and in the morning drew bubbling s-shapes on the surface as she tested her compasses, as if doodling or dawdling in advance of her last landfall – Ireland. Soon that dear isle swam into view, growing lighter, showing her cliffs and her fields, a lighthouse painted white and red. Harder to see were the hillside forts husbanding this harbour, but there they were, Fort Camden and Fort Carlisle.

She ran in a little way, unleashed the cacophony of her deep-seeking anvil, and watched the buoyant black forms that chugged towards her. These were the tenders *Ireland* and *America*, bringing fresh blood to appease the smoke-breathing beast.

A little after lunchtime on Thursday April 11, the *Titanic* bade adieu to Queenstown, final port of call before the narrows of New York. All that afternoon was spent rounding the Irish coast, past the Fastnet rock (with the beacon built upon that crag flying signal flags that spelled out 'Good luck!') on a slow swerve towards the start, and a great circle run to last 3,000 miles. Second Class passenger Lawrence Beesley, a science teacher, wrote: 'As dusk fell, the coast rounded away from us to the northwest, and the last we saw of Europe was the Irish mountains dim and faint in the dropping darkness.'

Friday April 12 passed into Saturday April 13 on the lonely ocean vastness. Sunday April 14 dawned windy and fresh. A planned muster by the ship's crew at the lifeboats – a drill, merely – was cancelled without explanation by the Captain, who nonetheless undertook the pleasant task of leading the principal passengers at morning worship in the First Class lounge. Similar supplications took place in Second Class, and certainly must have been emulated somewhere in the unseen steerage.

That Sabbath sank slowly into shadow, the passengers retiring to read, until at length dressing for dinner. Mrs George Widener held a party, at which the Captain came and smoked cigars, but held up his hand to decline the offer of alcohol. The line's Managing Director, Joseph Bruce Ismay, sat at table with the twinkle-eyed doctor, William 'Old Bill' O'Loughlin, salt-dated and many decades departed from his boyhood home of Tralee, Co. Kerry, now left at the edge of Europe in the ship's wake. Stewards wearing white waistcoats ghosted between and beyond.

The animated hubbub of conversation was replicated elsewhere in the ship's public areas, among the bridge players in the smoking room, and by giddy steerage dancing their set arrangements in a common cavern toward the stern of the vessel, all of it drowning the steady thrum of the engines.

By degrees that delirium faded, and as the dining tables broke up, many passengers remarked on how cold it had become as they repaired to their staterooms. The passageways themselves soon became deserted, shoes appearing outside cabin doors for stewards to buff for the morning.

In the lookout cage, Frederick Fleet and Reginald Lee wore double jerseys against the bitter cold, though they sheltered behind a weather cloth. Their eyes blinked frequently against the freezing air streaming in their faces, all the while cognisant of the message passed on by those they had relieved: 'Keep a sharp eye out for ice, particularly small ice and growlers. That's from Mr Lightoller.'

Their eyes grew sharp all right, bleared with the darting darkness and the endless tunnel of unrelieved night, moonless and monotonous, though the stars flung their steely glitter. An inordinate ordeal it was, after one hour and a half, but then an object grew form. Fred Fleet looked again, next goggled. He spun about. His gloved hand ripped upwards to clang a cloud of silver dust from the bell, shocking his companion. Three loud strikes, and he picked up the telephone and wound its arm quickly. Lee, his companion, shot looks from the front to Fleet and back again, until he saw it too.

Three strikes. Obstacle directly facing, and Fleet fairly bellowed it when the officer finally answered. 'Iceberg, right ahead!' The other end of the line murmured: 'Thank you.' Handsets replaced, the ship swept on.

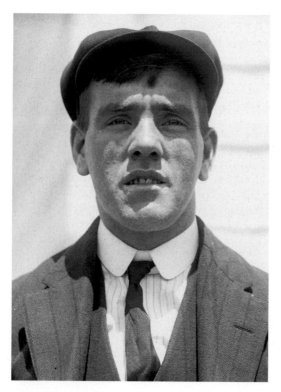

Frederick Fleet, the *Titanic* lookout who spotted the collision berg and sounded the warning, but who saw no light at all during his entire duty aloft.

Lee gazed from his guard post and said she would never make it. Fleet gripped him by the shoulder with his left hand, and mouthed that she should turn, turn, turn. The stem of the bow below them ticked a fraction to the left, not enough. Not nearly enough. Fleet pulled Lee, 'Get down,' and the other man knew it meant not to hunker, but to head inside the foremast, to gain the interior rungs leading down to the lower decks. This impact could fell a tree …

As they comically bustled in the breach, the sound of rending came at their backs, like a sail shroud ripping slowly in a gale off the Horn. But there was no pitching or tossing, only a short tremor that paused her, it seemed, not a jot. The mast did not fall. Feeling momentarily foolish, the men returned the step or two to their perch, and saw that great grey spectre passing on the starboard side into the murk.

'That was a narrow shave,' said Fleet.

But it was the drawing of a razor against the jugular. The headlong way came off the ship, and she drifted to a stop. A few minutes later, with little sign of activity except spectators in the wing cabs of the bridge, a dark form shooting down a companion ladder, and stray firemen larking in the well deck, she started up once more. She made slow ahead, and the white foam resumed. Then the engines cut again, and altogether. Fleet and Lee looked at one another in alarm.

The phone stayed silent, and there was nothing ahead. Nothing behind either, on the ship herself, but then came a gradual unfurling of activity. The men watched a beginning bustle that quickly became a hum of business. They saw figures climb on the starboard emergency boat, the 'man overboard' craft hanging overside, and start to throw back the covers. Stray cries mingled more frequently, until they threatened to become a din.

THE sea, and still more sea; liquid profundity buoying the folly of man. Supremely limitless, it drinks darkly of this unexpected morality play beneath studded stars. A pitiful radiance roofs the silent deep.

Miles below the suspended nebulae, miles above the bottom of the sea, and miles from anywhere that might be called land, is borne the grain irrelevant. A luminous pinprick, as if a sliver of astral light has fallen celestial heights to settle on the surface, the RMS *Titanic* is sinking.

The senior wireless operator of the RMS *Titanic*, Jack Phillips, who was lost.

'A light, dead ahead! – Sir, a light!'

'Thank you.' John Paul Moody's voice was once more politely nondescript. Replacing the telephone, he ruefully reflected that the last thing spotted dead ahead was the berg, and too late. But he was already walking the short few steps from the bridge to the port wing cab, where he could see the Captain's greatcoat.

'Sir, the relief lookouts are reporting a light! A light approaching dead ahead.'

'Thank goodness.' Captain Smith did not say more, but rushed to look from forward. A point off the bow, he thought he could discern it. Indeed, was satisfied he could at last. A smile allowed itself to creep across his whiskered features as he glanced with indulgence to a colleague nearby.

'Perhaps you won't need too many of those, Mr Boxhall,' said Edward John Smith to the Fourth Officer, nodding at the long rocket the latter was carrying in his cupped, gloved hands. The Master of the ship also nodded to Moody, who took his dismissal and snapped back to the bridge.

Captain Smith stood at the wing cab rail, studying whatever was straight ahead. 'What time is it?' he threw over his shoulder, before barking 'Enter it in the log,' when reply was given.

Fourth Officer Joseph Groves Boxhall now came to join him. Behind them came the creaks and clatters of boats making ready; the shouts, gasps and the muffled tumult.

Salvation.

Except we know the salvation did not come. Hundreds upon hundreds went instead to their deaths. The mystery ship did not manifest itself, and the light, though it came nearer still, stopped. What was the identity of this vessel?

Curiously, we need to know more about the *Titanic* first. Her identity – as a sinking ship – was communicated through the ether by means of wireless distress messages. A spark, controlled by her Marconi operators, Jack Phillips and his junior, Harold Bride, sent out the dots and dashes that identified the White Star liner not only by name, but also offered identity of place – the exact co-ordinates of where she was sinking.

The first transmissions were prefaced by the CQD emergency call, popularised as representing 'Come quickly, danger' even though the first two initials only meant: 'Attention all shipping.' The crucial aspect to the call for help would be the latitude and longitude that followed.

Latitude and longitude may seem off-putting concepts, but they amount merely to the crosshairs that specifically target any particular area. Longitude is the West-East axis, as if that hyphen between West and East was stretched to girdle the entire earth. Latitude is the North-South axis. The *Titanic*'s distress messages were to pinpoint the meeting place of both.

This then is the 'scene of crime' and a short explanation of how the spot is devised and described in surely warranted. Longitude and latitude are both broken up into degrees and minutes. The first distress call specified that the *Titanic* was sinking in Latitude 41 44 N, Longitude 50 24 W.

The N part after the latitude figures means North, signifying the 'top' hemisphere if the globe were cut in two at the equator like a grapefruit. The *Titanic* was going down in the North Atlantic.

How far north from the equator can be exactly determined by the specifics of 41 degrees and 44 minutes. As with the hour, there are sixty minutes in a degree. Latitude is a constant, and one of its minutes is equivalent to one nautical mile, anywhere on the globe.

Titanic therefore said she was sinking 41 times 60 miles (2,460), plus 44 miles, above the equator, no matter the curvature of the earth. She was exactly 2,504 miles north of the world's waist.

Latitude is constant, but longitude changes. Again it is divided into degrees and minutes, although the actual distances represented by a single minute of longitude will depend on one's particular location.

(The figure W just means west of Greenwich, that slice of London deemed to be zero longitude, just as the equator is zero latitude, with a mile either side of the latter being a mile north, or a mile south, as the case may be.)

It's all a way, in this case, of giving meaning to a featureless sea – turning unrelieved swells into a map, by means of a grid. Except that the sinking *Titanic*, having mistakenly calculated her position initially, was already revising it to a place substantially further east – from Lat. 41 44 N, Long. 50 24 W, to a latitude of 41 46, two miles further north, and a longitude of 50 14, or ten minutes less in westward progress.

This distress position, occasionally accompanied by the new SOS emergency prefix in *Titanic* transmissions, would not change thereafter. She was sinking, she insisted, in 41 46 N, 50 14 W, and she went down before any other vessel could reach her.

Yet she did not sink in 41 46 N, 50 14 W at all. The stricken maiden voyage had given out false information. She did it in good faith and wholly innocently, but it was mistaken nonetheless.

Hasty calculations, computed after the collision, had allowed too much progress west, even by the revised distress messages. When the *Titanic* wreck was finally found – in 1985, after her course and speed calculations had thrown searchers off the scent for decades – she was thirteen nautical miles further east (and a little to the south) of where she had claimed to be ...

Her wreck lies in 41 43 N (three miles south of the SOS latitude), and 49 56 W. The southern declination may be attributed to her heading to port to avoid the berg, and then drifting with the current over the two hours and forty minutes it took her to sink.

But look at the longitude. This is not remotely like 50 14 W (itself revised eastwards from the original 50 24 transmission). The *Titanic* never reached the major meridian of 50 degrees that straddled her path as she voyaged from east to west. She fell four minutes short of it – and a full eighteen minutes of longitude short of where she said she was sinking. Potential rescuers were sent on a wild goose chase.

It is rather an extraordinary thing for a sinking supership to transmit the wrong co-ordinates. The reasons she did so are still speculated upon, but have their roots in fallible human estimates based on assumed speed, allowances for any countervailing current, and the use of longitude tables, celestial observations and 'dead reckoning' from the last estimated position.

Unlike arriving at a position each local noon, thanks to the sun reaching its zenith, the night offered no guidance for progress along the West-East axis but a mariner's own guesswork and some night-sky observation tables, provided those observations were accurate or taken in the first place. Stellar observations were taken on the *Titanic* at 7.30pm that night, more than four hours before the collision.

Calculations were aided by a device trailed from the stern (confusingly called a log), which clicked-off revolutions and served to offer a clue as to the mileage travelled. But if, for instance, a reading were wrongly conveyed, perhaps with a single figure transposed, all other workings would be thrown into error.

There were many and various ways for the *Titanic* to get it wrong, and she did – by those eighteen minutes of longitude, equivalent to thirteen nautical miles in this vicinity of the North Atlantic because the value of longitude varies from one location on the globe to another.

The *Titanic* herself believed she was in 41 46 N, 50 14 W. No-one who sat in judgment at the subsequent inquiries doubted that position for one moment, even though it had been horribly misjudged throughout. Yet it became the gold standard by which all other information was assessed. The absolutely-wrong thus became the absolute.

Now consider inquiry findings in relation to another vessel, the Leyland liner *Californian*. The *Californian* was bound for Boston – much further north than the Statue of Liberty, goal of the *Titanic*. This 6,300-ton freighter's track was, in this particular setting, 19 or 20 miles further north than the track to New York. Her Captain, Stanley Lord, said as much in a 1914 newspaper article. The tracks never converged.

The *Californian* encountered not an iceberg, but an entire ice*field* that night. It stretched across the horizon and likely for many miles further south, blocking the passage to westbound voyagers, and eastbounders too. Captain Lord halted his vessel at the rim of the field to wait until morning. The ship's time was 10.21pm.

Californian wireless operator Cyril Evans. From the *Marconigraph* of June 1912.

He shortly thereafter worked out his ship's position, aided – most crucially in relation to latitude – by a stellar observation of Polaris, the northern star, so-called because it enables near exact latitude to be discerned from its angle of elevation.

Lord determined his ship to be in latitude 42 05 N, and longitude 50 07 W. In other words, he was indeed 19 miles further up the North-South axis than the *Titanic*'s transmitted latitude of 41 46 N (since 42 degrees was 14 minutes, or miles, above 41 46, and five further minutes were five further nautical miles).

He was also seven minutes of longitude past the major line, or meridian, of 50 degrees west. Thus he was seven minutes short of the longitude point, far to his southwest, of where the *Titanic* thought she was sinking – 50 14 W.

But he estimated himself as 11 minutes of longitude further west than the point in which the *Titanic*'s shattered hulk would actually be found decades later. This was to the far south*east*. It was as if the *Californian* had calculated herself at the apex of a pyramid, whose baseline would stretch from the erroneous SOS point in the west to the true point where she began to go down in the east.

Nobody knew this at the time, particularly not the *Californian* because she had reckoned her stop position long before the *Titanic* even collided. Captain Lord instructed his wireless operator to transmit a warning to all shipping. His youthful telegraphist, Cyril Evans, attempted to do so, subsequently transmitting to the *Titanic*: 'Say Old Man, we are stopped and surrounded by ice'.

He was rudely rebuffed by the unseen, but still-speeding liner. The maiden voyager's senior wireless operator, Jack Phillips, immediately interrupted Evans' message with the retort: 'Shut up, shut up! I am busy. I am working Cape Race.' The *Titanic*'s sending of the wireless chatter of paying customers, ostentatious First Class passengers in the main, was Phillips' immediate priority.

The *Californian*'s warning went unheeded. Cyril Evans may have scowled or shrugged. He subsequently told the US inquiry: 'At 11.25pm I still had the phones on my ears, and heard him [*Titanic*] still working Cape Race. About two or three minutes before the half-hour, ship's time, that was, and at 11.35pm, I put the phones down, took off my clothes, and turned in.'

At those inquiries, the *Californian* told of seeing distant rockets, which rose very low, in the southeast. We know now, thanks to the discovery of the wreck in 1985, that these smudges of light were the *Titanic*'s distress rockets, fired from where she was in fact sinking.

But in 1912, these assertions seemed farcical. The inquiries *knew* (or thought they did) that the *Titanic* had gone down in the transmitted SOS position, much further along the baseline of that explanatory triangle. The *Californian* should therefore not have been seeing lights on the southeastern horizon, but to the south*west*.

To the official line of thinking, the SOS position was sacrosanct. But the *Titanic*'s distress co-ordinates and the *Californian*'s claimed stop position could not *both* be right – or else two ships were firing distress rockets at the same time, many miles apart – yet relatively close together, given the enormity of the North Atlantic.

Officialdom assumed *Titanic* would not transmit false information when seeking to draw ships to her aid, and the assessors duly ignored many pieces of evidence pointing to such a mistake on the sinking vessel's part.

They reasoned that if the *Californian* was not seeing rockets to the south*west*, where they were assuredly being fired (or so the establishment rigidly believed), but was instead claiming to see them where they were very likely *not* being fired, then it was not hard to see which ship was bearing false witness.

Since the two accounts could not both be right, the validity of the *Titanic* – motiveless to deceive in her dreadful plight – was upheld. The *Californian* had to be in the wrong. Once her stop position was 'disproved' in this way, it was easy to relocate the Leyland liner to the west, so that the rockets she saw were in the 'correct' place. Once her navigational alibi had been torn away, as it were, she could be placed as the *Titanic*'s mystery ship – close in, seeing rockets high up, a witness to the sinking.

That's what happened. Yet it flew in the face of the evidence of an independent person aboard the *Californian*. Her wireless operator, whom we have just met, was employed by the Marconi company and was not a member of the crew, even though he appeared on the ship's articles. Frequently reassigned, such men as Cyril Evans owed no real loyalty to individual Captains or ships.

An honest broker then, Evans gave incidental credence to the *Californian*'s account in 1912, even though the latter has since been borne out by the discovery of the *Titanic* wreckage. Evans told how he came to understand that his ship was 19 miles north of the White Star liner before that vessel's collision.

Testifying as to how he had called up the speeding *Titanic* to say that the *Californian* was stopped, Evans commented that he was 'giving that [information] as a matter of courtesy, because the Captain requested me.

He was asked: 'You expected a reply from him, or an enquiry as to what your location was, where the ice was, did you not?'

Evans did not rejoinder that what he did not expect was the 'shut up' message he had been immediately sent back from *Titanic*. Instead he paused to consider whether the *Titanic* would want to know the precise location of the ice. He decided that the White Star ship, intending landfall in New York, need not want to know it – because she was too far away from a Boston-bound tramp and her surrounding ice.

And so the Marconi man declared: 'No, sir. I thought he was very much south of me, because we were bound for Boston, and we were north of the [New York] track.'

A little further on in this questioning, the independent Evans added: 'I can only work on that we were about 20 miles away.' When asked 'from what,' he replied; 'From the *Titanic*, and therefore he would be 20 miles away from us.'

The mystery ship, as we shall see from direct *Titanic* evidence, was by contrast very near.

In London, lawyers set out to tackle this troubling conviction – which was in the mind of Evans *before* the accident – that the *Californian* had been 20 miles from the *Titanic* while trying to warn the latter of ice

Asked if he remembered saying it in his American evidence, Evans replied easily: 'Yes, the Captain told me to expect the *Titanic* to be away to the southward of us.' He was not asked when exactly the Captain passed the remark, but he himself had it in his mind at the moment of the attempted last warning.

In his own American evidence, *Californian* Captain Stanley Lord had been asked: 'When did you notify the *Titanic* of your [stopped] condition? What was your purpose?'

He replied: 'It was just a matter of courtesy. I thought he would be a long way from where we were. I did not think he was anywhere near the ice. By rights, he ought to have been 18 or 19 miles to the southward of where I was. I never thought the ice was stretching that far down.'

But there was ice there, even if the *Titanic* found a stray sentry berg ahead of the main field – sinking to the southeast of the *Californian*, while the Leylander was to the north, stopped at the field's rim further west.

There are many other reasons why the *Californian* could not be the mystery ship. Captain Lord's vessel had transmitted previous wireless messages all that day, showing she was several miles north of the line of 42 degrees north (whereas the *Titanic* struck 14 miles south of there, in latitude 41 46, on the New York track, and would even sink a little south of there too.)

It's known the *Californian* was stopped, and her final warning message said so – as did everyone aboard her commonly maintain when questioned later. Yet the mystery ship would be seen to approach the *Titanic* … a fact that Captain Lord, interviewed years later, insisted 'clears everything.' A stopped ship could not be moving – but it seemed to officialdom that if the *Californian* were 'lying' about her stop position, then not only her location could be transposed at whim, but whether she was mobile or immobile tampered with too.

There are many other differences between the *Californian* and the mystery ship, were she not already disqualified. According to the evidence as to how she was facing, she would have been presenting only her green light (on a ship's starboard side, the port side light being red) to any vessel to the south of her. Instead, *Titanic* observation disclosed both lights being seen first as the mystery ship came on straight ahead, then a red light being seen 'most of the time,' as that vessel turned to starboard some miles away and stopped.

The *Californian* observers, for their part, had seen low-lying rockets. They associated them with a close-in steamer, small or medium in size, which was 'something like ourselves' (*Californian* 6,000 tons; *Titanic* 46,000). She had also arrived at the icefield, a few miles to the

A lifeboat's eye view demonstrating that the *Titanic*'s mystery ship must have been within a few miles because of the very limited horizon of her rowboats. There is extensive evidence that *Titanic* escapees continued to see the mystery ship for a long time while down on the water. Picture shows *Devonian* at Boston in 1914.

south, and stopped. But the *Titanic* rockets did not go a little up the mast, as seen by *Californian* in relation to their nearby counterpart. Instead they ripped up 'several hundred feet' into the air and burst with a cornucopia of stars and a sound akin to an artillery detonation. The mystery ship must have heard them. The *Californian* heard nothing at all.

Meanwhile, the *Titanic* lifeboats would make for the tantalising ship they could see – their only possible sanctuary on an otherwise empty sea. At least one of the escape craft burned green flares to attract attention. The lifeboats rowed aggressively towards the mystery ship, and did so on a flat calm sea – but could not make progress, indicating their goal was not stationary. Some saw the enigma's stern light as she went away – and when the sun began to come up at 4am, the mystery ship was nowhere to be seen.

The very restricted horizon for someone in a lifeboat (even a person of record height, standing on its highest point) at once proves conclusively that the mystery ship was close in to the *Titanic*. This is because her lights were seen, and continuously seen, by those cast adrift on the surface of the sea from the sinking maiden voyager.

That ship was near, but despite hours of pulling (bearing in mind that the *Californian* remained immobile until a very considerable time after the following dawn) the poor *Titanic* survivors could get no closer to their goal. This is an unalterable law of physics – if progress is made in distance towards a stationary object, it must soon appear larger. Instead, the *Titanic* survivors could not see the mystery ship in the following daylight, did not even espy masts or a funnel colour, and had eventually to be rescued by the RMS *Carpathia*, speeding up from an opposite direction.

And the *Carpathia*, with her enormous advantage of height, plus daylight, stability, binoculars and a crow's nest, could not see the eventually-blamed *Californian* either. Her Captain, Arthur Rostron, (who would be knighted for his rescue) testified that he first saw the *Californian* making for the scene at 8am, when he had all but completed the task of taking up those who had escaped what was by then the worst shipwreck in North Atlantic history.

The foregoing is a brief and potted history of why the *Californian* could not have been the mystery ship, even though she was later saddled with that reputation. The prosecution in the current case acted for the defence in that matter (*Titanic and the Mystery Ship*, Tempus, 2006), and the reader is referred to it if further evidence should be sought. A belated apology for a miscarriage of justice is offered in respect of the failings of both the American and British inquiries in this regard.

And so to return to the matter at hand, testing whether the *Mount Temple* might instead have been the mystery ship. What is crucial is that we begin again at the beginning – and learn from *Titanic* witnesses what it is possible to know about the ship they saw.

THE SCENE DESCRIBED

THE shaken *Titanic* lookouts had stayed in the crow's nest after the collision, because no-one thought to summon them to help. Fred Fleet and Reg Lee possibly considered it would be wise to stay out sight for a while in any case, but also knew that they were due to remain on duty for another forty-odd minutes.

The giant liner had struck at 11.40pm ship's time, but the partners were not due to end their shift until 12.23am. The extra 23 minutes from midnight were a quirk, to compensate for the clocks being put back to midnight at that point. This was because, as with every westbound vessel, the *Titanic* had to shed time regularly in order to coincide with local time on arrival in New York, which was five hours behind London, or Greenwich time.

So Fleet and Lee stayed where they were as the *Titanic* tentatively resumed progress following the collision. And they remained aloft when she stopped again. All this time they had been paying, one imagines, a keenly-renewed respect to their official duties.

'We are only up there to report anything we see,' Fleet told the US inquiry. He confirmed he was expected to report 'anything we see — a ship, or anything.' After the collision they 'kept staring ahead again.'

But Fleet and Reg Lee, the other lookout, did not see another ship or light on the horizon. They did not report anything of the sort during their whole time on watch, effectively dismissing the idea that the mystery ship could have been a stationary vessel all along.

Lee specifically denied (British inquiry transcript Br. 2564) that there was the light of any other vessel to be seen when his own ship struck. Apart from the fatal iceberg during his watch, 'there was nothing to be reported.'

Fleet was asked: 'Were there lights of any other vessels in sight when you came down from the crow's nest?' and replied: 'There was (sic) no lights at all when we was up in the crow's nest. This is after we was down, and [working] on the boats; *then* I seen the light.' The light of the mystery ship …

Fleet said he saw it on the port bow only after he left the crow's nest, which he did at 12.23am, and was down on deck 'It must have been about 1 o'clock,' he said, which would be very substantially after the 11.40pm collision. An hour and twenty minutes later was when he personally became aware of the light – colleague Lee did not see the stranger until he was down on the water.

The gleam was first reported by the relief pair that replaced Fleet and Lee in the crow's nest, sent there even though the *Titanic* was stopped. Indeed, it was perhaps vital that fresh eyes should go aloft, because full information was now needed – both from the magic of the Marconi-prompted ether, and from the visible, physical horizon.

The new lookouts were sailors named Frank Evans and Alfred Hogg. But they cannot be offered in evidence to describe the stranger, because they were never asked about it at the official inquiries. Hogg was dealt with peremptorily in London, hurried through his account with no mention of the light. Testimony from Evans was declined by the President of the Court, Lord Mersey, who commented that it would be 'of very little importance.' Thus it was never established when the glowing prospect of rescue for all was first discerned.

It is now time to call a prime witness, the *Titanic*'s fourth officer. He will recite his evidence to both the US and British inquiries. Joseph Boxhall is important, not only as one of just four surviving officers of the shipwreck, but as the man who was given the task by Captain Smith of summoning assistance – first by sending up distress rockets, and then the further duty of attempting to call up the mystery ship by Morse lamp, sending out flashes into the darkness – in the direction of this other ship – that represented the dots and dashes of that code.

Joseph Groves Boxhall, fourth officer on
the RMS *Titanic*, and her prime witness in
regard to the mystery ship.

JOSEPH GROVES BOXHALL

Twenty-eight years old, with a year's training in navigation school plus thirteen years' experience
at sea, Mr Boxhall was first an officer with the Wilson Line of Hull, followed by five years as
a junior officer with White Star.

'Where were you when the collision took place?'

Boxhall: I was just approaching the bridge ...

At the time of the impact I was just coming along the deck and almost abreast of the
Captain's quarters, and I heard the report of three bells. That signifies something has been seen
ahead. Almost at the same time I heard the first officer give the order 'Hard astarboard,' and
the engine telegraph rang.

It [the iceberg] seemed to me to strike the bluff of the bow ... a glancing blow. I was not very
sure of seeing it. It seemed to me to be just a small black mass not rising very high out of the
water ... The ship was past it then. It looked to me to be very, very low in the water ... I do
not think the thing extended above the ship's rail.

'When the order was given to clear the lifeboats, what did you do?' – I went around the decks
and was clearing the lifeboats; helping take the covers off ... and assisting generally around the
decks. Then I went into the chart room and worked out the ship's position ... I submitted her
position to the Captain. He said, 'Take it to the Marconi room.'

'What did you do after you left the operator's room?' – Went around the decks, assisting
to clear the [boats], and send distress signals off ... I was around the bridge most of the time,
sending off distress signals, and endeavouring to signal to a ship that was ahead of us ...

My attention, until the time I left the ship, was mostly taken up with firing off distress
rockets and trying to signal a steamer that was almost ahead of us.

'How far ahead of you?' – It is hard to say. I saw his masthead lights and I saw his side light.

Titanic fourth officer Joseph Boxhall, marked with an 'x,' right, testifying before the US Senate subcommittee inquiry into the catastrophe.

'On the same course [westbound], apparently?' – No, oh, no ... by the way she was heading, she seemed to be meeting us.

'Coming toward you?' – Coming toward us.

'You say you fired these rockets and otherwise attempted to signal her?' – Yes, sir. She got close enough, as I thought, to read our electric Morse signal, and I signalled to her. I told her to come at once, we were sinking; and the Captain was standing – I told the Captain about this ship, and he was with me most of the time when we were signalling.

'Did he also see it?' – Yes, sir. I went over and started the Morse [lamp]. He said, 'Tell him to come at once, we are sinking.' It was sent in the Morse key, the Morse code.

'And did you get any reply?' – I cannot say I saw any reply. Some say she replied to our rockets and our signals, but I did not see them. I cannot say that I saw any signals, except her ordinary steaming light. Some people (I think it was stewards) say they saw signals, but I could not.

'From what you saw of that vessel, how far would you think she was from the *Titanic*?' – I should say approximately the ship would be about 5 miles.

'What lights did you see?' – The two masthead lights and the red light. (The two masthead lights were first), and then, as she got closer, she showed her side light, her red light.

'So you were quite sure she was coming in your direction?' – Quite sure.

'How long was this before the boat sank?' – It is hard to tell. I had no idea of the time then; I do not know what time it was then.

'You would expect that this boat would pick up [the SOS transmission] if they had a wireless?' – If she had a wireless installation ... I would signal with the Morse and then go ahead and send off a rocket, and then go back and have a look at the ship, until I was finally sent away.

'The failure to arouse the attention of this ship was not due to any impaired or partial success of these [rockets]?' – Not at all, sir.

'You say you continued to fire the rockets and give the signals?' – Yes, sir.

(Recalled to the stand)

'What was the character of the light you saw; and did you see more than one?' – At first I saw two masthead lights of a steamer, just slightly opened, and later she got closer to us, until, eventually, I could see her side lights with my naked eye.

'Was she approaching you?' – Evidently she was, because I was stopped … I considered she was about 5 miles away. She was headed toward us, meeting us … Just about half a point off our port bow.

'And apparently coming toward you?' – Yes.

'How soon after the collision?' – I cannot say about that. It was shortly after the order was given to clear the boats.

'Did you continue to see that steamer?' – I saw that light, saw all the lights of course, before I got into my [life]boat, and just before I got into the boat she seemed as if she had turned around. I saw just one single bright light then, which I took to be her stern light.

'She apparently turned around within 5 miles of you?' – Yes, sir … I had been firing off rockets before I saw her side lights. I fired off the rockets, and then she got so close I could see her side lights and starboard light.

'What kind of steamer was that, which you saw, that apparently turned around, as to size and character?' – That is hard to state, but the lights were on masts which were fairly close together … She might have been a four-mast ship or might have been a three-mast ship, but she certainly was not a two mast ship.

'Could you form any idea as to her size?' – No, I could not.

'You know it was a steamer and not a sailing vessel?' – Oh, yes; she was a steamer, carrying steaming lights – white lights.

'She could not have been a fishing vessel?' – No, sir … a sailing vessel does not show steaming lights, or white lights.

'After you got in the water [in a lifeboat] did you see the light from this steamer?' – Yes; I saw it for a little while and then lost it. When I pulled around the ship I could not see it any more, and did not see it any more.

'Apparently that ship came within 4 or 5 miles of the *Titanic*, and then turned and went away in what direction, westward or southward?' – I do not know whether it was southwestward. I should say it was westerly.

'Almost in the direction which she had come?' – Yes, sir.

'You are very positive you saw that ship ahead on the port bow, are you?' – Yes, sir, quite positive.

'Did you see the green or red light?' – Yes; I saw the side lights with my naked eye … I saw this steamer's stern light before I went into my boat, which indicated that the ship had turned around. I saw a white light, and I could not see any of the masthead lights that I had seen previously, and I took it for a stern light.

'Which light did you see first?' – I saw the masthead lights first, the two steaming lights; and then, as she drew up closer, I saw her side lights through my glasses, and eventually I saw the red light. I had seen the green, but I saw the red most of the time. I saw the red light with my naked eye.

'Did she pull away from you?' – I do not know when she turned; I cannot say when I missed the [masthead] lights, because I was leaving the bridge to go and fire off some more of those distress rockets and attend to other duties.

I think I saw the green light before I saw the red light, as a matter of fact. But the ship was meeting us. I am covering the whole thing by saying the ship was meeting us.

'Your impression is she turned away, or turned on a different course?' – That is my impression.

'At a later time, when you were in the boat after it had been lowered, what light did you see?' I saw this single light, which I took to be her stern light, just before I went away in the boat, as near as I can say. I saw it until I pulled around the ship's stern. I had laid off a little while on the port side, on which side I was lowered, and then I afterwards pulled around the ship's stern, and, of course, then I lost the light, and I never saw it anymore.

'She was coming in toward your course?' – Yes, sir; she was slightly crossing it, evidently. I suppose she was turning around slowly.

'Is it your idea that she turned away?' – That is my idea, sir.

'She kept on a general course toward the east, and then bore away from you, or what?' – I do not think she was doing much steaming. I don't think the ship was steaming very much, because after I first saw the masthead lights she must have been still steaming, but by the time I saw her red light with my naked eye she was not steaming very much. So she had probably gotten into the ice, and turned around.

'What do you think happened after she turned around? Do you think she went away to avoid the ice?' – I do not know whether she stayed there all night, or what she did. I lost the light. I did not see her after we pulled around to the starboard side of the *Titanic*.

'And you saw her no more after that?' – No, sir. As a matter of fact, Captain Smith was standing by my side, and we both came to the conclusion that she was close enough to be signalled by the Morse lamp. So I signalled to her. I called her up, and got no answer. The Captain said, 'Tell him to come at once, we are sinking.' So I sent that signal out, 'Come at once, we are sinking.' Then leaving off and firing rockets. There were a lot of stewards and men standing around the bridge and around the boat deck. Of course, there were quite a lot of them quite interested in this ship, looking from the bridge, and some said she had shown a light in reply, but I never saw it.

I even got the Quartermaster, who was working around with me, to fire off the distress signal, and I got him to also signal with the Morse lamp – whilst I watched with a pair of glasses to see whether this man did answer, as some people said he had replied.

'You saw nothing of the hull of the boat?' – Oh no, it was too dark. I have already stated, in answer to a question, how far this ship was away from us, that I thought she was about 5 miles, and I arrived at it in this way. The masthead lights of a steamer are required by the Board of Trade regulations to show for 5 miles, and the [side lights] are required to show for 2 miles.

'You saw not only the mast lights but the side lights?' – I saw the side lights. Whatever ship she was, she had beautiful lights.

That was the evidence of Mr Boxhall, the prime witness as to the mystery ship, in the United States. The salient points are that this vessel was a steamer, and not a fishing boat, because she had identifier steaming lights. He was watching her through binoculars, and he and the Captain, a man of great experience but lost in the tragedy, both came to the conclusion that the ship was eventually close enough to be signalled by Morse lamp.

The mystery ship had beautiful lights. She was not a small ship, such as a two master, but of the larger type – either a three-master or a four-master. Which is also to say that she had only one funnel … the *Titanic* was something of an anomaly, with only two masts herself, but four giant funnels.

This steamer approached, came closer, on a meeting course. She then turned, showing her red light only (on her port side), rather than both the red and green as she closed head-on. Boxhall did not know why she slowed and stopped, but surmised that she had 'probably gotten into the ice.'

He knew that icefield was directly in the ship's path, running north to south as his vessel was heading east to west. Together, course and field formed a cross – but *Titanic* hit a stray berg.

Meanwhile the mystery ship eventually turned around, showing a stern light, and departed the way she had come – returning to the west, the same direction in which the *Titanic* had been headed.

In this same evidence, Boxhall remarked that after the sinking 'and the cries subsided, then I found out that we were near the ice.' He was asked if this statement also covered the field ice, and replied: 'Yes; it covers all the ice, sir. I heard the water rumbling or breaking on the ice. Then I knew that there was a lot of ice about; but I could not see it from the boat.' When darkness was banished by daylight, and Boxhall was safely aboard the rescuing *Carpathia*, 'I could see field ice then, as far as the eye could see ... '

In London, Mr Boxhall once more took the stand and recounted what he had seen:

I saw a lot of men come along — the watch I presume [starting at 12.23am by run-on time] ..I was just going along there and seeing all the men were well established with their work, well under way with it, and I heard someone report a light, a light ahead ... It was two masthead lights of a steamer.

I could see the light with the naked eye, but I could not define what it was, but by the aid of a pair of glasses I found it was the two masthead lights of a vessel, probably about half a point on the port bow, and in the position she would be showing her red if it were visible, but she was too far off then.

Br. 15394. Could you see how far off she was? — No, I could not see, but I had sent in the meantime for some rockets, and told the Captain I had sent for some rockets, and told him I would send them off, and told him when I saw this light. He said, 'Yes, carry on with it.' I was sending rockets off and watching this steamer. Between the time of sending the rockets off and watching the steamer approach us, I was making myself generally useful around the port side of the deck.

15400. Did you watch the lights of this steamer while you were sending the rockets up? — Yes ... I was paying most of my attention to this steamer then, and she was approaching us; and then I saw her side lights. I saw her green light and the red. She was end-on to us. Later I saw her red light. This is all with the aid of a pair of glasses up to now. Afterwards I saw the ship's red light with my naked eye, and the two masthead lights. The only description of the ship that I could give is that she was, or I judged her to be, a four-masted steamer ... by the position of her masthead lights; they were close together.

15403. Did the ship make any sort of answer, as far as you could see, to your rockets? — I did not see it. Some people say she did, and others say she did not. There were a lot of men on the

A quartermaster character preparing to fire a rocket from the deck of the *Titanic* – or in this case, the RMS *Asturias*, from the set of the 1958 movie *A Night to Remember*.

bridge. I had a Quartermaster with me, and the Captain was standing by, at different times, watching this steamer.

15404. Do you mean you heard someone say she was answering your signals? — Yes, I did, and then she got close enough, and I Morsed to her; used our Morse lamp.

15406. When people said to you that your signals were being answered, did they say how they were being answered? — I think I heard somebody say that she showed a light.

15407. Do you mean that she would be using a Morse lamp? — Quite probably.

15408. Then you thought she was near enough to Morse her from the *Titanic*? — Yes, I do think so; I think so yet.

I judged her to be between 5 and 6 miles when I Morsed to her, and then she turned round; she was turning very, very slowly, until at last I only saw her stern light, and that was just before I went away in the boat.

15410. Did she make any sort of answer to your Morse signals? — I did not see any answer whatever. Some people say they saw lights, but I did not. They did not say she Morsed, but they said the showed a light. Then I got the Quartermaster who was with me to call her up with our lamps, so that I could use the glasses to see if I could see signs of any answer; but I could not see any … Captain Smith also looked, and he could not see any answer.

15414. He also looked at her through the glasses? — Yes.

15415. After a. time you saw what you took to be the stern light of a ship? — It was the stern light of the ship.

15416. Did you infer from that that the ship was turned round, and was going in the opposite

direction? — Yes.

15417. When you first saw her, I understand you to say she was approaching you? — She was approaching us, yes.

15418. For about how long did you signal before it seemed to you that she turned round? — I cannot say; I cannot judge any of the times at all.

The picking-up of *Titanic* survivors. Captain Smith hoped his lifeboats would be able to row to a mystery ship that he could see at relatively close quarters.

Boxhall is the prime witness to the mystery ship – the only survivor to have studied her through binoculars. He repeated at a 1913 liability hearing his impression that the vessel was a steamer, and that she was approximately five miles away.

Fifty years after the disaster, in 1962, Boxhall further suggested in a BBC radio broadcast that he had used not only binoculars, but also a telescope, and that he could even see the portholes of the vessel:

'I heard the crow's nest report a light on the starboard bow. Well … I found this light with my own glasses – but I wanted the telescope to define what it was. And I realised then it was two masthead lights of a steamer below the horizon and the lights were very close.

'I went back and told the Captain: 'There is a steamer in sight, very nearly ahead but slightly on the starboard bow, and if she continues on her course she'll pass close to us down the port side.' Well I asked the Captain, 'Shall I send up some distress rockets, sir?' Then we started sending off these distress rockets …

'We also called up this ship, as she grew closer, with a Morse lamp, a very powerful Morse lamp that we had, and eventually this steamer approached and approached, until you could see her with the naked eye, and I should say that she must have been within five miles off.

'You could not only see her lights with the naked eye, but you could see the lights in her portholes. So I reckon she must have been within five miles. And then eventually she turned away and showed her stern light.'

The witness is offered to the defence.

Counsel for Captain Moore: The evidence offers no identification of any ship, other than to confirm that it is a mystery. The nature and location of that vessel, the compass directions offered, are also surmises. They must be as prone to error as the SOS position proved to be, which was wrong by 13 miles. Just one question to the witness:

15635. When the *Titanic* struck, of course it was necessary to ascertain her position in order that the distress messages might be sent out? — Just so.

15636. Who was it who did ascertain her position after she struck? — I did.

The witness withdrew.

VOYAGE OF THE *MOUNT TEMPLE*

THE SS *Mount Temple* was a sturdy workhorse of a ship. Built by Armstrong Whitworth & Co. of Newcastle-upon-Tyne, she was launched for the Beaver Line on June 18, 1901 – and named after a peer of the realm, rather than the peak of the same name in the Canadian Rockies.

The *Mount Temple* was 8,790 tons gross, or 6,661 net. She was 485ft long, had a beam of 59ft, and was outfitted with four masts and a single funnel. She sailed to New Orleans on her maiden voyage that September, but was soon commandeered for the British war effort in South Africa.

On November 4, 1901, she steamed from New Orleans to Cape Town in the first of two voyages as a transport ship in the Boer War campaign. Two years later the Beaver Line was taken over, and she joined the fleet list of the Canadian Pacific Railway Company, flying its distinctive red and white chequered house flag.

She was now put to use in the emigrant trade, arranged with accommodations for 1,250 third class passengers and just fourteen saloon passengers. Her first voyage on the Liverpool to Montreal route was on May 17, 1903.

Nine years later, and the *Mount Temple* lay moored in the bright light of an early morning at Gravesend in the Thames estuary. Smoke curled from her yellow funnel and drifted, dissipating, over the silver surface.

Originally envisaged as a livestock carrier – meaning cattle, before the British saw her as a means to ship hundreds of mules and horses to a faraway front – the *Mount Temple* had moved beyond the steers of the 'steerage.' Humans were her cash crop.

Her derricks had creaked and swung in recent days, taking stores aboard, a small general cargo, and quantities of ballast. Lighters had brought coal – a scarce commodity because of the miners' strike – to be shunted down the chutes as quickly as possible before someone suggested the black treasure be diverted to some more deserving hull. Fresh water was poured into her tanks, becoming water upon the water, but all of it would be vital to the well-being of the valuable freight anticipated at her first port of call.

There were the usual pre-voyage checks to be attended to, the hundred-and-one details, the reams of paperwork. It would be the vessel's sixty-second voyage west, and her Captain, James Henry Moore, doubted it would be any different from the sixty-one that had preceded it.

A portly, Falstaffian man, Moore was aged 51. A native of Birkenhead, he had been going to sea for 32 years – nearly a third of a century, he marvelled – with twenty-seven years thereof spent floating about on the North Atlantic. There was little, he fancied, he had not seen in all that time.

It had been his birthday a week ago, and he had been fortunate indeed to spend it at home with his wife Mary, mistress at a boy's school, at number 11, Neville Road, Waterloo, Liverpool. The lines beneath his grey eyes crinkled into a smile as he remembered it, entering his home address onto the front of the official log, as he was required to do when setting out anew.

Of course, Doris, the baby – at sixteen – had been there. But it was a surprise to see son Harry, who had followed him into the merchant marine and who had magicked some time off. The other two boys, William and Reg, were in Canada now, where he plied to himself – although he rarely saw them. They had gone under the Dominion Land Act of 1908, filing for their homesteads for a fee of just ten dollars, and both were now away out west. Emigrants, like all his passengers, every voyage, all 61 …

And wasn't he the son of an emigrant himself? William Moore, dock labourer, born 1820 in Ireland and lucky to escape the famine in 1847. Arrived in Liverpool with all the other hordes of starving, it being the nearest big city across the Irish Sea. Then there was his own brother,

Above: A broad portside view of the *Mount Temple* at Newcastle. *Titanic* officer Boxhall formed the view that the mystery ship he saw was a three or four mast steamer, and 'by the position of her masthead lights; they were close together.'

Right: Mount Temple sixth engineer Arthur Hugh Brenton Reed. Died in 1947 at Perth, WA, aged 56.

Below: Reed's discharge book. He was making his first sea voyage at age 20, signing aboard on March 29.

No.	*Name of ship and official number, Port of registry, and tonnage.†	*Date and place of engagement.	*Rating; and R.N.R. No. (if any).	Date and place of discharge.	Description of voyage.	Signature of Master.
5	**CERTIFICATE**		**OF DISCHARGE.**	6		
1	Mount Temple 113496 — £ L'pool 6661	29-3-12 London	6 Engr.	1 MAY 1912 DOCK ST. E.		Jas H Moo.
2				28 JUN.1912 DOCK STREET,		

William, who went to North America, worked as a cowboy, and was now moved to Argentina, enjoying his own ranch and every trapping of prosperity. Oh, there was a lot to be said for cattle – and a lot to be said for not going anywhere at all, least of all the sea, if it could be avoided. Another brother, Joseph, had the right idea. Went up the road and married a Northern Irish girl whose family had their own distillery.

Soon the pleasant reveries were banished and he had instead a nasty taste in his mouth. The Pearce brothers of Blackwall, John and George, hadn't bothered to turn up. He had signed them both, several days ago, as trimmers, or coal-ferrymen for the furnaces; they having been full of earnest talk about needing the work because of the effects of this strike. Family men both of us, they said, mature; 36 and 31, and they wouldn't let him down. Well, they did. He grimaced, and told the purser he may as well have their Discharge A books sent ashore, to the shipping master at Dock Street.

All else seemed in readiness. The Board of Trade surveyor had passed the ship while he was away home. He thumbed his white goatee beard once or twice in thought, wondering whether he was forgetting anything. The nagging sailor's superstition that it was unlucky to sail on a Friday – well it couldn't be helped. The pilot came aboard, was rather cheery, no doubt in anticipation of his weekend, and Captain Moore resolved to watch his every move carefully, even as he ordered the engines to stand-by.

Home waters were by no means safe, he reflected, and fourteen bodies were still missing. It would be exactly two weeks in just a few hours … a terrible tragedy. The P. & O. liner

The sinking of the
P & O liner *Oceana*,
as depicted in the
Illustrated London News
of March 23, 1912.

Mount Temple, left, pictured in the Tyne. Photographed at Newcastle early in her career.

Above left: Purser Harold J. Shaw of the *Mount Temple*, who also had a role in the apprehension of Crippen. Shaw (1887-1931) was torpedoed in the Great War, later became a collector of taxes, but died from pneumonia in Liverpool at age 43.

Above right: 'Miss Ethel le Neve – disguised as a boy – and Dr. Crippen. This snapshot I took secretly from my cabin in the *Montrose* as they were promenading the deck.' From *Adventures on the High Seas* (Hurst & Blackett, 1939) by Captain H. G. Kendall.

Oceana, sailing from the Thames for Bombay, passing him on the very day he had arrived in from St John – March 15 it was – had collided with the German barque *Pisagua* in the hours of darkness.

Passengers and crew had taken to the boats, but one boat swamped and several lives were lost. There was an attempt to tow the *Oceana*, which had valuable specie aboard, into Dover. But it failed and she sank six miles southeast of Eastbourne. Ten corpses had been recovered, against which all the gold bullion hardly weighed in the balance. But for the P. & O. company, it was the first time in its history that it had to record loss of life among passengers by shipwreck. Would not like to be the Captain facing that inquiry.

At 9.30am the screws turned, churning up the riverbed to a sandy wake, and they cast off in the cold. The vessel gave a low grumble of complaint and then moved past the marker buoy, out into the ever-deeper channel. Operating port-reverse, starboard-ahead, she neatly turned there – the sun glinting off her brasswork – and the avenue for Anvers, or Antwerp, whatever they may call it in their myriad tongues, lay clear ahead once more. Dutifully, *Mount Temple* moved for the open sea.

It took her all day and most of that night to trudge the 160 nautical miles across this small apron of the great grey widowmaker, but eventually the lights of Zeebrugge were seen to starboard, and *Mount Temple* could adjust her course to enter the Scheldt. She ran comfortably through the channel that narrowed into a passage as it drew her ever deeper towards the city.

It was in the dawn hours of Saturday that ropes were flung ashore to dimly-viewed figures on the Jordaens quay, with a new pilot barking bellicose French, then abruptly taking his leave.

Advancing morning brought desultory cargo work, but the vessel was mostly at ease. Purser Harold James Shaw came about some concerns, minor matters, customs and how many new crew should be taken on, because they had crossed with a light complement. Many crew were already sauntering into town, with time off due for all, but with it awarded the earnest injunction not to court any trouble.

'This is, after all, the scene of the crime,' said Moore knowingly to Shaw, who grinned at the recollection. Crippen, the English murderer, had fled to this city with his young lover after committing his dreadful deed at Hilldrop Crescent. Crippen, who disguised Ethel le Neve as a young lad, then booked aboard as Mr and Master Robinson, bound for Canada and a new life.

Ah, but that was the *Montrose*, Moore's old ship, of happy and unhappy memory. He had left her in 1908, two years before she became world-renowned – when the vessel carrying the fugitives, their true identities detected, was pursued by the faster *Laurentic* with Inspector Walter Dew of Scotland Yard aboard; a mass and ravenous readership equally following each and every new development.

It was the miracle of wireless, or at least another miracle from that new medium. And Harry Shaw had been aboard. The young purser had then admitted himself to the suspects' cabin after a suitable subterfuge, and had seen the revolver among the fleeing dentist's few possessions. Also on that same CPR ship, and aboard this one too, had been Chief Officer Alfred Henry Sargent. It was Sargent who had first raised suspicions about Crippen; Sargent who went to Captain Kendall, saying something was not right about this man and his 'son;' but Kendall, the glory-grabber, who had assumed control of the story, who had signed the wireless messages sending warning back home, who had been showered with all the honours. And the rewards, too.

'You had better study your passengers most carefully this time too, because now you enjoy a Captain who will share it out fairly,' joked Moore, knowing that while a criminal background was not to be doubted among at least some of those due aboard in coming days, there would be no international hue-and-cry over any of them. Hardly a tear to be shed if they all went to the bottom, in fact, crew included.

A couple of emigrants wandered to the quayside to inspect their impending home, although they were not allowed aboard. Passengers emigrating to the New World had to be in Antwerp

Above and middle: A Canadian Pacific liner tied up at the Jordaens Quay in Antwerp where *Mount Temple* moored in April 1912.

The high promenade above the Jordaens Quay in Antwerp where *Mount Temple* moored in April 1912.

at least two days before departure. They had a habit of selling their horse and cart on arrival, to help fund lodgings for a day or two. As a result, the price of horseflesh here was practically the lowest in Europe. Western Europe, that is ...

Belgian law stipulated that all cargo had to be on board before passengers were allowed to embark, while the owners of guesthouses were compelled to accompany their customers to their respective ships, a simple precaution against crimps – although sometimes the unversed emigrant misunderstood their close attentions.

In cases where legions marched to the docks in the morning or early afternoon it was not uncommon to wait until the next day to board, since loading the ship (not least with their personal belongings) could be a time-consuming affair. The scurvy clientele were forced to huddle under open hangars for hours, not pleasant in the biting wind of a harbour.

Prior to embarkation they also had to undergo strict medical inspection. Doctors could each see about 100 people an hour, although there were rarely more than two of them, even if a thousand intending passengers should wait. Those in questionable condition were ruthlessly rejected, because North America's guardians were even harsher – and would send them straight home as a charge on the company, although, in fairness, Canada sometimes let them in to die in quarantine. Instances of families being separated were not uncommon, particularly at what one might call the lower end of the market, wherein the CPR Antwerp liners seemed to specialise. The Magyars and Russians, Ruthenians, Poles. A lot of poor clothing, bad teeth, and low personal hygiene. Still, it paid.

Tuesday April 2, the day before the Atlantic sailing. An Austrian and a German were signed on as trimmers, wheelbarrow men for the furnaces, and a Swede was engaged as a fireman. Sixteen Belgians and Dutch, give or take, came aboard as assistant stewards. They could generally make themselves understood to the other crowd.

John Ehmig, an Austrian, came aboard to cook for the foreigners. Meanwhile George William Luxon, a solid Englishman despite the odd name, had shown a steady purpose in the stokehold and it had been noticed. It was proposed to promote him from trimmer to fireman, with a few extra bob a week.

But Torner, the Swede, had not impressed during his hour or two aboard. Why, his clumsy action showed he had never slung coal in his life, and it had all been a lie. He was going to be downgraded to a barrow boy, subsidising Luxon in effect, the latter grinning like a mudlark. When Torner was told the bad news, that his game was up, he replied 'All right.' At least he would be staying aboard, he consoled himself.

Sailing day: Spy Wednesday, April 3, 1912. They had all tramped up the gangway into Moore's ark, whole extended families, young couples, and entire enlistments of men in their twenties – brothers, friends, neighbouring villagers, strangers.

The *Mount Temple* would carry 1,466 passengers on this trip, with all but five of them in steerage. The below-decks amounted to a whole town in itself, a babble of tongues and a rabble of humanity. The overwhelming majority were adults – 1,304 – with just 157 children. It would be claustrophobic and cacophonous, as so many times before.

Canadian Pacific—s. LAKE MANITOBA, for Liverpool, left St. John, N.B., 10 a.m. Wednesday. MOUNT TEMPLE, London for St. John, N.B., signalled Lizard 9.15 a.m. yesterday 48 miles east.

The *Times* of London, April 6, 1912, notes the opening of the *Mount Temple*'s momentous voyage that would coincide with the *Titanic* disaster.

French language advertisement in a Belgian newspaper for the *Mount Temple*'s *Titanic* voyage – departing Antwerp on April 3, 1912, as part of regular and direct winter services for St John and Halifax.

Canadian Pacific Railway

Atlantic Steamship Lines

SERVICE D'HIVER

DÉPARTS RÉGULIERS ET DIRECTS POUR

ST-JOHN N. B. & HALIFAX (N. S.)

St. MOUNT TEMPLE, partira le 3 Avril

Connaissements directs pour

CANADA & LES ETATS-UNIS

Pour tous renseignements s'adresser à T. Mc NEIL, agent, 25, Quai Jordaens
Emplacement fixe   Hangar 23/24 (Sud)

An advertisement for the last departure of the season – the sailing of *Mount Temple* from Antwerp on April 3, 1912. From the Belgian newspaper *Neptune*.

Canadian Pacific Railway
ATLANTIC STEAMSHIP LINES

Saison d'HIVER

Dernier départ de la Saison

pour

St. John N.B. et Halifax N.S.

St. MOUNT TEMPLE,   3 Avril.

Fréts à forfait et connaissements directs pour :

Montreal, Quebec, Hamilton, London, Toronto, Ottawa, Kingston, Winnipeg, Portage, Brandon, Vancouver, Victoria, Chicago, St-Paul, Minneapolis, Tacoma, Seattle, Portland et Honolulu.

A starboard view of the *Mount Temple*.

But there was no concern, although outbreak of disease was often to be expected among the tightly-packed throng, even after their being passed by quayside medics. 'I have carried over 1,800 passengers,' shrugged Captain Moore. He could have carried more this very trip ...

And he had twenty lifeboats.

The RMS *Titanic*, eight times larger, had twenty lifeboats too. On her maiden voyage the new White Star liner would carry 1,316 passengers all told. The lowly *Mount Temple* held 150 more.

On Good Friday April 5, the *Mount Temple*, 'from London for St John, N.B.,' signalled the wireless station located at a famous lighthouse in southwest Cornwall. The Lizard, well known to mariners as the southernmost point of mainland Britain, had a colourful name that derived from the Cornish/Gaelic 'Lios Ard,' or 'high fort.'

It was 9.15am, and the Canadian Pacific liner transmitted that she was 48 miles east in the English Channel. This bare fact would be reported the next day in the 'Shipping Intelligence' column of the London *Times*, along with the news that her sister, the *Lake Manitoba*, had coincidentally just left St John for Liverpool.

But the report offers some meaning. It disclosed that the *Mount Temple* was in latitude 49 58 N, longitude 03 58 W, and had travelled some 358 miles since her 1pm departure from Antwerp, two days before.

The time elapsed was actually 44 and a quarter hours, giving the liner a speed of exactly eight knots. It made sense to show a little caution in these busy shipping lanes, and a touch more speed could be applied in the open Atlantic.

The temperature was about five degrees warmer than usual for the time of year, a pleasant turn of events. It had been dull and cloudy when leaving Antwerp, improving first to moderate, and then to fair, with good visibility in the Channel. A light westerly wind came against them, a further mercy when much worse might have been on offer.

Advertising for Canadian Pacific steamers, c. 1910, painting a tranquil deck scene. Some passengers loiter beside decorative lifeboats.

The ship had settled into her routine.

All day she steamed southwest on the Great Circle route, leaving England behind and capturing a horizon of unrelieved sea and sky. A few hardy souls among the passengers climbed the companion ladders from their bulkhead-divided compartments to take the air, but this was not a vessel in which they were encouraged to engage in jollity, playing quoits or deck games. Many remained stoically down below, content to while away the time in talk, or a Cyrillic book, or in dealing out a grubby set of cards – although monetary gambling was nominally forbidden.

Saturday was much the same, a piece of transatlantic tedium, although it was clear that some were enlivened by the prospect of Easter Sunday on the morrow, with many a mother smiling inwardly, having provided little treats for their offspring in the advance of the voyage. The large crowd of Orthodox aboard seemed particularly enthused, with knots of the men forming themselves into a choir, practising sacred and patriotic songs for the service. The significant complement of Jews had already seen Passover, the day before sailing, and took a detached interest, being more concerned with their own Sabbath, due to end that evening.

Captain Moore was of a mind that Easter should not be a day of any lesser effort by his crew. He scheduled a boat muster, as was his usual habit on a Sunday, and saw that it was carried out. The available men shivered by their stations, were inspected, and mostly dismissed. Two boats were readied and swung out. The lifesaving appliances were examined and certified fit and ready.

Twenty boats at 49 occupants each; 1,000 souls at most. Captain Moore certified that the duty had been carried out. They had wanted him to bring 2,200 this trip, until the 700 others were diverted to another sailing. He had not so much protested to the agent as sounded somewhat unhappy – it was more effective.

George William Luxon, stokehold
hand on the *Mount Temple*

The Allan liner RMS *Corsican*, original source of an important ice warning to the *Mount Temple*.

He squinted at the boats in the sunshine. Although well-built and buoyant, able to live in almost any sea, there was the question of getting them down into the water. Certainly, they could be shoved out easily enough by a couple of crew, and lowered by only two men, but if there was an emergency in a storm or a gale ... if the vessel were rolling or pitching, it should be a very dangerous operation.

If there was any rolling of the ship and the boat came back against the ship's side, I'm afraid there would not be any boat left, not at this great height.

Soon it was time for the noon observations. The position was entered in the log: April 7, Latitude 49° 27' N, Longitude 15° 35' W. Hieroglyphics to any of those passengers, but a long way from the Holy Land. Only a dead sea, it seemed eternally.

The ship's surgeon had been busy. William Arthur Bailey had been squinting too, checking the eyes of some of the ABs, a test of the sight of the lookouts for their own satisfaction. The ship put nobody in the crow's nest by day, but lookouts were certainly needed at night. Just as he was looking at one of them, word had come of an accident in the stokehold.

Big Bill Luxon was howling with pain, bubbles of blisters already forming on his seared left arm. Blowback from the furnace, a shot of superheated flame had savaged it in one second as he steadied the shovel, dropping it, recoiling wounded. Dr Bailey diagnosed burns of the second degree, and Luxon was placed off duty. Better for him to have stayed a trimmer, perhaps.

The days merged in monotony, amid the immutable murmur of machinery. Another Saturday came, being April 13 (what was happening in England? What in Canada?), with the only news that Luxon had resumed work 'of a suitable light nature.' A Hebrew injunction not to light a fire on the Sabbath, and yet they all depended on that coal-hungry combustion. Ships had run out of fuel before, that dreadful story of the *Atlantic*, same month as this, the last century. Half a thousand dead on the rocks of Nova Scotia, and the White Star Line nearly sunk altogether.

Noon. Latitude 43° 2' N, Longitude 44° 13' W. Total distance elapsed since Antwerp, two thousand and seventy nautical miles. An average speed of eight and two-third knots. And still the utter isolation; the humbling, numbing continuum of grey overhead and dark beneath.

It was late that night there was a surprise development. Wireless operator John Oscar Durrant, 'Jod' to some and Jack to his family, was still at his set. It was around 11pm ship's time, but since longitude 40 W the lad had been operating exclusively on New York Time, as if the Atlantic was parted down the middle between Britain and America.

How Dr Bailey might have cradled dead infant Dozko Oziro. This *Daily Sketch* picture shows an *Adriatic* passenger with *Titanic* baby Millvina Dean on her post-disaster return to Britain. Millvina, the last survivor, died May 31, 2009 – the 98th anniversary of *Titanic*'s launch.

The tousle-haired 21-year-old felt no fatigue at that hour. He generally kept working until one o'clock in the morning, because he had a good sleep each afternoon after the midday meal, usually for about three hours. There was method to it – his set had a range of 150 miles in the daylight, rising to somewhere above 200 at night.

His headphones suddenly fizzed and faded with the familiar staccato, his pencil roaming quickly across his pad. It was a message from the Allan liner *Corinthian*, a master service message, from one Captain to another. It was a warning about ice.

The *Corinthian*, eastbound for England from the *Mount Temple*'s intended destination, was passing on an important advisory notice from her sister ship, the *Corsican*. This latter vessel, westbound for St John, and now just a day from that port, had seen a huge swathe of field ice on her voyage.

The longitude and latitude was given. Durrant regarded the details, and although not a navigating officer, knew he was bound to take the formal message straight to the bridge. Putting the message in Moore's hand, he could see the Captain was quite astounded. The ice was nearly a full day's sailing away, but straight in their path.

The Master was particularly taken aback at the latitude, the position on the north-south axis. 'We are not making the corner where we planned any more,' he sternly instructed his Officer of the Watch, 'I am going to the chartroom to re-draw.'

He turned back to Durrant and thanked him. As the latter repaired to his wireless shack, he could hear the Captain remarking: 'I have never in all my experience known the ice to be so far south.'

Sunday April 14, 1912 – and further alarm in the early hours. A steward wakened the ship's surgeon with the news that a child was dead or dying in steerage. Dr William Bailey snapped on the light. Thirty-eight years old, the son of a butcher and cattle dealer, formerly the locum in a ladies' lying-in hospital, he was soon in rudimentary dress and had snatched his bag.

Mount Temple wireless
operator John Oscar Durrant
pictured in the *Marconigraph*
in June 1912.

He and the steward hurried down the companionways, into the narrow corridors, the pens of steerage, the desperate family gathered by other stewards and shepherded to a brightly-lit store room, where already the sound of a piteous keening assailed the hurrying help.

The eyes, livid with hope, brimming with tears, were what he first saw when he entered, then the blanketed, bare-headed form in the dark woman's arms. Ignoring the weeping man and the others, Bailey snatched the infant, tore up the swaddling woollens, and placed his stethoscope on the chest. But no stethoscope could make this child – this baby – any colder. The mite was dead, and had been for some time.

He ran through some other empty forms, as if to find the ghost-fled vitals, appreciated a glimpse of the steward's hand at the woman's shoulder as she stood stock still, staring, open-mouthed. He became aware of the devastated man searching his own face as he slowly ceased what he was doing. Bailey rearranged the clothes, he hoped respectfully, then offered the bundle back to the woman. 'I'm sorry, madam. Your dear child is dead.'

The steward stepped back from the cataract of pain, the howls, Bailey too outside this sudden clump of hugging humanity, the woman sagging down to the floor, drawing them all down with her. He swallowed drily, fumbled instruments back into his bag, knew the ghastliness indeed of it. His own young wife, but a few years earlier. Why he was at sea.

In due course Bailey remembered to look at his watch, entering the time it had been – 3.50am – in his pocket notebook. A legal requirement to enter every birth, death and marriage in the log. The crushed man, taken aside, repeating the name, saying it more slowly, eventually writing it. *Dozko Oziro*. Aged three months.

And who was he? Dozko's father. Yes, but your name, sir, the formalities. The stewardess was here now, easily interpreting between them. Luc Oziro, aged 24, a labourer, born in Austria. How long had the child been sick? He did not know the child was sick. He called to his wife, 'Horpyna – ' and then a rush of words, but her tear-streaked and upward-turned oval offered only a picture of despair. Regrets, regrets. 'She did not know the child was sick either,' said Miss Symanski, whether interpreting or inferring. The husband shook his head.

'You will have to explain to him that I will need the body to perform a post-mortem, but they will get it back in a few hours, and we will give the child a proper burial, I promise. I must carry out a p-m where there is no history of medical treatment on the voyage, no prior sign of illness. I must do it.'

The interpreter and steward undertook to see that it was done, and that the body would be brought to the infirmary. 'I will start at seven,' added Bailey, moving down the corridor. Probably nothing much, he thought to himself, or at least nothing notifiable. Slightest breeze can carry off these Slavic sucklings. Thin and weak to begin with. He returned to his bedding-strewn bunk, where the light was still on. It struck him he had not determined the baby's sex. Well, time enough.

Next day noon, and it had all been entered in the log, the details and the doctor's diagnosis. The early stages of broncho-pneumonia. Possibility of a little spread through the steerage, he mentioned to the Captain, and he would have a better idea from counting the coughs on his rounds. They had all signed the official entry – J.H. Moore, Master; W.A. Bailey, surgeon; H. Shaw, purser.

But now it was a matter of committing the body of Dozko Oziro to the deep. The boy was swaddled again, this time in a weighted, canvas shroud. He lay on a stretcher that rested on the ship's rail, the inboard handles easily supported by two sailors. There were muffled sounds of grief, somewhat incongruous clucking from a nearby hen-coop, and the stern and steady timbre: 'Insofar as it pleaseth Almighty God that this, the body of our brother -' the Captain paused momentarily – 'Dozko … '

The first body into the Atlantic this trip.

His last hour was up, John Oscar Durrant reflected. He stood from his chair, unbuttoned his tunic, and prepared for bed. Within minutes he was under the coverlet, his hand sneaking out for the headset he could not leave alone. He sat up, pulled his book from under his pillow, and flicked to the page with the turned-down edge. He fixed the headphones over his ears – in case anything came in while he was reading. Soon it would be time to let it all go, and turn in properly. Another day would pass into the ship's wake – indeed, had already done so. It was past midnight, ship's time. The bells calling the Middle Watch told him that, just as his consulted wristwatch could, adjusted every day to the governing ship's chronometer. But the clock in his shack, set to New York time, insisted it was but a quarter past ten. When clock and wristwatch met in harmony they would be tying up in British North America. New Brunswick.

He glanced at the pile of notes on the adjacent desk, exchanges of ships' times, called TRs, or time rushes. Nothing doing tonight. Cape Race had been busy lately, jabbering away, but the rest of the unseen shipping world was mostly quiet. No more direct ice reports to themselves, thank goodness. Nothing to bother the bridge about. Only some old Germans talking, one to another. Braunschweig – that's what Brunswick comes from, so they say. Probably some battle or other, for the Germans hardly got to Canada, although they were making up for it now.

Tell a lie, there was quite a bit of news tonight. He lowered the book absently and thought of that oil tanker adrift, another German. What was her name? The *Deutschland*, yes, not under power and needing a tow. A number of ships going after the prize. The *Parisian* racing against the *Asian*, or so it seemed. Pretty penny if you could pick up a salvage like that. Too far away for a slow old tub like us.

His first ship, now, that's what you'd want. The mighty *Mauretania*, win any race. Ocean greyhound and all that, but somehow they probably wouldn't lower themselves to give any old bucket a rope into port, no matter what the money. Too many first class passengers, all complaining that they would have taxicabs waiting in west Manhattan. Beastly lot, with their beastly boasts … thank God he didn't have to tap out their insufferable messages any more, nor on the *Victoria* either. A lot of showing off to shore-based friends, because the tidings were all claptrap. No news from a sea voyage anyway, so what to say? Except having a splendid time, and expect to arrive on such-and-such, and look at us, we are speaking from over the sea. How jolly! And how jolly expensive too, but that was all part of it. Exclusivity. And fellows like himself, the machine minder son of a machine minder, from old Buxhall in Suffolk, sending it out for all of them.

Bee-dip dip, dee-dee dip, here we go again. Some smart alec, no doubt looking for the baseball scores, – no, the big ship. *Titanic.* Good lord! She's sending CQD. Is she? C. Q. D., again. C. Q. D. God Almighty! 'Require immediate assistance. Position this-and-that north, and so-and-so west. Come at once. Iceberg.'

He sat stunned. Then he shot out of bed, standing hunched at the instrument alongside. His finger flashed at the key. 'Have you struck ice? Please confirm.' Silence. The great void. Then the flaring spit of reply: 'Cannot read you, old man. Here my position … Come at once. Have struck berg.'

He tore off his headset. Looked where he had written it. Queasily he peeled the page, then let it lie there until he had some clothes on. Oh please, do not be wrong! *Titanic* calling CQD.

CIRCUMSTANTIAL EVIDENCE

IT is now time to deal with circumstantial evidence, which is not to say that it is flimsy, indicative material, but rather that it relates to the circumstances. We now know, a century on, where the *Titanic* actually had been before she sank, because the wreck lies on the sea bed. Where was the *Mount Temple*?

The prosecution case is that the Official Log of the *Mount Temple*, or a document purporting to be such, contains false information. It shall be demonstrated that one of the positions certified by officers of that ship, at least, must be wrong. Then there will be what might be called sins of omission in relation to the entire *Titanic* affair, because the official log (or what is offered as such) contains not a word about the whole episode.

Thirdly, it will be shown that Captain Moore cited different positions for his vessel at a particular point crucial to his argument that he had not seen any ice until 'about three o'clock' – which was substantially *after* the *Titanic* had sunk. If he didn't see any ice at all to this point, then he could hardly have been the latter's mystery ship.

And fourthly, you will be satisfied that Captain Moore's description of his location at the time he received the CQD or SOS is absolutely inconsistent with his own testimony as to the speed of his ship in attempting, as he said, to render assistance – and with the time of arrival at the position indicated in *Titanic* distress messages.

Fifthly, there is the matter of Captain Moore's own suggestion that another vessel may have been the mystery ship, a steamer he describes in rudimentary terms – as an enigmatic foreigner, dark and indeterminate – which description led to a huge wild goose chase in 1912, at considerable cost to the British taxpayer in particular, but which also bothered various other bureaucracies to no possible avail.

This is because that steamer, fingered by Captain Moore, could not have been the mystery ship, unless – and this is crucial – his own vessel had an equally likely chance of fulfilling that role herself. These two ships, the *Mount Temple* and the 'foreign tramp,' are absolutely tied together, and out of Captain Moore's own mouth.

There are many more inconsistencies. The *Mount Temple* did a most unusual thing, at least according to her log, when warned of ice at night – she thereafter applied the highest speed of her entire voyage. If her own longitude and latitude positions are to be believed, she did this despite Captain Moore saying, in reference to the *Titanic*, that it would be 'most unwise' to approach an icefield at high speed, albeit that the latter's top rate was double that of his own ship. The usual thing, Captain Moore said, when approaching ice at night, was to stop and wait for daylight. He did not do this, but of course he will tell you that he did not see any ice. He just increased speed when told about unseen ice that lay in his path.

And the *Mount Temple* did not transmit her own position, or how many miles away she was, to the *Titanic* at any stage. She kept absolutely silent from the moment Captain Moore turned around to the rescue – despite many other liners and steamers giving their own positions and distances, all of which indicated that the *Mount Temple* was, as far as she knew, actually the nearest participant in the whole drama. Instead it would fall to the *Carpathia*, a ship that claimed to be further away than Captain Moore would have for his own vessel, which rescued all of the survivors.

So this is circumstantial evidence, all of it, and there is no absolute proof either way as to where the *Mount Temple* was during those fateful hours of darkness on the night of April 14/15, 1912. But the many myriad discrepancies, such as Moore's positional contradictions in evidence, his citing of that tramp, his impossible speeds, must all be taken into account and judged in the round, together with everything else.

23

OFFICIAL LOG of the
from *Antwerp*   *Mount Temple*
                          towards *St John NB*

Date of the Occurrence entered with Hour.	Place of the Occurrence, or situation by Latitude and Longitude at Sea.	Date of Entry.	Entries required by Act of Parliament.	Amount of Fine or Forfeiture inflicted.
Noon. *April 14*	*Lat 41-35N* *Long 48-20W*	*14/4/12*	*The body of Dozko Ozino, Coaled to the deep*	
			Jas H Moore Master	
			R H Cas Purser	
			W a Bailey (nurse) Surgeon	
Abris 19	*St John NB*	*19/4/12*	*J Wood, A Steinberg, & J Maguire*	

The Official Log of the *Mount Temple* shows no entries from noon on April 14, 1912 to arrival in St John five days later.

To dismiss individual matters of disquiet as 'not proving anything' in themselves may be to miss what the greater pattern sequentially discloses, and discloses inescapably. When one item after another is strung together in a necklace, it becomes inherently unlikely that the minority chance each time – the reasonable doubt – is the correct interpretation in every single instance. Not impossible, of course, but that likelihood progressively dwindles with each new consideration, and the circumstantial evidence adduced here will be supplemented by the testimony of a range of witnesses.

Counsel for Captain Moore: Witnesses we cannot test.

To take matters in order, refer to the exhibit that is the *Mount Temple* log, now held at the National Maritime Museum in Greenwich, London (CPR/10/18). The log is on an official form, No. 5, of which thousands were distributed, and consists of a series of loose, folded sheets (each consisting of four pages) that are numbered sequentially. These loose sheets have been bound together by thread.

It is not a gummed or stapled document, and instead the thread has been darned through the sheets and tied at the spine to hold them together. It is not possible to say, on cursory examination, whether all sheets originally belonged together. It is equally the case that there is nothing to say they have ever been apart, other than the fact that the 'darning' method could allow certain pages to be taken out, and fresh, but sequential, pages to be inserted.

Counsel for Captain Moore: To quote from my learned friend, Robertson Dunlop, representing the Leyland Line, owners of the *Californian*, at the British *Titanic* inquiry of 1912: 'The log, on the face of it, appears to be a perfectly genuine log.'

Be that as it may, we are faced with a log that has scant entries in places. From sailing day, April 3, and for each of the following three days, there are no entries at all. The position of the *Mount Temple* on April 5 is deduced from the report of the wireless station at the Lizard. The first positional entry is for April 7, followed by ones for April 9 and 13. It is to be assumed that each is a noon recording of latitude and longitude, which would be the most natural and the most appropriate.

The average speeds between these waymarkers, including from Antwerp to the Lizard position, are of 8 knots, 8.9kt, 9.18kt and 8.38kt. And in all this time, over these ten days, the

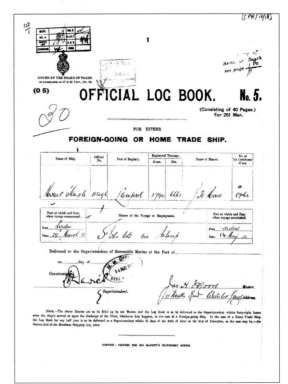

Cover of Official Log book, form
No. 5, 'consisting of 40 pages.' Signed
by Captain Moore to lower right, this
one for the *Mount Temple* has 32 pages.

Mount Temple has been journeying to the south and west, along a Great Circle route towards North America.

A huge change now takes place, and in relation to Sunday April 14, 1912, the very day on which the *Titanic* would strike ice. The official log suggests, not once, but twice, that the *Mount Temple* performed a very strange manoeuvre.

At noon on the previous day, she is in latitude 43 02 N, longitude 44 03 W. The latitude, to recap, is her distance north from the equator. The longitude is her distance west from Greenwich, which is designated zero.

But nearly sixteen hours later, at 3.50am when the doctor is called for little Dozko Oziro, the log records a position of latitude 43 56½ N, longitude 46 43 W. Look at the latitude – instead of continuing south and west since the previous noon, the log shows that the vessel has gone *north* and west.

This baffling diversion to the northwest is in the order of 121 miles – and would indicate a speed of only 7.64kt, if correct. There would be a strong inclination to write it off as an error inscribed in the early hours, were it not for the fact that this entry is certified with the signatures of the Captain, the ship's surgeon, and the purser.

But the death of Dozko Oziro is also recorded elsewhere in the log, in a space reserved for births, deaths and marriages on the voyage, and here the position is repeated as latitude 43 56½ N, longitude 46 43 W.

The latitude of 43 56½ N is astounding because it means a sudden dogleg to the northwest, as if the *Mount Temple* were seeking to eventually enter the Cabot strait (between Newfoundland and Nova Scotia), that would lead her towards the St Lawrence seaway, the river itself and ultimately Quebec and Montreal – with no possible way to obtain her destination (St John, New Brunswick), unless she became amphibious, landed south of Prince Edward Island, and took off cross-country towards the Bay of Fundy.

Yet there are two separate entries in the log, in different places, with this same longitude and latitude for the early hours of April 14. And both entries separately signed by these officers -

J.H. Moore, Master; W.A. Bailey, surgeon; H.J. Shaw, purser. It must be odd that not one of them noticed the discrepancy on either occasion, especially when they had all regularly sailed these waters and knew instinctively what the figures meant and what ought to have been the choreography of their changing daily position.

These six signatures by *Mount Temple* officers, in two different places of certification, would therefore amount to six individual errors in succession.

It would seem, looking at the long course since Antwerp, that the latitude should instead indicate a further declination, just as longitude would increase. The vessel should continue south and west, as it has been doing all the time – which would see the latitude come down from 43 02 N on the Saturday to 41 56½ N (rather than 43 56½) two-thirds of a day later. But if this is the case, it remains to be emphasised that an error of a full two degrees in latitude, one that was repeated in the official log, would represent a lapse in professional standards that is almost beyond comprehension.

On the face of the log, the problem gets worse if the two almost identical entries in respect of the shipboard death are compared with the next entry – that of noon on the Sunday that the *Titanic* collided. The midday position is latitude 41 38 N, longitude 48 20 W.

But this is a considerable distance away from the position twice logged for 3.50am on the same day. In those eight hours and ten minutes, the log would claim the *Mount Temple* sailed 156 nautical miles. But this would mean a speed of 19.11kt, gigantically more than for the rest of the voyage, and physically impossible for Moore's command. He was asked at question 9266 when giving evidence to the British inquiry, 'What is your highest speed?' and replied 'About 11 knots.'

Thus either the 3.50am entries are false, or the noon position is wrong, and there is no way that they can be reconciled.

Assuming, however, that an error of two degrees was made in the latitude for 3.50am on the Sunday, then the distance from the previous noon on Saturday would have been 128 miles, or a speed of eight knots, representing a slight slowing down.

To now reach the noon position on April 14 (From 41 56½ N, 46 43 W to the new 41 38 N, 48 20 W) represents 76 miles in 8.16 hrs. This is a speed of 9.31kt, which is much more reasonable.

But still there is a problem. The *Mount Temple* was warned of ice before the previous midnight in a Captain-to-Captain message from the *Corinthian*. There is no doubt both the wireless operator and the Master of the *Mount Temple* took it seriously, with an adjustment of course. But the speed had picked up considerably from 3.50am to noon, despite having been warned of ice, from a previous 8.38kt.

After being warned of ice during the night, the *Mount Temple* would thus have decided to go a knot faster than she had been doing!

This is very strange, and it will get worse. But first consider the import of Captain Moore's attitude to speeding in the wider vicinity of ice when asked about it in the case of the *Titanic*.

At question 9316 in London, he was asked, 'Now would you consider it safe in the neighbourhood of an ice field, provided your boat had the power, to go ahead at 21 knots?'

Moore replied; 'It would be most unwise to go that speed at night time.'

Speeding is naturally relative to the power of one's 'boat,' and Moore had been asked a similar question, responding similarly, at the US inquiry:

> Q. 'Suppose you had been warned in the afternoon of Sunday that ice was ahead; would you have considered it prudent or wise, under such circumstances, to have continued your speed as fast as 21½ knots?'
> Moore: 'I think it was very unwise, sir.'

In this same response, Moore acknowledged that on the same day he had been warned of ice himself, but unfortunately he made no reference to speed – specifically there is no disclosure that he may have speeded up:

'Before that, I received a message from the *Corinthian* saying that one of their vessels, the *Corsican*, had seen ice at 41 25 North, and 50 30 West. I immediately steered down to pass

Mount Temple at Gravesend in the Thames estuary. A number of small boats are dotted alongside. Had she rescued *Titanic* lifeboats, *Mount Temple* would be a celebrated ship today.

[longitude] 50° West in [latitude] 41 15 North, sir – that is, I was giving the ice 10 miles – and I came down and saw no ice whatever.'

Moore says he 'steered down,' indicating a change of course, which would suggest a precautionary change of direction involving steering only. There is no mention of the increase in speed that would be necessary at this point to even make sense of the overly-fair adjustment of his log to compensate for a giant error in indicated navigation.

The noon position is in the *Mount Temple* log, along with the crazy information relating to 3.50am that morning. But now Captain Moore is disclosing what he did that Sunday afternoon, having been warned about ice, in seeking to clear its southern limit so that he can resume his voyage – which would ultimately lead him back NW to pass south of Cape Sable at the southernmost tip of Nova Scotia, into the Bay of Fundy, and thence to St John.

Longitude 50 west is a very important meridian. The *Titanic* thought she sank a good deal beyond it, but she actually went down a little before the line was reached. Moore said he was coming down to a low latitude (or elevation on the north-south axis) in order to cross the line there.

He was 'giving the ice ten miles' because it had been indicated in latitude 41 25 N and he was aiming to reach 41 15 N, with each minute of latitude representing one nautical mile.

From the log's noon position, 41 38 N, 48 20 W, to an intended crossing point of 41 15 N, 50 W, is a distance of 78.6 nautical miles. At the typical speed of the voyage, he ought to have crossed in nine and one-third hours (8.38kt), which would mean 9.22pm, ship's time. Using an increased speed of 9.31kt would have shaved an hour off.

Now consider that Moore told both the American and British inquiries that he was in 41 25 N, 51 14 W when he received the *Titanic*'s distress call at 12.30am.

The distance from the crossing point to what might be called 'CQD point' is 57 nautical miles. This is interesting, because it means 78.6 nautical miles plus 57 miles, or a total of more than 135 miles, have been steamed since noon on April 14.

This distance, described by Moore himself, was covered in twelve and a half hours. But it represents a supercharged speed of nearly eleven knots (10.84kt).

The *Mount Temple* could not have been where her log says she was at noon on April 14, and where Captain Moore says he was just half a day and half an hour later. His ship's highest speed, he said, was 'about eleven knots.'

And he couldn't have been doing that at night, when he had been put highly on his guard about ice, and when his average speed, in the fair waters from Europe (from April 3 to April 13), over a distance of more than 2,000 nautical miles, had been just 8.66 knots.

Captain James Henry Moore of the *Mount Temple*

In an exchange at the British *Titanic* inquiry, Captain Moore suggested that he simply maintained his ordinary service speed, rather than significantly increasing it

Q. 9383. With regard to yourself, on this voyage did you get a Marconi notice that ice was about? — Yes.
9384. Was it fine clear weather? — Yes.
9385. Did you keep your speed? — I did.

There is no doubt, meanwhile, that Captain Moore turned his vessel around and attempted to reach the *Titanic*. The following morning, after the latter had gone down, he found himself in her distress-call latitude, but at an easternmost longitude of 50 09½ W.

The distance from here to St John is 840 nautical miles, which the *Mount Temple* completed in four days and three hours. She left the *Titanic* scene at 9am, according to Moore, and arrived at her quayside at noon on April 19.

This gives 99 hours to complete the distance, which can be seen to be an average speed over that time of just under 8½ knots. Even adjusting the parameters as much as possible results in a speed of only eight and three-quarter knots.

The indications, therefore, from the early part of the voyage (the first ten days) and the latter four days, it being a sixteen day trip, are that the *Mount Temple*'s speed would be very unlikely to suddenly substantially increase on the afternoon before the *Titanic* struck.

A major ramping-up of speed is needed to get his vessel to where he claimed it was when he received the distress call. Any more 'usual' speed and he is a lot closer to the *Titanic*. A more cautious attitude than earlier in the voyage would naturally mean a slower speed again – and even less distance travelled.

Captain Moore told the American Inquiry he crossed the major line of 50 W in latitude 41 15 N. But he told the British inquiry, held subsequent to the US investigation, that he crossed in latitude 41 20 N, or five miles further north.

This is no small matter – Captain Moore has changed his account from one official inquiry to another. And it is no use relying on his log for guidance, because the *Mount Temple* log contains no more navigational positions for the entire voyage after noon on April 14. Not a single one …

A postcard of the *Mount Temple* at Montreal.

Having told his listeners in Washington DC that he had been 'giving the ice ten miles,' Captain Moore was now blithely telling his audience in London that he was actually giving the ice just half that leeway, crossing in 41 20 N when the ice had been reported in 41 25 N.

It may be that this significant material difference in testimony by Captain Moore was not noticed by the British inquiry – although it is clear from the testimony that counsel in London had full access to the Washington transcripts. Indeed they quoted some of Moore's Washington evidence back to him. But not on latitude.

It is odd, on the face of it, that Moore should give different position s for crossing 50 W. Self-evidently, one of these positions (at least) is wrong, adding to the growing heap of contradictory claims for *Mount Temple* navigation.

A latitude of 41 20 instead of 41 15 would have meant 77 miles travelled since noon, not 78.6. The new, freshly-adjusted latitude would still have meant a distance of 56 nautical miles to the claimed position when the *Titanic* distress call was first heard. Taken together, the distance travelled in the 12½ hours to 12.30am is 133 nautical miles. The speed is 10.64kt, still very high, practically top speed – when top speed was not called for in the slightest, when Moore had instead been trying to project an air of caution and prudence.

Why the difference? Did Captain Moore consider that a more northerly crossing point might psychologically boost the story of reaching a claimed point for his ship (when the distress call was heard) that was almost beyond her maximum capabilities? Was he trying to trim as much as possible, having regard to the reality of the icefield he had manoeuvred around, while supposedly not seeing any ice?

The prosecution now calls Captain John Taylor Gambell of the Allan liner *Virginian*. He will testify in relation to Moore's new claim in London that he rounded the southern end of the icefield in 41 20 N instead of 41 15 N as he had said in Washington.

Captain Gambell reveals that the icefield instead extended as far south as 41 20 N, in other words five miles further south than had been indicated in the *Corinthian* warning (41 25 N) and that therefore Captain Moore had to have been skirting ice in 41 20 N, and must have seen it. He claims not to have seen any.

JOHN TAYLOR GAMBELL (1857-1936)

Aged 54 in 1912, and born in Liverpool, Captain Gambell lived at Mersey View in Seacombe on the Wirral. The son of a Plymouth-born sailmaker, he went to sea at an early age and was unfortunately widowed in 1886 after four years of marriage

He remarried in 1898 and had a long career with the Allan Line. Captain Gambell spoke to the press on his landfall in Liverpool in April 1912, and that report is tendered in evidence:

THE *VIRGINIAN*'S EFFORTS AT RESCUE
Press Association Special Telegram
Liverpool, Sunday.

The Allan liner *Virginian* arrived at Liverpool from Halifax this morning. Captain Gambell has made a report as to the wireless telegram he received in connection with the *Titanic* and his attempts to get to her. The report is as follows:

'Leaving Halifax at 8.51pm on the 13th inst., I came south of Sable Island, and steered a course to cross longitude 50 degrees west in latitude 43 30 north. Wind light N.W., and fine weather.

'At 12.40am ship's time on 15th inst. I received the following message by wireless from Cape Race – "*Titanic* struck iceberg, wants immediate assistance. Her position 41 46 north and 50 14 west." My position then was 43 27 north, 53 37 west. The *Titanic* bore from me south 55 [deg.] east. True distance 178 miles. I at once altered my course to go to her assistance and advised Cape Race and Messrs H. and A. Allan, Montreal, to that effect. At 1.20am I got a further message from Cape Race, which read: "*Titanic* reports ship sinking and putting women and children off in boats. *Olympic* making all speed towards *Titanic*, but much further off than *Virginian*. Her (*Olympic*'s) position latitude 40 32 north, longitude 61 18 west at 1.57am ship's time. The *Titanic*'s signals ceased abruptly as if power was suddenly cut off."

'At 3.45am I was in touch by wireless with the Russian steamer *Birma*, and gave her the *Titanic*'s position. She was then 55 miles from the *Titanic* and going to her assistance.

'At 5.45am I was in communication with the *Californian*, the Leyland Liner. He was 17 miles north of the *Titanic* and had not heard anything of the disaster. I Marconied her as follows – "*Titanic* struck iceberg. Wants assistance urgently. Ship sinking. Passengers in boats. His position latitude 41 46, longitude 50 14." Shortly after this I was in communication with the

The Allan liner *Virginian* in the St Lawrence.

Carpathia, the *Frankfurt*, and the *Baltic*, all going to the *Titanic*. At 8.10am I Marconied the *Californian*: – "Kindly let me know condition of affairs when you get to *Titanic*." He at once replied – "Can now see the *Carpathia* taking the passengers on board from small boats. The *Titanic* foundered about 2am."

'At 10am I received the following message from the *Carpathia*: "Turn back. Everything OK. We have 800 on board. Return to your Northern track."'

'At the same time the *Carpathia* sent the following message to the *Baltic* – "Am leaving here with all on board, about 800, chiefly third class and a lot of stewards. Proceed on your voyage to Liverpool. We are proceeding to Halifax or New York under full steam."

'I then altered my course to the eastward and continued on my voyage. In addition to the above messages, I learned from messages passing between the *Carpathia* and the *Olympic* that all the *Titanic*'s boats had been accounted for, and a careful search made for survivors among the wreckage and icefloes.

'I later learned that the *Californian* was going to remain in the vicinity for some time, and that the *Carpathia* had left for New York with 675 survivors on board.

'At 11am I sighted a field of ice and bergs to the north-east and at 11.20am, in latitude 42 30 and longitude 50 20, came up with a large field of heavy, close-packed ice with numerous bergs, stretching north and south as far as could be seen.

'I coasted around this to the south and south-west, and rounded the southern edge in **lat. 41 20, long. 50 02**, and steering east true finally cleared the ice in **lat. 41 20, long. 49 50**, the ice from that point trending away to the north-east. At 1pm I saw a steamer to the eastward, presumably the *Californian*, at the position of the wreck, but the icefield was between us and too heavy to take my ship through without incurring great risk of damage.'

In answer to questions, Captain Gambell said that from that point on he had clear weather. There was nothing eventful and nothing further to report. Later he heard a rumour that he had survivors on board. As soon as he heard that rumour he Marconied the *Olympic* that it was not so, and gave the Captain the substance of the Marconigram that he got at 10am from the *Carpathia*, and also the message which the *Carpathia* sent to the *Baltic*, and that he (Captain Gambell) had proceeded on his course. The *Olympic* replied that they would send them on to New York.

Asked if he could throw any light on the messages received on Monday that the *Virginian* had the *Titanic* in tow, and that other steamers were standing by, Captain Gambell said he knew nothing about that. He communicated everything as far as his own ship was concerned.

How near were you to the place where the *Titanic* went down?

'I passed it at a distance of about six or seven miles. I had to go around the iceberg (sic). There was a close, packed field of ice between me and the *Titanic*'s position. There were no boats, packages or wreckage to be seen.'

Captain Gambell, in answer to a further question, said his passage was lengthened by about 160 miles in trying to get to the *Titanic*. The ice certainly seemed to have gone further south than usual.

He agreed the wireless telegraphy had played an important part in the rescue. The *Virginian*, which carried two operators, was in a position to receive wireless messages day and night. She had 28 boats, including a collapsible.

An interesting incident occurred while the *Virginian* was hastening to the assistance of the ill-fated liner. The ship's boats were swung out ready for lowering if the necessity arose. There happened to be amongst the passengers on board the *Virginian* a party of bluejackets who were returning home from HMS *Algerine,* on the Pacific station. Lieut J.S. Morrell and the bluejackets, on learning the news of the *Titanic*, at once volunteered their service to man the *Virginian*'s boats in the event of these being required for the purpose of rescue.

(*Weekly Freeman*, April 27, 1912, p.15)

Captain Gambell says the ice extended quite a number of miles east and west in the latitude of 41 20 N, which he gives twice. Lest counsel for Captain Moore be tempted to interrupt with an argument about southern drift from the time the *Titanic* sank, it must be remembered that the drift is from the time the *Corsican* first reported the ice as being in 41 25 N, which was passed on by the *Corinthian* the night before to the *Mount Temple*.

Captain Moore could have been expected to anticipate any drift himself. If he had indeed diced with the ice in 41 20 N, he should certainly have seen it. It was his vessel's practice to have a lookout in the crow's nest when steaming at night – such a considerable height advantage ought to have yielded sight of closely-packed field ice even a few miles away.

It was also his practice, as he told the US inquiry, at least in relation to icebergs, to keep far away from the threat: 'Of course, my orders to my officers are to give them a wide berth; not to take any chances whatever.'

While Captain Moore appeared intent on such 'narrow shave' navigation in 41 20 N, as we might call it, together with considerably increased speed, we have to gloss this contention against what he testified in relation to his subsequent attempts to reach the *Titanic*.

The Master of the *Mount Temple* testified in Washington that after 3.25am he 'went slowly to avoid the ice, because it was too dark to proceed full speed on account of the ice.' And he had only addressed the issue of full speed in the first place because of the sudden emergency.

The prosecution contends that Captain Moore cannot earlier have full speed for his vessel in latitude 41 20 N, when it was dark and there was ice there, that the two ideas are mutually exclusive, and that the whole construct is a nonsense.

MOUNT TEMPLE'S ATTEMPT

ERNEST Meredith Pretty, not used to this sort of thing, hesitated for a moment before he rapped heavily on the door. Then the 18-year-old Londoner feared he might not have been decisive enough – until answered by an interrogatory groan.

Pretty opened the door and entered the darkness. 'A message from the Marconi man, Sir. Says it's urgent.'

A pause, then electric light bathed the room. Captain Moore, one hand on the fixture, was rubbing his face with the other. 'What time is it?'

'I don't know, Sir,' added Pretty with candour, offering the paper. The Master propped up, took it and regarded the slip an instant, tugging at his goatee. Then he shot across to the side of the bed, and blew the whistle to the bridge. He blew the voice pipe again, looking squarely at Pretty. 'Who's on?' he asked.

'The second officer,' said his steward, as Moore immediately diverted his attention. 'Yes, Mr Heald, put the ship on north 45 east, please. That's north 45 east, a ship in trouble, and come down at once when you've done. We'll need the chart.'

He replaced the pipe and swung his legs out of bed, completely alert, and suddenly spoke kindly: 'Thank you very much, Mr Pretty.' Gratefully closing the door, the teenager's last sight was of the abandoned Marconi message, buoyed on the bedclothes.

Descending the companionway from the lobby, Pretty could hear a clatter of feet coming from the flying bridge, Heald coming to heel, as it were. Only say the word. Hope he gets ready the chart. And then Pretty repaired up the steps, thinking perhaps that he should stand by for orders.

Moore came out of his cabin directly into the adjoining chart room, buttoning up his uniform jacket. Heald already had the North Atlantic spread out in diagram, and Moore asked the obvious question: 'Where are we?'

In a few moments they had pricked off the course, but then Kelly, the officers' steward, had brought a new position from the Marconi shack and they would have to do it again. Moore now briskly instructed the steward: 'Have all the officers turn out, immediately. In fact, call out all hands!'

Within a minute or two, the corridor was becoming crowded. 'I'm going down to Gillet,' the Master called over his shoulder as he strode from the chartroom, excused himself past a new arrival, hurried down a companionway and moved swiftly aft along the corridor. The night watchman soon encountered, Moore told him to summon all sailors to prepare the boats, and all firemen to the stokeholds.

John Noel Gillet, black-moustached, a stout-hearted fellow, was already up and lively when Moore reached the vicinity of the engineers' berths, abaft the funnel. 'Some trouble, Sir,' he offered, with hardly any inflection of enquiry, knowing the Captain would tell him. 'Yes, a ship in distress. Passenger liner, hit an iceberg. I want as many men at the fires as possible, as many men as you can handle.'

He noticed Gillet was in bare feet, and that his trousers were pyjama bottoms. 'After you are sufficiently dressed, Ginge, you might go down and try to shake up the leading fireman. If necessary, even give him a tot of rum if you think he can do any more. In fact, give a tot to the lot of them.'

Gillet aye-ayed immediately, and dived back into the open doorway of his room to fumble with socks and shoes. Moore leaned in at the jamb: 'Inform the firemen that we want to get back as fast as we possibly can. It's the *Titanic* sending out messages for help, a big new White Star boat.'

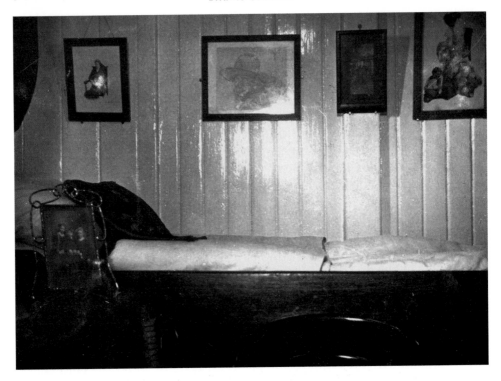

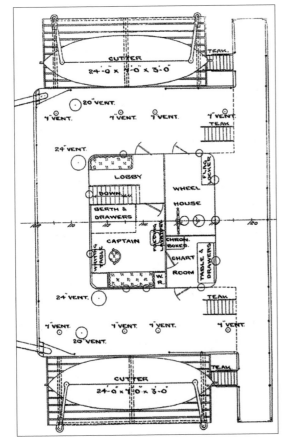

Above: The Captain's cabin of the
Mount Temple in 1913, showing the
Master's bunk.

Left: Plan of the *Mount Temple*,
showing *inter alia* the Captain's quarters
and chart room.

Moore turned away again, saw Pretty standing by, told him to 'Come with me,' and headed back forward. By this time, the fourth officer was coming down to meet them. 'Chief Officer is on the flying bridge now, Sir.' The Captain pointed ahead, walking briskly, indicating the officer should abruptly change course too, telling him loudly; 'I want all boats uncovered and swung out. All of them. Then checked and provisioned.'

The fourth officer spun on his heel and fairly ran away ahead of them.

To the upper housing, then, the exterior of his cabin and the door to the chart room, the teak stairs to the flying bridge, and the surgeon standing close. 'Another early morning for you, I am afraid Mr Bailey.'

The Captain came closer, contributed confidentially: 'This one could be serious indeed. The *Titanic* has struck a berg. If you could prepare rooms, the infirmary, everything put in readiness from a medical point of view. A potential emergency. Like the *Republic.*'

'How long before we are up with her, Sir?'

'Oh, quite some time yet. She's changing her position. Could be anywhere by now.'

He climbed the companion to reach the top, was gratified to see the Chief Officer, who turned immediately from the weather cloth and told him: 'Mr Brown and Mr Heald are turning out the port and starboard boats, Sir. Mr Notley is just gone to the wireless cabin.'

Moore could hear the yaw and clank of activity. He noticed the clear and frigid sky, the absence of wind, nothing to tear away the lung-smoke as Sargent spoke ... 'Very calm,' he managed, half in wonder. Then: 'Have you seen anything, any signals of any kind?'

'No, Sir. Possible ship's light to port, about five points on the bow, I mean a loom, but very low on the horizon. May be a star. We will know soon, I would imagine. Lookout called it a minute ago. Can't see anything from down here yet. He's not sure in any case.'

'Well it won't be the ship we want.'

'No.'

He noticed Sargent's gloved hands gripping binoculars. Still the creak and rattle of chains. 'We may want another man on the lookout soon. We should also have the gangway ready for lowering, and ladders ready to put over the side.'

He called to a seaman. 'Fetch Jacob's ladders and have them ready, and prepare Bosun's chairs, bridles and any nettings available. Tell the Chief Steward to have the galley ready to provide whatever might be needed for passengers who come aboard. And let the Bosun know I want lifebelts in heaps at hand, and everything made ready along the deck.'

The AB had barely gone when Officer Notley appeared at the stairhead to the flying bridge, ascending, nodding respectfully to his superior. 'Wireless says the *Titanic* is now working the *Carpathia*, Sir. And still calling CQD,' he added. 'Wireless had *Carpathia* earlier, eastbound. Wireless thinks she would have passed us about half past nine.'

Moore exclaimed. 'Good lord, have the poor souls nothing nearer? That Cunarder will be doing a good clip – not bothered by ice where she is. Must be a good distance away by now.'

Notley murmured: 'We might be the nearest ourselves, Sir. Wireless is just listening, and says that they're not getting much response at all. Lot of operators have already gone to bed, of course. Fluke that we caught it ourselves.'

'We must pray they'll be all right. Last until daylight anyway,' it was Sargent commenting now, his face a picture of concern.

'I wouldn't be too confident of that. Latest from wireless is she's in a sinking condition.'

'Sinking!'

'Yes, Sir. Wireless says she's sent out that she's sinking.'

'Can't be sinking. Plenty of bulkheads. Go down a lot in the water, maybe. A sad sight by daylight. But probably a fleet around her by then.'

Télégraphie sans fil, à bord de tous les vapeurs, pour la sécurité des passagers.

Period advert for Canadian Pacific liners, noting that all steamers in the company's fleet are equipped with wireless for the security of passengers.

Moore moved forward to check the compass in the binnacle. 'Large opportunity anyway. Big prize to the first to get a line on her, if she needs it. Remember the *Dart*.'

His eyes flickered over the weather cloth, noticed for the first time the pronounced lines of foam to either side of his vessel. Banging along at a good rate now. Getting along at a splendid pace …

WHEN the *Mount Temple* finally reached the SOS position, at 4.30am as Captain Moore told it, she saw no sign of the *Titanic*. Such was not surprising, at least in the retrospect of century's passing, because that vessel had sunk no less than 13 nautical miles further east, and a little south.

All the way along, the Canadian Pacific vessel had been audience to an increasingly desperate series of transmissions from the distressed maiden voyager, as well as eavesdropper to a confused set of responses and queries from other shipping, all anxious to help.

Her Marconi operator, John Oscar Durrant, gave a sample of the transmissions to the British inquiry, confirming that he heard the *Titanic* working the *Carpathia* at 12.21am by his own ship's time — having first got the distress message at 12.11am, which was some nineteen minutes before Captain James Henry Moore testified that *he* received it.

9463. Then five minutes after that, 12.26, is your next entry '*Titanic* still calling CQD'? Have you noted there about that time that you had turned your ship's course?
Durrant: — Yes.
9464. And started to their help? — Yes; that was about 15 minutes after we got the signal. It may have been sooner.
9465. At any rate by that time you had turned round? — Yes.
9466. Then eight minutes after that, I think that will be 12.34 … did you hear the *Frankfurt* answering the *Titanic*? — Yes … '*Titanic* gives position and asks, 'Are you coming to our assistance?' *Frankfurt* replies, 'What is the matter with you?' *Titanic* says, 'We have struck iceberg and sinking. Please tell Captain to come'; and then *Frankfurt* replied, 'O.K. Will tell the bridge right away.' Then the *Titanic* said 'O.K., yes, quick!'
9472. The Solicitor General: That was the first time you had overheard a message from the *Titanic* that she was sinking? — Yes.
9473. Just about 25 minutes to 1am? — That's it.

9474. Then following on that, I think another eight minutes later, did you hear her calling SOS? — Yes.

9478. After that could you hear the *Titanic* talking to these other ships? — Yes, she was calling the *Olympic*.

9479. When was she calling the *Olympic*? — 12.43 …

9481. Now tell us your next entry? — The *Caronia* … a long distance away. 12.45 ship's time.

9484. You have got one a minute later, 12.46. What is that? — '*Titanic* calling *Virginian* and CQD.'

9489. The Commissioner: And all this time you were making your way towards the position of the *Titanic*? — Yes, the Captain had doubled the watch down below.

9490. The Solicitor General: Now pass on to the next entry … ? — 1.06 ship's time. '*Titanic* is answered by the *Olympic* and tells him 'Captain says get your boats ready, going down fast at the head.''

9494. You notice that message which you hear is within a few minutes of an hour from the time when you had first heard the *Titanic*'s CQD? — Yes.

9495. Six minutes past 1. Then five minutes after that, 1.11am, did you hear a message from the *Frankfurt*? — Yes. 'Our Captain will go for you.'

9498. And the next one? — Two minutes afterwards the *Titanic* was working the *Baltic*.

9501. You have a record of that going on again three minutes later? — Yes.

9502. Now, 1.21 is it not? — 1.21am. '*Olympic* sends to *Titanic*' … it was an official message, something about lighting up all boilers.

9506. Did you hear the reply of the *Titanic* at 1.21? — Yes. 'We are putting the women off in boats.'

9508. Then six minutes after that, at 1.27? — '*Titanic* calling CQD, says 'engine room flooded.'' I remember distinctly the *Olympic* asking him, 'Captain says 'How is the sea around there?'' and he replied 'Sea calm.'

9534. That takes one down to 1.29? — Yes.

9535. Now two minutes after that, 1.31, did you hear the *Frankfurt* sending a message? — Yes, he asked, 'Are there any boats around you already?'

9537. Did the *Titanic* make any reply? — No.

9538. Two minutes after that again, 1.33, did you hear the *Titanic* send a further message? — No. I heard the *Olympic* send a message to the *Titanic*. The *Titanic* acknowledged it.

9540. I had better ask you now: Is that the last message that you heard from the *Titanic*? — Yes.

9541. What is the time? — 11.47 New York time, that is 1.33am.

9542. 1.33, your ship's time? — Yes.

Durrant did not hear again from the *Titanic*, and it would be three further hours before his ship reached the site indicated in the distress transmissions, according to Captain Moore.

The wireless operator said he presumed the flooding of the engine room 'put the wires out of commission,' rendering the *Titanic* speechless, although storage batteries were available in the wireless shack as emergency power and could be switched to 'in a minute.'

As time had ticked by, he heard the *Frankfurt* and the Russian ship, *Birma*, both calling the *Titanic* with no reply. At four minutes to 2am, he heard the *Olympic*, the *Frankfurt*, and the *Baltic*, all calling the *Titanic*, and no reply. A quarter of an hour later the *Birma* told the *Frankfurt* he was 70 miles from *Titanic*, and Durrant dutifully logged it.

Perhaps he slowly became more pessimistic. At 2.36am, Durrant wrote in his *Procès Verbal* (wireless log): 'All quiet now.' He added the ominous words: '*Titanic* has not spoken since 11.47pm.' It was a recording of New York time and meant 1.33am ship's time. The White Star liner had whispered her last wireless message over an hour before.

Durrant's next entry was at 3.11am, a full three hours after he first received the distress call. '*Carpathia* calls *Titanic* and says, 'If you are there, we are firing rockets.''

A further fifteen minutes thereafter – 3.26. '*Carpathia* calling *Titanic*, no reply.'

And at 3.44am: '*Birma* tells *Frankfurt* that he thinks he hears the *Titanic*, so calls him and says, 'Steaming full speed to you, shall arrive [with] you six in morning. Hope you are safe. We are only 50 miles now.''

Then, two minutes after that, he heard the *Carpathia* calling for her again. There was no reply.

One exacting hour later, Durrant made the entry in his log: '4.46am. All quiet. We are stopped amongst pack ice.'

The prosecution contends that it is distinctly odd that the *Mount Temple* was The Ship That Stayed Silent in this entire affair. When she got to the SOS co-ordinates that were given, at whatever time it was, finding that there was nothing there, why did the *Mount Temple* then not use her wireless to ask the *Titanic* where she was?

Couldn't it be that she would not make any transmission at all *only* if she already knew, suspected or believed that the *Titanic* was in fact elsewhere ...

The failure of the *Mount Temple* to send any kind of wireless message at this time would seem to suggest that she already knew where the *Titanic* actually was – lending credence to the proposition that she may have actually seen the latter's rockets on the other side of an icefield that she herself chose not to attempt to enter.

Durrant was asked about this oddity at the British inquiry, the only place where he gave evidence. It came after a solicitous Solicitor-General suggested the *Mount Temple* had been 'doing her best.'

> 9486. If you had broken in and tried to talk to the *Titanic* yourself, you would only have interrupted her talking to other people? — I should.
> 9487. So you keep quiet and only listen? — Yes, I never said a word after I got his position.
> 9488. And you told your Captain of the *Mount Temple* the place, and then you spent your time in recording what you could hear? — Yes, that is the first rule in wireless telegraphy, to avoid interference.

But it will be plainly seen that the time for such circumspection has passed, especially when the *Mount Temple* believes she is in the immediate area indicated, and yet there is nothing to be seen in the darkness. Durrant's vessel surely must, in these changed conditions, do her best to raise the *Titanic*? The chatter has fallen away – and there is no question of interference.

Counsel for Captain Moore: '*Titanic* messages had ceased by the time the *Mount Temple* arrived at what she thought was the SOS position. Mr Durrant saw no point in trying to engage the *Titanic* and presumably had drawn his own conclusions. I would point out that in response to a contact from the *Californian* at 5.11am *Mount Temple* time, Mr Durrant gives that vessel the distress position and informs her; 'The *Titanic* has struck an iceberg and sunk.'

He has formed that opinion over time, having known that she was sinking, and then hearing nothing at all from her. It is three hours from the last *Titanic* transmission that *Mount Temple* arrives ... I presume Mr Durrant is not in the habit of attempting to make contact with sunken ships, although it has to be acknowledged that spiritualism was all the rage in 1912.'

I am grateful for my friend's assistance, and indeed Durrant was asked in London why he stated, long after dawn, that the *Titanic* had sunk. He replied indeed that he 'came to his own conclusions.'

It is a pity, however, that he didn't convey that conviction at the time to other shipping – and not only because it would have assisted us, but because it may have assisted the escapees that Durrant knew had been put off the sinking ship in lifeboats.

For instance, Captain Rostron of the eventual rescuer *Carpathia* was evidently hoping *Titanic* was still afloat as he approached the scene. A full 36 minutes after Durrant noted on his own ship 'All quiet now,' the *Carpathia* was calling the *Titanic* and saying: 'If you are there, we are firing rockets.'

Durrant did not use this *Carpathia* information as the cue or prompt it was. If the *Mount Temple* was in any doubt as to whether they were on the scene indicated, and it is clear they were not in any such doubt, then the wireless operator should have been telling this *Carpathia* news to the deck personnel.

He should have warned them that any rockets now seen would not be *Titanic* ones; he should have alerted them to look out for these *Carpathia* rockets, as that ship was approaching the scene, and that they might to report to him, as well as the Captain, as to whether and when any were seen ...

Why didn't Durrant transmit, in response to this message: '*Mount Temple* now at indicated spot. No sign *Titanic* or lifeboats. Can [or cannot] see your rockets, *Carpathia*.'

This would have provided reassurance to the Cunarder as she fired those signals, that at least she was on the right track, if they were acknowledged as being seen. If the *Mount Temple* had transmitted the opposite, 'Cannot see your rockets, *Carpathia*,' then it would equally have provided the valuable information that something might be wrong with the reckoning of the *Titanic's* position and that the Cunarder should beware of running down lifeboats as she sped to the given junction of latitude and longitude.

It is perhaps strange that wireless operator Durrant remained silent when he suggests his ship was actually at the position, while other ships were saying they were 'only fifty miles' away and coming hard. They, at least, despite being hours away, were offering hope – but the *Mount Temple* was denying any support, despite her own closest proximity. Nor did the *Mount Temple* herself at any stage fire any rockets.

Perhaps this is like a policeman, sent to a pitch-black city square on the report of another ghastly Whitechapel murder, who gets there first, and who uses neither his torch nor his whistle.

Counsel for Captain Moore: 'One hates to interrupt this somewhat indulgent Jack the Ripper reverie, but the question was put to Captain Moore in his American evidence – Q. Let me ask you right there, did you see the rockets from the *Carpathia*? And his reply is, 'I never saw any rocket whatever, sir.'

The prosecution appears to be suggesting the *Mount Temple* should report something it hadn't seen, which might be like its policeman blowing a whistle and waving his torch for no crime at all. At any rate, Captain Moore goes on – and I quote –

> Moore: 'If the *Carpathia* was farther away, it is not likely you would see her rockets. But you see, this ship says she is sending rockets up. So it is possible that other ships may have seen them. I do not know. I thought of sending rockets up, but I thought it far better to let it alone, because if other ships – they thought they saw them – might be coming to me, and I had not seen anything of the *Titanic* and did not know exactly where she was; because I think, after all, the *Titanic* was further east than she gave [in] her position, or, in fact, I am certain she was.'

I am again obliged to my friend, and it is true Moore said that – but it is a pity he did not have his wireless operator transmit this very salient conclusion (at the time these rockets were being fired) that other ships were, in his opinion, in his later *certain* opinion, hurrying to the wrong place. It is an important matter, is it not?

The Captain says instead that it would have been far better to let the situation be, even though he believed the *Titanic* was much further east than she indicated, and therefore her freezing survivors, in tiny craft, would equally be much further east than any other ships imagined.

Why not increase the chances of those survivors being found earlier? Why not improve the odds for the many who were suffering from hypothermia, and the unknown numbers who may have been dying from it?

Captain Moore's statement is a plain nonsense. If he had sent up rockets, he said, other ships 'may have been coming to me,' thinking that he was the *Titanic*, perhaps. But they were already coming to him, because he says he was already at the SOS position, and that is where they were headed too – and where they appeared to him hours later, long into the daylight.

Above left: The wireless log, or PV, of the *Mount Temple*, with what appear to be amendments. The statement suggesting the ship was 'about 50 miles off' appears to be an obvious later addition.

Below: A Library of Congress photograph shows a view of the icefield taken on the morning of April 15, 1912 by RMS *Carpathia* passenger, and Brooklyn art tutor, Lewis Skidmore.

A Canadian Pacific officer on an unknown ship of the line. The *Mount Temple* made no sound during the hours of the emergency and was curiously inert in the morning.

There can be no possible explanation for his inaction, which allowed other ships to come to a place where he was, but where he was certain the *Titanic* was not. He could have fired rockets, if only to illuminate the scene to look for lifeboats – this was where the *Titanic* had said she was, and if the ship had gone down, as Durrant apparently quickly concluded, then they should have been looking for lifeboats. At least they might have sounded a foghorn, or done anything to indicate their presence.

The *Mount Temple* had plenty of pyrotechnics aboard, as Moore acknowledges. Why did they not fire them for illumination, or even as a signal to the lifeboats? How does Moore not look for lifeboats, nor indicate his presence, when he is at the SOS position ... and we are brought back to the original question, as to why Durrant did not transmit any wireless message at all, once they had reached there?

Durrant and his Captain are bound together in this. The Captain did not fire any rockets – but it was dark. He had no searchlight. He was asked, at the US inquiry, if he had a searchlight, or anything of that kind, and said 'No, Sir.' We may take it he did not use 'anything of that kind,' and we know he could not see through the dark. How did he know there were no lifeboats to be seen? If he didn't know, why did he not search for them, or at least, advertise his presence by rockets, that they might row to him?

If clarification were needed for other ships, and there is no doubt they could have done with some of the certainty Captain Moore had, then he could have transmitted, for instance, 'I am at the position given, and I am firing red rockets.' Or blue, or green, as the case may be.

The question has to be addressed as to whether Captain Moore already knew in the hours of darkness that not only was there no *Titanic* to be found in the SOS position, but no lifeboats either, because he had earlier seen rockets that he knew to be *Titanic* distress rockets, and in an entirely different area.

That is a matter for the jury readership. The prosecution merely notes that operator Durrant was extraordinarily reluctant to provide any 'interference' when nobody at all was transmitting, but much later – at 5.11am, immediately responded to a general shipping enquiry from the *Californian* that could have been answered by any ship, and indeed was addressed to all and sundry, and formulated in such a way that it was seeking a response from anyone. Durrant suddenly chose to answer straight away, and even said *Titanic* had sunk. He did not hesitate to respond.

It is thus an ineffably weak argument to say Durrant saw no point in trying to raise *Titanic* once the *Mount Temple* felt she was on the scene. In that case why see any point in turning around in the first place?

A huge passenger liner had sent out an SOS. Hundreds upon hundreds of people were aboard. The *Mount Temple*, by her own account, gets there ... and transmits nothing. The point is that you at least try.

If the imperilled ship's signals have been weak, power failing, one might at least be able to hear faint signals if one is in the immediate area. If there is a tiny chance the *Titanic* is still afloat, one must surely take it.

Not transmitting is being self-protecting - before any question of defensiveness arises. That is, unless one already has a sense of guilt ...

It is also to be noted that it is not for Durrant to decide. He is under Captain's orders when they reach what should be the scene. Durrant's natural instinct will be to transmit, indeed must be to transmit. Others are doing so.

Someone, the prosecution contends, told him not to transmit. We invite the jury, relating the situation to their modern lives, to consider an arrangement to meet someone. You have a cellphone, and they have a cellphone. They want to see you urgently. You arrive at the rendezvous and find they are not where they said they would be. What would you do?

The *Mount Temple* would have us believe that it is perfectly reasonable to do nothing.

It is an old adage that 'silence gives consent' to whatever is happening, and in this case that would be the sinking, not that *Mount Temple* actively consented to it, but perhaps did so unwillingly because of intervening ice. It may have been a moral dilemma, but those aboard the

Canadian Pacific liner actively decided not to draw attention to themselves, and the suspicion must be that something *caused* them not to want to draw attention.

Was it the case that one large piece of cowardice engendered a second, smaller, piece of cowardice? If so, we can at least see the second one. It is manifested by the unsent message at the SOS position. The corollary is that if there was no larger, earlier piece of cowardice, then there is no reason whatever not to send a message to the *Titanic*, asking where she was, as soon as the *Mount Temple* reaches the distress co-ordinates.

Why not send up a rocket for illumination, if you are half-expecting to see a disabled hulk or lifeboats? Why skulk? It is an old precept of the law that one is presumed to know the natural and probable consequences of one's actions. In this case there is no searching, and there is no interrogation of the ether. The question 'why not?' is put, and it is submitted that there can only be one answer.

Meanwhile, Captain Moore has an antidote for this silence and this calm, this inaction and this muteness, at the SOS position. He is about to astound you with rip-roaring tales of action and intrigue *on the way* to the empty area. Don't look at the uninteresting final location of the *Mount Temple* – listen instead to her derring-do in the hours earlier!

Captain Moore garnished his tale of how he responded to the *Titanic* SOS with stories of encounters with two other vessels en route – although he never learned the name of either.

STRANGE SHIPS

A SALIENT question was asked of Captain Moore early in his testimony to the American *Titanic* inquiry, carried out by a subcommittee of the US Senate Committee on Commerce.

Chairman Senator William Alden Smith of Michigan asked: 'After satisfying yourself as to her position, how far was the *Titanic* from your vessel?' Moore replied: 'About 49 miles, sir.'

> Q. After you got well under way, what speed were you making?
> Moore: 'I should imagine perhaps 11½ knots. Of course, perhaps she would have a little of the Gulf Stream with her too, sir.'
> Q. What occurred then?
> Moore: 'At about 3 o'clock we began to meet the ice, sir.'

The commander indicated that his vessel was trying 'to get back as fast as we possibly could.' His vessel was designed for a maximum 13 knots, which he didn't achieve. His average voyage speed had been considerably less – it may be that, as Captain Stanley Lord of the *Californian* remarked of this night in an article two years later: 'the steamer was making the voyage under owners' instructions, on reduced coal consumption.' There had recently been a coal strike and the fuel was in short supply.

Captain Moore did not stint – but consider his reply to the second question above: What next happened after he had got well underway? Moore mentions nothing except meeting ice from around 3am.

There follows this further long exchange in testimony, before Moore suddenly thinks to reveal that in fact there *had* been something happen between 12.30am and 3am. Why, he had encountered one ship (a steamer) and then a second vessel (a schooner), shortly after 3am:

> Moore: At about 3 o'clock we began to meet the ice, sir.
> Q. Where? From what direction?
> Moore: We were passing it on our course. We met ice on our course. I immediately telegraphed to the engine room to stand by the engines, and we double-lookouted, and put the fourth officer forward to report if he saw any ice coming along that was likely to injure us, or, in fact, any ice at all.
> Q. You say you doubled the lookout? – Yes, Sir.
> Q. Let us get into the record exactly what you mean by that.
> Moore: Before this we had only one man on the lookout, sir.
> Q. One man in the crow's nest?
> Moore: One man in the crow's nest, and we put another man on the forward bridge, and the fourth officer we put on the forecastle head, so, if the ice was low down, he perhaps could see it further than we could on the bridge.
> Q. Did you take any other precautions to avoid danger or accident?
> Moore: Not at that time, sir. We had the lookout, and the engines were at stand-by, sir.
> Q. So you were simply protecting yourself against ice at that time?
> Moore: That is all, sir.
> Q. And you had stopped your boat?
> Moore: Oh, no, sir. We had only the engines at stand-by.
> Q. Were you stopped at any time?
> Moore: We were stopped; yes.

Q. So I understand you.
Moore: At 3.25 by our time we stopped.
Q. Where were you then; in what position was your ship?
Moore: I should say we were then about 14 miles off the *Titanic*'s position.
Q. Can you tell me just what your position was; did you take it?
Moore: I could not; I could not take any position. There was nothing – I could not see –
Smith (interposing): You judged you were 14 miles from the *Titanic*?
Moore: That is what I estimate.
Senator Fletcher: What time was that?
Moore: At 3.25 o'clock.
Senator Smith: Was it dark or was day breaking?
Moore: It was dark, then, sir.
Q. What did you do then?
Moore: I stopped the ship. Before that I want to say that I met a schooner or some small craft, and I had to get out of the way of that vessel, and the light of that vessel seemed to go out.

Dramatic information at the end, involving a potential collision that he had to avoid, but which he had not previously mentioned. And it should be noted that the *Mount Temple* wireless operator, and his PV, or wireless log, makes no mention of the ship stopping at 3.25am. John Oscar Durrant instead records his vessel being stopped at 4.46am, after daylight, and amongst pack ice.
    But for now, enjoy the story of the schooner:

Q. The light of the schooner seemed to go out?
Moore: The light of the schooner; yes. When this light was on my bow, a green light, I starboarded my helm.
Q. The schooner was between you and the *Titanic*'s position?
Moore: Yes, sir.
Q. And in your track?
Moore: She was a little off our bow, and I immediately starboarded the helm and got the two lights green to green, sir. [starboard light to starboard light, heading in opposite directions.]
Q. Was this schooner coming toward you?
Moore: I was steering east and this green light was opening to me.
Q. Was he evidently coming from the direction in which the *Titanic* lay?
Moore: Somewhere from there, sir. Of course, had he been coming straight he would have shown me his two lights, sir. [sidelights, red and green]
Q. I have been informed that a derelict schooner was in the sea in that vicinity that night without anyone aboard her. Can you tell me whether or not this schooner was inhabited? [Shades of the *Flying Dutchman*!]
Moore: I could not say, sir. All I could see were the lights. It was dark.
Q. You saw a light on the schooner?
Moore: A light on the schooner; yes, sir.
Q. Where was that light?
Moore: I could not say where the light was on the schooner, but I daresay -
Senator Smith (interposing). Whether it was fore or aft?
Moore: No, sir; I could not say.
Q. The light, however, would indicate that it was inhabited?
Moore: At that time; yes, sir.
Q. You had no communication with any person, and did not see any person, on that schooner, yourself?
Moore: Oh, no, sir. It was quite dark.
Q. How much nearer the *Titanic*'s position do you think that schooner was than your boat at the time you have?

Moore: I should say this light could not have been more than a mile or a mile and a half away, because I immediately put my helm hard a-starboard, because I saw the light, and after I got the light on the starboard bow then the light seemed to suddenly go out. I kept on, and then the quartermaster must have let her come up toward the east again, because I heard the foghorn on this schooner. He blew his foghorn, and we immediately put the helm hard a-starboard, and I ordered full speed astern and took the way off the boat.

Issuing this order, of 'full speed astern,' is nautical hard braking – an emergency stop. Moore was previously asked if he was stopped at any time, and he did not mention this urgently attempted arrest, speaking of only the later 3.25am stoppage.

Furthermore, he got 'little' notice of this schooner. He repeatedly says it was a little distance away. Yet Moore also told his inquisitors previously that at 3am, with one man already in the crow's nest, because they were meeting pieces of ice, 'we put another man on the forward bridge, and the fourth officer we put on the forecastle head.'

Yet none of these three lookouts was able to provide sufficient early warning of an approaching schooner to avoid this seriously dangerous incident ...

Meanwhile Captain Moore had excited Senator Smith, Chairman of the US inquiry, as to the schooner's possible link to the *Titanic*:

Q. You think the schooner was within a short distance of the *Titanic*?
Moore: I thought she was within a short distance of *us*, because I put the engines full astern to avoid her.
Q. Now, let us see if we understand one another. How far was this schooner from you?
Moore: Well, I should thank at that time we could not have been so far apart. I could not judge, because you cannot judge by a light at sea.
Q. At 3.25am you think you were 14 miles away from the *Titanic*?
Moore: Yes, sir.
Q. At about that time you saw this schooner?
Moore: Oh, no; it was just shortly after 3 o'clock when I saw the schooner, sir.
Q. That is what I say – about 3.25?
Moore: No; just shortly after 3 o'clock I saw the schooner. That was before I stopped her on account of the ice getting so thick, sir. As a matter of fact, I did not stop her altogether; I simply stopped the engines and let the way run off the ship and then proceeded slowly.

Captain Moore says he say the schooner 'within a short distance of us,' which suggests the three lookouts he posted at 3am, shortly before this incident, were somewhat lax in attending to their duties.

Then there is the other odd matter, that of a schooner having a foghorn, which was usually an accoutrement of only large passenger steamers (like *Mount Temple*), so that they might avoid one another. Not only did this sailing ship have a foghorn, but she was lackadaisical herself – she did not use it until practically the last minute, perhaps to wake up the many *Mount Temple* lookouts, whereupon Captain Moore took immediate emergency action.

Q. One light, you said, was on the schooner?
Moore: One light. I just saw the one light. He would have his starboard light [green] open to me.
Q. What did you do then, after the schooner passed and got out of the way?
Moore: I put her on her course again, sir.
Q. I want to be certain that the schooner was as near the *Titanic* as I thought I understood you to say it was. [Note the Chairman's assumption]
Moore: I should say the schooner, from the position of the *Titanic*, would be, perhaps, 12½ to 13 miles [away, at this time].
Q. Exactly; and from you at the same time?

Moore: At that time it would be farther off, because it was 3.25 when I stopped the ship; I reckon it was shortly after 3 o'clock. I could not give the times, because I did not take them; but at 3.25am I was 14 miles off. This was shortly after 3 o'clock, when I met the schooner, and had to starboard to get out of the way. That meant I starboarded about two points.

Q. About how fast was that schooner moving?

Moore: He could not have been moving very fast.

Q. How fast? Just give your best judgement.

Moore: I dare say she would be making a couple of knots an hour. Some time after that the breeze sprang up until we had quite a fresh breeze.

Q. This schooner came from the direction of the *Titanic*'s position?

Moore: Fairly well, sir. You see, I was going north 65° east, and he angled a bit to the south, because if he had come directly from the other, of course, he would have shown me two lights, sir.

A strange tale. The schooner had only been making 'a couple of knots.' Instead of this pedestrian vessel menacing the *Mount Temple*, the steamer pounding at 11½ knots had instead allowed herself to surge at the schooner such that the latter was forced to use her 'foghorn.' But this is not the way that Moore had earlier told it, when he gave the impression of reckless behaviour on the part of the sailing craft.

Separately, notice that Captain Moore also subverts much of what he had earlier said by saying he 'could not give the times, because I did not take them.' But he had given them, and quite specifically too.

Thirdly, if Moore didn't take times, then he could not have been judging the distance he was away from the *Titanic* SOS location when any particular incident happened. But he was able to give mileage estimates, while later suggesting that his frailty on times should perhaps give him a free pass on being held to account for any of them.

"At dawn the lights of the rescuing ship, Carpathia, appeared on the horizon"—As told by the survivors

A contemporary portrayal of a *Titanic* lifeboat making for the *Carpathia* offers a 1912 image of a nocturnal encounter. Nobody but Captain Moore spoke of the *Mount Temple* meeting a strange schooner the same night ... Meanwhile this picture underlines again how close the mystery ship must have come, as she was visible a long time from the launched boats.

Maybe he already realised his contradiction – he said he encountered the schooner 'shortly after 3am.' Let's assume this is 3.10am, which allows a further fifteen minutes before he stops his ship (for the first, or second time?) because he is encountering very much heavier ice.

At 3.10am, therefore, which may even be a late estimate, Moore says the schooner is 'perhaps, 12½ to 13 miles' from the *Titanic*'s transmitted position.

Maybe the schooner is 12½ and the *Mount Temple* 13 miles away. Moore does say that the separation was a mile to a mile and a half, but that was when the light was first seen by him, and not when later bungling (blamed on his quartermaster) caused that emergency manoeuvre.

The maximum separation from the *Titanic* SOS position for the *Mount Temple*, assuming she was half a mile away from the schooner, and the schooner was at a maximum of 13 miles, is then 13½ miles. This is practically what Captain Moore has said above in evidence.

But he then states, and quite categorically, 'at 3.25am I was 14 miles off.'

Thus, we are left to imagine that *Mount Temple*, far from engaging full speed astern merely to stop or brake the ship at 3.10am, thereafter made sure she continued to engage reverse gear so that she was actually further away from the *Titanic* SOS position fifteen minutes later. And a quarter of an hour is a significant time when rushing at full speed to the aid of a sinking liner.

What a gigantic mess this evidence is – and yet the US inquiry, made up of landlubber Senators, noticed nothing awry.

They certainly were not familiar with the fact that Captain Moore had given quite a number of interviews on his landfall in St John, over the space of nearly a week, before he travelled to the United States to give evidence.

MOUNT TEMPLE'S CAPTAIN TELLING OF EFFORTS TO AID TITANIC

CAPTAIN MOORE BEFORE SENATE COMMITTEE
The skipper of the steamer that was caught in the ice while trying to reach the sinking White Star liner is shown in the left of the etching, giving his account of the efforts to force his vessel through the pack to the scene of the disaster.

Captain Moore in the only known picture of his *Titanic* testimony, seen at the US inquiry with his wireless operator, John Oscar Durrant, sitting alongside with arms folded. The caption reads: 'The skipper of the steamer that was caught in the ice while trying to reach the sinking White Star liner is shown in the left of the etching, giving his account of the efforts to force the vessel through the pack to the scene of the disaster.'

View of the port bow of the *Mount Temple*, location unknown. Has a certain nocturnal flavour.

In not one of these interviews about his dashing action did the Captain disclose his near-thing with a schooner ...

In fact he seems to have been particularly slapdash in an interview he gave to the *Evening Times & Star* of St John, dated April 25, 1912, in which he was reported as stating firmly: 'From the time we first turned at half past twelve o'clock until very early in the morning we could see no lights at all, as it was pitch dark ...'

Captain Moore said repeatedly in his testimony that he had met the wild schooner 'shortly after three o'clock.' But in this same reported interview, Captain Moore is seen to declare: 'Shortly after three o'clock, I brought the ship to a standstill, as we had encountered a floe of ice that was at least five miles wide and utterly impassable.'

His press interviews can be returned to, schoonerless as they are, but Senator Smith, the Chairman of the US Inquiry, was next turning to another matter in his examination. In doing so, he provoked Captain Moore to fresh feats of confession.

The Master of the *Mount Temple* produced a new vessel, one he had not mentioned at any time before, but which had apparently been in view from the very earliest:

> Q. What I am trying to get at is this: One or two of the ship's officers of the *Titanic* say that after the collision with the iceberg they used the Morse signals and rockets for the purpose of attracting help, and that while they were using these rockets, and displaying the Morse signals they saw lights ahead, or saw lights, that could not have been over 5 miles from the *Titanic*. What I am seeking to develop is the question as to what light that was they saw?
>
> Moore: 'Well, it may have been the light of the tramp steamer that was ahead of us, because when I turned there was a steamer on my port bow.'

This is breathtaking. Moore actually offers that another vessel, a tramp steamer, which coincidentally crossed his path, could have been the *Titanic*'s mystery ship.

Asked what identity the *Titanic*'s visible light five miles away might have had, Moore brazenly declares that the mystery ship might have been a tramp steamer that was very close to him when he turned. But Moore also said (see the beginning of the chapter) that when he turned he was 49 nautical miles away from the distress position!

The tramp steamer, in that case, must also have been practically 50 miles from the SOS position, which Moore later said was inaccurate – and that the *Titanic* must have sunk even further east, as we now know she did, and by 13 miles.

Yet Moore, while saying that this vessel was going in the same direction as himself, and despite already knowing by the time he testifies that the SOS position was not accurate, is happy to implicate a steamer that was virtually beside his own. The *Titanic*'s mystery ship, seen at five miles, 'may have been the light of the tramp steamer that was ahead of us.'

Perhaps he has been emboldened by the stupidity, or lack or maritime understanding at best, that had thus far been displayed by the Senators, but he has surely now put his foot in it.

The difficulty for Moore, obviously, is that if the tramp steamer that was going in the same direction could very easily be the *Titanic*'s mystery ship, then an unkind critic could claim that the *Mount Temple* herself, proceeding alongside in the same direction, could also – just as easily – have been the mystery ship.

But despite this thunderclap claim, the questioning proceeds, in leaden, dull-witted fashion

Q. Going in the same direction?
Moore: Almost in the same direction. As he went ahead, he gradually crossed our bow until he got on the starboard bow, sir –

Senator Smith interrupted at this point. But he did not discern that this 'gradual' crossing could have put this new steamer in a position to be collided with by the schooner that Moore later says passed on his starboard bow!

No, Smith's interruption was of a far more mundane and unthinking nature.

Smith (interposing): Did you see that ship yourself?
Moore: I saw it myself. I was on the bridge all the time.
Q. Did you communicate with it by wireless?
Moore: I do not think he had any wireless; I am sure he had no wireless, because in the daylight I was close to him.

A steamer with wireless, of course, could identify herself. Not that Captain Moore, as seen earlier, chose to have his vessel make any wireless transmission at all during those hours of darkness.

And he could not know that this steamer had no wireless during the night, when he only saw lights. Moore is instead using something he gleaned from the daylight (lack of aerials?) to deflect a question, asked of him in relation to the timeframe of the night, which he had not perhaps anticipated.

Q. How large a vessel was it?
Moore: I should say a ship of about 4,000 or 5,000 tons ...
Q. Did you come close enough to that ship, to which you have just referred, to determine what she was?
Moore: No, I did not get her name.
Q. Or her character?
Moore: I think she was a foreign ship, sir. She was not English. I do not think she was. She did not show her ensign.
Q. Do you know the vessel *Hellig Olav*?
[A Danish emigrant ship, not anywhere near the scene.]
Moore: No, sir.
Q. Have you seen that ['foreign'] vessel since you saw her early that morning – Monday?
Moore: I saw her until after 9 o'clock, sir.
Q. But no communication with her?
Moore: Had no communication with her. We were trying to pick him out in the signal book, and we were trying to signal with him, because I think he was under the impression that I was

going to the eastward, that I was bound to the eastward, and I think when I turned back after we both stopped, when we found the ice too heavy, he followed me, because when I turned around, after finding the ice too heavy to the southward, after I went to the southward later on in the morning, when it got daylight, and I went down to where he was, thinking he perhaps had gotten into a thin spot, when I got there he had stopped, he had found the ice too heavy. I went a little further, and I turned around because it was getting far too heavy put the ship through. But that would be about 5, or perhaps half past 5, in the morning, sir.

A long and rambling answer. Is Captain Moore dissembling? He is accepting, nay, declaring, that the tramp steamer, has steamed like himself for a number of hours towards the scene – and therefore this foreign freighter must have been going at 'emergency' speed, like Moore's 11½ knots, because she remained ahead of him all the time.

Arguably, the foreigner may have been going slightly faster, at least as Moore describes it. She crossed the *Mount Temple*'s course, from port to starboard, heading in the same direction. The *Mount Temple* at no point overhauled her … yet, if it was a reasonable assumption – from her frantic speed in the night – that this steamer must also have been responding to the SOS (and would therefore indeed possess wireless), well then, why not try to contact or reach her?

Moore said she had no wireless and no ensign, but was charging powerfully for an icefield at night, and at something far beyond the routine tramp rate. If cut off from the world, she could have known nothing of unfolding events. It was therefore emergency speed, for no reason.

These were not the only curious aspects to her character. Captain Moore was about to offer another.

Q. You have no means of determining what the name of that vessel is, or what the name of the commander is?
Moore: I had no communication with him whatever, sir.
[Why not approach in daylight and attempt semaphore?]
Q. Were you close enough to see whether her funnel was of any special colour?
Moore: If I can remember rightly it was black, with some device in a band near the top.
Q. You have never seen her since that night?
Moore: I have not seen her since the morning I saw her, 9 o'clock in the morning, because she followed me right around this ice pack, you know, sir.
Q. Did you get any nearer the *Titanic*'s position given you in the wireless CQD message than the point you have just mentioned?
Moore: At 3.25am I stopped the engines, and then went slowly to avoid the ice, because it was too dark to proceed full speed on account of the ice.
Q. Did you reach the *Titanic*'s position?
Moore: I reached the *Titanic*'s position. I reckon I was very close to that position, either that position or very close to it, at 4.30 in the morning, sir.
Q. Was there any other vessel there at that time?
Moore: None except the tramp, sir.

If the tramp had been present all the time, it would seem to contradict Moore's earlier evidence – which conveyed that when stopped at 3.25 he could not take any position (despite later offering confident estimates) because 'there was nothing – I could not see –'

Asked was it dark then, he confirmed that it was, and made no mention of any steamer's lights that he could see. Earlier, at 'shortly after three,' Moore testified, 'All I could see was the lights. It was dark.' But these were the lights of the schooner, not the steamer.

He was later tackled (in a rare moment) with it being pointed out to him that he had said there was only one light, not 'lights,' on the schooner. Moore then replied: 'One light. I just saw the one light.' No mention at all of the tramp steamer ahead, the one that constantly accompanied him, the vessel that crossed from port to starboard ahead of him (when he was doing 11½ knots), the steamer that could have been the *Titanic*'s mystery ship …

Captain Moore fleetingly mentioned a steamer in his landfall interviews. It came just once, in the same article cited earlier, in which he had compromised his schooner story. Considerably after daylight, when they could see 'the *Carpathia* on the other side of the floe, and later the *Californian* and one or two other liners,' Moore then immediately remarks: 'We met a tramp liner also trying to make her way through the ice from the same side we were on, but she was unsuccessful.'

So he strongly implies he first saw the tramp steamer long after daylight (*Californian* reached *Mount Temple* at the SOS position at 7.30am) ... and this was the same article in which he was quoted as saying: 'From the time we first turned at half past twelve o'clock until very early in the morning we could see no lights at all, as it was pitch dark ...'

If he didn't first meet her long into the morning, then he is contradicting himself in virtually the same breath. But this account itself contradicts his sworn evidence.

Continuing that US testimony, Moore said of the tramp with the black funnel that had 'cut across my bow' in the early part of the night that he 'could see him then,' when I arrived at the SOS position at 4.30am. 'He was a little to the southward of me, but ahead of me, sir.'

The bridge of the *Mount Temple*. What might navigating officers have seen from here?

Q. When you were at that point what did you do and what did you see?

Moore: I saw a large ice pack right to the east of me, sir; right in my track – right in my course.

Q. How large?

Moore: In consulting my officers as to the breadth of this, one said it was 5 miles and another said it was 6 miles ... Of course it extended as far as the eye could reach, north and south, sir.

Q. Twenty miles or more?

Moore: I should say 20 miles, perhaps more than that. It was field ice and bergs.

He saw nothing of the *Titanic*, only the tramp steamer. There was 'nothing whatever in the way of wreckage,' no floating bodies, and no abandoned lifeboats, according to his answers.

'We searched around to see if there was a clear place we could go through, because I feared the ice was too heavy for me to push through it. Of course, I reckoned I was somewhere near, if not at, the *Titanic*'s position that he gave me, which afterwards proved correct, when I got observations in the morning, sir. I searched for a passage to get through this pack, because I realised that the *Titanic* could not have been through that pack of ice, sir. I steered away to the south-southeast true, because I thought the ice appeared thinner down there, sir. When I got down, I got within about a mile or so of this other ship, which had already stopped, finding the ice was too strong for it to go through.'

Q. What did you do after discovering that there was no wreckage, nor any service you could render?

Moore: 'When I found the ice was too heavy, I stopped there and just turned around – slowed down and stopped her – and searched for a passage, and I could not see any passage whatever, sir. I had a man pulled up to the masthead in a bowline, right to the foretopmast head, and I had the Chief Officer at the mainmast head, and he could not see any line through the ice at all that I could go through.'

Before leaving Captain Moore in his quandary of being in the *Titanic* distress co-ordinates long after daylight, with nothing to be seen, it is worth examining another discrepancy about the black-funnel steamer. This vessel had been doing at least Moore's emergency speed, because she beat him to the ice rim. He testified to seeing her from shortly after he turned around at 12.30am, and from then until 9am, when he decided to leave the scene after being advised that nothing could be done.

Moore says the tramp followed him in some of his nosing around the icefield the following morning, looking for any leads in the ice that could offer a passage through to the east side. 'I think he was under the impression that I was going to the eastward, that I was bound to the eastward' – as if, in the tramp's view, both she and the *Mount Temple* were two casual, eastbound steamers.

It is Moore, in a ship half as large again as that tramp (6,661 tons versus 4-5,000 tons) who conveys the idea that this unknown steamer is a uncomprehending ordinary voyager. He has already told inquisitors that she had no wireless, and therefore could not have known of any emergency. If this is the case, why then is Moore's curiosity not piqued at what he says he saw – a much smaller steamer rushing urgently at night at eleven and a half knots, or better. He cannot have it both ways – that she is frenzied, but casual; that she is speeding but routine. Yet it is Captain Moore, and no-one else, who is advancing both these entirely contradictory ideas about that steamer, and doing so on his oath.

Yet if Moore in the morning loses interest in his fellow traveller from a wild and dramatic night of headlong impulse, then the supercharged tramp, for its part, has no inclination to discover why it was she was so powerfully pursued. Whatever prompted her own boosted performance, the small tramp suddenly had no rage about her, nor even any mild interest in the *Mount Temple*. She had switched, however unexpectedly, to listless mode.

It may be interesting to observe that at no time does Captain Moore put these two vessels – the schooner and the tramp – together with his own. His evidence treats the schooner and the small foreigner as completely separate episodes, as if one actor has left the stage to allow the other to interact with the *Mount Temple*, only to leave the stage herself and be replaced by the re-entering earlier protagonist.

In his brief London evidence, which came weeks after his American performance, Captain Moore was questioned in the most cursory manner about what he had said about these vessels.

Once again he was allowed the opportunity to separate one from the other, and it may be that he was grateful to take it. There was no mention of the schooner having to slalom between two steamers shortly after three o'clock – and no mention of the drama of having to throw his engines into full steam astern.

This is all that was involved:

9245. Now I want to ask you with regard to two matters I think you mentioned in your evidence in America. Whilst you were on your way to the position, which had been given to you as to the disaster of the *Titanic*, did you fall in with a small schooner? — Well, I could not say it was a small schooner or a large one. I simply saw the green light of a sailing vessel.

9246. I want you to tell me a little more about it. At what time was that? — Shortly after 3 o'clock.

9247. How far do you think you were from the place where the *Titanic* foundered? — At that time?

9248. Yes? — I should think about 15 or 16 miles.

9249. Were you on your bridge at the time? — All of the time.

9250. You saw a green light? — Yes, of a sailing vessel.

9251. Did you see the ship herself? — Not at all; it was dark.

9252. You could only see the green light, and I suppose beyond that you know nothing more about the schooner? — No.

9253. Later on did you see a light or lights of any other vessel?
[Notice how counsel has fallen into the trap of assuming, from the American evidence, that these were separate ship episodes. He asks if 'later on' there was another incident.]
Moore — I had seen the lights of a vessel proceeding the same way, but steering a little more to the southward than mine; I could see a stern light.

9254. At what time was that? — Shortly after we turned round.

9255. That is earlier than this. About what time was that? — Say one. Between one and half-past one.

9256. You only saw a stern light? — We saw a stern light, and then the masthead lights as she was crossing our bows to the southward.

9257. Beyond that you know nothing of her? — I saw her afterwards in the morning, when it was daylight. She was a foreign vessel — at least, I took her to be a foreign vessel. She had a black funnel with a white band with some device upon it, but I did not ascertain her name.

9258. How are you able to say that the vessel that was showing you a stern light was the vessel you saw at daylight? — We saw her all the time.

9259. You kept her under observation? — Yes.

9260. Was she going west? — She was going east.

This line of questioning terminated at that point. The interrogating counsel eventually realised that the tramp steamer had preceded the schooner – 'this is earlier than that.' Moore himself had stuck to his story in America, in which he offered dramatically – and at a late stage – that a steamer he had seen very early in the night could have been the *Titanic*'s mystery ship. In England he appears curiously reluctant to elaborate on these matters, and his answers are short and staccato – whereas in Washington he had waxed expansively.

Moore has indirectly conceded that because 'we saw her [the steamer] all the time,' that three ships – *Mount Temple*, schooner and steamer – were in close proximity at one time. At times it was very dangerous, because 'I had to get out of the way of that vessel,' being the schooner.

He also said he 'had to starboard to get out of the way' first, followed by a manoeuvre of full speed astern, and that both actions had to be executed 'immediately' because of the critical nature of the situation.

There is no mention of that incident here, even though the schooner had been 'within a short distance of us.' Look at Moore's tersely economical answer in London to question 9252. 'You could only see the green light, and I suppose beyond that you know nothing more about the schooner?' — 'No.'

He had known plenty about the schooner in America, this sailing ship of a few knots that had twice offered to collide with him. Now he 'simply saw' that vessel. He simply saw it. In a way, however, he was by now even more anxious to get safely past her …

And despite two ships being within a short distance of another, as he now obliquely acknowledges, we must remember Moore's earlier testimony, where all he could see was the one light (on the schooner), because 'it was dark.' Two questions then – where is the light of the tramp steamer that he could see 'all the time'? And if he only ever saw a light in the dark, how did he diagnose that light as a schooner in particular? Was it the foghorn gave her away?

Moore is the only man on the *Mount Temple*, in newspaper report or evidence, to suggest anything about ever encountering any schooner, much less any emergency evasion thereof. Meanwhile there was one similar report of a black-funnel steamer in the vicinity the next morning, but it does not follow that any such vessel was Moore's nocturnal escort, in sight all the time, barrelling along, whose identity he does not bother to establish the next day when both are similarly blocked by ice and are making little progress.

There is also a change. In Washington, the tramp had a black funnel, with some device in a band near the top. In London, the steamer has a white band. She has gone from black to black and white.

Yet even though the above extract is Moore's entire account of these incidents to the British *Titanic* inquiry, it should be pointed out that there are further contradictions with his sworn evidence to the Senate subcommittee.

He appears to have grasped some of those mistakes, and is correcting where he can. Moore repeatedly told the US inquiry that when he stopped at 3.25am, he was 14 miles from the SOS position, but also that the schooner he met had been 12½ to 13 miles away 'from the position of the *Titanic*' at 'shortly after three o'clock.' The mistake is obvious.

Here in Britain the thinks the schooner encounter occurred when he was 'about 15 or 16 miles' away. At least there is a reduction in the distance by 3.25am, although only of the order of a mile to two miles. If we assume that 'shortly after three o'clock' means 3.10am, as we did earlier, then this further quarter of an hour represents a speed of only 8 knots at best, 4 knots at worst – and he has not yet been stopped by any ice at all. He is certainly not doing anything like the 11½ knots that he testified – so he is once more condemning himself out of his own mouth.

Meanwhile he now states that he saw what turned out to be the tramp steamer at 1am, then immediately suggests 'between one and half past one,' while simultaneously claiming this was 'shortly after we turned round' – an event he has always insisted was at 12.30am, and yet this 'shortly' could now mean up to an hour afterwards …

Yet it is a complete and utter contradiction of his American evidence: 'When I turned, there was a steamer on my port bow.'

This was the same vessel he confidently proposed could have been the *Titanic*'s mystery ship. Despite the extreme importance of that entire matter to the British inquiry (and we will see just how much effort was expended on it), Moore does not offer this opinion in London *at all*.

DAYLIGHT DOUBTS

IN THE cold light of day, certain things are clear. One is that Captain Moore's navigation numbers on the night of the *Titanic* sinking do not add up.

As seen at the start of the last chapter, he claimed to have been 49 nautical miles away from the SOS position when he turned at 12.30am. He supplied his own position at the time of the alert, in longitude and latitude, which was consistent with that distance.

He also insisted he had arrived at the SOS position at 4.30am, which neatly offers four hours of steaming. The Master of the *Mount Temple* said he was making 'perhaps 11½ knots,' which would give a total distance travelled of four times the speed – 46 nautical miles; close enough considering his mention that his vessel might have had 'a little of the Gulf Stream' with her too, on the way back.

Funny that the Gulf Stream did not impede the *Mount Temple* in her surge in speed the afternoon before, when voyaging in the other direction – and managing to make nearly 11 knots then also, despite not responding to any disaster.

In any case, his initial mathematics seem nothing much to quibble about. But it is the detail of his evidence that throws up fresh disturbing considerations.

For instance, Moore affirmed to the US inquiry on no fewer than four occasions that when he stopped at 3.25am, he was fourteen miles from the SOS position. Up to that point his vessel had been travelling at 11½ knots, but then he stopped. 'At 3.25 I stopped the engines, and then went slowly to avoid the ice, because it was too dark to proceed full speed on account of the ice.'

He stopped for a time (five minutes? That would bring him to 3.30am), then went slowly. Yet he got to the SOS position an hour later at 4.30am. It was 14 nautical miles away ... even if he had been going top speed, instead of slowly, he couldn't have got there in the available time. With a five minute stop, it would have represented a speed 14 knots, when his ship's very maximum was rather less. No amount of Gulf Stream (Moore elsewhere considers the current might have been the order of half a knot) could have got him there in time.

Needless to say, the American probing was so ineffectual that Moore was not asked to say how long he stayed stopped at 3.25am, but even with a split-second stop on encountering ice, the problem with Moore's navigation is obvious: He was 14 miles from the SOS position at 3.25am, and an hour and five minutes later he had completed that distance. His ship has to work back up to speed after stopping. Many vessels of the time took up to half an hour to reach top service speed from a standing start.

But Moore also said he went slowly (four or five knots?) during this time – in which case he might not even have got one-third of the way.

Captain Moore has thus significantly misled the US inquiry. He could not have achieved the distance cited in the time stated. Either he arrived much later, long after dawn (it is estimated to have long been broad daylight at 4.30am), or else the mileage was not as great as purported. This would mean he was closer to the sinking *Titanic* than he claimed.

Moore condemns himself elsewhere. He must significantly lose speed – and therefore time – if he slams his engines into full speed astern to avoid colliding with a schooner shortly after 3am.

In London he changed his earlier estimate for the distance the schooner was from the *Titanic* (and therefore the SOS position) at 'shortly after 3am.' He himself, in the *Mount Temple*, was now 15 or 16 miles away at this time.

But this change means that he only completed one or two miles of steaming from then until 3.25am, when the distance was 14 miles. This would seem to indicate a maximum speed, in this brief timeframe at least, of 8 knots – again, nowhere near enough to get him to where he said he arrived at 4.30am.

There had been even earlier caution too, which indicates further moderation of speed. Moore said in Washington that at about 3 o'clock 'we began to meet the ice.' This is before the encounter with the schooner.

'We met ice on our course. I immediately telegraphed to the engine room to stand-by the engines, and we double-lookouted … '

Moore said that she never actually stopped at this time – but it seems tempting to imagine his vessel was not pressed on at full speed, given that 'scattered ice' had now been seen and he had already taken a precaution.

Certainly from 3 o'clock until 'shortly after 3' he could not have achieved very much before he was forced to throw his engines completely into reverse as a result of the schooner's malevolent intentions.

These considerations do terrible things to his ability to complete 49 nautical miles in four hours, as he said he did. That's so, even if his later stop (at 3.25am) was not a prolonged one. But he told the Senators: 'At 3.25, by our time, we stopped.' He actually mentions immobility five times, in one way or another, but this is a clear example: 'I stopped the ship.' The first newspaper interview with him, published on the day of his landfall reports that they were 'compelled to stop for a time' before reaching the scene. He does not give the duration.

Typically, Captain Moore later contradicts himself on this very point. He said elsewhere in his US evidence that this stop was not really a stop, even though the ice was 'getting so thick.' His explanation was: 'As a matter of fact, I did not stop her altogether; I simply stopped the engines and let the way run off the ship, and then proceeded slowly.'

This would seem to be a claimed repetition of what he had earlier done at 3am. Both cases seem to imply his ship losing speed all the while, until he chose to proceed again. But adding in the schooner incident naturally means three stops, or practical stops, in this four-hour rush at 11½ knots to a position that is 49 nautical miles away.

And then there is the issue of working back up to speed each time, followed at last by about an hour of picking one's way slowly along.

Moore's stated evidence is therefore a physical impossibility. It could not have happened, and it did not happen.

His wireless operator does not record being buffeted around by this stop-go navigation. John Oscar Durrant does not specify any stops before 4.46am, when he records that: 'We're stopped amongst pack ice.'

The same Durrant told the *Saint John Globe* (April 25, 1912) that: 'It was not until 4.30 that we arrived at the position of the *Titanic*, having been much delayed by the thick field ice.'

'Much delayed' suggests periods of slow or very slow progress, rather than outright stops. It utterly contradicts four uninterrupted hours of steaming at 11½ knots, particularly since Captain Moore decided to revise the top speed of his vessel downwards in his London evidence. She lost half a knot, to be 'about eleven knots' highest speed (Br. 9266).

This suggests that this American account of 11½ knots might have been *inclusive* of the Gulf Stream effect, so that his very highest range, in four hours of maximum speed in the calmest and most trouble free of water, is a 44 to 46 miles – without stopping, or going slowly, or taking emergency evasions.

Add in the latter considerations, which are admitted by the *Mount Temple* and this range is very considerably further reduced. The vessel plainly could not have been 49 miles from the SOS position at the relevant time. Her actual location was much closer.

Much delayed ourselves by these considerations, let the narrative be returned to Moore's account of his morning dilemma in finding himself as the very first ship on the scene of nothing at all

We searched around to see if there was a clear place we could go through, because I feared the ice was too heavy for me to push through it. Of course, I reckoned I was somewhere near, if not at, the *Titanic*'s position that he gave me, which afterwards proved correct, when I got observations in the morning, sir. I searched for a passage to get through this pack, because I realised that the *Titanic* could not have been through that pack of ice, sir. I steered away to the south-southeast true, because I thought the ice appeared thinner down there, sir. When I got down, I got within about a mile or so of this other ship, which had already stopped, finding the ice was too strong for it to go through.

When I found the ice was too heavy, I stopped there and just turned around – slowed down and stopped her – and searched for a passage, and I could not see any passage whatever, sir. I had a man pulled up to the masthead in a bowline, right to the foretopmast head, and I had the Chief Officer at the mainmast head, and he could not see any line through the ice at all that I could go through.

There was nothing in sight. No reports were apparently made by any of these observers, including two men raised to the top of the two forward masts. But Moore could see the tramp steamer that he had seen 'all night' while speeding to the rescue. Half an hour after his arrival – at 5am – he decided to go down to her:

… And I went down to where he was, thinking he perhaps had gotten into a thin spot. When I got there he had stopped, he had found the ice too heavy. I went a little further, and I turned

Arthur Henry Rostron, Captain of the rescuing Cunard liner *Carpathia*, in the uniform of aide-de-camp to the King, one of his numerous honours.

around because it was getting far too heavy put the ship through. But that would be about 5, or perhaps half past 5, in the morning, sir.

Captain Arthur Henry Rostron of the rescue ship *Carpathia*, the Cunard liner that picked up over 700 survivors on the eastern side of the icefield, would testify in London:

> (Br. 25551).'It was daylight at about 4.20 a.m. At 5 o'clock it was light enough to see all round the horizon. We then saw two steamships to the northwards, perhaps seven or eight miles distant. Neither of them was the *Californian*. One of them was a four-masted steamer with one funnel, and the other a two-masted steamer with one funnel. I never saw the *Mount Temple* to identify her.

But if the *Carpathia* could see the silhouette of the *Mount Temple*, a four-master, in this period after 5am, Captain Moore's vessel had yet to detect any other ship – apart from the smaller steamer with a black funnel 'with some device in a band near the top.' Asked if there had been any other vessel 'there at the time' – which admittedly was earlier, at 4.30am – Moore replied 'None except the tramp.'

The Master of the *Mount Temple* now concluded that the *Titanic*'s actual sinking position must have been at least eight miles further to the eastward. He formed this view because of the extent of the blocking icefield ahead. 'In consulting my officers as to the breadth of this, one said it was 5 miles and another said it was 6 miles.'

A sketch of Captain Moore giving evidence to the US *Titanic* inquiry, carried by the *Washington Post* in April 1912.

'When I came to this great pack of ice, sir, as I remarked, I went to the southeast to try to get around them because I realised that if he [*Titanic*] was not in that position – I had come from the westward – he must be somewhere to the eastward of me still. Of course, I had no idea that the *Titanic* had sunk. I had not the slightest idea of that.'

Moore says he went to the southeast, being the same manoeuvre that brought him down to the tramp steamer's locality at 'about 5, or perhaps half past 5,' when he still had not the slightest idea that the *Titanic* had sunk.

It is a curiosity however that at 5.11am, *Mount Temple*'s wireless operator, John Oscar Durrant, was telling the questioning *Californian*: '*Titanic* has struck an iceberg and sunk.' He was asked if he 'had been told by anyone that she had sunk, or was it your own conclusion?' Durrant did not initially reply directly, but then offered: 'I came to my own conclusions.' He had a firm idea at the same time his Captain entertained not the slightest one.

'It was not until I received word from the *Carpathia* that she had picked up the boats and the *Titanic* had sunk,' testified Moore as to when he was finally seized of the conviction. That wireless message came from the *Carpathia* at 8.30am *Mount Temple* time, advising of the sinking and the fact that Captain Rostron's vessel had rescued 20 boatloads, and that there was no need for other ships to stand by. "Nothing more can be done."

At half past five however, the *Mount Temple* had not seen the *Carpathia*, even if the red-funnel Cunarder had discerned two distinct steamers that were seven or eight miles distant.

Moore had made sure he was in the right position transmitted in the distress messages, taking navigational observations. 'When I got the position in the morning I got a prime vertical sight. That is a sight taken when the sun is bearing due east.

'That position gave me 50° 9½' west (longitude – *Titanic* had claimed to be further west, in 50 14 W). I got two observations … we took these two positions, and they both came within a quarter of a mile of each other; so that the *Titanic* must have been on the other side of that field of ice, and then her position was not right which she gave.'

The two observations were not taken in the same place, or at the same time. The second was taken when *Mount Temple* was 'steering north at the time, steering north to go around this pack again, to look out, to see if we could find a hole through the ice.' It was after the visit to the tramp steamer, in other words.

'My fourth officer [William Sydney Brown] took two observations, and of course, he is a navigator, and also, an Extra Master's certificate is held by him, which is a better certificate than mine, and he took those observations both times, and both of them tallied. One came 50° 9½' west and the other came 50° 9 ¾'.

'Of course, it proved afterwards when, after coming southward and trying to find some place I could get through, on the way back again – I suppose about 6 o'clock in the morning – I sighted the *Carpathia* on the other side of this great ice pack, and there is where I understand he picked up the boats. So this great pack of ice was between us and the *Titanic*'s position … I was to the eastward of the position the *Titanic* gave me, but she must have been to the eastward still, because she could not have been through this pack of ice.'

Moore's view as to where the *Titanic* really went down is of course correct, even though such indications were comprehensively overlooked by both inquiries, with the British one in particular deciding that the accuracy of the SOS position was enshrined beyond question.

But it is now 6am, and Captain Moore says he has sighted the *Carpathia* on the other side of the icefield. The red funnel of the Cunard line may have been reported by one of his lookouts. In any case, it is an assumption on Captain Moore's part that this is the *Carpathia*. It could be any Cunarder. He at no point uses his wireless to check.

Two and a half hours will go by before Captain Moore learns – verifiably from the *Carpathia*, one of many red-funnel Cunard liners – that the *Titanic* has sunk. He can see a liner he assumes to be the *Carpathia* across the 'great ice pack,' but all he knows reliably from wireless reports is that the *Carpathia* was one of the prime response vessels, second only to himself in proximity to the disaster, and that it was the *Carpathia* that was transmitting to the *Titanic*: 'If you are there, we are firing rockets.'

It is 6am and Captain Moore's operator has not heard from the *Titanic* in four and a half hours. The 'Sparks' may have formed his own conclusions, but Captain Moore has no idea … and is not taking any steps to clarify matters. He has a probable Cunarder across an icefield from him, but Cunard is the largest passenger line in the western world with scores upon scores of steamers. The idea that the vessel over there is the *Carpathia* can only be a working assumption.

Why does he not take steps to check? Moore knows for a fact – he has been told many times in the night – that the *Titanic* was evacuating her passengers into tiny lifeboats. They have presumably been afloat on a freezing sea for several hours. It is a life or death situation, and he has no firm idea of where these lifeboats may be, except the presumption that they are on the other side of the great ice pack.

Why did he not use his wireless?

Moore instead offers the astoundingly limp comment: 'This pack of ice between us and the *Carpathia*, it was between 5 and 6 miles [wide]. She did not communicate with me at all. When we sighted her she must have sighted us.'

He implies that the onus of communication was on this red-funnel Cunarder … yet he had no solid guarantee himself that this was indeed the *Carpathia*. It might possibly have been an entirely different and *unknowing* participant. How is it responsible of Moore to say, 'She did not communicate with me at all,' if he did not use his own wireless?

If Moore was acting with a high sense of duty during this emergency, then it was surely a matter of being *actively* engaged in trying to pluck those survivors, likely to be suffering the ravages of hypothermia, from the jaws of death. Yet he took no positive action himself at this point – such an obligation was left to what might have been, probably, the *Carpathia*.

Perhaps there was a tiny chance the vessel across the pack was the *Birma*, a Russian East-Asiatic vessel. Moore did not know her funnel colour, but he might have expected to see her at this time. This was because the *Birma* had sent a wireless message for the *Titanic* during the night, received and logged by Durrant at 3.44am, *Mount Temple* time, or just over an hour before the latter stopped for her long wait – 'Steaming full speed to you; shall arrive with you 6 in the morning. Hope you are safe. We are only 50 miles now.'

The Russian East Asia company's *Birma*, which rushed to the aid of the *Titanic* although of too great a distance away to be of practical help.

It was now past six in the morning, but there was no sign of the *Birma*. An hour and a half before this 50-mile message, at 2.11am by Durrant's log, the *Birma* had told the *Frankfurt* she was 70 miles from *Titanic*. Twenty miles in an hour and a half was a speed of over 13 knots, so she was truly coming like a train. Perhaps she had been forced to slow down in the heavier ice ...

Moore did not know it, but the *Birma*, had just been working to the *Californian*.

Ah yes, the *Californian*. Durrant had woken up this vessel at 5.11am with the startling news that the *Titanic* had sunk overnight. The Leyland liner had then been told the SOS position by the *Frankfurt* and had signalled that she was responding. *Californian*'s wireless had next been working to the *Virginian* – and Captain Gambell, previously cited, later told how the *Californian* was 17 miles north at the time.

Most recently she had been talking to the *Birma*, whose wireless operator, Joseph Cannon, would note in his log:

> 6.00am. MWL [call-sign for the Californian], proceeding for Boston, informs she is only 15 miles away from the position given by Titanic. Birma 22 miles.

So the *Birma* would not be next on the scene after all; the *Californian* would. These other ships – *Frankfurt*, *Virginian*, the *Titanic*'s sister ship *Olympic* – remained too far away to be of any assistance.

Moore knew all about them. He told the US inquiry, referring to the sheaf of wireless messages he had accumulated and was describing in evidence: 'He (Durrant) sends these up to me as he receives them, sir.' Elsewhere he said: 'As I received them I put them in my pocket.'

Moore later read his wireless operator's log into the record of the US *Titanic* inquiry in its entirety. He was already familiar with the sequence of events, and was now briefed by his wireless operator that a new source of assistance, closer even than the *Birma*, had just become alive to the situation. From seventeen miles away to fifteen miles away, she could be expected in an hour.

She was heading for the SOS position and a rendezvous with the *Mount Temple*. Hearing all this wireless traffic, learning of the *Californian*'s intentions, the *Mount Temple* did not burst onto the airwaves to point out one rather important fact – that they were already at the place pinpointed, and that it was empty. Wherever the *Titanic* was sinking, or had gone down, was in another place entirely.

The *Mount Temple* simply allowed the *Californian* to fling herself into a reckless dash towards a pointless position ... the Leyland liner, on the eastern side of the ice pack, was attempting to get across the dense field to the west, where the *Titanic* had mistakenly reported herself.

Yet Captain Moore already knew, or very strongly suspected, that the *Californian* would have been better advised staying on the eastern side of the icefield, because many miles directly south – on the same side of a field at least 20 miles long and studded with bergs – was stopped a vessel that was very probably the *Carpathia*.

Californian never got that 'better advice.' Perhaps it was because there was nothing to say that the *Carpathia* – if it was the *Carpathia* – had had any luck finding *Titanic* survivors at all. She hadn't said anything about it, but neither had anybody asked her.

In any event Captain Moore – physically in receipt of messages about the *Californian*'s intention to respond – never conveyed his own strong belief at the time, which was that the *Titanic* – whether afloat or vanished – was definitely somewhere even further east than that red-funnel liner. Somewhere over there, in other words, in the *Californian*'s half of the ice-divided globe.

Captain Moore never used his wireless. And so the *Californian* charged onwards, towards him, towards nothing at all, risking the field and her own hull. And Moore knew it.

This failure to deter the *Californian* and other vessels from coming towards him is utterly at odds, remember, with Moore's excuse for not sending up rockets when he arrived at the SOS position in darkness at 4.30am.

'I thought of sending rockets up, but I thought it far better to let it alone, because if other ships – they thought they saw them – might be coming to me, and I had not seen anything of the *Titanic* and did not know exactly where she was, because I think, after all, the *Titanic* was farther east than she gave her position, or, in fact, I am certain she was.'

Now it was three hours on and the situation was unchanged. But Moore's supposed concern for other shipping, and the best deployment of life-saving effort, apparently has altered. Again he does nothing – but one piece of inactivity is now in contradiction of another.

The Master of the *Mount Temple*, who did not dare enter the icefield himself, resumes evidence:

Q. As I recollect, the Captain of the *Californian*, who was sworn yesterday, and who went to the position given by the *Titanic* in the CQD, also said that he found nothing there, but cruised around this position.

Moore: I saw the *Californian* myself cruising around there, sir.

[Meaning 'the position given by the *Titanic* in the CQD' – the SOS position.]

Q. She was there when you were there?

Moore: She was there shortly after me, because when I came to this great pack of ice, sir, as I remarked, I went to the southeast to try to get around them because I realised that if he was not in that position – I had come from the westward – he must be somewhere to the eastward of me still. Of course, I had no idea that the *Titanic* had sunk. I had not the slightest idea of that.

Q. At that time?

Moore: No, sir. It was not until I received word from the *Carpathia* that she had picked up the boats and the *Titanic* had sunk.

Q. And then you gave it up?

Moore: I stayed there until 9 o'clock.

Q. It was not until that time that you gave the ship up?

Moore: That I gave up hopes of seeing her, sir, because I was cruising around all that time.

Q. How near the *Carpathia* did you get that morning?

Moore: This pack of ice between us and the *Carpathia*, it was between 5 and 6 miles. She did not communicate with me at all. When we sighted her she must have sighted us.

Q. On which side of the ice pack was the *Californian*?

Moore: The *Californian* was to the north, sir. She was to the north of the *Carpathia* and steaming to the westward, because, after I had come away and after giving up my attempt

The Leyland liner *Californian* meets the *Carpathia* on the morning of April 15, 1912.

to get through that pack, I came back again and steered back, thinking I might pick up some soft place to the north. As I was going to the north the *Californian* was passing from east to west.

Q. And you were also cut off from the *Carpathia* by this ice pack?

Moore: Yes, sir; by this ice pack. He was then north of the *Carpathia*, and he must have been, I suppose, about the same distance to the north of the *Carpathia* as I was to the westward of her.

Moore uses the words 'I suppose' and 'must have been' about where the *Californian* was, and knew only that she was on her way. The *Mount Temple* had been marking time all these hours, and was staying ineffectual, silent. Arguably she was next allowing others to make mistakes, even as lives remained hanging in the balance.

Moore said, self-servingly, that the *Californian* was at the SOS position 'shortly after me.' But this second arrival (ignoring the tramp steamer) took place at 7.30am – a full three hours after the *Mount Temple* reached the spot. Yet the use of the word 'shortly,' in this context at least, subtly makes it look as if the *Mount Temple* was doing her best.

Before these ships met, the next news had come, once again, by wireless. Operator Durrant received a message from the *Californian*. It was 7.06am on the *Mount Temple* as Durrant recorded: 'Sigs. *Californian*. Wants my position. Send it. We're very close.'

The *Mount Temple* breaks her silence, but does not offer any intelligence about other matters. The two vessels were indeed becoming closer to each other, but the CPR liner was effectively doing nothing while the *Californian* hastened towards her.

Moore describes the eventual rendezvous very tersely in evidence, saying that the *Californian* passed him at about a mile off, but the Master of the Leyland liner elaborated a little more. From the evidence of Captain Stanley Lord:

Br. 7256. You came to the point where the *Titanic* had been reported as having foundered, 41 46 N, 50 14 W? — Yes.

7257. How far from that point was the *Mount Temple*? — I think she was very close to it. I should think she had been looking for the *Titanic* boats or wreckage, or something. She was stopped there … I passed her somewhere about half-past seven, somewhere in the vicinity of half-past seven … .

7261. What rate were you going at? — We were driving all we possibly could. The chief engineer estimates the speed at 13 and-a-half [knots]. I estimate it at 13.

7262. You were about an hour [getting there, having crossed the field]? — We were an hour.

The *Californian*, driving all she possibly could, reached the stopped *Mount Temple*, which had been in the vicinity three hours. Then the *Californian*, shooting passed the stationary CPR liner, spotted a four-masted liner to the south east, on the other side of the icefield. The same field that she had already picked her way through, tempering speed against the risks involved in crossing from east to west, 'pushing the ice' as her log book would say.

Captain Lord asked one of his officers, Charles Victor Groves to study this vessel through a telescope. 'After I had been looking at her, I made out she had her house flag at half-mast,' testified Groves later. 'She had a red funnel, with a black top.' He told his Captain everything, knowing the house flag – a golden lion rampant on a red ground – had been 'half-masted for death.'

At that point the Commander of the *Californian* realised that he would have to cross the icefield again, from the west side back to the east. He continued in testimony:

7401. After 7.30am had you to navigate through the field ice again? — Yes, I ran along until I got the *Carpathia* bearing north-east, and then I cut straight through the ice at full speed.

At full speed he did it, ramming through five miles of ice from 8am until his vessel was visible to the *Carpathia*. The *Californian* saw, as she drew nearer, the empty boats at the Cunarder's side. At 8.30am, just as Captain Lord arrived, the *Carpathia* wirelessed that she had rescued 20 boatloads of *Titanic* survivors.

'I think he was taking the last boat up when I got there.'

The *Mount Temple* did not see any of this. She did not follow in the *Californian*'s decisive wake. She stayed where she was. Perhaps she had been paralysed with shame, or instead by astonishment at this display of daring before her eyes.

Actually that is not quite true – the *Mount Temple* did not stay where she was. She moved off – to the southwest.

'About 8 o'clock we sighted the *Birma*,' Captain Moore told the US inquiry. 'We could just see smoke when we first sighted her. We just saw the smoke, and then we saw the yellow mast and yellow funnel. I thought it might possibly be the *Olympic*, and we steered toward her … '

He steamed in a direction distinctly *opposite* to where he himself was convinced the *Titanic* lay or had appallingly foundered.

'Shortly after she was coming up very fast,' said Moore of the *Birma*'s effort to reach the scene. He could see that she was not a four-funnelled city on the sea – like the *Olympic* was, and as the *Titanic* had been.

'We saw she had only one mast – that is, one funnel, rather.'

EXCUSES AND ACCUSATIONS

WHEN the *Californian* rams through the ice the next morning to go to the *Carpathia*'s side, why did the *Mount Temple* not follow her lead?

Only shame or guilt can have caused Captain Moore to remain on the western side of the icefield, whereas he knew the *Titanic* had sunk to the east.

It is against this single fact, in the pure brightness of the morning, and in the dead calm of that deathly panorama, that all Moore's exciting references of the night before must be judged – 'we wanted to get back as fast as we possibly could,' his serving out of rum to stimulate stokers to greater exertions, and his desperate measures to avoid a rogue schooner 'whose light seemed suddenly to go out' …

Whatever about any of that, whether any schooner ever existed, *Mount Temple* had witnessed the *Californian*'s Captain 'cut straight through the ice at full speed.' Ice that the CPR vessel had passed by at lower speed – at least twice – when cruising down south in the early dawn, looking for a 'soft place' to nudge through, then returning north to the SOS position from the place where she had seen the tramp steamer at close quarters.

Moore said: 'I had come away … after giving up my attempt to get through that pack.' He had searched for a passage, but the ice was 'too heavy,' 'too strong,' and in fact so impassable ('utterly impassable,' he told a New Brunswick newspaper) that 'I realised the *Titanic* could not have been through that pack of ice.'

The *Californian* had just cut through it at full speed, this white beltway that Moore estimated as five to six miles wide with dozens of bergs interspersed in the pack. 'There must have been between 40 and 50 I counted that morning' – it seems he had time on his hands to enumerate them all.

Moore had been unable to seize the bull by the horns in the way the *Californian* had. He said: 'When I found the ice was too heavy, I stopped there and just turned around – slowed down and stopped her – and searched for a passage, and I could not see any passage whatever, sir. I had a man pulled up to the masthead in a bowline, right to the foretopmast head, and I had the Chief Officer at the mainmast head, and he could not see any line through the ice at all that I could go through.'

He added: 'I feared the ice was too heavy for me to push through it.'

Whence had fled all his determination and bravado of the night before? The terrors of the darkness were gone, but now he had fear. He quailed at the test in daylight.

This is an important consideration when assessing the prosecution contention that it is abundantly likely that he in fact quailed at the test the night before too.

Now his ship slunk away: 'About 8 o'clock we sighted the *Birma* … and we steered toward her … '

It is not clear when exactly he steered towards her, but it would appear to be long before the *Carpathia* transmitted (at 8.30am) that she had rescued 20 boatloads. Thus Moore was distancing himself from the scene before he knew any confirmed facts at all … and the effect of this order on his officers and crew, men who had striven valiantly the whole night through, can only be imagined.

He was steering for a ship he said he thought to be the *Olympic* (actually the *Birma*), which would mean encountering a giant White Star liner whose sister was the one actually in trouble. What was he hoping to do, exactly? Curry favour by finally telling this giantess that he knew nothing about anything? Or was it simply an opportune excuse to depart?

S. S. MOUNT TEMPLE, LIVERPOOL.

The *Mount Temple* at Liverpool, a real photo postcard from the collection of Patrick Mylon.

Captain Stulping of the *Birma*

The North German Lloyd liner *Frankfurt*, which went to the assistance of the *Titanic* from some 170 miles away.

The *Birma* – what few accounts exist from her – makes no mention of meeting the *Mount Temple*, but she soon would also realise what Moore long knew, that the *Titanic* must have been to the east of the ice barrier. *Birma* went to the empty SOS position, then had to steam south around the icefield, then back north to where she could eventually see vessels in the recovery vicinity.

'We had to get around the icefield by devious courses,' her Captain, Ludwig Stulping, wrote. 'About 12.15pm we met the ss *Carpathia* going at full speed to the west, and we exchanged flag signals with her.' They noted that the house ensign was still at half-mast.

So a Russian East-Asiatic vessel, which was still 40-odd miles away when *Mount Temple* was at the SOS position, made sure she reached the *Carpathia*'s side, even if they chose to steam laboriously around the southern end of the icefield in order to do so. Latecomers perhaps, they nonetheless surpassed Captain Moore's effort in that regard.

He was instead like the Grand Old Duke of York, marching his men up to the top of the hill, or at least the edge of the icefield, only to wilt in resolve and creep away again. Is this evidence in itself of his excessive caution?

Other ships converged on the scene. The North German Lloyd Co. later issued a statement saying that 'on receiving the call for help, the *Frankfurt* at once steamed north, and after covering 140 miles, arrived at 10.40am at the scene of the disaster, where [she] found the steamers *Birma*, *Virginian* and *Carpathia*.'

The *Californian* had met the *Frankfurt*, as Captain Stanley Lord described: 'I met him five or ten minutes past 12, after I was leaving the *Titanic*, the scene of the disaster. He was running along parallel with the ice, apparently trying to find an opening, and he saw me coming through and he headed for the place I was coming out, and as I came out he went in. He went through the same place toward the scene of the disaster.'

This piece of opportunism by the *Frankfurt* is exactly what Captain Moore could have done. But unlike her commander (Captain Hattorff) and Captain Lord, he chose not to enter the ice – despite testifying how he had pushed through 'thick' ice the night before.

The evidence is that the *Frankfurt*, like the *Birma*, had earlier gone to the empty SOS position, and had wasted time in doing so. From the evidence of Captain Lord:

Q. Where was the *Frankfurt* headed? – 'He was running about south-southeast, when I saw him, coming away from the northwest.'

The meeting is chronicled by *Frankfurt* third officer Karl Herbert, in an article written for a German weekly news magazine *Die Woche* in May 1912 (translation): '12 o'clock noon: We passed close to the English four-master [*Californian*] and turned southeast to search the ice frontier.'

These ships crossed the ice barrier (and in Captain Lord's case, crossed it three times). The *Mount Temple* did not. She did not go to where the *Titanic* passenger and crew escapees were, just as the mystery ship had ignored those people and their now-dead shipmates earlier in the night.

Captain Moore stated twice in evidence he had seen his 'foreign' black-funnel steamer until 9am, or just after, which may have implied that he remained close to her, and therefore on the scene himself. But of course his vessel could still discern the other's presence if he had left her in his wake from shortly after 8am. He had lookouts scanning the whole horizon, reporting what they saw.

At 9.26am, the *Mount Temple* received another report from the *Carpathia* which Moore saw as the final word on matters. Operator Durrant recorded: '*Carpathia* calls CQ and says: 'No need to stand by him; nothing more can be done.' Advise my Captain, who has been cruising around the ice field with no result … '

Well, exactly – no result. But why did Moore not press the issue to its finality if he had been so fearless and resolute the night before? The excuses he offered were as cold as ice.

'My instructions from my company are that I must not enter field ice, no matter if it seems only light. Those are my explicit instructions from my company. If I was to go through ice and my ship was damaged I would have pointed out to me that those were the instructions, that I was not to go into any ice, no matter how thin. As a matter of fact, I would not attempt to go through field ice if it was thick.'

He fervently declared the above towards the end of his US evidence. He would also comment: 'Of course, I have been fortunate myself. I have never yet had any injury from ice, although I have been Master in this trade for a very long time.'

In London, a month later, he again relied on this company instruction, even though he knew at the time that men, women and children were likely dead, dying or adrift.

> 9405. Your instructions seem to be that you are not to enter field ice? — Not to enter it on any account.
>
> 9406. You meet constantly field ice on your way to Montreal, do you not? — Yes, but we go round it.
>
> 9408. The Commissioner: And you have never gone through field ice except when you went to the position where the *Titanic* was lost? — No; I did not pass any ice at all.
>
> 9409. You never in your life have been in field ice? — Yes, I have been through field ice when I was in other companies, my Lord, but not with the Canadian Pacific Railway.
>
> 9410. Did you consider it was dangerous when you were with the other company? —Of course, we took every precaution. If it was very heavy, we would not attempt to go through it.
>
> 9411. But you did go through it? — We did go through it, but still we would never attempt it if it were heavy. Light scattered field ice we would go through without any trouble.
>
> 9412. But with the present company you would not even do that? — We have instructions not to go into field ice no matter how light it may appear. On my voyage before last, I went 30 miles south to clear some ice. I saw some ice and went down 30 miles to the south, and I wrote to my Marine Superintendent and told him what I had done and he said I was quite right in doing so, my Lord.

The answer to question 9408 seems ambiguous, as if to deny he went through any ice, even when he answered the *Titanic* distress call. But equally the answer may be referring to the past, and it can be left lie.

Nonetheless, consider what Moore now relies on – a company general operating instruction for routine voyages. In extreme situations, rules are made to be broken, but in this Captain's world-view they should be adhered to in such a crisis, indeed clasped to one's bosom for dear life. And it was dear life, on an unparalleled scale in the history of shipping, that weighed against the rule on the other side of the scales.

It was not enough to outweigh the rule, apparently, even though Captain Moore knew what he was capable of doing as a mariner. Question 9411 seems to take him up to the *Titanic* voyage, to challenge him over past evidence (in Washington) of meeting ice in the darkness that was 'getting so thick,' even though in the same breath he says he 'proceeded slowly' through it.

Had he already broken his company's rule that night? Moore now relies on degrees of weight and encrustation – the ice was thick, but it was not *heavy*, even though he had stopped for a time on account of it, before making further progress and eventually reaching the SOS position. Perhaps it now constituted 'light scattered field ice,' although this would run counter to the 'so thick' impression he gave to interrogating Senators.

And he had 'been through field ice when I was in other companies.' Many other firms were not so scrupulous or so punctilious as the Canadian Pacific Railway (CPR). They were the exception, he suggests. But this was not so exceptional a circumstance that he could do what other mariners, in other companies, routinely did – on *ordinary* voyages – when there was not extreme peril on the sea for 2,200 human beings who might have been within reach.

Joseph Bruce Ismay, the Managing Director of the White Star Line, not a seafarer by any means, was tackled in London about his company's failure to give any similar standing instruction of the type that Captain Moore had testified about:

J. Bruce Ismay, Managing Director of the White Star Line, with *Titanic* blueprints at the US inquiry. The Line's instructions to its Captains allowed them a wide latitude to act on their own initiative.

18699. I take it you do not issue any similar instructions to your Captains? — We do not.
...
18708. But don't you think it is a matter on which you might give instructions to your Captains? — I think it is unnecessary to give those instructions.
18709. You think the Captains should do it themselves? — If they think it necessary.

Ismay's first answer can be seen to be slightly embarrassing for him, in light of the fact that his firm had lost a prestige liner and two-thirds of her complement on her maiden voyage. But seconds later, when referring to other matters relating to the issue of possible standing instructions for White Star Captains on meeting ice (such as being required to double the lookouts), Ismay recovers ground. It is unnecessary to give such instructions. Captains, who are dealing with ever-changing situations, must rely on their own judgement. To give them ironclad rules could in fact restrict their freedom of movement and prove much more costly. How costly might it have proved on this occasion?

Captain Moore, a man of nearly one-third of a century's experience, would have been precisely the kind of Master that Ismay would have trusted to apply his own assessment of any situation.

But Captain Moore, in this instance, instead of railing against hard-and-fast rules created by landlubber bureaucrats with no front line experience, instead treats inflexible regulation as his friend, repeatedly citing the rule. Does the rule now absolve him of any personal responsibility?

The British inquiry was interested in the various operating procedures adopted by different companies in relation to ice, and canvassed them all on the issue. On the 28th day of proceedings, the Attorney General, Sir Rufus Isaacs, was able to tell the Wreck Commissioner's Court that he had received a reply, dated June 11, 1912, from Captain Moore's employers.

It was the manager of the Canadian Pacific Line writing — 'Our Masters know that they must not enter even light field ice or touch ice of any kind.' The Attorney General, if given careful pause on his receipt of this letter, showed no hesitation in open court ten days later (Friday, June 21,1912) in immediately adding: 'This bears out what the Master of the *Mount Temple* says.'

But in fact it reveals that Moore was already subjectively interpreting the rule for himself, partially applying it, and partially ignoring it. If it was an inflexible rule, he was nonetheless already breaking it. Therefore he did not consider himself absolutely bound by it at all.

You ask for information as to whether there is among ship masters any general practice as to the course to be adopted in the event of meeting ice.   I have no knowledge of what other shipmasters do, but our masters know that they must not enter even light field ice or touch ice of any kind.

Letter from the Canadian Pacific line to the British *Titanic* inquiry, dated June 11, 1912, saying their Masters know they must not touch ice of any kind.

Circumstances alter cases. Moore did enter ice, made progress through it, and it was praiseworthy on the night of April 14/15, 1912. He did 'touch ice,' and move through it – whether it was 'so thick' or actually just 'light scattered field ice.' The letter from the company formally stated that he and other Masters 'must not enter even light field ice.' Moore broke the rule.

How can he then rely on its shattered shards for his failure to reach the *Carpathia*'s side the next morning? Why did he not 'go round it,' as *Birma* had, when he did this in the CPR's own service on voyages to Montreal?

Mount Temple left the area, resuming her voyage to St John, even if she was already underway when told by the *Carpathia* that there was no need to stand by him as 'nothing more can be done.' Marconi operator John Oscar Durrant nonetheless stayed at his instrument for the rest of the day. He noted in his PV that the *Carpathia* and *Olympic* were 'very busy' dealing with the aftermath.

There is nothing in the *Mount Temple*'s official log describing the events of that night. The entry relating to noon on April 14 and the burial of little Dozko Oziro is followed by an entry for April 19, five days later, recording the vessel's arrival in St John.

Thus the death of a three-month-old is faithfully registered by Captain Moore in compliance with an Act of Parliament requiring births, marriages and deaths to be entered in the log. But there is not a word, not a letter, not a scintilla, about the deaths of more than 1,500 others in the same vicinity and within the same day.

There will be claims, however, that log entries were indeed made about the ship's response to the *Titanic* disaster, an incident which does not trouble the Official Log for inclusion even as a footnote.

Captain Moore was, however, quite prepared to be interviewed about this event, to which the world accorded importance, when he made landfall. The following is his first newspaper account, published by an evening newspaper on the very day he arrived in St John:

MOUNT TEMPLE HEARD
THE CALL AND HURRIED
TO AID OF THE TITANIC

Within fifty miles of the giant *Titanic* when she sent out calls for succour before being engulfed in mid ocean, and one of the first to go to the doomed liner, the CPR liner *Mount Temple*, Captain Moore, arrived here at noon today from London and Antwerp with a graphic account of the race to aid the ill fated White Star monster.

Captain Moore said that it was about 12.30 when his Marconi operator picked up the 'CQD' call for help. The first call was 'We have struck iceberg, come to our assistance at once.' The *Mount Temple* was put about at once and with all possible speed headed for the *Titanic*, her position having been indicated in the first message.

In reply to a message sent by the *Carpathia*, the *Mount Temple* heard the *Titanic* reply: 'We want all the help we can get.' To get to the position of the *Titanic* the *Mount Temple* had to go through an immense field of ice with more than fifty bergs. As Captain Moore had about 1,600 people aboard, including crew, the undertaking was a hazardous one. In fact they were compelled to stop for a time. About 4.30 in the morning the *Mount Temple* arrived at the position of the *Titanic* to find her gone.

The *Carpathia* was sighted on the other side of a row of bergs and she advised the *Mount Temple* that she had picked up twenty boats. As she came up with the *Titanic*'s position, Captain Moore had his lifeboats swung out from their davits ready to lower away and the gangway lowered over the side ready to take on any passengers that might be found.

At the ocean grave of the *Titanic* at one time were the *Mount Temple*, *Carpathia*, *California* [sic] and the German steamer *Burmah* [sic]. The *Mount Temple* picked up the following message from the *Olympic*: 'We are putting the women off in boats.' The steamer *Frankfurt* asked the *Titanic*: 'What is the matter,' and the reply came back: 'We have struck an iceberg and are sinking; tell Captain to come.'

After cruising about the vicinity for some time the *Mount Temple* proceeded on her way. Captain Moore said that in all his experience he had never seen so much ice so far south. Before he received the call for help from the *Titanic* he was in a course clear of ice, but in the locality where the big liner foundered there were gigantic bergs and the heaviest kind of field ice. While going to the *Titanic*, men were kept in the 'crow's nest' and every point of vantage scanning the ocean for signs of the ill-fated liner or her boats. The commander and his officers used their glasses continuously. 'In fact, our eyes were sore from looking,' said Captain Moore.

(*Evening Times & Star*, Friday April 19, 1912)

It may be useful to deconstruct this account, bearing in mind that Captain Moore's speech is being reported second-hand, but also that the reporter going aboard could not previously have known anything of the *Mount Temple*'s experience that night.

Moore said it was about 12.30am when his Marconi operator picked up the call for help. This is untrue – Durrant's PV proves to this day that he picked it up at 12.11am, nineteen minutes earlier. The same PV notes fifteen minutes later, at 12.26am *Mount Temple* time, that: 'Our Captain reverses ship.' The word 'engines' is crossed out and replaced with 'ship,' the latter word written in heavier penmanship. Alongside, in the right hand margin, is an addition – also in heavier ink – stating 'We are about 50 miles off.' The line above notes that the *Titanic* is 'still calling CQD,' and the line above that again, her plea: 'Come to our assistance at once.' There is a fifteen-minute gap between receipt of the distress call and the *Mount Temple* reversing either engines or ship. Moore says in this newspaper interview however that the '*Mount Temple* was put about at once.'

The next paragraph contains the statement; 'To get to the position of the *Titanic* the *Mount Temple* had to go through an immense field of ice with more than fifty bergs.' It ought to have more accurately read that, to get to the actual position, the *Mount Temple* 'would have had to go through an immense field.' She didn't do it.

The construction of the account, with mention of being 'compelled to stop for a time,' links this to the ice barrier, whereas Moore subsequently testified that this happened earlier, when meeting ice that was 'so thick' or just 'lightly scattered.'

The *Mount Temple* 'arrived at the position of the *Titanic* to find her gone.' There is no mention of Moore's realisation that the distress co-ordinates did not amount to the true sinking position, at which his vessel never arrived.

Nor is there any mention, in this account, of a close-run thing with a schooner. No mention, either, of the black-funnel steamer. The *Carpathia* was sighted, and the impression is given that the *Mount Temple* made rendezvous with her. Again, this did not happen.

A series of names of other steamers is cited, as if the *Mount Temple* was a member of a college of the concerned that gathered at the 'ocean grave of the *Titanic* at one time.' Despite being at the grave and appraised of a full understanding, the article may also give the impression that the *Mount Temple* cruised 'about the vicinity for some time' in search of further survivors or anything she might see. It would appear that it was with reluctance that she proceeded on her voyage.

The interview was published the same day after the *Carpathia* finally docked in New York with *Titanic* survivors, making that city the epicentre of a gigantic world story. The Cunarder has arrived in Manhattan in a thunderstorm, the lightning offered the puny assistance of press flashcubes, with the newspapers churning out special editions of unprecedented print runs.

Fifteen hours later, on a noon flood, the *Mount Temple* arrived at St John to the most modest attendance of the press – a single reporter. Her picture wasn't even taken as she lay amid the familiar Gloucester schooners, named after a Massachusetts port down the coast.

The emigrants swarmed off, corralled into queues to undergo entry inspection. There were 1,304 steerage adults and 157 children, and passing them all took four and a half hours for Dr Ellis, the medical examiner. A small number were detained for further examination, while the rest passed down to the civil examiner, J.V. Lautalunn, nervously unfolding their papers.

Ship's surgeon Bailey produced his certificate to the shore authorities, declaring: 'I hereby certify that I have daily during the present passage made a general inspection of the passengers on this vessel, and that I have at least once during the passage made a detailed individual examination of each immigrant on board, and that I have seen no passenger thereon who I have reason to believe is, or is likely to become, insane, epileptic, or consumptive, or who is idiotic, feeble-minded or afflicted with a contagious, infectious or loathsome disease; or who is deaf, dumb or blind or otherwise physically defective or whose present appearance would lead me to believe that he or she might be debarred from entering Canada under the Immigration Act.'

He was obliged to provide details of the lonely death en route of Dozko Oziro, and did so, having already supplied the medical examining officer with a list of those disembarking who had been treated for sickness. Thus prepared, officialdom could not be bluffed.

Inspections were completed at 6pm, and the dog-tired *Mount Temple*'s passengers, their legs exhausted and uncertain from the long hours of standing on unfamiliar hard ground, still somehow feeling the roll of the sea in their limbs, could at last prepare for their journeys to the interior. Virtually no-one was staying in St John.

The CPR passengers left by special trains – the earliest at two minutes to eight, another at twenty minutes to eleven – many parents boarding with sleeping children in their arms, returning to the platform to secure their suitcases – with the last train of the day leaving half an hour before midnight. All day had been spent in this debilitating epic.

The stern of the RMS *Carpathia* as she makes her way into New York in April 1912 with *Titanic* survivors and many of the sunken vessel's lifeboats aboard.

1.—Every passenger or other person seeking to enter or land in Canada shall first appear before and make application to an immigration officer at a port of entry for permission to enter or land in Canada and shall be detained for examination, which shall be conducted forthwith on shipboard, or on train, or at some other place designated for that purpose.

2.—Every passenger or other person seeking to enter or land in Canada shall answer truly all questions put to him by any officer when examined under the authority of this Act; and any person not truly answering such questions shall be guilty of an offence and liable on conviction to a fine of not more than one hundred dollars or to a term of imprisonment not exceeding two months or to both fine and imprisonment, and if found not to be a Canadian citizen or not to have Canadian domicile, such offence shall in itself be sufficient cause for deportation whenever so ordered by a Board of Inquiry or officer in charge, subject however to such right of appeal as he may have to the Minister.

3.—Every passenger or other person so examined shall be immediately landed unless the examining officer has reason to believe that the landing of such passenger or other person would be contrary to any provision of this Act.

4.—Every passenger or other person as to whose right to enter or land the examining officer has any doubt shall be detained for further examination by an officer in charge, or by a Board of Inquiry and such examination shall forthwith be conducted separate and apart from the public, and upon the conclusion thereof such passenger or other person shall be immediately allowed to enter, landed or shall be rejected and kept in custody pending his deportation.

Above: Passenger-number papers filed with the Canadian authorities on landfall, showing the *Mount Temple* was carrying 1,461 steerage and five saloon passengers – or 150 more in total than the *Titanic.*

Right: A landing information card for would-be immigrants to Canada that warns of circumstances that could lead to their deportation.

An immigrant inspection card of the Canadian Pacific line. This one was issued in August 1912 at Liverpool to an intending passenger on the *Empress of Ireland.*

A Canadian vessel had caused a flap, a few days before. The steamer *Bruce* had been cited as the source for stories published in New York purporting to describe vivid scenes at the wreck of the *Titanic*, having supposedly been wired by her. They were a pure invention. The *Bruce* arrived in St John's, Newfoundland, two days before *Mount Temple* arrived in New Brunswick. She had sailed from Sydney and Cape Breton – on an ordinary inshore voyage that could not have sent her far out into the North Atlantic. Her Marconi operator informed the reporters of all the St John's newspapers that he had picked up no messages at all from the *Titanic*. They left disappointed.

Perhaps this helps explain why the *Daily Telegraph* of St John relegated Captain Moore's newsworthy interview with its sister paper the evening before to page ten of the Saturday morning edition – alongside a story noting that 'Plans for the river steamers are uncertain,' which itself stood over an article about 'St John people off to Europe.'

The headline for Moore's interview was slightly more prominent, but almost as banal – 'Great Fields of Heavy Ice Where *Titanic* Went Down.' But the *Daily Telegraph* had also sent its own reporter to the ship, and he added: 'Captain Moore expressed the view that Captain Smith of the *Titanic* was taking no short cut, as had been inferred, and from his chart pointed out the *Titanic*'s position, showing that she had been making every effort to escape ice.

'In fact the *Titanic* seemed to have been going to the southward to clear the ice fields,' as indeed Captain Moore had done himself. 'The *Mount Temple* brought out 1,488 passengers of many nationalities. The steamer landed two passengers at the Island yesterday, seriously ill, a Bulgarian suffering from typhoid pneumonia, and an Italian suffering from pneumonia.'

On the first day in St John, three cattlemen who had been part of the ship's crew, promptly deserted. Moore entered their names in the log – Flood, Stamberg and Maguire. He noted that they had taken their kit.

The day of the *Daily Telegraph* article, Saturday April 20, there had been trouble. Firemen Sidney Simpkins and Timothy O'Brien had sworn at a customs official and verbally abused him. The origin of the row is obscure, but the local police weren't having any lip or 'profane language' from a pair of cocky Londoners. The pair were arrested and conducted to jail, tough East End men, 29 and 31, though they were.

That same day, in a separate incident, as people were still digesting all the *Titanic* news, the ship's assistant passenger chef, Arjen de Ruijter, was imbibing a little too much for himself. Found drunk, if not quite as obstreperous as the other pair, he too was lodged in St John jail.

A quiet Sunday intervened on the 21st. The prisoners cooled off, but they were not set free. Ships came and went in the harbour mouth.

Cattlemen aboard the *Mount Temple* in October 1907. From the collection of Campbell McCutcheon.

Monday, April 22, was quiet aboard ship. A man named Klacker was signed as a trimmer, and a fellow called Walter taken on as an assistant steward. Meanwhile there would be three further desertions – by Berndt Englischer, an assistant steward, and trimmers Thomas Meinschad and Daniel Driscoll. That brought the number of runaways to six.

And on this same day, most mysteriously, Arthur Howard Notley, the ship's third officer, was paid off. He was no trimmer or cattleman, not a waterfront roisterer, and not intent on using inaccessible St John as a striking point for anywhere else. A family man with a young son in London, with five years' service on this route, he hardly intended making Canada his home. So why on earth did he demand his wages, receive his discharge papers, and leave the *Mount Temple*?

Monday, April 22, 1912, was also the day that *Titanic* Fourth Officer, Joseph Boxhall, revealed to the world that his ship's agonising demise had been attended by another vessel's mute vigil.

Something else happened that day too – a man who had arrived in Toronto made allegations to the *Star* newspaper in that city, having sought out its offices. He was a respectable man, dapper, groomed, with spectacles – evidently a person of refinement. A telegram was sent to the American inquiry.

Whether the man's visit preceded or followed the dramatic news from Washington – which had not yet been printed in any newspaper – the *Toronto Star* newsdesk found itself with two stories that clearly seemed to knit together. One was of a mystery ship, seen from the *Titanic*, the other a claim that it was the *Mount Temple* that had been within sight of the sinking liner. Sensation upon sensation!

It is impossible to judge the speed with which a message was flashed to St John, but the *Toronto Star* harnessed all the means of urgent communication at its disposal that day. It led to the *St John Globe* seeking out Captain Moore for further comment – and led to a story printed on April 23, 1912, but on page nine.

CAPT. MOORE MAKES INDIGNANT DENIAL
Says There Was No Basis for Passenger's Statement

Captain Moore, of the S.S. *Mount Temple*, when interviewed by a *Globe* representative this morning regarding the statement made by one of the passengers who came out on his ship, who claimed that he (Captain Moore) arrived within sight of the *Titanic* and instead of offering help, ordered all lights out and steamed away from the scene, gave out the following statements –

There followed a recital of his tale of frustrated assistance. But then the reporter, having listened sympathetically, perhaps having only asked Captain Moore to tell again what had happened, now produced a scrap of paper:

... Captain Moore was wrathy when he was shown the telegram stating that he steamed away from the *Titanic*. He said that as soon as he turned about he ordered all hands on deck and immediately put them to work getting the boats ready to be lowered at a moment's notice, also getting ropes and accommodation ladders in readiness for service. He said that he also placed men in the crow's nest, and had one sailor hoisted to the very top of the mast, instructing them to keep a sharp lookout. He said that he and his officers almost strained their eyes in a hope to catch some glimpse of the *Titanic*.

When he turned his ship and rushed back among immense fields of ice he was doing so at great risk, for he had on board 1,451 passengers beside his crew. Nevertheless, he promptly answered the call for help.

'Now,' said the Captain. 'I had turned back and steamed for fifty miles. I kept my crew on deck all night, working and preparing to render any assistance possible, and I and my officers paced the bridge, keeping a sharp lookout during the remainder of the night; we cruised about for five hours and never saw the ship. Had I seen her, would I have done as this man says? No. The man must have been a fool. The above statement shows I never caught a glimpse of the steamer.'

Capt. Moore said that when he turned away from the scene to continue on his course the steamers *Carpathia, California* [sic], *Burma* [sic], *Frankfurt* and a tramp were in the vicinity. 'Furthermore,' he said, 'what do the people who were on board my steamer know what I was doing or where I was going? How could they tell in what direction I was sailing? It was past midnight, and they were below. The statement is not only false, but absurd.

'Another thing,' said the Captain. 'leaving the humanity side of the question, do you not think that I would have liked to have been the lucky one to pick up those people?' The man who made the statement against him must have done so out of spite.

But what possible spite? A 'fool' passenger who is piqued by a Captain he never sees, could lodge a complaint directly to the port agent in St John. Why would he journey all the way to Toronto, putting over 1,000 miles of railtrack behind him, before resurrecting a personal hurt? If it was merely the perception of some insult or injury, it seems on the contrary absurd for a passenger not to put it behind him with those two days of train journey, human nature being what it is. Why then take the first opportunity spill out a false story about a now-remote ship?

The passenger accusation is stark, but it has an arresting detail. The ship that appeared to the *Titanic*, claimed to be *Mount Temple*, 'ordered all lights out and steamed away from the scene.' Why does this sound familiar? Ah, because it is Captain Moore who supplied a strange feature of the schooner he met coming from that direction.

He would say it in two places at the American inquiry: ' … and the light of that vessel seemed to go out,' he said, later repeating: 'then the light seemed to suddenly go out.' In London, asked if he saw this vessel itself, he only offered: 'Not at all, it was dark.' Whether this is a passive observation about the quality of night, or a direct reference to the hull of the unknown is unclear.

Titanic Fourth Officer Joseph Boxhall had seen 'beautiful lights' on the mystery ship, which he identified as a three or four-masted steamer, when she first approached. He later lost the light when he got down on the water. Yet quartermaster Arthur John Bright, who left *Titanic* from the port side in a very late collapsible lifeboat, remarked that when he finally got afloat; 'There was a light … possibly 4 or 5 miles away, off the port bow of the ship. It looked to me

Mention in the *Toronto Star* of May 1, 1912, that Dr Quitzrau has subscribed a sworn affidavit of what he knew about affairs on the *Mount Temple*.

like a sailing ship – like a fishing boat. There were no lights to be seen about the hull of the ship [steamer], if it was a ship.'

Nobody in sworn evidence suggested that the lights of the mystery ship suddenly went out. But survivors occasionally made reference in newspaper reports to a lack of lights along the hull, such as Caroline Bonnell of Ohio, who spoke of seeing two lights on the mystery ship when she was down on the water, being a red light (port-side light) and a white light (masthead light or stern light) – with thus no lights along her superstructure.

Sailor Albert Horswill, who left the *Titanic* relatively early, on the contrary told a newspaper that his small lifeboat started to pull 'in the direction of the light, which it transpired was but one of a number of lights, thus indicating that the ship was a large one. Unfortunately the lights seemed to get further away.'

Fifteen-year-old passenger Edith Brown was on the *Titanic* with her mother and father, the latter doomed to died in the sinking. In later years she insisted she had seen the mystery ship, and pointed it out to her father. As she looked back at it, she saw 'the lights in that ship go out.' Having married and become Edith Haisman, she even allowed her story to be recorded for posterity by the oral history unit of Southampton City Council. In that recording she can be heard to say: 'I turned round and said to my father, 'Look, there's a ship over there, see the lights,' and then the lights went out.'

Perhaps she is dreaming – considering that, in advanced years, before her death in 1997, she also claimed her father had looked down on her in the lifeboat from the rail, with cigar and brandy in hand.

None of this was relevant when Captain Moore was wrathful in April 1912. Who on earth was this man making such preposterous allegations?

Above: Photograph of Mount Temple lights.
Below: Design drawings for the foremast and mainmast of the *Mount Temple*, showing oil and electric lights on the former and an electric lamp on the latter. Fourth officer Boxhall of the *Titanic* said the mystery ship was displaying 'beautiful lights.'

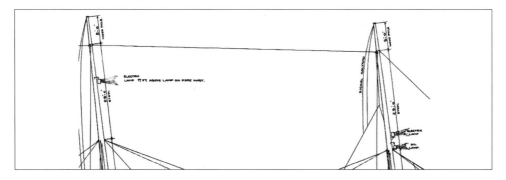

THE QUITZRAU AFFAIR

THE narrative of the *Mount Temple's* voyage from London to Antwerp and thence to St John has been concluded. The prosecution will now adduce witnesses as to what may have happened on that voyage. The first is Dr Frederick Charles Quitzrau.

FRIEDRICH CARL QUITZRAU (1887-1946)

Born May 23, 1887 in Germany. Aged 24 on the *Mount Temple* in 1912.
Died January 9, 1946, in New York, aged 58.
Had been living at 92 Bödeker Street, Hannover, Germany.
Quitzrau, who later anglicised his forenames, had also been living in Pittsburgh in 1910. He was a graduate of medicine at the Charité University in Berlin, and was on his way to the University of Toronto to attend a postgraduate course.

It was initially reported on the front page of the *Toronto Star* (April 23, 1912) that Dr Quitzrau:

> ... told the *Star* that the wireless operator on the *Mount Temple* had informed him that they were the first boat to get the *Titanic*'s CQD, and that they were only about forty miles from her at the time. The *Mount Temple* is a slow boat, making ordinarily about eleven knots.
>
> Dr Quitzrau also states that the story among passengers and ship's staff was that the lights of the *Titanic* had been visible for some time before she sank. These statements have a particular interest in view of the fact that it is the first mention that has been made here of the *Mount Temple* as one of the boats within the *Titanic*'s range on the night of the tragedy.

The newspaper immediately sought comment from Captain Moore, who wired to 'the *Star* newspaper, Toronto,' a statement for inclusion in the same day's edition:

> St. John, NB, April 23 – Could not possibly have been my ship. Did not receive CQD until 12.30am Monday. Was then 50 miles west and south of *Titanic*'s position. Did not arrive at that position until 4.30am. It is very evident that passenger is mistaken. Captain Moore, CPR steamer *Mount Temple*.

After Quitzrau had broken this provocative story to the *Star*, the newspaper's Managing Editor, John R. Bone, cabled his newspaper's special correspondent in Washington, Eldred James Archibald (who was there to report the Senate investigation into the *Titanic* sinking) alerting him to the development.

The result was that reporter E.J. Archibald furnished a telegram from Editor Bone to Senator Smith, chairman of the American inquiry, which read as follows:

> Dr Quitzrau, a passenger on the CPR *Mount Temple*, arriving at St John, NB, last Friday, tells us here that passengers say they saw lights of the *Titanic* before she sank.
>
> The Captain states to our correspondent at St John that he laid to, on account of ice; denies that he saw lights. If investigating committee wants evidence of Captain and officers it should communicate with Ottawa immediately.

Frederick Charles Quitzrau, pictured soon after
his arrival in Canada when he was working as a
doctor at the isolation hospital, Toronto.

We shall see that the US inquiry did contact the Canadian authorities on foot of this intelligence, but meanwhile its chairman also wrote directly back to the *Toronto Star*, which printed the telegram it received:

> Washington DC, April 24 – Can you put me in touch with Dr Quitzrau? Have wired Captain of Canadian Pacific Railway vessel *Mount Temple* to ascertain something of position of ship Sunday night, April 14, in vicinity of *Titanic* at time she sank. (Signed) William Alden Smith, chairman, Senate investigating committee, *Titanic* disaster.

Dr Quitzrau was communicated with, and immediately replied by telegraph as follows:

> Toronto, April 24 – Senator William Alden Smith, Washington DC. Have received your message sent through Editor of the *Toronto Star*. Shall be glad to appear before your committee if you instruct me that my testimony is needed. (Signed) F.C. Quitzrau, M.D.

The newspaper report of this exchange, printed the next day, further remarked: 'Dr Quitzrau, who was in the *Star* office late this afternoon, did not say he saw the *Titanic*, but that employees of the ship told him that they saw the vessel's lights and witnessed their disappearance.'

There next came a fuller newspaper report, quoting Quitzrau, which went around the world, and was printed, *inter alia*, in the *New York Times*:

> TORONTO, Ontario, April 25 – Dr Quitzrau, who has been asked to testify before the Senate investigation of the *Titanic* disaster, today described his experiences aboard the *Mount Temple* when that steamer was near the sinking White Star liner. He said that he was going to Washington tonight.
>
> 'I only know from hearsay what transpired previous to my being awakened, but I prefer to say nothing more until I testify before the Senate committee,' said Dr Quitzrau.
>
> 'I retired about 9pm on Sunday. I was awakened by the sudden stopping of the machinery. I asked what was wrong and was told that the *Titanic* had struck an iceberg and was sinking, and that the lights of her distress signals had been seen.

'I dressed, and coming on deck shortly after daybreak, I saw a tramp steamer about half a mile north in the field of ice. She was cruising around, evidently in an attempt to get out.

'A Russian boat came alongside, but did not give any word. She made a circle around where the *Titanic* was supposed to have sunk, as well as around us. A little later, at 6 o'clock, we sighted the *Carpathia* to the south east.

'We made a circle around what was said to be the scene of the wreck, but did not see any kind of wreckage or bodies.

'At 8 o'clock we got a general message from the *Carpathia* that the *Titanic* had struck a berg and was at the bottom of the sea. The *Carpathia* said that 700 people have been saved, all the others being lost, and that there was no need to stand by.'

(*The New York Times*, April 26, 1912, p. 4)

In any event, Dr Quitzrau did not attend at the US inquiry in person, a matter which shall be looked at later. But in consequence of his raising these allegations, he visited the offices of William James Elliott, a notary public for the province of Ontario. There he attested a sworn deposition dated April 29, 1912.

Sent to the inquiry in Washington, where it was read into the record, it declares:

Dr. F.C. Quitzrau. being first duly sworn, deposes and says that he was a passenger, travelling second class, on the steamer *Mount Temple*, which left Antwerp April 3 1912;

That about midnight Sunday, April 14, New York time, he was awakened by the sudden stopping of the engines; that he immediately went to the cabin, where were already gathered several of the stewards and passengers, who informed him that word had been received by wireless from the *Titanic* that the *Titanic* had struck an iceberg and was calling for help.

Orders were immediately given and the *Mount Temple* course changed, heading straight for the *Titanic*.

About 3 o'clock New York time, 2 o'clock ship's time, the *Titanic* was sighted by some of the officers and crew; that as soon as the *Titanic* was seen all lights on the *Mount Temple* were put out and the engines stopped and the boat lay dead for about two hours;

That as soon as day broke the engines were started and the *Mount Temple* circled the *Titanic*'s position, the officers insisting that this be done, although the Captain had given orders that the boat proceed on its journey.

While encircling the *Titanic*'s position we sighted the *Frankfurt* to the northwest of us, the *Birma* to the south, speaking to both of these by wireless, the latter asking if we were in distress; that about 6 o'clock we saw the *Carpathia*, from which we had previously received a message that the *Titanic* had gone down;

That about 8.30 the *Carpathia* wirelessed that it had picked up 20 lifeboats and about 720 passengers all told, and that there was no need for the *Mount Temple* to stand by, as the remainder of those on board were drowned.

Quitzrau's affidavit was subscribed and embossed with a seal. There is a major error within it, being the suggestion that New York time was ahead of ship's time, which could not have been the case.

If the reference to 'about midnight' is actually ship's time on the *Mount Temple*, the story may proceed. Quitzrau said he was roused 'by the sudden stopping of the engines,' and in the wireless log of Marconi operator John Oscar Durrant the entry 'Our Captain reverses engines' has the last word crossed out and replaced with 'ship.' Captain Moore's claimed full speed astern on the engines (when encountering a schooner), which would create judder and vibration, but this is apparently later than now described.

Quitzrau says he went to the 'cabin,' presumably the second-class saloon directly outside his stateroom in an amidships section of the ship. This area also housed accommodation for the chief and second offer, and George Henry Scott, the chief steward. There he met stewards and passengers, he says.

It is next claimed that the *Titanic* was sighted by 'some of the officers and crew' at 2am ship's time. There was considerable difference between *Mount Temple* and *Titanic* times, and *Titanic* would certainly have been afloat at 2am *Mount Temple* time. However the mystery ship was seen earlier in the night by the *Titanic* clock, but in any case the time is approximate.

Then follows the contention that all lights on the *Mount Temple* were put out while the ship was in sight of the *Titanic*.

In neither of these assertions, the alleged seeing of the *Titanic* and the claimed putting out of lights, does Dr Quitzrau indicate that he personally saw anything, and in point of fact he never advanced that claim, indicating instead that his knowledge came from hearsay.

The deponent does appear, however, to have a good grasp of what transpired in the wireless shack, having claimed from the earliest that he was directly given information by the Marconi operator, John Oscar Durrant.

There are some differences with the earlier version of events ascribed to him in the extract from the *New York Times*, but the sworn affidavit must be taken as Quitzrau's settled account, and of course it is a major consideration that this man, who had been branded a fool, actually took the enormous step of going to a notary public and making a sworn legal statement on an event that had been dominating the newspapers for days.

This was a course of action taken with all seriousness and due deliberation. Quitzrau does not appear to be a sensation seeker – in his soberly phrased telegram to Senator Smith in Washington, he writes that he shall be glad to appear before your committee *if you instruct me that my testimony is needed*. No self-publicist would offer such a negating clause. Then there is the fact that Quitzrau presents himself only as a facilitator of the story emerging – and no self-publicist would exclude himself from personally witnessing what is important.

As to the two versions, in the *New York Times* account, Quitzrau says he had retired for the night at the relatively early hour of 9pm that Sunday. He does not say when he was awakened, but when he emerged to enquire about 'the sudden stopping of the machinery,' he was told that

Dr Quitzrau and daughter Gladys splashing in the surf at Atlantic city, New Jersey, *c.*1921. Less than a decade earlier his ocean voyage had involved a deadly seriousness.

the *Titanic* was sinking – with the emphasis on the ongoing sinking process – and at this point that 'the lights of her distress signals had been seen.'

This latter phrase can only mean one thing – distress rockets. These signals had been seen, he said, but it is a curiosity that there is no mention of visible distress signals from the *Titanic* in his subsequent sworn affidavit.

Quitzrau's newspaper account says he came on deck 'shortly after daybreak,' which was not before 4am, and it means that he personally could not have seen any rockets or other signals from the *Titanic* herself. It would appear, therefore, that if he had learned of the emergency in its early stages, he then simply repaired to bed – rising early to then hear tales of what had been seen by others, just as he could not himself have known the names of particular ships seen later that morning, or what would be transmitted by wireless.

What is interesting, parenthetically, is his sighting of a 'tramp steamer about half a mile north in the field of ice.' This is Moore's 'foreign' steamer, on the same side of the icefield in the bright morning.

It is a great pity that Quitzrau was not seen and questioned by the US inquiry. Perhaps it would have been a personal inconvenience for him to attend, or it could be that it was agreed with Washington that an affidavit, at least in the first instance, would suffice. These circumstances are unclear.

The US inquiry was, however, distracted by apparently rival claims – just as sensational – at this time, which turned out to be untrue, and which could have coloured attitudes to the Quitzrau claims. Chairman of the inquiry Senator Smith was also issued with a flat denial of the story from the *Mount Temple* herself, and his interest in the mystery ship would later be fixated on the *Californian*, a vessel that admitted seeing low-lying rockets, whereas Captain Moore denied seeing any lights or signals at all.

George Eulas Foster, Acting Prime Minister of Canada, who liaised with the Chairman of the US *Titanic* inquiry, Senator William Alden Smith.

But when he first learned of the allegations from the Editor of the *Toronto Star*, Senator Smith pursued them with the Canadian authorities, writing to Prime Minister Robert Laird Borden of the Dominion Government:

'It is reported that Canadian Pacific Railway steamer *Mount Temple* was within five miles of *Titanic* at the time she sank. This steamer is scheduled to sail from St John, NB, Friday. Can sailing be stopped by your Government until Captain of ship can be interrogated concerning the statement of passenger who claims to have been on board and until rumour can be established as a fact or successfully denied?'

Unfortunately for Senator Smith, the Canadian Government was then in a temporary state of flux, with Prime Minister Borden suffering from a bout of ill-health. Secretary for Trade and Commerce George Eulas Foster had assumed the role of Acting Premier, and no doubt had his hands full.
He first cabled:

Message received. Making immediate enquiries and telegraph later. (Signed) Geo. E. Foster, Acting Premier.

He later wired to Senator Smith the text of a wire that Captain Moore had himself sent to the *Toronto Star* in response to the *Titanic* allegations, and strongly implied that he was reluctant to bestir himself much –

'Captain of *Mount Temple* reports having received CQD message from *Titanic* at 12.30am ship's time Monday. Was then fifty miles west and south of position sent out by *Titanic*. Immediately altered course to reach *Titanic*, but did not arrive at her position until 4.00am when could not see *Titanic*'s lights. Saw no sign of ship or boats. Cruised around position until

Senator William Alden Smith of Michigan, chairman on the subcommittee of the Committee on Commerce charged with investigating the *Titanic* wreck, on the steps of the Capitol.

received message from the *Carpathia* at 8.44am that she had picked up twenty boatloads and that the *Titanic* had sunk. Received another message at 8.50 from the *Carpathia*: 'No need to stand by, as nothing more can be done.'

Under these circumstances it does not seem necessary to detain boat due to sail Friday evening. If considered necessary, commission could be appointed to take Captain's evidence. Will no doubt be examined later by British commission.'

Senator Smith pressed his point however:

I will greatly appreciate it if depositions of Captain of *Mount Temple* could be taken by commissioners, as suggested by you, and forwarded to me at Washington, relative to the movements of the ship on Sunday evening, April 14, stating relative positions to *Titanic* and *Carpathia*, together with a detailed report on all wireless messages sent and received. I thank you for your kind and prompt attention to my former telegram, and especially hope that this additional request may be complied with.

Smith then got into communication with Captain Moore, and a telegram was received by his committee, signed by Moore, other officers and the wireless operator. It largely repeated the information sent by the Acting Premier, concluding: 'Names of passengers who claim they saw lights of *Titanic* unknown.'

But there were again slight differences in detail. The *Toronto Star* journalist in Washington, E.J. Archibald, having the inside track, reported on April 24 that a long despatch had been received by Senator Smith from the *Mount Temple*, 'the whole contents of which he would not make public.

Publicity seeker Luis Klein made a series of outrageous allegations, claiming to have been aboard the *Titanic* and to have personally sounded the warning of a berg ahead. His deception made the US inquiry wary of being similarly hoodwinked.

The despatch is signed by the Captain and all the officers of the *Mount Temple* and says in part that the vessel was 53 miles south and west of the *Titanic* when the accident happened, about the same distance away as was the *Carpathia*, and that she arrived at the scene of the disaster at 4.20am, having been compelled to lay to for a while on account of the ice at 3.25.

Ignoring the impossibility of these figures and assertions, the *Star* next quoted the Chairman of the US *Titanic* inquiry himself:

'The information thus furnished has been most valuable,' said Senator Smith to *The Star*. 'It is too early as yet to say anything about its results, but it may be that it will completely clear up this phase of the case.'

Senator Smith's drifting interest in the Quitzrau claims was already evident. On May 1, the *Toronto Star* would put on its front page a report of the sworn affidavit being received in Washington, with the headline: QUITZRAU SWEARS TO REMARKABLE STORY, 'Declares *Mount Temple* Put Out Her Lights When the *Titanic* Sank.'

The report said the affidavit, sworn two days previously, had been 'received today by Senator Smith.' In fact it had been enclosed in a letter that was sent express, not by Quitzrau, but by as high a personage as the United States vice consul at Toronto. Yet Smith only read it into the record of the US Inquiry on the afternoon of Thursday, May 9, over a week later, along with a number of other submissions and depositions received, and Quitzrau was never called.

In the meantime the inquiry had heard from Captain Moore in direct evidence, the Chairman being somewhat charmed by him, and a story had also emerged about the *Californian* seeing rockets. But it appears that a separate, and somewhat embarrassing, incident – in addition to the downbeat reaction of the Canadians and Moore's pro-active use of cables – had dampened Smith's initial enthusiasm for the Quitzrau story.

The parallel incident involved a claimant named Luis Klein. It began in a Cleveland bar, and concluded in high farce before Smith's committee. By the time the affair had run its course it had also embroiled a United States senator and high profile members of America's Austro-Hungarian diplomatic community.

Baron Hengelmüller, Austro-Hungarian envoy to the United States, who became embroiled in the farcical Luis Klein affair.

Jack Lavin and John Schrieber, residents of Cleveland, came across Klein in a saloon in Woodford Avenue on Saturday, April 20, 1912. Klein, who claimed to be Hungarian, was 24 years old, slightly built, and spoke only German. As his two new friends listened the young seaman told an epic story of monumental malfeasance on the bridge of the *Titanic*, negligence of such vast dimensions that it led almost inevitably to catastrophe. One hero emerged from the story, however – Klein himself.

Nor was this the first time he'd proved himself a man of mettle. He had been a seaman for four years before joining the *Titanic*. His discharge papers had, so he said, gone down with the ship – along with 500 German marks and a gold medal from the Hamburg-American line, presented to him in August 1910 for rescuing a girl at sea from the *President Lincoln*.

His new friends took him to the offices of the *Cleveland Plain Dealer*, which the next day (the day before Quitzrau went to the *Toronto Star*) published his tale:

> Klein alleged that the entire watch on deck, excepting himself, was drunk. The liquor, he said, was supplied by the stewards from the leftovers at the banquet and ball on the *Titanic* the night of the crash.
>
> Secondly, Klein asserted that the White Star line had given him a suit of clothes, shoes, shirt and a hat, plus two $10 gold pieces and that he had been told to leave New York City with speed ...
>
> His third declaration was this: that he, Klein, personally and alone, first saw the berg and sounded 'half of the alarm.' From the promenade deck, where he was on duty, he said, he ran forward, past the bridge, climbed into the crow's nest, where the lookout was asleep, and rang the alarm bell ...

Titanic second officer Charles Herbert Lightoller aboard the *Oceanic*.

The lookout awoke on the first sound of the bell, and hammered out the second stroke, which told the bridge that there was danger ahead. Then, said Klein, almost instantly the ship struck, and he jumped overboard.

This story was patently absurd, including Klein's assertion that, without a lifebelt and in his heavy clothing and boots, he struck out for a cake of ice and lay there until picked up by a lifeboat.

That Saturday night, before the story had even been published, Assistant United States District Attorney Cary Alburn contacted Washington with the news that there was a reported *Titanic* survivor in Cleveland who had explosive information. Senator Smith returned instructions to Alburn to hold Klein on a technical charge.

Soon after Saturday midnight Klein was turned over to the United States marshall's office, pending the arrival of a subpoena. On Sunday April 21, Smith admitted that 'Klein did not appear on the list of the *Titanic*'s crew.' He told reporters: 'I do not know whether Klein is what he claims to be. I have no opinion, but am going entirely on statements from Cleveland. It will be easy to establish whether Klein is telling the truth once he takes the witness stand.'

Smith's comment that he had 'no opinion' on Klein's story was accompanied by a comment to the *Plain Dealer* reporter that it sounded 'fishy,' but he was still determined to call him. Austro-Hungarian ambassador, Baron Hengelmüller, had meanwhile also called on Smith personally to draw his attention to Klein's story.

At 1.30pm on Monday, a telegram arrived at the office of US Attorney U.G. Denman, summoning Klein to appear as a witness, signed by Senate Sergeant at Arms Daniel M. Ransdell:

Please serve process on Luis Klein, Cleveland, O., to appear before subcommittee on commerce, United States Senate, No. 414 Senate office building, forthwith. You are hereby authorized and deputised to serve this process.

Deputy Marshal Harry T Brockman had meanwhile subjected Klein to six hours of questioning on Sunday, taking him repeatedly over the events leading up to the collision and his alleged escape from the ship. Klein proved unshakeable in his story, and attempts through an interpreter to trap him into admissions that would prove him an impostor failed. Federal officers holding him in custody were, so the *Cleveland Plain Dealer* reported, convinced that he was indeed the man who sounded the lookout bell on the *Titanic*. Government officials stated that Klein – without the ability to speak or read English – had had no opportunity to learn the details of the wreck from newspaper accounts. Nor did he seem alarmed when the federal officers held the possibility of a prison sentence over his head if his allegations proved to be without substance.

'I have told the truth,' he replied. 'If they can put me in jail for that, I do not care. I did not come to Cleveland to tell my story. I came to get work.'

His story was, however, undergoing modifications from its original form. Changing the account he had originally given on Saturday, Klein on Sunday dropped some of the more racy elements. No longer was the lookout man and practically all the rest of the crew drunk or asleep, and the claim that the White Star Line had paid him to get out of New York was abandoned.

On the evening of Monday April 22, just as Smith was receiving a certain telegram from Toronto, Klein left Cleveland for Washington under the charge of Deputy Marshall Charles Morgan. The pair arrived in the capital on Tuesday morning and booked into the Hotel Driscoll.

Klein must have felt the net closing around him when he was faced in Senator Smith's office the next day by the *Titanic*'s Second Officer, Charles Lightoller – and was not recognised as one of the crew saved aboard the *Carpathia*. Lightoller had never seen him before.

When later questioned in open committee hearing, Lightoller stated that as far as he knew there was only one crewman named Klein on the *Titanic* – and it wasn't Luis. 'I am given to understand that there was one man named Klein, who was a second-class barber. That man is personally known to me. He is the only Klein who was on board, so far as I know.'

Senator Duncan Fletcher asked if the man Lightoller had met in Smith's office could have been a stowaway in a lifeboat. 'I really could not say, sir,' replied the officer, as the session threatened to dissolve into farce.

On the Wednesday morning Klein saw his chance to escape. When Deputy Marshall Morgan came to rouse him at 8am, he found the room empty. He learned that Klein had left an hour before, simply walking out of the hotel to vanish.

Nonetheless, Senator Smith attempted to hear his controversial witness the following day:

Senator Smith: I would like to ask the sergeant at arms if the witness Luis Klein, who was subpoenaed and brought here by the marshall's office of Cleveland is here; and tell him, if he is here, we are ready to use him.

Notary Edgar L. Cornelius: He is not here, Senator.

Senator Smith: Where is he?

Mr Cornelius: He left his hotel yesterday morning. We do not know where he is. We have been unable to locate him.

Senator Smith: Have you made every endeavour to locate him?

Mr Cornelius: Through our officers here; yes, sir – through the marshall's office here.

Senator Smith: Are you continuing your efforts?

Mr Cornelius: Yes, sir.

Senator Smith: You may continue your efforts to find him, and if you can find him, it is the wish of the committee that you should do so.

Morgan had to appear before the investigating committee to explain how Klein had managed to escape his custody. Called before Smith, Morgan stated that he had been attempting to find the absent witness. 'I immediately notified the people here, and have been following instructions, trying to locate the man.'

On Friday and Saturday, Smith again called for Klein to appear. The sergeant at arms dutifully called for the witness outside the committee room, and received no response. On May 2, the *Washington Post* reported in a small paragraph: 'No further effort will be made to find Louis Klein, who was brought here from Cleveland, and disappeared before being called to testify

Dr F. C. Quitzrau in later age. He became a prison surgeon and travelled extensively in the United States.

about a story he told in an interview regarding the disaster. The committee learned that Klein was not aboard the vessel.'

After Smith's impatient questioning of the *Titanic*'s senior surviving officer, Lightoller, about the wretch, he had immediately turned to taking evidence from his next witness – Captain James Henry Moore of the *Mount Temple*, who had kindly come down from St John to tell his story.

Much mollified by Moore's testimony, in which the latter praised the Senator's opinions, Smith thanked him ardently for his attendance, with the latter gushing: 'I was only too glad to come, Sir.'

Senator Smith then replied: 'I do not want any wrong impression to get out concerning the course of the *Mount Temple* …'

The comment was made two days before Frederick Charles Quitzrau swore his affidavit. Moore had got his retaliation in first, and Quitzrau would never be called. In fact, reporter E.J. Archibald reported:

> As a result of Moore's testimony, Dr F.C. Quitzrau of Toronto, a *Mount Temple* passenger, will not be called here, Senator Smith stated. It was thought today that Dr Quitzrau had only heard gossip on the *Mount Temple* that the *Titanic*'s distress rockets had been seen and ignored, but he had no personal knowledge of the alleged incident.

Counsel for Captain Moore: This gentleman admitted from the first that his story was hearsay. He indicated an intention to present himself in Washington, and then never arrived. On the contrary, Captain Moore was energetic in his indignant defences, and eventually made the much longer journey to Washington, from St John, than would have been the case from Toronto.

We can hear the ringing anger of the Captain, for instance in an interview given to a reporter from the *St John Globe*: 'I certainly would have done my best. Any statement to the contrary is untrue, and I don't care how damned strong you make it.'

Quitzrau says he had direct information from the wireless operator, but why Mr Durrant would take a strangely-named foreign passenger into his confidence is not explained. Whereas it might be highly unlikely, if we accept it at face value we must then also accept what Quitzrau

Claims in the *Boston Globe* that Dr Quitzrau was making claims 'out of spite.' Quitzrau's name does not appear on the surviving steerage manifest and the five-person saloon list is missing.

"SPITE" SAYS OFFICER.

Dr Quitzran Ordered From Deck on Which He Did Not Belong, It Is Declared.

ST JOHN, N B, April 26—One of the officers of the Mount Temple says only Dr Quitzran could have been responsible for the story that the steamer did not do its best to reach the Titanic. Dr Quitzran, he says, was a steerage passenger who because of the crowded condition of the steerage was given second cabin accommodations. The officer says that Quitzran was found on the saloon deck during the voyage, and when it was found he had a steerage ticket he was ordered from that deck. This officer says the passenger is making untrue charges against the ship for spite.

said the operator told him, which was that the *Mount Temple* was 40 miles away and therefore could not have been the mystery ship by any stretch of the imagination.

If this passenger had really emerged from his bed on Sunday night and been told, as he claimed in his newspaper interview, that distress signals had been seen, it seems rather more likely that he would have gone out on deck to try to see rockets for himself, rather than merely return nonchalantly to his slumbers. And if the rocket allegation disappears from his sworn deposition, then its mention in the first place is all the more suspicious.

There is also the matter of pique, or spite. Although Dr Quitzrau was accommodated as a second-class passenger, there was a story in *the New York Tribune* that he had been ordered at one time from a part of the ship where he shouldn't have been. No doubt it was all a mistake.

Similar indulgence might be needed in the matter of a border crossing at Niagara Falls in 1942, thirty years after the sinking. Asked whether he had ever been 'arrested and deported, or excluded from admission,' Dr Quitzrau answers 'Yes, misdemeanour June 1941.'

SHEDDING LIGHT

THE Quitzrau claims touched off a newspaper descent on the *Mount Temple*, lying at Sand Point in St John, to search for corroboration. Those who attempted to coax stories from the crew quickly found there was an air of division among the ship's complement.

The *St John Globe* reported that 'the officers are reticent, refusing to divulge just what took place a week ago Sunday night when, it is declared, the *Mount Temple* came within a few miles of the *Titanic* and refused to go to her aid.'

The *Boston Globe* reported:

St John, N.B., April 24 – Marked differences of opinion exist between the officers and crew of the Canadian Pacific steamer *Mount Temple* in regard to what occurred a week ago Sunday night when the *Titanic* foundered.

In the first place, some members of the crew who are supposed to know more than their comrades are not inclined to tell all they know, evidently believing that their officers are the ones to make whatever statement is necessary.

But some of them declare that the *Mount Temple* deliberately sailed away after reading the *Titanic* distress signals and did not attempt to render assistance.

Under a headline entitled 'SAILORS' TALK,' the *St John Globe* reported on April 25:

The *Standard* this morning says:

There are members of the crew who are outspoken in their condemnation of the failure of the *Mount Temple* to reach the scene of the wreck.

Sailors, firemen and others declare that they sat on deck for hours and watched the *Titanic* sending up rockets and burning red and blue lights until the *Mount Temple* steamed so far away that these signals were lost.

One of the sailors, who says he was on watch Sunday night, says that he heard Third Officer Notley tell the Captain of the distress signals, and that instead of the steamer heading directly to the wreck, she steamed away on her own course, so that the lights were soon lost.

An oiler named Pickard, who was on duty at the time, declares that the second engineer came below and asked the men to keep her fired up to the limit, as it was a case of life or death.

Another engine room hand adds that when his watch was over he went on deck and with a lot of others, passengers and crew, leaned over the rail and saw the almost steady stream of rockets being sent up by the *Titanic*.

He adds that in spite of the cold of the night, he remained on deck until almost 2 o'clock, watching until the signals were lost in the distance. At the time of the accident the *Mount Temple* was between five and ten miles from the scene.

The *Boston Globe* the same day reported:

Second Officer Heald says that if he wanted to talk he could tell a lot, whatever that means, but it is not his business to talk and if anyone wants information to go to the Captain.

Third Officer Notley, who was the officer of the watch when the wireless messages were received, could not be found. The statements of the crew agree with those of Capt. Moore in so far as the reports of preparing the lifeboats, etc., are concerned.

View towards the grain elevator at the Canadian Pacific dock in St John, New Brunswick, where the *Mount Temple* tied up in April 1912.

> Capt. Moore has been besieged with enquiries, telegraphic and otherwise, since the *Mount Temple* docked.

Moore had responded with cables of his own, of course, the one to the American inquiry bearing his signature and that of A.H. Sargent, his Chief Officer, wireless officer Durrant, and his second officer, Herbert Heald. But this was by no means 'all the officers' as E.J. Archibald had confidently reported in the *Toronto Star*, even though Senator Smith had kept the full contents of the wire to himself.

Meanwhile the fact that Third Officer Notley 'could not be found' was due to his having left the paid employment of the ship in St John – a fact of which the newspapers were unaware. But the *St John Globe* was becoming anxious:

THE *MOUNT TEMPLE* AND THE *TITANIC*'S LOSS
Contradictory Statements Made – Inquiry Ordered

Can it be possible the S.S. *Mount Temple* was close to the *Titanic* when she went down, and failed to render assistance? That is the question asked on all sides today.

It is impossible to believe that the two steamers were so close together that one might have rendered help to the other and failed to do so. The only charitable view to take of statements of those passengers on the *Mount Temple* who are making grave charges is that they are mistaken, and that the steamer they saw was not the *Titanic*, but some other of the steamers rushing to her assistance.

The interesting statement on page two of today's *Globe* made by the wireless operator shows clearly that those on the *Mount Temple* knew full well the perilous plight of those on the sinking steamer. They knew she was going down rapidly, and that all hands were in danger.

Capt. Moore and his officers must also have known, what all seamen knew, that the ship had not sufficient [lifeboat] accommodation for even one-half her passengers.

It is inconceivable, under the circumstances, that they could have failed to make the greatest possible effort at succour. Capt. Moore's own statement is that he did his utmost to reach the *Titanic*, and did not get to the spot until two hours after she sank.

If he can demonstrate that he was fifty miles away when the call for help came, his story will need no other confirmation, because it is known the *Mount Temple* could not cover better than fifty miles in four hours.

There are the statements of some of the *Titanic*'s crew that they saw a steamer's lights, and there is the statement of passengers of the *Mount Temple* that they saw the *Titanic*. This suggests that the two steamers were closer together than the *Mount Temple* officers admit.

There are also rumours afloat that members of the *Mount Temple* crew have told shore friends of seeing the lights of the sinking ship. It is impossible to get verification of such stories at the present time, and it is only through an official investigation under oath that such reports can be sifted.

Crew of the *Mount Temple* are alleged to have watched on deck for hours as the *Titanic* frantically signalled her distress.

> Ottawa reports say such an investigation will be held, but so far no orders to that effect have reached local officials.
>
> (*St John Globe*, April 25, 1912, p. 7)

Crew such as 'sailors, firemen and others' were claiming to have seen red and blue lights and rockets sent up by the *Titanic*, essentially corroborating Quitzrau's newspaper statement about distress signals being seen. Some had also, apparently, told shore friends of seeing these lights.

Did the *Titanic* burn red and blue lights?

Witnesses from that ship would indeed talk in evidence of having fired coloured rockets, at least besides the solely white ones seen by the *Californian*. Third officer Herbert Pitman said they were 'Various colours.' Quartermaster Robert Hichens opined: 'Some were green, some were red, and some were blue – all kinds of colours – and some white, Sir. I think, if I remember rightly, they were blue.'

Col. Archibald Gracie, a first class passenger, wrote a book in which he spoke of white rockets, but added (p. 28, *The Truth About the Titanic*, Mitchell Kennerley, 1913): 'these were followed by the Morse red and blue lights.'

Lookout Reginald Lee specified 'coloured rockets,' and passenger Major Arthur Peuchen 'different colours flying down.' But officer Joseph Boxhall said his threw out 'just white stars, bright ... not red,' while officer Charles Lightoller said they were 'principally white,' whatever that meant. Quartermaster George Rowe said he brought up detonators, green lights and blue lights from the stern to supplement the rockets on the *Titanic*'s bridge. The evidence of various colours in the *Titanic* rockets is therefore plentiful.

Quartermaster Hichens told the *New York Times* that rockets were going up 'every few seconds,' while sailor George Symons used the word 'simultaneously,' as if in corroboration of the 'steady stream of rockets' allegedly sent up.

But Captain Moore denied absolutely seeing any lights at all in the night sky.

Moore was asked in the US inquiry:

> Q. Some passengers on your vessel, Sunday night about midnight, claim to have seen these rockets from the decks of the *Titanic*. Have you heard anything about that?
> Moore: I have read it in the papers, sir; but as a matter of fact, I do not believe there was a passenger on deck at 12 o'clock at night. I am positive, because they would not know anything at all about this, and you may be sure that they would be in their beds. I know the steward tells me there was nobody on deck; that is, the night watchman at the aft end. At the forward end there was nobody on deck.

Mount Temple crew members. It was alleged that many sat casually on deck and watched the pyrotechnic display of distress from the RMS *Titanic* as she sank

He was not asked about his *crew* allegedly seeing lights and rockets – and the midweek tales that were emanating from the *Mount Temple*, from sailors, firemen and others, including at least one engine room hand, did not include any passengers, who had all left during the previous weekend.

Later on, he was asked again about 'signal lights':

Q. Do you wish to be understood as saying that you did not see, on Sunday night or Monday morning, any signal lights from the *Titanic*?
Moore: I can solemnly swear that I saw no signal lights, nor did my officers on the bridge see any signal lights.

On the face of it, this answer adds only bridge officers and the Captain to the excluded passengers, and makes no reference to other members of crew ... but Senator Smith immediately passed on and asked about the *Mount Temple's* wireless apparatus.

Moore took the opportunity thereafter to read out and discuss his operator's long list of logged messages. He eventually got to the one received at 3.11am *Mount Temple* time from the *Carpathia*, telling *Titanic*: 'If you are there, we are firing rockets.'

Q. Is it possible that this passenger from Toronto, who claims to have seen rockets, may have seen the rockets from the *Carpathia* at that time?
Moore: I do not think it possible, sir, because if the *Carpathia* was farther away it is not likely you would see her rockets.

Leaving aside Moore's estimates of how far away his ship was from the scene (14 miles at 3.25am, less than a quarter of an hour after this *Carpathia* message) it should be remembered that *Mount Temple* was at the distress position at 4.30am, and could later see the *Carpathia* in daylight.

The *Carpathia*, by her evidence, first stopped at the scene at 4am. Captain Arthur Rostron said in his US evidence: 'At 4 o'clock I stopped. At 4.10, I got the first boat alongside.' He said the same in Britain (Br. 2540½).

And Rostron indicated why he had begun firing rockets in the first place:

25394. — At 20 minutes to 3 I saw the green flare, which is the White Star company's night signal, and naturally, knowing I must be at least 20 miles away, I thought it was the ship herself still.

...

25401. —At twenty minutes to three I saw a night signal, as I was saying, and it was just about half a point on the port bow, practically right ahead.

He had similarly declared in America:

'At 2.40, I saw a flare, about half a point on the port bow, and immediately took it for granted that it was the *Titanic* itself, and I remarked that she must be still afloat, as I knew we were a long way off, and it seemed so high.'

The *Titanic* had sunk, and the flare was actually from a lifeboat. But as a result of seeing it, Captain Rostron ordered that rockets to be fired 'at 2.45 and every quarter of an hour after to reassure *Titanic*.'

He therefore fired five rockets at 2.45, 3am, 3.15, 3.30, and 3.45am, with possibly a sixth at 4am when he arrived. The *Mount Temple* maintains that did not see any of them – even though they were separated at 4am only by the width of an icefield and half an hour's slow steaming for Captain Moore (to stop at 4.30am).

This denial seems hard to believe when set against what Captain Rostron said. He had seen a flare at twenty minutes to three. Captain Rostron also mentioned that at 'a quarter to three' (in other words, five minute later) his ship was doing 14 knots. He did not indicate that he slowed his speed at any point from then on, despite seeing a few icebergs.

It took Rostron an hour and a quarter thereafter to arrive (2.45am to 4am), which suggests a distance of 17.5 miles for him to see a flare that was burned from a lifeboat after the *Titanic* had sunk.

This distance of visibility is based on one hour at 14 knots, plus a further one-quarter of 14, being 3.5 miles, for the additional fifteen minutes. These are Rostron's claims, and he has no particular axe to grind.

It's even worse for Moore if *Carpathia* was slower (and therefore closer, backtracking from her 4am arrival) as her rockets would have been seen at a greater radius to the west. It is doubtful the *Carpathia* was steaming at full speed from the turnaround until the very moment she stopped. Second officer Bisset wrote that she went half-speed and then slow during the last half hour.

In any case, the *Carpathia* had seen green flares from a point of origin that was right down on the water, in a lifeboat, from a maximum of seventeen and a half miles away, and probably less. She was a commanding ship, high above the waterline, and her response was to fire rockets from the imposing elevation of her decks.

RMS *Carpathia* in a Cunard company postcard.

Watching brief: An adapted image from *The Graphic* of May 4, 1912, indicating how *Mount Temple* may have looked at the rim of an icefield at night.

Captain Moore said he stopped in ice at 3.25am, when 14 miles from the distress position. He later suggested the actual sinking site was eight miles further east, so that is a maximum of 22 nautical miles to where the *Carpathia* stopped.

Perhaps he stopped for five minutes, and if so, this would have coincided with the *Carpathia* firing her 3.30am rocket, and from the height of her superstructure. She was a maximum further seven miles away, bringing the outer separation between the two ships to 29 miles.

Of course it may have been very much less, particularly if a rocket was fired at 4am by the *Carpathia*, which would also mark her arrival and stop. Dawn was just breaking.

Moore's evidence is that he closed the distance from his 3.25am stop to the distress position, that is, 14 miles, in just an hour and five minutes. At 4am, is it reasonable to suppose he might be halfway along, say seven miles? Adding the remaining seven to the eight miles further away that Moore later reckoned *Titanic* sank, gives 15 miles between them.

The Captain of the *Mount Temple* had placed three lookouts, staring east, from 3am when he began to meet heavier ice. When the *Carpathia* was firing rockets from her bridge deck, Moore had a lookout in the crow's nest. He later 'had a man pulled up to the masthead in a bowline, right to the foretopmast head, and I had the Chief Officer at the mainmast head.'

And still he saw no rockets, or signal lights of any kind.

Carpathia second officer James Bisset, in a 1959 memoir (*Tramps and Ladies*, p. 282) wrote that the green light sighted at 2.40am was on the horizon. 'But then the light vanished, and we knew that it had been a pyrotechnic rocket, flaring at 500 feet above sea level.'

The *Times* of London noted in its columns on May 23, 1912. (p. 6) that: 'Rockets fired from the bridge of the *Titanic* must have risen to the height of at least 300ft above sea-level, and should therefore have been visible at a distance of nineteen miles. From the bridge of another ship they would be visible at a greater distance still.' Nineteen miles ...

If the *Carpathia* bridge was slightly lower than that of the *Titanic*, it should also be allowed that the crow's nest of a steamer would always be considerably higher than its bridge. But the *Times* is being conservative by offering a height of 'at least' 300ft, and then calculating a visible range only to that figure.

Modern calculations for the ranges at which a sea-level observer could see a rocket-burst fired to various altitudes are as follows (Michael Baldwin, UK Pyrotechnics Society).

Rockets fired from the bridge of the Titanic must have risen to a height of at least 300ft. above sea-level, and should therefore have been visible on the water-line at a distance of 19 miles. From the bridge of another ship they would be visible at a greater distance still.

Extract from the *Times* of London of May 23, 1912, giving its opinion as to the range at which *Titanic* distress rockets could have been seen

Height of Burst (feet)	Distance Visible (nautical miles)
100	13
200	18.7
300	22.5

But these are sea-level calculations, and Moore was considerably higher … he told the US inquiry: 'On my boat, when she is light, it is about 50ft from the water line to my bridge.'

The *Carpathia* bridge height was similar (Br. 25428), as may be judged in photographs. The combined height of both will make rockets visible over a very great distance.

Captain Rostron's rockets would probably have been based on Tonite, which was a mixture of guncotton and barium nitrate. The propellant was more powerful than the gunpowder-based rockets used previously.

Alan St H. Brock, in his 'A History of Fireworks' (1949) reports that Swiss military trials with gunpowder rockets in 1831 gave ranges of 1,800 to 1,900 yards. (The maximum range is obtained by firing at an elevation of 45 degrees, and the maximum height if the rocket had been fired vertically would be half the maximum range. These are calculations based on ballistics). Brock also reports that a two-pound rocket rises to a height of approximately 2,000ft in six seconds. Altitudes of at least 1,000ft could be reached by signal rockets in 1912, but the nature of *Carpathia*'s rockets is not known.

Yet there is evidence that the *Californian*, perhaps nineteen miles to the north (she told the *Virginian* at 5.45am that she was 17 miles away) saw *Carpathia* rockets. She did so when the *Mount Temple* was considerably closer to their source. *Californian* had also, of course, seen low-lying *Titanic* rockets, but had always been stationary and was not the mystery ship.

Apprentice officer James Gibson saw three rockets from 'about 3.20am,' which may be 3.30am by the *Carpathia*'s clock and would mean the other two were at 3.45 and 4am. If it was actually 3.15am *Carpathia* time, it would mean a final rocket at 3.45am. But while *Californian* and *Carpathia* ship times were very similar, it may not be that the ordered rockets 'every quarter of an hour' resulted in precise intervals.

In any case, *Californian* second officer Herbert Stone mentioned only two rockets, not three, seen from the same time, 'about 3.20am.' They were faint, he said, and a little distance apart, which would chime with *Carpathia* progress. Gibson said (Br. 7596): 'It was right on the horizon.'

Stone, in evidence in London, said he was told by Gibson of a rocket 'just before half past three.' He next saw another one, 'at a very great distance, I should judge.'

Above left: The height advantage of the ship's crow's nest offered an extended horizon.
Above right: Second engineer Robert Cragg reportedly came down to the engine room to tell the men to 'keep her fired up to the limit' as it was a case of life and death.

> Br. 8010. What do you mean by a very great distance? — Such a distance that if it had been much further I should have seen no light at all, merely a faint flash.

The two men were on the flying bridge of their steamer, which was slightly smaller than the *Mount Temple*. Because they had been stopped, drifting since 10.20pm, there was no crewman in the crow's nest at all. But they still saw the rockets (which were described as white, rather than the green flares seen by Rostron), and they did so at a 'very great distance.'

The *Mount Temple* did have someone in the crow's nest throughout, but Moore insisted that he and his officers saw no rockets or signal lights, and that no passengers were ever on deck during the hours of darkness.

If the CPR vessel had indeed seen *Carpathia* rockets, fired long after the *Titanic* had sunk, what would be the point of denying them? The overall story was still valid – the *Mount Temple* had hastened to the spot, arriving at 4.30am, and was separated from what was the real scene by an ice barrier.

But Captain Moore had denied seeing any lights from the first, and his story did not change.

Titanic officer Boxhall had been burning green lights in his lifeboat, having ordered a box of them be put into it before lowering. 'I had been showing green lights most of the time. I had been showing pyrotechnic lights ... the *Carpathia* was steaming toward our green lights.

'He saw our green lights and steamed down for them.'

But the green light on the schooner, which suddenly went out, is the only light of any kind which Moore mentions seeing during the night.

There now follows what may be a truly shocking fact: it is that the British *Titanic* inquiry did not ask Captain Moore any question at all about whether rockets or signal lights had been sighted from his ship. Not one, even though he was examined by no fewer than eight legal counsel during his appearance.

Described as an oiler, Pickard was named in a report about men who watched 'a steady stream of rockets' from the *Titanic*. Pickard was not stated to be among the spectators, yet 'another engine room hand' was. Journalists sometimes cloak informants thus.

The sole ordinary member of crew named in these midweek despatches from St John, which described what some aboard had confessed to seeing, was 'an oiler named Pickard.' But this man only made the uncontentious statement that the second engineer (Robert Grisedale Cragg. 1877-1956) had come below and asked the men to 'keep her fired up to the limit,' as it was a case of life or death.

It may be worth noting, in assessing the overall reliability of these reports, that there was indeed a man named Pickard aboard the *Mount Temple* on the voyage in question:

CHARLES NORTON PICKARD (1878-1949)

Aged 33, born in Peckham, London. He signed on as an assistant steward, not an oiler. His address in 1912 was at 30 Ruskin Avenue, Manor Park, in the East End.

Pickard later turned up as third class waiter on the RMS *Aquitania* in 1920, as night watchman on the *Lancastria* in 1924, and as night steward on the *Ausonia* in December 1929, by which time he had 22 years' service at sea.

Lest counsel for Captain Moore be forced to mention it, let it be disclosed that Pickard first went to sea in 1907 – after being let out of jail.

In 1905 he pleaded guilty to feloniously wounding his wife, Louise Emma Pickard (whom he divorced in 1917) and Edith King, her mother. He was sentenced to three years' penal servitude by Mr Justice Grantham.

CHARGE OF ATTEMPTED MURDER

At Stratford, Charles Norton Pickard, 26, a cellar-man, of Rutland Road, East Ham, was brought up on remand, before Mr Burnett Tabrum, charged with feloniously wounding Louisa Emma Pickard, his wife, with intent to murder her at Arragon Road, East Ham, on April 12 (1905), and he was also charged with attempting to murder his mother-in-law Edith King, at the same time and place.

Mr F.A. Stern prosecuted, and Detective Inspector Nicholls, of the K Division, represented the Police Commissioner. The evidence showed that the prisoner, who had left his wife on February 19, went to the house at 12pm at night on April 12. He asked his wife whether she would live with him, but she refused, saying: 'No, not to be starved.' He then threatened to murder her, and struck her four or five times on the neck with a knife. Her screams brought Mrs King and others into the room, and the prisoner stepped forward and stabbed Mrs King also in the neck.

The prisoner, who pleaded 'Guilty' to wounding without intent to murder, reserved his defence, and was committed for trial at the Old Bailey.

(*The Times*, Friday May 5, 1905, p. 3)

The couple had married in 1903 at West Ham. Charles Norton Pickard, a retired merchant seaman, died of lung cancer on May 23, 1949, aged 71.

Meanwhile, in this crucial midweek of late April 1912, three members of the *Mount Temple* crew remained in jail in St John. And, unknown to the press, there continued to be further desertions.

There were also demands to be paid off, so that crew members could part company with the vessel. On Tuesday April 23, the day the thunderclap first testimony about the *Titanic*'s mystery ship had appeared in morning newspapers, assistant stewards Krause and Bomberg took their leave.

So too did 'J. Ehlig, assistant cook,' as he was called in the log, although his name was John Ehmig, and we shall meet him again later. Jan Van Almen, the third baker, Aerts the assistant baker, and a ship's cook named Jones completed the list of half a dozen terminations of employment.

On the same day, the following men deserted without notice – ABs Gerhard Pfuhl and K.A. Andersen, and seamen J.W. Penna and A.P. Janssen. The four discharge books involved were deposited with the St John shipping master.

This amounted to a total of ten severances on the one day. There had been six earlier desertions, plus the departure of the Third Officer, Arthur Howard Notley, who would subsequently be mentioned in despatches. The total reduction in the *Mount Temple* crew since landfall now stood at 17 – or twenty if the trio in jail was included.

Note by the Shipping Master of St John, listing ten members of the *Mount Temple* crew deemed to have deserted in the port.

It was a wastage, or casualty rate, of virtually one man in seven.

The pressure on numbers got worse the next day, Wednesday April 24, although not as a result of an active desire to leave the ship. At 6.30am, assistant steward *Lodewijk (Ludovic)* Michiel loss his balance and tumbled into No. 6 hold.

Numbered backwards from the bow, number six was immediately abaft the third, or mizzen, mast. Michiel could have been knocked over by the boom of a derrick while at cargo work, or he may simply have tumbled over a coaming while crossing the deck. In any case he fell some 25ft, sustaining injuries to his arms and back. He was removed to the general hospital in St John, where the pronouncement was that he would certainly miss the homeward sailing.

A couple of replacements were signed in the course of the day, being two trimmers and a seaman named Thorpe, all at wages of £5 per month. One of the trimmers, whose name was given as 'C. Lightening' (somewhat ironic in light of the alleged sighting of signals) subsequently broke his commitment and failed to join.

By Thursday, Captain Moore had resolved to travel to Washington to deal with the Quitzrau accusation, thankful perhaps that there was absolutely no sign of any Canadian commission being formed, or depositions being taken from the men still on his ship. His absence could even help by heading off that possibility entirely, he may have reasoned.

He had also been fighting back in the local press, and an interview had been carried on page three of the *St John Globe* that morning, April 25, 1912 –

CAPTAIN Moore expressed much indignation at the reports circulating to the effect that he had in any way been derelict in his duty in rendering aid to the *Titanic*.

'I don't know what people would have, or what they mean,' he said. 'I steamed out of my course fifty miles and then cruised around for five hours keeping a sharp lookout for any survivors or wreckage, and then because I did not succeed in rescuing the passengers they demand to know why I did not get there before the ship sank.

'I did all that it was possible to do. I doubled the watch of the firemen below and served out rum to incite them to greater exertions. I had all my people up on deck and although on the bridge all of the previous night I remained there with the rest of the officers, all of us keeping a keen lookout.

'There were men in the crow's nest and a watch was even set at the mast head. Even the ship's cooks were kept on deck for fear they might be wanted to get warm food for survivors.

'All my boats were swung over the ship's sides, ready to lower at a moment's notice and the ladders and gangways were all in position if required.

'Remember, too, that I had 1,600 people on my own ship who were neither Englishmen, Americans nor Canadians, and if the *Mount Temple* had struck a berg there would have been a terrible panic and probably we would all have been lost.

'A passenger on my ship says he saw the *Titanic* at 12 o'clock when we were forty miles away. All I can say is that his eyesight must have been extraordinary. But then there was no passenger on the deck at 12 o'clock; none was allowed to come up, as they would have been in the way of the sailors and hindered the preparations going forward.

'I did not see the *Titanic* in the first place because it was dark, and in the second because there was a great ice field between us. I did not launch the lifeboats as it would have been silly to do it, knowing that they would have been crushed like eggshells.

'I repeat I did all it was possible for a man to do under the circumstances. I steamed out of my course fifty miles, cruised around five hours and only left the place after the *Carpathia* had assured me that no more could be done.

'It is pretty hard after all that to have mud slung at me. What do the members of my crew know about it, let alone the passengers? They might see the lights of a tramp steamer and imagine they were those of the *Titanic*. I have told my story before and can add no more.'

This account reflects Moore's increasing frustration, but while singling out the ship's cooks for mention, he did not disclose that a couple of them had already deserted. His assertion that a passenger was claiming to have seen the *Titanic* at midnight was doubly inaccurate – the distress message was only received at 12.11am, and it was only claimed from hearsay that crewmen were insisting shortly thereafter that they had seen rockets from the stricken liner, rather than the ship itself

Moore, for the first time, seems to touch on what stories certain members of his crew may have been peddling to the eager (and indiscriminating) ears of the press. The lights of a tramp steamer in the night are offered as a substitute *Titanic* – and Moore had seen such a freighter at the ice barrier the following morning. He does not address the issue of rockets.

It can also be seen that he seems to strike a note of caution as part and parcel of his response – if his ship had struck an iceberg there would have been a panic. If he had launched boats, they would have been crushed like eggshells; although all the launched boats of the *Titanic* remained untroubled that night.

These perils of ice are not what he will later rely on in evidence. Instead he cites the company rule, that he should not enter any ice, no matter how thin. There is no mention of the possible attitude of steerage passengers, whose numbers he slightly exaggerated.

Nonetheless, the passion of this interview indicated there was still newspaper mileage in Captain Moore, and the *Evening Times and Star* once more sent down to the ship that morning.

They found the Master of the vessel still bristling over developments and ready to talk:

> 'There is not another man sailing the high seas today that would have been more pleased or any more glad than I to have been able to go to the *Titanic* and render assistance to the passengers and crew,' said Captain Moore of the CPR liner *Mount Temple*, in an interview with a *Times* reporter on board his steamer this morning.
>
> Captain Moore feels his position keenly in view of the reports that have been circulated to the effect that he disregarded the *Titanic*'s calls for help and sailed in the opposite direction.
>
> 'The stories circulated,' said the Captain, 'are without foundation, and I and my officers are ready at any time to prove them so. Why the whole thing is utterly preposterous and there is not a single word of truth in any of the reports that are being sent out.'

Captain Moore then went on to state that: 'on the night of the accident we were sailing along at the rate of about ten miles or more, or maybe less.' This more-or-less statement, on an issue untested in evidence, contradicts the level of speed needed to get the *Mount Temple* from the noon position (which appears in the official log for April 14) to the spot where Captain Moore said he turned around at 12.30am on April 15. This has been discussed in an earlier chapter.

Captain Moore went on to contradict his wireless operator, and the latter's PV or ledger of messages, by claiming the distress call had been caught at 'about half-past twelve o'clock,' when it is shown in the PV at 12.11am and Durrant likewise testified that it was received nineteen minutes earlier.

He then describes his response once again, mentioning a 50-mile distance, but says that 'soon after three o'clock I brought the ship to a standstill, as we had encountered a floe of ice that was at least five miles wide and utterly impassable.'

But 'shortly after three o'clock' is the time he later relies upon in evidence for meeting the rushing schooner. That schooner was coming from the direction of the *Titanic*'s distress co-ordinates, but by this account it could not have done so because there was a floe of ice here than was five miles wide and utterly impassable.

Could Captain Moore possibly have forgotten his near-thing with this irresponsible other seafarer so soon? The one that caused him to twice take evasive action, one an emergency 'full speed astern' on the engines, and which had put out her illumination in guilty fashion?

In this account, Moore's 'utterly impassable' ice barrier has been brought forward by fifteen minutes or more. But his sworn evidence would be that he journeyed on from here, stopping at 3.25am because the ice was getting 'so thick.' But even in this instance it was not 'utterly impassable,' because he pressed on from there again, and finally reached the SOS position at 4.30am.

This interview, about which Moore was never asked, then proceeded to give further hostages to credibility and consistency. The Captain declared: 'From the time we first turned at half-past twelve o'clock until very early in the morning we could see no lights at all, as it was pitch dark, and I do not see how any of the passengers could.'

What does the phrase 'very early in the morning' mean? If only 1am, it seems a ridiculous matter to even mention. If it means daylight, that the morning has arrived, then Moore is forgetting not only his schooner but also the lights of the tramp steamer that crossed his urgent course.

But Moore was warming to his indignation, finishing:

> I had at least 1,600 people on board my steamer, and it would have been very foolish for me to try to force my way through five miles of ice floe, for undoubtedly I would have met with the same disaster as did the *Titanic*. The ice was so thick that it would have cut through the iron plates on the ship like paper, so I decided that it was useless. I would have been very thankful if I could have been of any assistance, but God knows I did all that I could.

The good Captain has subtly changed his stance once again. No longer is it the panic of steerage that could have presented the greatest risk in the event of an ice strike or dent, but the extreme danger of that ice itself. Not content with possibly crushing lifeboats like eggshells, it would now have cut through the iron plates of the ship like paper.

Captain Moore decided on this basis, not under any company rule, not to attempt this ice. But we recall that Captain Lord, of the *Californian*, cut through it at full speed and not only survived intact but actually reached the side of the *Carpathia*.

In the view of the Master of the *Mount Temple* however, he had safeguarded 1,600 lives, not sacrificed 1,500.

He added to the reporter that, as of that morning, he had 'not received any official notification as to attendance before a commissioner in regard to the movements of the *Mount Temple* on the night of the accident.'

But that day he would sign clear of the ship's articles and take himself to the train station in St John, accompanied by his wireless operator, bound ultimately for Washington.

WITNESS PASSENGERS

STRATHCONA, Alberta – What may amount to a very serious charge against Captain Moore of the CPR liner *Mount Temple*, which passed close to the *Titanic* during the four hours preceding the ill-fated steamer's sinking, is contained in a statement made here yesterday by E.W. Zurch, who crossed from Antwerp on the *Mount Temple*.

According to Mr Zurch, the passengers heard of the *Titanic*'s distress at 12.15 o'clock Monday morning, when the wireless call for help was caught. Captain Moore altered his vessel's course at once and headed for the *Titanic*, lifeboats being swung from the davits meanwhile, and other preparations made for lending assistance.

The northern course was not held long, however, says Mr Zurch, because of a great field of ice looming up ahead. It was reported among the crew and passengers that the Captain refused to make further efforts to penetrate the floes, asserting that he could not afford to take the risks of endangering the two thousand souls aboard his ship.

The statement of Dr. Quiterau [sic] to the effect that passengers and crew believed they could see the lights of the unfortunate *Titanic* is borne out by Mr Zurch. With two companion passengers he disobeyed the Captain's orders, which forbade passengers entrance to the upper deck at the time.

He is fairly positive that they saw the masts of the *Titanic* and is not ready to accept the assertion that their ship was at least forty miles from the wrecked liner at the time. At any rate, he thinks the *Mount Temple* might have reached the spot before the *Titanic* sank, and this opinion seems to have been entertained by others on board.

In fact, says Mr Zurch, it was rumoured among the crew that the ships' officers even discussed the advisability of taking temporary command from the Captain and making an attempt to answer the wireless calls for help which were being received.

Their vessel sighted the *Carpathia* the next morning and, by keeping in touch with the wireless communications to land, were conversant with the whole story of the wreck, even hearing that Captain Smith and two officers had shot themselves. While this information came from out on the Atlantic, [it] adds mystery to the already most peculiar circumstances surrounding the first reports of the disaster.

Mr Zurch says that the *Mount Temple* sighted immense fields of ice during the Sunday and Monday on which the *Titanic* went down. Their ship was entirely surrounded at times with gigantic bergs, of which he at one time counted fourteen.

Mr Zurch comes from The Hague, Holland. He is a brother-in-law of C.J. Vanvelzen, of this city.

(*News-Plaindealer*, Edmonton, Alberta, Friday April 26, 1912, p. 1)

This fresh marvel broke while Captain Moore and wireless operator Durrant were entrained for the US Senate inquiry. Both men travelled, but only Moore would give evidence, quoting extensively from Durrant's wireless log as the latter sat alongside.

A new passenger was contradicting Captain Moore, and from as far away as Alberta. Mr Zurch was quite accurate – saying the wireless call for help had been caught at 12.15am, whereas it was actually 12.11am. Still a sharp contradiction of Moore's oft-quoted 12.30am.

Zurch now spoke of a 'northern' course ... and while a passenger could not of his own faculties detect which direction a ship was travelling in (unless he was very familiar with Polaris,

Ernst Wilhelm Zurch, a passenger on the *Mount Temple,* who came forward with serious allegations.

the northern star), this was a further contradiction of the claimed diagonal that *Mount Temple,* to the 'south and west' of the *Titanic* position, said she steamed to the north and east.

The course described by Zurch suggests his vessel had scarcely rounded the southern extremity of the icefield, rather than achieved significant progress away to the west. Obviously, if this were the case, the *Mount Temple* would be in the immediate vicinity – and naturally Zurch would not be willing to accept that his ship was 40 miles away at the time.

The new report opens with a strange reference: that the *Mount Temple* passed close to the *Titanic* during the four hours preceding the sinking. But the foundering took place two hours and forty minutes after the collision, at 11.40pm *Titanic* time. To extend the timeframe out to four hours would mean the *Mount Temple* being close to the *Titanic,* the latter still speeding, at 10.20pm *Titanic* time.

Zurch does not mention seeing rockets, but he does claim to have been able to discern the masts, mentioned in conjunction with lights, which suggest masthead lights and possibly deck lights. At this point he anticipates Moore's fears about the huge population aboard his own ship – quite prescient, as this interview was given on the same day that Moore gave his, the latter printed in the *Evening Times and Star,* and that of Zurch in the next day's dailies.

The new witness seems to have also realised what had not been disclosed yet – that the *Mount Temple* had maintained wireless silence. Zurch suggests that officers discussed a virtual mutiny, so that they could 'answer the wireless calls for help which were being received.'

Finally Zurch mentions that the *Mount Temple* sighted immense fields of ice ... and what is particularly striking is that he says they was seen 'during the Sunday,' as well as on the Monday morning after the *Titanic* had gone down.

Captain Moore's evidence throughout was that he saw no ice at all until he was on his way back, towards the co-ordinates transmitted by the sinking White Star liner. Yet Zurch claims differently, and a sighting of ice during Sunday would materially affect Moore's ability to be where he said he was when he turned about.

Meanwhile there are close overall similarities between Zurch and Quitzrau – the two men equally suggest that both crew and passengers were alive to the situation shortly after the wireless report was received. More importantly, they state that the *Titanic* was actually seen, putting the vessels close to each other in the early hours – and it was early because the *Titanic* had not yet sunk.

The prosecution calls Mr Zurch.

ERNST WILHELM ZURCH (1881-1964)

Ernst Wilhelm Zurch was born in Bürg, Saxony, on April 29, 1881. He died of a heart attack on April 30, 1964, aged 83, while watching a Stanley Cup hockey game at home in Edmonton, Alberta, where he is buried in Mount Pleasant cemetery beside his wife Adriana.

Ernest William Zurch, a 30-year-old shoemaker from The Hague, Netherlands, still used the Germanic form of his name when he travelled alone to Canada on the *Mount Temple* in April 1912.

Married eighteen months before to the former Adriana Lochmans (whom he wed in October 1910), he was nonetheless father to three children.

His wife and children – sons Ernst Jr, 4; Johannes, 3; and baby Adolph, eleven months – followed him to Canada on the *Megantic*, three months later, sailing from Liverpool on July 20 and arriving at Quebec on July 28, 1912.

By 1914, he was trading as Ernest W. Zurch, a shoemaker, living at 10553 Whyte Avenue in South Edmonton, Alberta. He was an amateur boxing trainer for 34 years, and many of his charges went on to win Alberta and national boxing championships. He was the Alberta boxing team coach at the Canadian championships in 1927.

Valerie Wissinger, granddaughter of Ernie Zurch, says she has always known that her grandfather's ship heard the SOS distress call from the *Titanic*. 'Somehow I had been told this in the past, and that small piece of knowledge stayed with me.'

Ernst was a shoemaker by trade. He was registered at The Hague in 1898, having come from the small town of Voorburg. His two eldest children, born out of wedlock, were legally acknowledged by him on August 25, 1909.

He brought his shoemaker trade with him to Canada, and page 13 of the *Mount Temple*'s steerage manifest, filed on April 19, 1912, shows his named clearly, specifying his ticket number as 00457, and his age 30. He is shown to be a 'Hollander' by race, and his destination is indicated as Strathcona, Alberta – whence his story was later datelined.

The source of the steerage manifest is microfilm T-4826, covering ship arrivals at St John, New Brunswick, from March 29 to July 5, 1912, and held at the National Archives of Canada in Ottawa.

Zurch was unable to speak a great deal of English on his arrival, according to his descendants, and it may be that his story was mediated to a newspaper by his brother-in-law, Christian Vanvelzen.

Counsel for Captain Moore: 'I would like to read into the record Captain Moore's reaction to this man's allegations. When shown the despatches, he said: 'It is an utter falsehood. Why, how would that passenger know anything about what I and my officers were doing?

'And then again, there was not one passenger on deck all night long. The man that is circulating stories like that is looking for cheap notoriety and has an utter disregard for the truth.

'To think that after all that I did to render assistance I should have such statements as these hurled at me is more than I can stand, and it just shows you what some people will do.'

It is evident this man saw no rockets, which rather contradicts previous claims rather than strengthening them. It is also quite possible that, in seeing masts, he was only discerning the tramp steamer in the night that my client gave evidence about.'

Evidence that Ernst Wilhelm Zurch was aboard the *Mount Temple,* a shoemaker bound for Strathcona, Alberta, whence his story later emerged. (Microfilm T-4826, National Archives of Canada)

Ernst Wilhelm Zurch in his shoe repair shop in Edmonton, nineteen years after the *Titanic* calamity.

I thank my learned friend – Captain Moore indeed suggested that Zurch was a man looking for cheap notoriety. Of course Moore knew nothing about him, but at least it can be positively stated that Zurch was indeed a passenger on the *Mount Temple*.

Quite what benefit the 'notoriety' could have brought to the 30-year-old shoemaker, a *pater familias* who was acting as a pathfinder for his dependents in Canada, is difficult to see. But Zurch was never called to any inquiry, and certainly the Dominion Government had lost interest in having a commission take depositions from anyone.

Mr Zurch worked with an Edmonton shoemaker in the north of that city, and eventually opened his own shoe shop. He went on to have eight children in all, but never said anything in detail to them about his voyage, other than that his ship responded to the *Titanic*'s call.

He was, at least, not seeking any particular notoriety from posterity.

ON THE very same day that Zurch's story was printed, two other Canadian newspapers, far to the west, were printing an arresting story from a different individual. But this was another Dutchman, and he can be clearly linked to Zurch. These were his allegations –

IF THIS STORY IS TRUE
THE PASSING OF 1600
SOULS LIES AT THE
DOOR OF MOORE

Keurvost, Passenger on Mount Temple, Charges Captain With Responsibility.

Says the Ship Was Only Five Miles Away From the Scene When Titanic Went Down.

Frantic Messages Came From Titanic Telling of Distress, But Moore Stopped.

His Officers Urged Him to Proceed to Prevent Certain Loss of Life.

Nelson, B.C., April 25. – W.N. Keurvost, a passenger on the *Mount Temple*, one of the ships in the neighbourhood of the sinking *Titanic*, passed through Nelson tonight on his way to Fruitvale, where he will settle on a fruit ranch..

He declares that he does not wish to pose as the judge of Captain Moore of the *Mount Temple*, but that he is personally convinced that if anyone is responsible for the loss of life on the *Titanic*, it is Captain Moore.

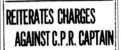

REITERATES CHARGES AGAINST C.P.R. CAPTAIN

Man Arrives at Nelson Who Says Captain Moore Let People Drown

Special dispatch to The Herald.

NELSON, B.C., April 25.—If there is any one who should be punished for the frightful loss of life in the Titanic disaster that person is Capt. Moore of the Mount Temple. Although not more than five miles from the foundering steamer half an hour before she went down, and while he was in possession of wireless messages saying the White Star liner was sinking and that the women and children had been put off, Capt. Moore hove to his ship in spite of the entreaties of his officers that he rush to the aid of the doomed passengers and crew.

This was the statement made here tonight by W. N. Kenrvorst, who crossed the Atlantic from Antwerp on the Mount Temple. "Of course I am not Captain Moore's judge, but I do think that there facts should be known," he said. "I think every light should be thrown on the calamity and blame placed where blame is due."

Kenrvorst declares he received his information as to the wireless message and the attitude of Captain Moore through a friend, the Marconi operator. Kenrvorst states he saw lights from the Titanic and twice emphasized the point that officers, clothed in high boots and heavy overcoats, and in readiness to lower the lifeboats, had besought Capt. Moore to rush to the aid of the drowning hundreds. Moore's answer was that the ice was too dangerous and that he would not risk the lives of his passengers.

A Calgary newspaper details the extraordinary allegations against Captain Moore by Willem Keurvorst, a passenger on the *Mount Temple*. The 'u' in his surname has been inverted, leading to references to 'Kenrvorst' throughout.

Keurvost declares that the *Mount Temple* heard the first calls for aid from the *Titanic* and that Captain Moore immediately turned his ship toward the scene. At two o'clock, half an hour before the *Titanic* sank, and when only five miles from the wreck, Captain Moore stopped although the *Mount Temple* had received the last messages from the *Titanic* saying that she was in desperate straits and although his officers implored him to proceed to prevent otherwise certain loss of life. The Captain was obdurate, saying that it was dangerous and that he declined to risk the lives of his passengers.

Wants the World to Know

Keurvost shipped on the *Mount Temple* at Antwerp and has lived at The Hague and in England. He is a Dutchman but speaks excellent English. He says that he learned the facts from the wireless operator on the *Mount Temple*, and is convinced that they are correct, and is anxious that a true statement shall be given to the world.

(*The Morning Albertan*, Friday April 26, 1912, p. 1)

REITERATES CHARGES
AGAINST CPR CAPTAIN

Man Arrives at Nelson Who Says Captain Moore Let People Drown.

Special dispatch to *The Herald*.

NELSON, B.C., April 25. – If there is any one who should be punished for the frightful loss of life in the *Titanic* disaster, that person is Capt. Moore of the *Mount Temple*. Although not more than five miles from the foundering steamer half an hour before she went down, and while he was in possession of wireless messages saying the White Star liner was sinking and that the women and children had been put off, Capt. Moore hove to his ship in spite of the entreaties of his officers that he rush to the aid of the doomed passengers and crew.

This was the statement made here tonight by W.N. Keurvorst, who crossed the Atlantic from Antwerp on the *Mount Temple*. 'Of course I am not Captain Moore's judge, but I do think that the facts should be known,' he said. 'I think every light should be thrown on the calamity and blame placed where blame is due.'

Keurvorst declares he received his information as to the wireless messages and the attitude of Captain Moore through a friend, the Marconi operator. Keurvorst states he saw lights from the *Titanic* and twice emphasised the points that officers clothed in high boots and heavy overcoats, and in readiness to lower the lifeboats, had besought Capt. Moore to rush to the aid of the drowning hundreds. Moore's answer was that the ice was too dangerous and that he would not risk the lives of his passengers.

(*Calgary Herald*, Friday April 26, 1912 p.1)

To deal with the last point first: Keurvorst says the officers were in readiness to lower lifeboats. The previous day, Moore had declared in the *St John Globe*: 'I did not launch the lifeboats as it would have been silly to do it, knowing that they would have been crushed like eggshells.' Yet Captain Moore was at least entertaining the proposition of lowering lifeboats – and then giving his reason against. The question is why the idea of putting boats in the water would even be raised in the first place if the *Mount Temple* was in fact many miles from the actual place of the wreck, and in complete darkness.

In both the reports, which seem syntactically to have been written by different journalists, which in turn suggests that Keurvorst spoke to more than one at the same time (and which would verify that he did at least say it), the witness says he is not Captain Moore's judge – again, as in the case with Quitzrau, not something that a mere self-publicist would say.

Both Zurch and Keurvorst also give credit, that Captain Moore turned 'at once' or 'immediately' on receiving news of the distress call. But whereas Zurch says the course was not held long before ice loomed up, it was 2am, says Keurvorst, when the *Mount Temple* came to within five miles of the *Titanic* – the same distance away as the mystery ship.

In both of his accounts, Keurvorst is quoted as saying that the Captain resisted the entreaties of his officers by saying it was dangerous to attempt the ice and that he would not risk the lives of his passengers. Zurch does not have the claim of danger, but does insist that Moore was unwilling to risk the lives of those aboard his ship. He also clearly states a near-mutinous mood among the officers, whereas Keurvorst has the Captain deaf to all their supplications.

There are resonances also with Quitzrau's affidavit, the latter stating that the *Mount Temple* officers had insisted the next day that their vessel cruise the vicinity, 'although the Captain had given orders that the boat proceed on its journey.' Quitzrau, like Keurvorst, had it that at 2am ship's time the *Mount Temple* stopped within a short distance of the *Titanic*.

Counsel for Captain Moore: One might have copied it from the other; that is, Keurvorst from Quitzrau. It is also noticeable that Keurvorst claims to have seen lights from the *Titanic* in only one of these articles. One hopes he was not improving his story as he went along, or having it improved for him, without his knowledge.

WILLEM NICHOLAS KEURVORST (31)

Born July 24, 1880. Died March 31, 1958, aged 77.
Keurvorst's name appears in the *Mount Temple* passenger manifest, where his destination is given as Nelson, BC (British Columbia). He is indicated as 'Ret'd [returned] Canadian,' having previously been resident from 1906 to 1908. His religion is Evangelical Protestant.

Keurvorst was well-travelled and it should be no surprise that he had 'excellent English.'He had previously lived in Amsterdam and Chicago, and his surviving family also know that he lived for a time in Burnley, England.

Willem Keurvorst, who had 'excellent English' and lived in that country and Canada prior to 1912, said he learned his facts from the wireless operator on the *Mount Temple*, John Oscar Durrant.

This fact is borne out by a passenger manifest for the *Cymric* on a voyage from Liverpool to Boston, arriving on October 14, 1906, in which he stated residence in the English town.

There is also evidence to show his parents left Holland for Burnley on February 11, 1899, with Keurvorst joining them there on September 1 of that year. The family is seen at 13 Plover Street in the town in the 1901 census, where his father's occupation is given as a gardener.

Wilhelm Nicolas Keurvorst was a bookkeeper, from The Hague, 5ft 10in in height. His grandson Brad said he had been to Canada for a short time two or three years previous to the *Mount Temple* voyage, 'on a visit or perhaps to check out the possibilities prior to moving over.'

His daughter Barbara wrote that her father 'spoke five languages and was a real old fashioned gentleman.' He was an accomplished rider, and explored much of the interior of British Columbia on horseback.

In 1913, in the town of Ashcroft, BC, Keurvorst married a Scottish woman, Louise Shepherd. They moved to Medicine Hat where a son named William Henry was born in 1914. They then had two girls, Marie and Christina. Keurvorst did some farming at first but later went to work for the railroad.

His wife died after fifteen years of marriage and the family relocated to Verdun, near Montreal, in the early 1930s. Nicholas remarried and had a daughter from that union, the above-quoted Barbara.

There is a connection between Keurvorst and Zurch, both of whom are from The Hague. Zurch says that he and 'two companion passengers' defied orders in order to look at the lights. Wilhelm Zurch's ticket was number 00457, and it turns out that Keurvorst's ticket is numbered 00456. Friends commonly bought tickets together, and these tickets are sequential.

It may be a coincidence that Kuervorst ended up in British Columbia and Zurch in the adjoining province of Alberta, although there are hundreds of miles between them. Nonetheless, the only conclusion must be that the men were friends. They watched the lights together.

Zurch suggested he and his 'two companions' had borne out Quitzrau's contentions, which would indicate Quitzrau was not one of the three men, although Keurvorst must have been. The 'third man' may instead very well have been one Phillip De Vries, a 24-year-old Dutchman whose surname is very common in the Netherlands.

Above left: Willem Keurvorst in later life, in a photograph possibly taken in Quebec. A sign in the background is bilingual.

Above right: Willem Keurvorst made his allegations while passing through Nelson, British Columbia, to work on a farm in Fruitvale, BC. He said he saw the *Titanic*'s lights and that *Mount Temple* crew were standing by to lower their vessel's lifeboats.

The ticket held by De Vries was number 00458, making it the third in sequence. But his entry on the *Mount Temple* manifest is stamped: 'To be deported.' He was apparently not admitted to Canada, and appears to have been sent home.

Although his hometown is not shown, De Vries was bound for Winnipeg, Manitoba, which is similarly in the Canadian west, like the others. And because Ernst Zurch's wife's mother was born Akke de Vries (she married Johannes Cornelis Lochmans in The Hague on April 1, 1885), there is the possibility that Phillip and Ernst were cousins. A cousin might indeed be a 'companion' passenger, rather than a mere acquaintance.

In any case, Keurvorst, De Vries and Zurch appear one after another at the bottom of p. 12 and the top of p. 13 of the steerage manifest – and there are no other like tickets in this sequence, either afterwards or before (such as up to 00455, or 00459 and later).

A further key connection between Zurch and Keurvorst is that both are aware of wireless reports. Keurvorst, who was fluent in English, 'says that he leaned the facts from the wireless operator on the *Mount Temple*.' In a parallel report, he says he learned certain information 'through a friend, the Marconi operator.'

The Marconi man, John Oscar Durrant, was then accompanying Captain Moore to Washington …

While the wireless man might not have been a close 'friend' of the chatty Keurvorst, it has been independently stated that the latter had excellent English. The Dutchman further states his direct interaction with the Marconi man as a simple fact, in a take-it-or-leave-it fashion. It is this information, from an impeccable source, which convinces him that the 'facts' are correct.

Could wireless operator Durrant have told inner secrets to Keurvorst, which the latter appears to have relayed to Zurch? Both passengers had knowledge of wireless-derived information, as had Quitzrau from the signs in his affidavit.

Here it is important to note that it was specifically the Marconi man's job to interact with passengers, at least in terms of transmitting any messages they may have paid for through the purser. He was not aloof in the way that a navigating officer might be – Durrant was not in the employ of the ship, but of the Marconi company.

It may round out this portion of the story to realise that while Zurch and Keurvorst were separately giving interviews to newspapers far removed from each other (and, who knows, De Vries might also have done, had he been allowed entry), wireless operator Durrant was himself giving an account to the press.

The interview was printed the same day, and Captain Moore and Durrant may even have read it as they took the train that evening. Furthermore, the very fact that it was given at all may demonstrate that the 'Sparks' was a genial and gregarious individual:

Wireless Operator's Very Interesting Statement

Mr J. Durrant, Marconi wireless operator on the steamer *Mount Temple*, now lying at Sand Point, in conversation with the *Globe* on Wednesday evening related a story, simple and direct, and yet full of wonderful pathos.

Sitting in his cabin and referring to his record, he related the successive messages sent out by the doomed ship *Titanic*, after the disastrous collision with the iceberg. None of them were lengthy, indeed for the most part they consisted of only a few words, or even of the code letters. And yet it was easy to perceive in them the successive stages of the heart-rending calamity, the first shock of the fatal impact when the thrilling 'CQD' message was flashed everywhere into the chilly air, then the gradual settling of the giant liner by the head, the nervous appeals for aid, the quiet chivalric heroism which prompted the men to yield their place without a murmur to helpless women and children, and finally the flooding of the engine rooms precluding all further hope of [the *Titanic*] communicating with the steamers which were even then frantically steaming towards her, and finally of the terrific plunge into the darkness of the ocean depths.

Mr Durrant explained that on the *Mount Temple* there is never any great necessity for the operator to sit up late at night. For all that he never retires much before midnight, whiling away the time either writing letters or reading. It was owing to this habit that he caught the 'CQD' message from the *Titanic*. Said he, 'I was lying in bed reading, with the telephone over my ears at 10.25 New York time, or 12.11 ship's time, when I caught the first call. Immediately getting out of bed, I answered, asking the position of the stricken ship. This was sent back with the addition, 'Come at once, have struck berg.'

'As soon as I got the message, I notified the Captain who at once doubled the watch of firemen below, called all hands on deck and changed the ship's course towards the position of the *Titanic*. Then I went back to my instrument and sat there. I did not call the *Titanic* again because other ships which I judged to be closer were working and I did not wish to jam them. At 12.21 I heard the *Carpathia* answer the 'CQD' calls of the *Titanic* and heard the operator on that ship give his position, adding 'Have struck iceberg. Come to our assistance at once.'

At 12.34 I heard the *Frankfurt* answer the appeals of the *Titanic*. That ship asked 'What is the matter with you?' The answer was, 'We have struck an iceberg, please tell the Captain to come.'

To this the operator on the *Frankfurt* replied: 'O.K. Will tell the bridge right away.' The answer to this was, 'Yes, quick.'

'All this time the CQD message was being sent out incessantly from the sinking liner and at 1.06 I heard the *Olympic* answer the call. To this steamer the *Titanic* said, 'Captain says get your boats ready. Going down fast by the head.'

Five minutes later the *Frankfurt* struck in with 'Our Captain will go for you.'

At 1.21 the *Olympic* sent another message which the *Titanic* answered, saying, 'We are putting the women off in the boats.' Another five minutes of anxious waiting passed, when the agonised CQD signal again cut the air, accompanied by the words 'Engine room flooded.' Out of the darkness the *Olympic* again asked, 'How is the sea around you?' to which the reply was, 'The sea is calm.'

Another four minutes passed when the operator on the *Frankfurt* was heard asking the *Titanic*, 'Are there any boats around you already?' To this there was no reply and two minutes afterwards the *Olympic* sent a message to the *Titanic* which the latter barely acknowledged by the code words 'R.D.' That was the last message I heard and I presume the flooding of the engine room had put the wireless out of commission.

'Meantime everything that was possible was done on the *Mount Temple*. All hands were on deck, the boats were swung clear of the davits and the gangways and ladders were got ready to lower at a moment's notice. It was not until 4.30 that we arrived at the position of the *Titanic*, having been much delayed by the thick field ice. At that time we saw no sign of the ill-fated ship, nor any wreckage.

At 5.11 I had a call from the *Californian*, and told that boat of the disaster and gave the position in which it had occurred. Shortly after the *Frankfurt* also called me. About forty minutes later we saw the *Carpathia* and *Californian* with the Russian steamer *Birma*. There was also a tramp steamer cruising about, apparently going in the same direction as us, but as she had no wireless installation and never approached very near, we could not find out what she was.

As soon as I saw the *Carpathia* I asked for news of the *Titanic* and if she had seen anything, but got no reply. Other ships asked the same question, but she kept silent to all. It was not until 8.30 that the *Carpathia* gave out anything and then the only information was that she had picked up twenty boats. There was not a word as to the number of survivors. At the time I received the first message I would judge the *Mount Temple* to be fifty miles from the *Titanic*'s position, and when the big ship went down there was still twenty or twenty-five miles between us.'

(*St John Globe*, Thursday April 25, 1912, p. 2)

It can be seen that there is no room for compromise between what Durrant is stating and what Keurvorst has averred. Whatever about the sights that sailors and fireman may claim to have witnessed, the wireless operator is clearly no more Captain Moore's judge than Keurvorst says he would want to be. But the simple truth is that one of them must now be lying.

FURTHER ALLEGATIONS

ANOTHER passenger meanwhile emerged, one who was of an entirely different nature to the German and three Dutch. He was of a different generation, being a 58-year-old Slav, and not the typical young bachelor emigrant, because he was travelling with his daughter.

The front-page headline of the *New York Journal* of Thursday April 25th, 1912, blared:

Mount Temple Only 5 Miles Away
WATCHED *TITANIC* SIGNALS FOR HOURS.

The statements about the *Mount Temple* were made by John Mlynarczyk, now in Toledo, Ohio, and by Dr Quitzrau, who is in Toronto.

Mlynarczyk and his daughter sailed from Antwerp for Toledo. They are convinced, as are others, that the *Mount Temple* is the vessel referred to by Fourth Officer Boxhall of the *Titanic*, and others, who described seeing the lights of a ship nearby as the *Titanic* was going down and which neglected to respond to the signals for aid.

Mlynarczyk said: 'The morning after the *Titanic* struck the iceberg, three lifeboats from the *Mount Temple* were lowered and one man, a *Titanic* sailor, was picked up and taken aboard the ship.' What became of the sailor when the ship docked at Boston [sic] they do not know.

'The *Titanic* passed us late on Sunday night, April 14,' Mlynarczyk said through an interpreter. 'She was going at a good rate of speed. We could see her lights far away.

'I think it was about two o'clock in the morning that we heard coming over the water the noise of lowering boats and cries of people. The ocean in that vicinity was full of lifeboats. Later on, we could see the lights of the *Titanic*.

'The next morning, three lifeboats from our boat were lowered, and when they came back they brought one of the *Titanic*'s sailors. We were not allowed out of steerage, so what went on up above, I don't know.'

(The *New York Journal*, Thursday April 25, 1912, p.1)

There are a number of obvious contradictions in Mlynarczyk's account. His ship docked in New Brunswick instead of Boston, for one thing, but it may be that language difficulties led to misunderstandings in the interview.

The passenger notably admits he was not allowed up from below deck, but perhaps this refers only to the daylight part of the morning and not the night before. He does state that 'we could see' the lights of the *Titanic* 'late on Sunday night.' This would seem to recall the statement of Ernst Zurch that the *Mount Temple* passed close to the *Titanic* 'during the four hours preceding the ill-fated steamer's sinking.'

There is no evidence, however, that Captain Moore's vessel lowered lifeboats the next morning, and it is absurd to suggest that they picked up a *Titanic* sailor. He frankly admits that he doesn't know what went on at that time.

But his daughter appears to support her father in that something unusual did occur, and thus Ohio joins Ontario, British Columbia and Alberta as a theatre for *Mount Temple* allegations. A similar version of this story was carried by the *Washington Post*:

John Mlynazk and his daughter, who were passengers on the same ship [*Mount Temple*], said at Toledo, Ohio, last night that the *Mount Temple* was so near the *Titanic* that they heard the creak of

A stark lead story headline in the *New York Journal* of Thursday April 25th, 1912.

John Mlynazk and his daughter, who were passengers on the same ship, said, at Toledo, Ohio, last night that the Mount Temple was so near the Titanic that they heard the creak of chains as the lifeboats were lowered, and also heard the commotion on board the sinking liner. Also, he said, the Mount Temple lowered a boat and picked up a sailor from the Titanic.

Above left: Clipping from the front page of the *Washington Post* of April 25, 1912, that refers to a new claimant – Stanley Mlynarczyk, recently arrived in Toledo, Ohio.

Aboe right: Stanley Mlynarczyk, older than the usual immigrant, who made allegations concerning the conduct of the *Mount Temple*.

chains as the [*Titanic*] lifeboats were lowered, and also heard the commotion on board the sinking liner. Also, he said, the *Mount Temple* lowered a boat and picked up a sailor from the *Titanic*.

(*Washington Post*, Thursday April 25, 1912, p. 1)

The prosecution does not rely on this gentleman, but he is tendered in evidence to demonstrate that he was indeed on the *Mount Temple*, as were the others cited, which indicates they were able to satisfy the newspapers concerned, whether by contract tickets or other documentation, that they had indeed been on the vessel for the voyage concerned.

STANISLAW MLYNARCZYK (58)

Born in Galicia in 1853. Died June 12, 1932 in Toledo, aged 78.

Toward the end of the *Mount Temple* passenger manifest is a section headed with the words 'To USA,' indicating transit passengers for the United States landing in Canada. Here is seen one Stanislaw Mlynarczyk – not 'John' – travelling with a 15-year-old female named Angeline, who is identified as his daughter. Their destination was Toledo, Ohio.

Three of Stanlisaw's sons had preceded him to Toledo, the first being John and Thomas who established themselves under their Anglicised names. John set up a wholesale and retail meat business, and Thomas worked for him. A third brother, Frank, arrived two years later and became a grocer.

Frank then sponsored his father (Stanislaw) and sister (Angeline) to come over to the United States in 1912. Stanislaw's wife, named Malgorzata, did not travel as she was taking care of other family members.

Above left: Angeline Mlynarczyk, who accompanied her father in the Atlantic crossing aboard *Mount Temple*.

Above right: Stan Krolczyk, grandson of Stanislaw Mlynarczyk, in US Navy uniform.

Stanley Krolczyk, a grandson of Stanislaw, whose mother was his daughter Angeline, confirmed the pair came over on the *Mount Temple*. The family knew the Captain received the SOS message from the *Titanic* and started towards her but stopped because of the ice.

When they came on deck after daylight his mother personally saw the ice field and that the *Mount Temple* was stopped, Stanley said. 'They did not know how long the *Mount Temple* had steamed before she stopped.'

A former US navy officer, Krolczyk opines: 'It seems Captain Moore did not utilise all the tools he had to assist the SS *Titanic*. Sea conditions were optimum with sea-state at zero. In an icefield with all-ahead slow, the ship at general quarters and visibility good, the overall risk to the *Mount Temple* would have been very low.'

Counsel for Captain Moore: 'Motion to strike from the record. The reader must ignore irrelevant opinions offered by descendants of persons not relied upon because of their own inconsistencies.'

This concludes the evidence of passengers, none of whom was called to give evidence in person. Had they been, Quitzrau, Zurch, Keurvorst, and the two Mlynarczyks might have been joined by Philip De Vries, or indeed others who would be awakened by the opportunity to be taken seriously in what they had to say, and which they may have said in private, but which is now lost to history.

The prosecution now calls a crew witness from the *Mount Temple*, one who left the ship at St John after requesting to be paid off, and who then journeyed to Detroit.

JOHN VINCENT EHMIG (1882-1947)

John Ehmig's name appears in the *Mount Temple* Crew Agreement, held at a university in Newfoundland for the April 1912 voyage. He is listed as a 29-year-old Austrian, with an address at 21 Rue d'Amsterdam, Antwerp. He served as an assistant cook.

John Ehmig in later life.

Ehmig was in fact born in Prague, then part of the Austro-Hungarian Empire, on May 17, 1882. He was naturalised as a US citizen in New York in 1907, having emigrated to the USA on the *Vaderland*, from Antwerp, in November 1901 at age 19.

Extant records show him as being of medium height, with black hair, brown eyes, and a moustache.

MT. TEMPLE STEWARD
BLAMES THE CAPTAIN

Says He Skirted Ice Floe Instead
of Making Direct for the *Titanic*

ONLY FIVE MILES AWAY

Carpathia, Eastward Bound, Had
Passed a Little While Before
  -- Lost His Nerve.

Detroit, April 29 – John Ehmig, of Trenton, Michigan, a suburb of Detroit, who says he was a steward on the steamship *Mount Temple* when she passed within easy range of the *Titanic* disaster, yesterday charged that weakness on the part of Capt. Moore was the reason for the loss of at least a thousand lives when the *Titanic* went down.

'The *Mt. Temple* was the ship which the passengers of the *Titanic* saw in the distance, and which rendered no assistance,' said Ehmig. 'We were only about five miles from the *Titanic* when we received the aerogram that she was sinking. A short time before we received word of the accident we passed the *Carpathia*, eastward bound. She was fifty miles from the *Titanic* when the distress message was flashed.

'There were about twenty-five big icebergs between the *Mount Temple* and the *Titanic*. Captain Moore got all the lifeboats ready and headed for the *Titanic*, but had not gone far when he evidently lost his nerve and changed his course so that he skirted about the outside of the big ice field and went nowhere near the scene of the accident.

With the *Mt. Temple* so near at the time of the accident, I am sure she could have saved nearly all of the passengers.'

(*Toronto Star*, Monday April 29, p. 3)

Ehmig's charges are stark. He is the first *Mount Temple* crewman to publicly go on the record with an assertion that his own vessel was the *Titanic*'s mystery ship.

Although only a cook, it should be remembered that Captain Moore himself had told the *St John Globe* four days earlier: 'Even the ship's cooks were kept on deck for fear they might be wanted to get warm food for survivors.'

Ehmig (described as a steward, not a cook, in the report) gave his interview on Sunday, April 28, which was the day after Captain Moore had testified to the United States investigation of the disaster.

His public identification echoes clearly what was being reported from anonymous 'sailors, firemen and others' from St John, who said they sat on deck for hours and watched the *Titanic* sending up rockets.

In particular it would back up 'one of the sailors' who was reported as saying that Moore 'steamed away ... so that the lights were soon lost.'

The word 'sailor' may have been used loosely, and no such job description exists in the crew agreement or log, which both differentiate instead between roles of 'AB' and seaman. An AB was an 'able-bodied' sailor, and it is an AB that seafarers would have understood by the specific use of the 'sailor' in 1912, as distinct from a 'seaman.'

John Ehmig, assistant passenger cook on the *Mount Temple*, wearing a steward's uniform.

Perhaps it is to credit one word with too much meaning, but there were nine ABs aboard the *Mount Temple* that voyage, and three of them – a very high proportion – deserted at St John, being a German named Pfuhl, a Dane named Johansen, and a Swede called Reidersson.

Equally it is possible that one of the three Londoners in the AB list could have been the sailor who was on watch on Sunday night and 'says that he heard Third Officer Notley [who had a London address] tell the Captain of the distress signals.'

Counsel for Captain Moore: 'The prosecution is attempting to expand its paucity of alleged witnesses by the most outrageous sleight of hand. We have not the slightest evidence that any of these unnamed individuals ever existed.'

Ehmig did exist, and so did Captain Moore, and the former's charges against the latter are those of weakness and loss of nerve. The prosecution contends that Captain Moore in fact indirectly corroborates those charges by his own repeated references to the terrifying capacity of ice, its ability to crush lifeboats like cockleshells, and to cut through the iron plates on the ship like paper.

Ehmig is as strong as Moore is weak – he lays responsibility for needless deaths at the door of the Captain, just as Keurvorst unequivocally does, and these accusations are directly and plainly put, with no attempt to blame extraneous, indirect factors that could cloud judgment or muddy the water.

Counsel for Captain Moore: 'Arrant speechifying. Tell us about Ehmig.'

Ehmig is not someone who can be damned by Captain Moore or anyone else as having a grudge. He was paid off at St John and departed. His ability and conduct are both shown as 'very good' in the log, which is neither more nor less than duty satisfactorily performed.

He did not hawk himself around Washington as any angel of the truth, but told his story once and returned to anonymity. He stayed as a ship's cook, working on other vessels, and is listed on the *Thuringia*, from Hamburg for New York, in January 1927. He appears in the 1920 census, living in Hartford, Connecticut.

The 1930 census shows him in New Haven in the same state, a 47-year-old chef dwelling at Front Street with his Finnish-born second wife Alice and their six month old son, John Arnon.

A WW2 draft registration card next shows the family living in Akron, Ohio. Ehmig now works for the Works and Public Administration agency, a New Deal creation, and perhaps it is in tribute to FDR that the youngest of his four children is named Franklin.

His son, John Arnon, has confirmed his father's long service as a ship's cook, but has no specific recollection of any *Titanic* stories.

Counsel for Captain Moore: 'This galley hand has cooked up a story indeed, but it is the poor ingredients that give him away. We should suspect his determination to invent when he elevates himself from a passenger cook, and an *assistant* passenger cook at that, to the position of steward, which sounds altogether more grand. That may be his own weakness.

He next tells us that the *Mount Temple* was but five miles away – but this is when the wireless call, or 'aerogram' to bestow another enhanced title, is first received. This suggests that the *Mount Temple* did no steaming at all, because that was the final separation of the *Titanic* and mystery ship, and Captain Moore says the ice barrier itself – when finally reached after hours of steaming – was at least five miles in width.

Ehmig thus contradicts everyone else and renders his account unacceptable. The cook can haughtily dismiss the danger of the 25 icebergs he says were between his vessel and the *Titanic*, but these are not meringues. He is not qualified to judge the challenges posed, and it is weak-minded of him to imagine he is, and that his ship was so near that she might have rescued all aboard.

He asserts that it was but 'a short time' before they received word of the accident that his ship passed the *Carpathia*, but that she was fifty miles from the *Titanic*. It is either this – that the *Mount Temple* was effectively just as far away, because these ships passed before whatever time elapsed; or else the time really was short, in which case the *Carpathia* might have been the mystery ship, for goodness' sake.

Captain Moore is fortunately quoted in the *New York Times* of Friday April 26 as saying 'about 9.30 on Sunday night the steamer *Carpathia* passed us.' There can thus be no 'shortly before' for Mr Ehmig, and he is inventing matters on the hoof.

A time of three hours elapsed since this passing, from 9.30pm until 12.30am when the *Mount Temple* turned – and even allowing for the *Carpathia* to be going at a greater rate of speed, it

ST. JOHN, N. B., FRIDAY MORNING, APRIL 26, 1912

CAPTAIN OF MOUNT TEMPLE WILL TELL HIS STORY AT WASHINGTON

Commander to Be Given a Chance to Refute Yarn of Toronto Doctor Who Said He Saw Titanic's Signals

Above: Page 1 headline from the *Daily Telegraph* of St John, New Brunswick, April 26, 1912.

Left: Stanley Mlynarczyk in later life.

supports my client's case. It is Ehmig who gives the *Carpathia* 50 miles.

It may be that the *Mount Temple* knows the *Carpathia* to be passing, not from visual identification, but by wireless exchanges of time and course, with perhaps the inference of a particular speed. If so, well and good.

But if they actually sighted one another, that would allow for the unfortunate Mlynarczyk to perhaps see the *Carpathia*'s lights on a late night stroll before retiring, and to later imagine that those were the lights of the *Titanic*.

Captain Moore, incidentally, says it was not 'shortly after' passing the *Carpathia*, headed in the opposite direction, that he received the first distress call. He says that was 'some time later,' which naturally accords with 12.30am. The Master of the *Mount Temple* has these facts, but Ehmig is decidedly short of them.'

On a point of information, the 50-mile distance of the *Carpathia* from the *Titanic* at the time of the emergency does not mean that the Cunard vessel has done that distance since meeting or passing the *Mount Temple*.

The *Carpathia* in fact estimated her distance from the distress position to be 58 miles. To do over 50 miles in three hours would be over 16 knots, emergency speed. There is no relationship whatever between her distance away and how far distant the *Mount Temple* might be, because it all depends on where the *Titanic* actually was. Furthermore, Captain Moore himself admits his ship was doing ten knots or less before the distress call was heard. Counsel for the defendant has himself engaged in sleight of hand in advancing an argument that does not stand up.

In fact, the wireless operator of the *Carpathia*, Harold Cottam (Br. 17068) records at 11.50pm, by his ship's clock, saying 'Good night' to the *Mount Temple*, and only 35 minutes later receives his first word about the disaster. He further states in evidence that he did not know the *Mount Temple* position at any time, which discounts any idea that they passed in view of each other.

We shall pass on, as ships in the night. When Captain Moore left for Washington, the log records that he signed clear of the ship's articles on April 25. He was temporarily succeeded as Master of the ship by Alfred Henry Sargent, his chief officer.

Captain Moore gives evidence on April 27. In the meantime the official log shows that 'all papers' have been turned over to Sargent as the new Master, and specifically declares as much and in those terms.

How can it be, then, that all entries in the log are signed by Moore – for April 26, 27, 28 and 29 – even though he did not rejoin the ship until April 29 at evening?

The entries for these days, when Moore is away, are signed by Moore, not Sargent. In fact the new Captain signs the log only once, to indicate he has superseded to command. His only other entry in the log is to certify that a boat drill has been carried out on May 12, two days before landfall on the return voyage.

All the entries in the official log are made and signed by Captain Moore. His handwriting is the same as on an official letter he writes in his own hand on ss *Mount Temple* stationery. The official log is therefore not a contemporaneous sequence of entries. It must have been written up subsequently.

If it is written up subsequently, what possible reliance can be placed upon it? In such circumstances new items may be introduced ... and other matters deleted.

The *Mount Temple*, while Captain Moore is away, now engages in a positioning sailing from St John, New Brunswick, to Halifax, Nova Scotia, a journey of a little under 300 nautical miles. But nothing will ever appear in the official log to show when it was begun or completed.

It appears to have taken place on Saturday morning, April 27, when Captain Moore was making his personal appearance in Washington. The *Daily Telegraph* of St John announced on page ten of that day's edition:

The CPR liner *Mount Temple* is scheduled to steam for London and Antwerp via Halifax at an early hour this morning. In the absence of Captain Moore in Washington, Chief Officer

Shipping Master's Office
Halifax, N.S. APR 29 1912
This agreement was deposited on the APR 29 1912

been discharged at the Port by Mutual Consent and has signed his release in my presence. I further certify that WH Baker and AH Sargent have been signed at this port in the terms of this agreement. I also certify that H Moore has become Master and AH Sargent has been transferred to 2nd Mate.

Above left: Halifax harbour, 1912. From a contemporary postcard.

Above right: Certified note by the Shipping Master's officer in Halifax that officer Arthur Notley has left the *Mount Temple* and been replaced by officer William Henry Baker for the homeward trip.

Sargent will be in command and the other officers will be given a temporary promotion for the trip. It does not seem clear whether Captain Moore will join his steamer at Halifax or not. It is possible that he will not, but will go over on the *Empress of Britain*.

Sailing at an early hour, the *Mount Temple* would have arrived in Halifax in the afternoon of Sunday, April 28. Captain Moore and wireless operator Durrant had left by train on Thursday evening, April 25, so the vessel was undertaking the positioning voyage without benefit of a Marconi man.

On the day before sailing, the day after Moore and Durrant's departure, there was an odd development. Third officer Arthur Howard Notley, who had abruptly left the ship four days earlier, now once more signed articles, this time as second mate. He would leave the ship again in Halifax, before Captain Moore returned.

That Saturday too, on their fine being paid, Sid Simpkins, Tim O'Brien and Arjen de Ruijter returned to the ship from St John jail. But it was only for a short time in the case of Simpkins – disgusted, he promptly collected his kit and deserted. He quit the ship with a greaser friend named Charles, who was also from Canning Town, and who had signed on for the *Mount Temple* on the line above Simpkins in the crew agreement.

Their 'Discharge A' books, or seafarer service papers, were later taken out of safe keeping by Captain Sargent and turned over to the shipping master at St John, probably the next morning, after a night flit by the two gentlemen. This notation is signed by Moore!

With that, Sargent sailed.

Monday, April 29 – Halifax. A man named Carroll was signed on as a seaman, but officer Notley once more took what was coming to him and signed clear of the ship. He was replaced by one William Henry Baker, who came aboard as fourth mate on wages of £8 a month.

Meanwhile Captain Moore was making his way to Nova Scotia to rejoin his vessel, having given his evidence in Washington, and having read out his wireless operator's notes – such that the latter was effectively spared from giving testimony.

Moore passed through St John on his way back, and the local *Evening Times and Star*, realising that events appeared to have taken a particularly favourable turn for the Captain in the American capital, and that the paper may have gone out on a limb in drawing attention to the adverse claims made about his command made by *Mount Temple* crew, now opted to over-compensate:

CAPTAIN MOORE IN CITY TODAY ON WAY TO HALIFAX

Entirely exonerated of whatever shadow of blame might have been attached to him for what he was alleged to have done on the night of the sinking of the *Titanic*, according to the statements made by Dr Quitzman [sic] of Toronto, Captain J.H. Moore of the steamer *Mount Temple* passed through the city at noon today on his way to rejoin his ship at Halifax.

The hardy shipmaster was publicly thanked in Washington for the directness of his testimony, and the manner in which he replied to the questions of the investigating committee, whom he greatly aided in their work by his experience and familiarity with the sea.

The master mariner had noting further to say today regarding the action of the *Mount Temple*, other than that he was pleased with the reception given him in the American capital, as well as with the fact that little credence had been placed in the statements of Doctor Quitzman, which the latter had been obliged to admit were from hearsay.

Captain Moore produced a letter, which he had received from F.J. Swift of Montreal, who, with his son Horace, had recently crossed with the skipper on the *Mount Temple*. The latter expressed surprise that such remarks should be made against Captain Moore, as from the experience which they had on board the boat they knew him to be an honest, straightforward and courageous man, who would do all within his power to aid any other steamer in distress.

Another passenger to the city this morning was Henry L. Mulligan, passenger manager o the White Star line offices in Boston, who was passing through to join Mr [Percy] Mitchell, of the Montreal office, in Halifax to aid as far as possible in the work of identification, claiming, attending to, embalming, etc, of the bodies recovered by the cable ship.

In journeying to Halifax, Moore and Durrant were venturing to a city of mourners, where over 300 bodies of the *Titanic* dead would eventually be landed, with many more being buried at sea. In the same train as the *Mount Temple* pair was W.L. Prizer of New York, seeking the body of oil executive Howard Case, in company with Timothy Woods of Brockton, Mass. The latter was an embalmer, and there were two other embalmers from the National Casket Company of Boston taking the same connection.

Flags were at half mast along the waterfront at Halifax, where the chartered cable ship *MacKay-Bennett* was due to make port with a heavy freight of human remains the next day. Captain Moore would surely have been the most good humoured man in the city when he arrived, pleased indeed with how things had turned out in Washington.

It had been a simple matter of simpering to all the Chairman Senator's ludicrous ideas and opinions … Asked early on by Senator Smith if sounding the steam whistle would give an indication (through echo) as to whether or not icebergs were ahead, Moore had answered tactfully that he did do not think it was generally done. A moment later he was denying ever hearing any 'explosions' from icebergs.

He had also been asked whether the schooner he met had been 'inhabited,' whether he could see, in daylight, further than a mile from the bridge of his vessel, and whether the very last message his ship had received from the desperate *Titanic* was 'regards,' whereas it was merely RD – an abbreviation of 'Received,' in terse acknowledgment of another's message.

Moore had also been asked by Smith whether ships should have, as part of their equipment, a permanent buoy made 'indestructible material, fastened to an indestructible chain or wire,' so that, in the event of a sinking at sea, the buoy 'might register on the surface of the water its exact burial spot.'

He murmured that there was a depth of over 2,000 fathoms, two miles of water, where the *Titanic* went down, but then three times agreed that the notion was feasible. 'If it could be provided by having a good flexible steel hawser, sir, that would be quite possible,' offered Moore, ignoring the size of a buoy that might be needed to suspend the weight of two miles of metal cable, no matter how thin.

Moore fended off a question about whether Arctic ice ever ended up in the South Atlantic, then praised as 'very feasible' a Smith suggestion that the movement of the icefield could have covered the bodies generated by the disaster.

The Chairman, suitably charmed, responded as follows, and Moore's official US inquiry evidence proceeded to an unctuous end:

> Senator Smith: I am very much obliged for the compliment, because I am not generally regarded as a mariner, nor an authority on sea conditions.
> Moore: I think you are perfectly right, sir.
> Q. Is there anything further that you can think of?
> Moore: There is nothing further, sir.
> Q. I am very much obliged to you for your kindness in responding to our request to come here.
> Moore: I was only too glad to come, sir.
> Q. I do not want any wrong impression to get out concerning the course of the *Mount Temple* after receiving this [ice] warning.
> Moore: I assure you that I did everything that was possible, sir, consistent with the safety of my own ship and its passengers.
> Q. While it may not be any consolation to you, or anybody else, I want to compliment you upon your care and solicitude for the passengers and the property that have come under your care.
> Moore: I thank you, sir.

On the day when he would rejoin his ship at Halifax, the morning when he was briefly seen by the *Evening Times & Star* at St John, the syrup and sycophancy had affected E.J. Archibald, the 30-year-old *Toronto Star* special correspondent at Washington who had first brought Quitzrau's claims about the *Mount Temple* to the attention of Senator Smith.

A front page opinion piece appeared in that day's edition (and may have alarmed the St John evening paper into following suit) that was gushing in its praise for the Captain that Senator Smith may have conveyed had been needlessly forced to Washington to defend his reputation.

Headlined CAPTAIN MOORE, FINE OLD, RUDDY, CHEERY SEA-DOG, it declared in sub-decks: Skipper of the *Mount Temple* Hates But Understands Icebergs, and Is No Fool – TELLS COMMITTEE ALL; IS COMPLIMENTED.

Datelined Washington, April 29, Eldred James Archibald wrote:

> Of all the fine old, red-cheeked, thin-necked, outspoken, cheery old sea-dogs which the present investigation has brought to Washington, Captain James Henry Moore of the CPR liner *Mount Temple*, is the finest type.
>
> For a number of days now an impression has been abroad that the *Mount Temple* should be called on to explain her movements on the night of the *Titanic* disaster. Captain Moore came down here and did it. He did it so thoroughly and satisfactorily that when he was through he got the warmest thanks and highest compliments of Senator Smith – just as from one mariner to another as it were.

At this point, Archibald added yet another mariner, and the mistake was not noticed but printed – and then replicated exactly in the syndicated newspapers which took his copy. He inadvertently substituted for 'Captain Moore' the name of Smith, ill-fated Captain of the *Titanic*:

'You don't catch Captain Smith taking fool chances with icebergs ... '

If Moore saw that on the train, he must have burst out laughing, especially considering his description in evidence of Smith's full speed as having been 'most unwise.' Perhaps he did not then realise that his own official log's noon position and his claimed turnaround position after hearing the distress call would indicate that he too must have been doing full speed that day.

> When Captain Moore knows there's ice about at night he stops his engines and waits for daylight. The *Mount Temple* may be a little late at St John or Liverpool, but she will eventually land at the port she sailed for, and not at the bottom of the sea.

Ignoring Moore's evidence that he did *not* in fact stop in the seven hours of darkness until 12.30am, when ice was certainly about, despite having apparently swerved the southern tip of a vast field, Archibald was building to a crescendo.

He had heard only one witness – Moore – in evidence about the *Mount Temple*, but yet he ringingly declared:

> 'Now the *Mount Temple* was not the 'phantom ship' whose lights raised in the breasts of the *Titanic*'s passengers a hope doomed to disappointment. She did not lie to, five miles away from the sinking ship, refuse to recognise signals of distress, and then sail away when the catastrophe had occurred.

But some ship did.

BACK IN BRITAIN

CAPTAIN Moore officially signed back onto the ship's articles at 11pm on Monday April 29, 1912. The vessel had been readied to return to Europe as soon as he and Durrant went aboard, and the moment of his return to command was followed just twenty minutes later by the *Mount Temple* casting off for the return voyage.

The log also shows that the remaining two members of the crew who had been in St John jail – fireman O'Brien and assistant cook de Ruijter had their shipboard wages forfeit by Moore for the six days in which they had been incarcerated. The additional penalty of £1 and two shillings apiece seems harsh, although it is unclear who paid the official fine that secured their release for the minor crimes of profane language and being found drunk, although presumably disorderly with it. A particular curiosity is that neither man made a court appearance, or at least none that made the local press.

There was nothing ever cheery about shipboard discipline, and one crewman – yet another – had managed to escape its rigours shortly before sailing. Frans Mees, a 20-year-old Belgian assistant steward, was found to have deserted in Halifax some time earlier that day. He had taken his belongings from the ship with him, becoming the 14th member of crew to be listed as a deserter. Half as many again had left by mutual consent.

Whether the return voyage to home waters was a happy one or not, there were no further matters of concern to be written up in the ship's log. In fact, from the moment Halifax was left behind in darkness, nothing at all was entered in the official log, even though the ship would be over two weeks at sea.

The document mysteriously ends with the following ink-stamped text (with some handwritten entries in the spaces provided), which was impressed upon it on arrival in London:

'The above entry, dated the 29th April 1912, is the last entry made or contained in this logbook. Dated 14 May 1912. Signed *Jas H. Moore*, Master. I hereby certify that I have carefully examined this Log Book and that the above statement of the Master is correct. Dated 14 May 1912. Signed *W.H. Williams*, Mercantile Marine Office, Dock Street, London.'

There was a notation, elsewhere, confirming a lifeboat drill two days before arrival in Gravesend, but this was not an entry per se, merely a confirmation in a reserved space on the form that the drill had been carried out and life-saving appliances inspected, with both found fit and ready.

There are blank pages remaining in the log. It is, on the face of it, inexplicable that there should be 35 entries made for the voyage from London to St John, via Antwerp, but not a single one for the crossing from Halifax to London.

The question is especially puzzling since Moore rejoined his vessel with just one hour left of April 29 before April 30 would arrive, and yet there are four log entries since a notation of 11pm indicating that he resumed command at that hour, and all are dated that same day.

Obviously there could be no more desertions after 11.20pm when the darkened citadel and Haligonian wharves were left behind, but even the more routine developments aboard are utterly absent. When Halifax next saw daylight, she would also see the *MacKay-Bennett*, her stern crammed with freight coffins and her foc's'le piled high with canvas-covered corpses. Perhaps that realisation made mundane matters seem unworthy of inclusion, or it may be that the likes of George Luxon never so much as scorched a finger, nor someone like Lodewijk Michiel (who had been paid off and left behind in Halifax) took so much as a tumble.

The atmosphere on board can only be guessed at, but in any case the *Mount Temple* arrived back in British waters in the ordinary way, and may possibly even have landed a few eastbound passengers at Gravesend.

Above: A letter from Captain Moore to the Mercantile Marine office after his return to Britain, stating that if a complaint had been made by a crewman during the voyage it would have been entered in the log 'as usual.' But the Official Log had no entries for the return crossing and a total absence of any from the time of the *Titanic* incident until landfall in New Brunswick.

Fresh from the Senatorial investigation at Washington, Capt. Moore of the Canadian Pacific liner Mount Temple reached Halifax this evening to take charge of his ship, which sprang into fame when the genuineness of his effort to aid the Titanic was called into question.

The Mount Temple put into this port last night and sails for Liverpool before dawn. In the interval those lingering near the docks heard from the crew much the same story of those on the Mount Temple having seen the Titanic's distress lights. It is known that when communicative one of the officers and several of the crew tell the same story, but for the most part the ship's company vows that Capt. Moore did his best in the sea of floating ice with 2,000 passengers to protect. Durrant, the Mount Temple's young English operator, was of this opinion. He was eager for news of his friend, Harold Bride, the Titanic's second wireless man, with whom he used to share lodgings in Liverpool. He mourned the lost Phillips.

"I knew that 'C. Q. D.' was his," he said, "his was a musical spark."

Right: The *New York Times* of April 30, 1912, makes it clear that crew members of the *Mount Temple* were continuing to make allegations at Halifax, Nova Scotia, as they had done originally at St John, New Brunswick.

A glimpse of unhappiness then becomes apparent. The very next day, Wednesday May 15 – a full month after the *Titanic* disaster – Captain Moore writes a letter on ship's stationery, complete with an embossed red-and-white chequer CPR flag, to the Superintendent of the Mercantile Marine Office, the same inspectors who had come aboard the previous day, overseen the payment of wages – and stamped the log.

The letter, in the Captain's distinctive hand, reads as follows:

Dear Sir,

Referring to claim brought forward by H. Torner, trimmer, whilst being paid off yesterday, I beg to report that no complaint was made by this man during the voyage to either the Surgeon or myself. If the man had reported same, an entry would have been made in the Official Log as usual.

Regarding J. Carroll, fireman, this man was signed on the articles as a substitute just prior to leaving. Yours faithfully,

James H. Moore, Master.

This letter remains with the log. It may be that Moore does not realise the irony of his saying that any complaint – which Torner felt he needed to voice in front of officialdom – would, if made, have been entered in the log 'as usual.'

He had made no entries in the log for the entire homebound crossing, so there was nothing usual about it. In a way, Moore had simply officially confirmed just how unusual it was to have no log entries at all in over a fortnight's run.

What of Torner's complaint? It seems it may be linked to Torner's being demoted from fireman to trimmer within hours of being hired as a stoker. His wages dropped from five pounds and ten shillings a month to £5 a month.

If this is his cause for complaint, he is making it six weeks later. The drop in his wages, half a pound sterling, is a loss of only 9pc of salary, and worst things had happened since. The ship was still at the quayside in Antwerp, and if dissatisfied, Torner could simply have left. Instead he may have stored up resentment. But it was not sufficient to make him desert the ship at St John, nor at Halifax, nor just seek to be paid off at either port.

The mention of the ship's surgeon suggests he might have intended making some medical argument in defence of his apparent poor performance as fireman before he was reduced in rank – but such a point would be unlikely to cut any ice. If he could not perform those duties, then he could not do them. He had just been taken on that very day, and the ship did not owe him a living.

Perhaps Torner made some other complaint. If so, its nature is now unknown. Then, did James Carroll, similarly mentioned in this letter, make a separate complaint of his own – or why is he mentioned at all? Did Liverpudlian Carroll, 33, inflict injury on Torner, a 24-year-old Swede, during the crossing? Yet any such serious incident would surely come to the attention of engine room supervisors, and would naturally merit mention in the log.

There is another oddity; Carroll was signed on at Halifax as a seaman, not as a fireman. His wages as a deckhand – distinctly different from being a member of the Black Gang – were five pounds and four shillings per month. It seems bizarre that he might have converted from one role to another (unless Moore erred in his description), but if so he would hardly have made complaint about wages, because firemen earned an extra six shillings a month over seamen.

If Carroll was a seaman and stayed a seaman, any complaint must have been different in nature to that of Torner, a stokehold worker. And if Carroll changed duties to become a fireman, this ought to have been recorded in the log. The westbound log entries contain a bewildering number of notations relating to promotion, demotion and reshuffles, with particular changes in wage entitlements always scrupulously described in pounds and shillings – and always signed off by the Master and the purser, the latter responsible for shipboard finances.

Even more oddly, and elsewhere in the log, Carroll's name in the crew list has his role of 'seaman' crossed out and replaced with 'AB,' with Captain Moore's initials alongside. This was a higher paid role, and if he was promoted to higher deck duties then there was a requirement by law that his elevation and new rate of pay be entered in the log. But there are no such entries at all – and it is as if the *Mount Temple* has been a kind of *Mary Celeste* all the way home from Halifax.

There is another disturbing element to the log. It states on its face that it is an Official Log book, form No. 5, 'consisting of 40 pages.' The inside cover is page 2, and each succeeding page is numbered. But the *Mount Temple* log, whose pages are sewn together, consists of just 32 pages. Is there anything significant about the eight missing pages?

The Mercantile Marine office appeared unmoved by it. Not only was the official log stamped in receipt, but the separate crew agreement was rubberstamped on May 15, the day of Moore's

Bow view of the *Mount Temple* replenishing at a dock in north east England.

letter, with its long list of desertions – uncommonly long – for which money had been retained, because there wasn't the band of seafarers there to be paid what they were owed.

Pay for the crew had been dispensed on the day of home arrival, but here there is further cause for perplexity. A 37-year-old German trimmer named Klacker walked down the gangway without being paid, and Marconi operator John Oscar Durrant similarly 'did not appear.'

The remaining crew, all but a skeleton few, then left the ship after receiving their wages, having also been handed back their Discharge A books on completion of the voyage.

Durrant was only paid a nominal shilling a month by the ship, his wages actually coming from the Marconi company, but the fact that he did not appear may have indicated that he was elsewhere.

Both Captain Moore and John Oscar Durrant were presumably seen by emissaries of the British *Titanic* inquiry immediately on landfall, because they both gave evidence on the next day, May 15, which is the same date as Moore's letter. Durrant would actually be recalled to the stand the following day, having commenced giving his relatively brief evidence very late in the evening, after Captain Moore had testified.

But Durrant did not appear for the next sailing of the *Mount Temple* three days later, on May 19, to Montreal. The ship was given a replacement 'Sparks.'

Meanwhile, if Captain Moore had been wondering how this mystery ship business had been going in his absence, all he had to do was buy the *Daily Sketch* on the morning of his British inquiry appearance. It showed that the home investigation had the steamer *Californian*, of the Leyland line, very much in its sights:

DRAMATIC DAY AT THE INQUIRY
Did the *Californian* see the *Titanic*?

Subtly, yet surely, the dramatic element in the *Titanic* inquiry is quickening.
From the region of dry technical details, vital of course, but prosy enough, and of plain unvarnished narratives such as have already been told to Lord Mersey and his five assessors by members of the *Titanic*'s crew, the court is passing to the knot of puzzles in which the whole tragedy still seems hopelessly tangled.

When the Commission resumed at the Scottish Hall yesterday, there were many more eager listeners than at any previous sitting, though the ladies' gallery was sparsely tenanted. The spacious floor was well filled, from the back row of the seats assigned to counsel to the big red curtains which screen the entrances. Here, women in all the colours of bright summer frocks and millinery, were more conspicuous than men, though as the day passed men too turned up in ever-increasing numbers and contentedly took standing places where they could at least see all that is to be seen, though they could hear little.

Expectations of seeing Mr Bruce Ismay and the surviving officers of the *Titanic* had called together this larger muster of onlookers, and though these leading figures in the tragedy were not yet to be seen, the day's evidence was sufficiently exciting to hold the close attention of every man and woman in the hall.

It was exciting, and to that extent dramatic in a strangely suppressed sort of way, because one felt that at last one was reaching the heart of things, getting to an understanding of many points about which the world is curious.

The puzzle of the *Californian*, for instance. This was the particular question in which Lord Mersey, with the aid of the Attorney General and other leading counsel, directed attention throughout the day, quite half of which was spent at the witness table by Stanley Lord, the Captain of the *Californian*, the Leyland Line steamship which was somewhere in the neighbourhood of the *Titanic* on that fateful Sunday night.

As the Master and men of the *Californian* told their story, an element not so much of the sensational as the sheer inexplicable quivered the endless string of questions and answers. There were mysteries of lights seen across the waters, of rockets flashing into the sky, and other usual and unusual things to be explained.

Somehow, in spite of the efforts of a keen questioner like Sir Rufus Isaacs, or of the quietly-uttered but deeply-searching interjections of Lord Mersey, the sense of the inexplicable remained and even deepened.

It was 'inexplicable' and a 'puzzle,' because the evidence from the *Californian* was not fitting the presumptions in the line of questioning. Captain Lord's ship had seen lights in the sky, but they were low-lying, over a coincidental steamer nearby. If they were the rockets from the *Titanic*, they were infuriatingly seen in the wrong direction. The nearby steamer was small to medium, something like the 6,200-ton *Californian* herself, but should have been eight times larger to fit with the theory being advanced – that the lights seen meant the ship sending them up was seen, that it was this coincidental steamer, and if she was the *Titanic*, then the mystery ship was the *Californian*, even though the latter claimed to be on the Boston track. Worse than all of these inconsistencies, the *Californian* was stationary throughout, although the *Titanic* evidence was clearly to the effect that a previously unseen vessel had approached and stopped.

The British Inquiry was impatiently trying to square the circle.

The American inquiry had been just as inclined to run with a theory. On Thursday April 25, two days before Captain Moore appeared before him to pour soothing oil on troubled waters, Senator William Alden Smith, presiding, had been prepared to advance the argument that the *Mount Temple*, then only a figment of newspaper stories, had been the mystery ship.

Smith was examining the *Carpathia*'s wireless operator, Harold Cottam, at 2pm on that day when he ran with the speculation. Cottam had simply advised that he had not heard from the *Mount Temple* during the whole of the emergency. Just before the adjournment, the chairman of the inquiry had been trying to tease out whether it was right for the *Titanic*, during the emergency, to tell the *Frankfurt* operator that he was a fool and to keep out, even though the sinking White Star liner had no idea of the *Frankfurt*'s position.

Knowing that the *Titanic* had earlier, prior to her collision, rebuffed the *Californian*'s ice warning because she was taking private messages from Cape Race, Smith wanted to know if Cottam would have dismissed another ship's operator in such a crisis just because the other man seemed slow on the uptake.

Cottam replied 'I would have told him the same,' arguing that the CQD and position were all that any other ship should require, not an explanation to each new entrant to the airwaves as to why the summoning ship was sinking. Moments later, Senator Smith then came out with this:

Senator Smith: Suppose this ship that was just ahead of the *Titanic*, the *Mount Temple*, and was in sight of its officers from its deck, was itself stuck in a field of ice and could not at that moment move, would that change your view of your duty?

Cottam: You mean in sight of the *Titanic*? I do not understand it. I do not understand the question …

Q. Well, if the help, which was called for, and was within easy reach of the ship that was sinking, was itself struggling with the ice and quite busy and could not respond to the CQD call as promptly as you might think it ought to do, do you not think it would be desirable [for the *Titanic*] to explain to them the circumstances under which the message for help was sent?

Cottam: The operator on the ship has no duties on the bridge to perform, with regard to keeping a lookout or anything like that. His duty in a case of that description is to keep a constant watch …

Smith: Wait a minute, now. Suppose that this ship was stuck in the ice herself and he was taking business for his Captain. [*Mount Temple* receiving routine messages]

Cottam: I know he was not, sir.

Smith: How do you know he was not?

Cottam: Because, as I say, when the communication with the *Titanic* was going on there was not a sound otherwise.

Smith: But you were passing from your room to the deck delivering these messages … suppose that during the time you were temporarily absent from your apparatus a call had gone out from the *Mount Temple* that they were in the ice, and having a little difficulty – you would have missed it?

Cottam: If I had not been in the room, certainly I would have missed it.

Smith: And therefore you would not know all that was taking place; and when you came back you might get the second message instead of the first one. And, as a matter of fact the only one you did get was the 'goodnight' message from the *Mount Temple*.

Cottam: That is right, sir. That was at 10.40 o'clock.

Smith: I want to get into your mind the fact that there are people who were on the *Mount Temple* who say they saw the lights of the *Titanic* when it went down and there are people who were on the *Titanic* who say they saw the lights of a boat ahead when the *Titanic* was sinking, and in that situation it is no time to be flippant or discourteous, in such a responsible position as you held.

Cottam: I was not flippant. Nobody was flippant with the *Mount Temple*. The *Mount Temple* was off watch.

Smith: I understand that; you were not discourteous to the *Mount Temple*. But you say you would have made the same answer to the *Mount Temple* that was made to the *Frankfurt* if the *Mount Temple* had asked the question the *Frankfurt* asked. [Pause] I do not think I will pursue this any further …

Senator Smith's assumptions are clear, but two days later he had performed a *volte face* and was positively swooning over Captain Moore by the end of his testimony, the two attitudes together being possibly one of the more alarming aspects of a ramshackle American inquiry.

Now, here was Moore in London with another commission apparently hell-bent on furthering its own ideas, but in this case he was off the hook. The *Californian* was the ship under pressure. All that would be needed from him, he surely reflected, would be another mollifying meander through various bits and pieces – as long as he kept out of the choppy waters that, on reflection, he may have generated in aspects of his American evidence.

Moore did not give evidence until the afternoon of May 15. If he had been in court that morning, he would have heard the third officer of the *Californian* grilled about whether the *Titanic* could have been the small steamer close to his own ship on the Boston track, although the corollary, that the *Titanic* (bound for New York) would therefore have been vastly off course, was ignored. The officer, who had not seen any rockets or lights because he was off duty after midnight, succumbed. And then there had been pressure too on the next witness, *Californian* chief officer George Stewart, over the fact that the signals seen had not been entered in the log.

If Moore was feeling slightly uncomfortable about his own log, with no mention of the *Titanic* incident at all, no entries from noon on April 14 until landfall in St John five days later, and then no entries for the homeward sailing, he may have perked up at hearing an intervention by Lord Mersey, addressing the Solicitor General of the United Kingdom, at question 8705. 'Do your questions suggest this [*Californian*] log has been doctored?'

Harold Cottam, wireless operator of the *Carpathia*, at the US inquiry. He fended off a theory from Chairman William Alden Smith, lower left (smudged). British Ambassador James Bryce, partly hidden, listens at top left.

The query was smoothed away, but it had perhaps been a rhetorical signal to turn up the heat on the witness. A short time later, at Br. 8838, Lord Mersey confessed that it was by then his attitude of mind that the *Californian* and *Titanic* were in sight of each other.

The *Mount Temple* was thus in the clear, before Moore had even given evidence. There could only ever be one candidate at any time for the *Titanic*'s mystery ship. And with the next witness, the *Californian*'s wireless operator, Cyril Evans, things would get even brighter from Moore's point of view.

Evans, like Cottam of the *Carpathia*, had not heard from the *Mount Temple* all night, even though operator Durrant had not been 'off watch' as Cottam imagined. But Evans now told how the *Californian*, the next morning (at 5.11am *Mount Temple* time) had sought contact with other shipping:

9071. Did you get an answer from anybody? — Yes.
9072. From what ship? — The *Mount Temple* first.
9073. That is a Canadian Pacific vessel, I think? — Yes.
9074. Did you get any information from her? — He said, 'Do you know the *Titanic* has struck an iceberg, and she is sinking,' and he gave me her position.
...
9078. Did you say, 'She is sinking?' — He said, 'She is sinking.'
9079. The *Mount Temple* said, 'She is sinking?' — Yes.
9080. Did he give you the position of the *Titanic*? — Yes.
9082. Did the *Mount Temple* say what she was doing? — No. The *Frankfurt* jumped in then. He told me the same thing and gave me the same position.

This was useful, because Evans had just indicated that the *Mount Temple* believed the *Titanic* was still sinking, even though it was by now the broad daylight and Moore had already gained the empty SOS position.

On the contrary, however, Durrant had by this stage formed his own opinion that the giant liner had long since gone down, and would the next day confirm that he told Evans in this message that the *Titanic* had definitely sunk, rather than that she remained in distress.

As such, the evidence of Evans was a positive boon.

Captain Moore, called in the mid-afternoon, would spend about three quarters of an hour in the witness box. It was a gentle examination: the early five mile difference (as compared to his

Captain Moore in civilian clothes in a photograph that may have been taken close to his retirement from the sea.

American evidence) as to how far north he crossed a major line of longitude was not spotted. The inquiry was not interested in when exactly he turned, nor when he reached the distress position transmitted. His schooner and steamer tales, as seen previously, were dealt with perfunctorily, and then his first questioner handed the witness over to another.

Moore next unveiled, making it a central theme, his instructions never to enter ice. He spoke about lifeboats, and the best way to load and lower them. A third interrogator asked seven desultory questions. A fourth asked ten that were equally dull. A fifth counsel tried four questions on the manning of lifeboats. It was all rather pleasant.

A sixth and a seventh asked general occupancy and operational questions. Altogether there were 115 questions on seafaring generalities (out of less than 200 put to Moore all told) before matters returned to the voyage in question. Even then it was the briefest of scrutiny, and matters veered away again.

It was staggeringly the second-last question before he was asked what his position was when he received the first *Titanic* signal. He replied with the longitude and latitude, but did not mention the distance between the two places. Nor had the inquiry elicited the timeframe involved, although Moore had said his top speed was eleven knots. In short, Moore's version of events, even though the British already possessed his American evidence, was not remotely tested.

Moore stepped down gratefully. He had not been asked a single question about his log, nor had any of the allegations made in Canada or the United States been put to him. The inquiry was simply not much interested in him. His wireless operator followed him into the box.

The 21-year-old first confirmed that his name was John Durrant, then described his work practices, and how he was off duty 'for about three hours' after his midday meal. While he took at nap at that time, he presumably also had a lot of time to wander at will around the ship, and perhaps meet passengers such as Keurvorst, with whom he could strike up a conversation.

He was next taken through his wireless log, just as he had shown it to a reporter at St John, and as Moore had described it to the US inquiry. There was one notable confirmation of a fact disclosed in that record – he confirmed at Br. 9464 that his ship had turned back towards the *Titanic* 'about fifteen minutes after we got the signal. It may have been sooner.' Moore had claimed that both signal and turn had happened practically simultaneously, at 12.30am. Durrant's record showed his ship received the first distress call at 12.11am.

There was a mildly diverting moment when Lord Mersey, in response to one of the wireless messages, asked: 'What does OK mean?' and heard in reply from the Solicitor General, Sir John Simon, that it stood for 'Orl Korrect.' A minute later, and it was the turn of the Attorney General, Sir Rufus Isaacs, to tell the bench that the new distress code of SOS stood for 'Save Our Souls.'

Durrant had only got as far as 12.46am, *Mount Temple* time, as the *Titanic* was calling the *Virginian*, when the Court President, Lord Mersey, suddenly made a pronouncement: 'This boat, the *Mount Temple*, was never in a position to render active assistance.'

Mersey could not have known this, unless he had been privately briefed to that effect, which would raise serious questions about possible manipulation of his fact-finding process. No evidence had been given by Moore about how far he was away, or how long it took him to get there, and at what speed, although he did mention the extent of his vessel's top speed.

Moore had of course spoken of other matters in Washington, but Lord Mersey was supposed to hear all the evidence afresh and not be aware of foreign testimony. In response to his observation, however, the Solicitor General did refer to the mileage involved in the claimed separation, which had not been given in evidence by anyone in London.

Sir John Simon declared in response to Lord Mersey: 'It was 49 miles away and was making for her.' Neither Moore nor Durrant had mentioned that mileage in evidence. Sir John might have drawn it out, but instead he relied on American testimony that was not properly within the court's competence.

In further reply to this information, Lord Mersey opined compendiously: 'She [*Mount Temple*] could not possibly have reached her [*Titanic*].' Once more, the Solicitor General was not found wanting: 'No, not possibly. She was doing her best.'

What this indicates is that the *Mount Temple* was not just being discounted as the mystery ship in mid-evidence, but that she had actually been dismissed in advance, before a single witness from that vessel had opened his mouth. Hence the lack of voyage-specific questions to Captain Moore.

Unfortunately this in turn indicates that counsel cannot have read the US evidence too closely or interrogated its meaning and implications. In a deeply ironical sense, the *Mount Temple* could indeed 'not possibly have reached' – because Moore had given a top speed of 11 knots, he had completed the journey from turnaround to arrival in four hours, yet the distance was 49 nautical miles and he had been stopped or going slow for considerable periods.

And in this same breath, the Solicitor General proceeded to offer Durrant unsought reassurance that his ship's silence throughout was not a matter for concern either. Sir John told him: 'If you had broken in and tried to talk to the *Titanic* yourself, you would only have interrupted her talking to other people.' But this statement is, on the face of it, illogical – why shouldn't the *Mount Temple* have been among the 'other people' if she could ask relevant questions or pass helpful information?

The rehearsal of wireless messages continued, and Durrant's 4.46am notation 'we are stopped amongst pack ice' might have given rise (since they had the US evidence) to a query as to why he hadn't noted Moore's testified stop in ice at 3.25am, an hour and twenty minutes earlier. In London Moore confirmed that he met 'heavier ice' at that time, but didn't actually mention whether he had stopped or not, in contrast to what was said in America.

Meanwhile it is known that Durrant had been regularly sending messages up to Captain Moore. And a case could be mounted that *Titanic*'s crowning error that night may have been not to answer the question from the 'fool' *Frankfurt* at 1.31am – 'Are there any boats around you already?'

Titanic may have been impatient with the *Frankfurt*, as previously seen, but the unanswered question seemed to hang in the ether. The failure to answer this question, coupled with an earlier *Titanic* reply (cited in evidence by Moore) that 'We want all the help we can get,' may have led the latter to assume that the stricken vessel indeed had one protector alongside, but did not want to disclose the fact in order to attract more.

In a scenario of such an assumption, it may have seemed to Moore that he was entitled to break off his efforts at assistance. The *Titanic* had not replied: 'No, there are no ships around us already.' Perhaps that would have been, strictly speaking, untrue. There is evidence the wireless operators of the *Titanic* knew the mystery ship had appeared, although they knew nothing further about her. The White Star liner never told other shipping that there was another vessel in sight close at hand. Did her silence make Moore suspicious that his ship might not be so urgently needed after all?

'CQD got a good name in the time of Jack Binns,' said Durrant in one part of his British evidence. He was referring to the wireless operator of the White Star liner *Republic* who, three years earlier in 1909, had sent out a distress message following collision with the *Florida* which resulted in a fleet of ships being around the stricken vessel by daylight and the safe transhipment of all passengers. It was hours before the *Republic* finally sank.

Now, with many ships responding by wireless, Moore may have concluded that a similar rally of vessels was unfolding. If he was reluctant to turn in the first place, he may have been reluctant to persevere if there was any inkling of the *Titanic* not being completely honest. That liner was not saying whether there were any ships around her already.

In his US evidence Moore declared that his operator sent a message to him at the bridge somewhere after 1am that the *Titanic* was still calling distress. He read aloud from what he had been told: '*Carpathia* asks if he wants any special boat to wait on him. *Titanic* says, 'We want all we can get.''

Moore immediately added: 'I do not think anybody realised at the time that it was so bad, sir.' There is a clear implication there, although he refers to the *Carpathia*, that he himself did not know the situation was so critical. Even in the morning light, Moore would maintain in his testimony that he had 'not the slightest idea' that the *Titanic* had sunk.

If Moore thought the *Titanic* was certainly good for many more hours yet (as many passengers on the sinking liner thought too) there would have been an understandable temptation not to take too many chances with his own ship.

The *Carpathia*'s question had commercial overtones … . *Titanic* had been working by wireless with the *Olympic* of the same line. Fleet mates could succour each other with no salvage cost implications. But the involvement of a ship from another line, in towing for instance, would cost the White Star Line money. On a psychological level, with the *Florida* case the only parallel in anyone's memory since the advent of wireless, the *Carpathia* question may have raised the unfortunate notion: that the *Titanic* could pick and choose.

While Captain Moore had recent experience of a club of vessels assisting each other, he also had a record – that very year – of breaking off aid attempts and leaving it to others.

In January 1912, after initial assistance, the *Mount Temple* had left a vessel named the *Dart* to the ministrations of other shipping. The *Washington Post*, in a short report headlined ABANDONS DISABLED SHIP related in a subhead: '*Mount Temple* Forced to Leave the *Dart* in Midocean.'

While bound from New Orleans and Norfolk for Copenhagen, the rudder of the 3,207-ton *Dart*, built in 1898, was carried away. She was days later spotted drifting helplessly off Newfoundland by the *Mount Temple*. Moore planned to tow her to St John's, but the cable parted and a rich salvage prize was lost.

It was reported from St John's that Moore had been obliged to abandon the *Dart* and had proceeded on his way to London. Arrangements had been made to despatch the steamer *Belleaventure* to the assistance of the disabled steamer, the report added.

But the *Times* of London (January 27, 1912, p.13) made clear: 'With reference to the disablement of the British steamer *Dart* off Cape Race, the Captain of the British steamer *Mount Temple* reports by wireless that when he left the vessel a steamer was standing by and that the steamer *Montezuma*, bound westward, had been notified of the position of the *Dart* and was going to her assistance with gear ready for towing.'

The *Montezuma* was a sister ship of the *Mount Temple*, also serving on the Belgium-Canada route. The *Dart* was eventually towed into St John's, Newfoundland (a distance of 774 miles) by the Leyland liner *Georgian*, then under charter to the Atlantic Transport Line. The rescue took five days.

The case went to court in London in June 1912, with the *Times* reporting that 'this action was brought by the owners, Master, officers, chief steward and carpenter of the steamship *Georgian* to recover salvage remuneration for services rendered to the steamship *Dart*, her cargo and freight, in the North Atlantic.' Mr Justice Bargrave Deane awarded £3,500, with £250 to the Captain alone, equivalent to nearly a year's wages, tax-free. It is no wonder, then, that salvage races were always keenly contested when they occurred, and that it was a deep disappointment to finish as an also-ran.

ABANDONS DISABLED SHIP

Mount Temple Forced to Leave the Dart in Midocean

From the *Washington Post* of Monday, January 22, 1912, p.5.

THE FINGER OF BLAME

THE British inquiry's interest in the *Mount Temple* ended with a final question to wireless operator Durrant as to whether the words 'engine room' had been abbreviated in a message he had received from *Titanic* ... and they hadn't, he said.

The question seems innocuous, but it may reflect an unspoken desire for an abbreviation, because then a mistake might have been made. No-one cared to dwell on the horror encapsulated by a message received by the *Mount Temple* at 1.27am that spelt out in full: 'Engine room flooded.'

As a final official word on the *Mount Temple*, it is chilling in another way. The CPR vessel was at the distress position three hours later but made no further effective efforts. Yet the last lifeboat would not be picked up for a further four hours again, or seven hours after that grim message had been sent.

Moore did not even risk minor damage to his ship in daylight. The words echo from his evidence: 'If I was to go through ice and my ship was damaged I would have pointed out to me that those were the instructions, that I was not to go into any ice ... '

So Moore did not just put the lives of his passengers first, as he claimed. He also put the inviolability of his hull from a dent or a scrape ahead of the desperate needs of humanity in a monumental disaster. One man's service record would remain unblemished.

'Of course, I have been fortunate myself,' Moore remarked at the end of his US testimony. 'I have never yet had any injury from ice, although I have been Master in this trade for a very long time.' It may have struck a note of being just a little self-concerned, given the context in which he was making it.

But Moore did not have an unblemished record. Five years earlier he had been criticised by an official inquiry and warned to 'be more careful in future.' There is no doubt that a chastened Moore responded to the rebuke – he was indeed careful beyond the call of duty, as defined by his shipping line, on the night of April 14/15 1912.

The rap on the knuckles came after a keel-scouring incident while Moore was Captain of the Canadian Pacific liner *Montrose*. She was stranded on the Red Island Reef in the St. Lawrence river on July 2, 1907, when on a voyage from Antwerp to Montreal.

It was no small matter – the vessel sustained 'considerable damage,' and a Wreck Commissioner's Court was convened in Montreal. The *Montrose*, over 6,000 tons but a shade smaller than *Mount Temple*, had been under pilotage at the time.

The court, in which commissioner O.G.V. Spain sat with assessors, ruled that the pilot, Joseph H. Talbot, was guilty of a grave error of judgment, 'insomuch as he continued at full speed and on too fine a course, without first ascertaining, by the lead or otherwise, that the vessel was in a safe position to clear a thoroughly well-known danger.'

But bad news was to come for the Master. Even though navigation was not in his hands at the time, he had a duty to oversee and make sure no unnecessary risk was run:

> At the same time the Court cannot exonerate the Master, J.H. Moore, from blame, as this officer accepted the actions of the pilot as correct, and allowed him to alter the course and continue at full speed without first assuring himself of the actual position of the vessel ...
>
> The Court, taking into consideration the excellent record as a pilot held by Joseph H. Talbot, fines him the sum of one hundred dollars, which is to be paid in four quarterly instalments of twenty-five dollars each; Captain J.H. Moore, Master of the s.s. *Montrose* is admonished and warned to be more careful in future. The Court exonerates the other officers of the s.s. *Montrose*.'

The bows of the *Montrose*, famous for her role in the apprehension of wanted fugitive Hawley Harvey Crippen. James Henry Moore was her Captain when she ran aground on a reef and was told by a subsequent inquiry that he could not be exonerated from blame. He was admonished to be more careful in future.

clear a thoroughly well-known danger.

At the same time the Court cannot exonerate the master, J. H. Moore, from blame, as this officer accepted the actions of the pilot as correct, and allowed him to alter the course and continue at full speed without first assuring himself of the actual position of the vessel, which might have been so easily and conveniently found out by taking the departure from the lightship and running a course that would determine a safe offing from the Red Island reef. The Court, taking into consideration the excellent record as a pilot held by Joseph H. Talbot, fines him the sum of one hundred dollars, which is to be paid in four quarterly instalments of twenty-five dollars each ; Captain J. H. Moore, master of the s.s. "Montrose," is admonished and warned to be more careful in future. The Court exonerates the other officers of the s.s. "Montrose."

(Signed) O. G. V. SPAIN,
Wreck Commissioner.

Mount Temple on the rocks at Ironbound island in Nova Scotia, five years before the *Titanic* disaster.

Judgement in the matter (Board of Trade inquiry No. 7102) was handed down in August 1907. It is not known if the CPR line imposed a separate punishment, but since he was allowed to return to the *Montrose*, it is likely he suffered from no more than slight embarrassment among his fellow Captains of the line.

Certainly he would not be in disgrace for long, as another CPR Captain would have a much worse accident within a few months – aboard a vessel known as *Mount Temple*:

Bridgewater, N.S., Dec. 2 –

Seven hundred and thirty-two persons stared death in the face yet came through the ordeal unscathed when the C.P.R. liner, *Mount Temple*, driven far out of her course in a blinding snow storm was wrecked on Ironbound Island, at the mouth of the La Have river on Sunday night.

It was between 11 and 12 o'clock when the steamer went ashore. For several hours she had been in shoal water and immediately she struck, a tremendous sea swept her broadside on against the rocks. Sea after sea swept over her and when the frightened emigrants, who were chiefly Austrians, Russians, Poles, Gallicians, ands Jews, rushed up from below, the decks were waist deep in water.

Pandemonium broke out. In an instant the frightened foreigners were panic stricken and cries and shrieks arose above even the howling of the gale and the crash of the waves as they surged over the ship.

Quickly the officers and crew calmed the frenzied passengers; life preservers were served out and a line shot ashore, while the old order, the first thought of a British seaman, 'Women and children first!' rang out.

There were about one hundred women and children on board and these were sent ashore in the breeches buoy while the men were transferred in boats. Only a portion of the passengers could be landed during the night as the seas were running very high.

Those that did get ashore spent a very uncomfortable night. Fires were lit and the lightkeeper and his family did everything in their power to relieve their sufferings, but nevertheless the night proved a terrible hardship to many. In the morning assistance was received from Lunenburg fishermen and local steamers.

The citizens of Bridgewater looked after the comforts of the unfortunates until they could be transferred to Halifax.

(*The Spectator*, December 4, 1907)

The *Mount Temple* had left Antwerp with a cargo of supplies for Christmas, along with more than 600 emigrants to Canada. Bound for St. John, New Brunswick, she mistook Ironbound lighthouse for Halifax harbour and duly went ashore. Miraculously, no lives were lost in the incident, although much of the cargo was spilled – including potatoes, which have seeded successive local crops such that they are known to this day as 'Mount Temples.'

The vessel was firmly wedged on the rocks, and it was believed she would become a total loss when December gales pounded the helpless ship and broke her up. She had been insured for £95,000, and there seemed little hope. But in the event, the weather was clement, and she remained where she was. The cargo was removed, and matters appeared more promising.

She was successfully refloated by the salvage company Beazley Brothers on the evening of April 15, 1908 – exactly four years before the *Titanic* sank. 'The *Mount Temple* Saved – Liner That Was Abandoned by Underwriters is Pulled off Rocks,' championed the *New York Times*. It reported that the big liner was proceeding for Halifax under her own steam, convoyed by six ocean tugs. There she would be dry-docked for further repairs.

It had all ended very happily for everyone – apart from Captain Hubert Boothby, Master of the ship, who had remained at Ironbound with his officers all winter. He was now relieved of his duties and left the company — the sole victim of a terrifying occurrence. His fate stood as a stark warning to all in the line's employment.

STEAMSHIP "MOUNT TEMPLE" IN DRY DOCK.
HALIFAX GRAVING DOCK CO. LTD.

The *Mount Temple* in dry dock in Halifax in 1908 following her floating from the rocks at Ironbound island, where she had run ashore the previous December.

And it would no doubt have entered the mind of Captain Moore later that year when he was asked to take command of the *Mount Temple*, an unlucky ship, in December 1908. He would hold her captaincy for another five years, though he went aground again in 1913.

Meanwhile the British inquiry had awarded itself an additional question to answer towards the end of its proceedings. That question, 24 (b), was as follows:

'What vessels had the opportunity of rendering assistance to the *Titanic*, and if any, how was it that assistance did not reach the *Titanic* before the ss *Carpathia* arrived?'
(Br p.839)

The new question was first mentioned on June 28, which was the 33ʳᵈ day of the inquiry. The Attorney General, Sir Rufus Isaacs, told Lord Mersey that afternoon: 'I amended it so as to include the *Californian*,' thereby demonstrating not just his own prejudice, but a complete violation of procedure in altering the commission's terms of reference in the middle of its work.

Even if the question itself was a perfectly valid one, had the court originally been asked to address it, and even though framed in terms of vessels in the plural, the highest law official to the British Government – leading a case whereby the Board of Trade was investigating itself – had put only one vessel into play.

A couple of days later, on July 3, the Attorney General was blithely declaring that he had added the question to 'purposely' address the *Californian* seeing rockets but failing to act. The added question, it should be noted, was not directed towards establishing the identity of the ship seen off the *Titanic*'s bow, because at this late stage British officialdom was going to satisfy itself with half measures and a nod and a wink.

Later that month, the answer delivered to this question in the official report was stark: 'The *Californian*. She could have reached the *Titanic* if she had made the attempt when she saw the first rocket. She made no attempt.'

This finding made no mention of any other vessels. It did not mention the *Mount Temple*, nor the ice barrier that prevented Moore from joining the *Carpathia*, nor indeed his company's rigid rule.

Remarkably however, while the British provided a scapegoat for public opinion in the shape of Captain Lord of the *Californian*, they also pursued a vessel which they thought *could have been* the mystery ship.

And it is all the more extraordinary that they did so, not on the basis of any evidence adduced in their own court, but instead by relying on second-hand transcripts of what was said in America. And it was Captain Moore himself who sent them off on this wild goose chase.

Moore had been available for scrutiny in the witness box in London, but he was not asked about the mystery ship and did not venture any opinion. He did see an eastbound vessel 'all the time' from when he turned around, but of course – in the opinion of Lord Mersey and the Solicitor General – his ship 'could not possibly' have reached the spot. Therefore neither could the other steamer.

The Master of the *Mount Temple* answered precisely one question as to the nature of that vessel in London: 'I saw her afterwards in the morning, when it was daylight. She was a foreign vessel ... She had a black funnel with a white band with some device upon it ... I did not ascertain her name.'

Now the British tried to identify her, even though Moore in London had carefully avoided repeating the words he had blurted out to the Americans, that the *Titanic*'s mystery ship 'may have been the light of the tramp steamer that was ahead of us, because when I turned there was a steamer on my port bow.'

But the British, from their US transcripts, now thought that vessel could be the villain of the piece, even though her constant proximity to Moore might have led them to question *him* more closely, his ship being automatically another candidate thereby. The Admiralty and the whole of Whitehall, the heart of the United Kingdom Government, now engaged in a huge and costly exercise to try to pinpoint a steamer consistent with Moore's description – which had changed from Washington, where he had only mentioned the colour black, omitting white.

Customs officials, diplomats, and ports across the eastern seaboard of the United States and Canada, including Newfoundland, were asked to check sailings of a 4-5,000 ton 'foreign' steamer with a black funnel containing a white band with some device. Sworn statements were taken from Masters and port officials in many countries, including those where such a ship might have made landfall.

Embassies were telegraphed and instructed to begin investigative undertakings in France, Germany, Norway, Sweden, Holland, Belgium, Italy, Russia and Greece. The files of the old

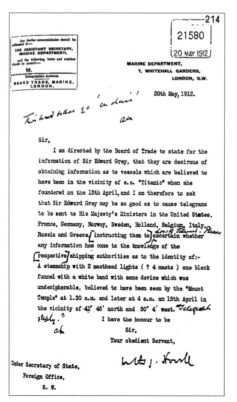

Letter outlining the extensive, but unproductive, efforts the Board of Trade was prepared to initiate as a result of information supplied by Captain Moore in America, but about which he was not questioned in London.

Board of Trade remain packed with a bewildering amount of paperwork on this single issue, which was all in vain.

Captain Moore is solely responsible for that fruitless search. He must have known that what he was suggesting was untrue. It could only have been true if both he and the tramp were within a few miles of the *Titanic*'s distress position between 1am and 1.30am, which was the later timeframe he suggested in London, having asserted in America that she was there when he turned at 12.30am.

Moore could not resile completely from what he said in America without being accused of misleading an official inquiry, but the British drew inferences about this tramp that would send them off on a prolonged wild goose chase.

There was such a vessel at the ice rim the next morning. Durrant had mentioned her in an early interview, and she was also seen by the *Californian* when responding the next morning. Third officer Charles Victor Groves said:

> Br. 8349 Did you see any other vessel? — I saw another vessel a little on our port bow, she was coming down almost end-on.
> 8350 You do not know her name? — I do not, but as far as I remember she had a black funnel She was a small steamer.
> ...
> 8458 — A small steamer, yes.
> 8459 Was she a passenger steamer? — That I could not say.
> 8480 Have you tried to find out her name? — No, I have not ... I took no further interest in her.
> 8461 — I never saw her broadside, I only saw her end on.
> 8462 You told me it was a very small boat? — It was a small boat. I judged that from her end-on view.
> 8464 Was she a vessel about your own size? — No, in my opinion she was considerably smaller.

Moore said she was a vessel of 4-5,000 tons. Groves said she was 'considerably smaller' than the *Californian* (6,230 tons), which would suggest a steamer of perhaps 3,000 tons. As a general rule, smaller vessels have much lower top speeds than larger ones

We recall what Fourth Officer Boxhall, the prime witness, said about the *Titanic*'s mystery ship. While he declined to offer any guide as to her size, he declared: 'She might have been a four-mast ship or might have been a three-mast ship, but she certainly was not a two mast ship.'

But Groves saw only a small steamer, and one of three or four thousand tons would almost certainly have only two masts – therefore being doubly disqualified from possibly being the mystery ship. And while Moore at no point specified how many masts this 'foreign' steamer had (and was not asked!) the evidence of Captain Rostron of the rescue ship *Carpathia* is of direct relevance. He said:

> Br. 25551. — At 5 o'clock it was light enough to see all round the horizon. We then saw two steamships to the northwards, perhaps seven or eight miles distant. Neither of them was the *Californian*. One of them was a four-masted steamer with one funnel, and the other a two-masted steamer with one funnel.

Moore's stranger tramp was in all likelihood a two-masted steamer, and thereby exempt from becoming the suspect sought so assiduously by the British. And Moore's suggestion was effectively ruled out by prime eyewitness Boxhall, thus leaving open the question of why Moore had suggested her in the first place.

The British did not search for Moore's erratic schooner. Perhaps this time they had been a bit more attentive and realised Boxhall had been emphatic in mentioning a steamer as the mystery ship, rather than a sailing vessel.

It may be a small mercy to now draw a veil over the schooner episode, even though Moore had specified that she was coming 'somewhere from there,' referring to where the *Titanic* lay. The schooner was moving to the west, while Moore and his sinister tramp steamer were both apparently rushing to the east.

Captain Lord was meanwhile furious at the judgment made against him by the British inquiry, which had called him as a witness, not as a defendant, meaning he had no power to adduce evidence to his own benefit – while the inquiry itself seemed satisfied with as little evidence as possible on the matter.

He wrote to the newspapers that the publication of the report 'ends a compulsory silence on my part on points raised in the course of the proceedings which affect me as the late Master of the steamer *Californian*.'

He said he owed a duty to himself to give publicity to circumstances which the inquiry failed to elicit, 'to show that the deductions which have been drawn, reflecting upon my personal character as a seaman, are entirely unfounded.'

Among those circumstances, listed in an admittedly 'lengthy' explanation, was 'the evidence of the *Titanic* officer who was firing her distress signals [and] states the steamer he had under observation 'approached' — obviously not the *Californian*, as she was stopped from 10.30pm until 5.15am.'

He also pointed out that his ship's position was Marconigramed to other steamers at 6.30pm the night before, five hours before the accident, 'and also at 5.15am, before I had heard of the position of the accident, proving my distance from the disaster as given by me to be correct.' An 'undeserved stigma' now rested upon him, he protested.

Captain Lord also wrote directly to the Board of Trade, on August 10, 1912, saying that at 'about 5.30am, I gave my position to the *Virginian* before I heard where the *Titanic* sunk [and] that gave me 17 miles away. I understand the original Marconigrams were in court.'

The letter, preserved in the UK National Archives (document MT9/920E, file M23448), adds dolefully: 'My employers, the Leyland Line, although their nautical advisers are convinced we did not see the *Titanic*, or the *Titanic* see the *Californian*, say they have the utmost confidence in me, and do not blame me in any way, but owing to Lord Mersey's decision and the public

Captain Stanley Lord of the *Californian*, pictured some years prior to 1912.

opinion caused by this report, they are reluctantly compelled to ask for my resignation after 14½ years' service without a hitch of any description, and if I could clear myself of this charge, would willingly reconsider their decision.'

While the Board of Trade was deaf to such entreaties, and didn't even reply for six weeks, something dramatic happened almost as soon as Captain Lord had mailed that letter. He received another one – not from officialdom but from a most unusual source.

The letter that dropped in his letterbox at 10 Ormond St, Liscard, was dated August 6, but had taken some time (at least two weeks) to arrive from Canada. These were its contents:

August 6th 1912
Empress of Britain
Quebec

Dear Lord,

You will be surprised to get a letter from me after all these years, but when I mention the old *Conway* you will then remember me. My wife had heard that you were living quite close to us in Liscard & sent me your address, so I am writing to tell you how deeply sorry I am for you with regard to the *Titanic* affair, for I know how you must have suffered. I came home in the *Mount Temple* from Halifax that voyage, having been taken out of the *Empress* at ten minutes notice to fill up a vacancy as one of her officers had been given a shore billet on her arrival at Halifax homeward bound.

The officers and others told me what they had seen on that eventful night when the *Titanic* went down, & from what they said, they were from ten to fourteen miles from her when they saw her signals. I gather from what was told me that the Captain seemed afraid to go through the ice, although it was not so very thick. They told me that they not only saw her deck lights but several green lights between them & what they thought was the *Titanic*. There were two loud reports heard, which they said must have been the 'finale' of the *Titanic*; this was sometime after sighting her, I gathered.

The Captain said at the inquiry in Washington, that he was 49 miles away – but the officers state he was not more than 14 miles off. I must tell you these men were fearfully indignant that they were not then called upon to give evidence at the time, for they were greatly incensed at the Captain's behaviour in the matter.

The doctor had made all preparations, & rooms were turned into hospitals, etc, & the crew were standing ready to help, on deck, watching her lights, & what they said were the green lights burnt in the boats.

On our arrival in Gravesend the Captain & Marconi officer were sent for, also the two log books, Scrap and Chief Officer's. What they wanted with the scrap log I cannot understand, for there was only about a line and a half written of what occurred during the four hours, and quite half a page in the Chief's book! I saw that myself. These fellows must feel sorry for you – Knowing that you could not, in the face of this, have been the mystery ship!

I have been residing in South Africa for some years with my wife & family & have only within the last five years returned to England, & have taken up the sea again, & have once more had to begin at the beginning, but I live in hopes of getting promotion sometime. You will of course have heard all about our collision.

I hope to see you when I get back. By the way, Rostron was also on the *Conway* with us, as you will of course remember.

Well, no more now. All news when we meet. Wishing you a happy issue out of all your troubles,

Believe me,
    Sincerely yours,

    W.H. Baker

The effect of the above letter on Captain Lord can best be imagined. He knew his was not the mystery ship, and now here was confirmation of that fact with mention of the dramatic involvement of the *Mount Temple*. But at one level he was mystified, because he didn't know any W.H. Baker, and Lord had not been an apprentice on the merchant marine training vessel *Conway*, which was a familiar sight moored in the river Mersey.

With Captain Lord rooted to the spot in his house in Cheshire, amazedly re-reading the four-page folded lettercard in his hand, the prosecution now calls a former officer of the *Mount Temple*.

WILLIAM HENRY BAKER   (1869-1955)

Aged 41 in 1912, Baker appears in the Official Log of the *Mount Temple* as a replacement fourth officer on the homeward-bound trip from Halifax to London. His arrival, from the *Empress of Britain*, allowed fourth officer W.S. Brown to move up to third officer, replacing A.H. Notley, who quit the ship in Canada.

Baker was born at 33 Charles Street, Reading, Berkshire on December 28, 1869. Suitably for someone of such a surname, he was the son of a confectioner, William Sr, and his wife Mary, nine years his senior.

The family moved to Wednesbury in Staffordshire, where they had a shop in the High Street. This address appears in Baker's register entry for his sea apprenticeship aboard the *Conway*, which he joined from James Longstaff Higher Grade School in 1885.

The young William Henry attended the *Conway* from September of that year, when he was aged 15, until July 1887. He then joined a ship belonging to Herron, Dunn and company, his final certificate from the *Conway* describing his conduct as 'Very Good' and his ability as 'Fair.'

William Henry Baker, replacement fourth officer of the *Mount Temple*, in 1912.

Above: The Union Steamship Company vessel RMS *Greek*, whereon William Henry Baker met his future wife.

Below: The training ship *Conway*. Both Captain Rostron of the *Carpathia* and *Mount Temple* replacement officer W.H. Baker attended here, but Baker was mixing up the Captain of the *Californian* with other boys named Lord when he thought he was a student too.

W.H. Baker obviously applied himself thereafter, because ten years later he successfully sat examinations and was awarded Officer Certificate No. 024646 at Cardiff, duly recorded in Lloyd's register.

Baker joined the Union steamship company, later Union Castle, which ran a mail service between Southampton and Cape Town. He served aboard the *Greek*, of 4,757 tons, built a few years earlier, and in 1899 was smitten by a singer and musician who had been engaged to entertain the passengers.

Rejoicing in the name of Henrietta Kate Marie Anne Krüger Velthusen, she was a noted soprano, professor and teacher of music, aged 30, with a diploma from the Royal Conservatoire of Music in Leipzig. Her family was German, but she had grown up in England.

Her father, Alexander, had once been aide-de-camp to Emperor Wilhelm I of Germany, but later joined the French Foreign Legion and was decorated for 'acts of gallantry during the Italian war of independence.'

The couple were married in East London in what was then the Cape colony, on September 4 1899. The Boer War had broken out, and Baker left the sea for a staff role in its prosecution. In Pietermaritzburg they set up home, Hetty giving birth to five children while also finding time to give lessons as a singing teacher.

William and Hetty decided to return to England after she was offered a prestigious appointment as a concert pianist. They arrived with their brood in late 1907, and Baker returned to the sea the following year while his wife achieved glittering success. According to her 1938 obituary, she was 'personally thanked by King Edward VII after a Covent Garden command performance' and 'held audiences spellbound from New York to Cape Town.' How they managed it all with five children, even in an era of service, is a wonder.

Hetty Baker appears as a passenger aboard the *Mauretania* for one of these engagements, arriving in New York on July 30, 1909 from Liverpool. She gave an address of 87 Seaview Road, Liscard – which establishes what Baker says in his letter to Captain Lord: 'My wife had heard that you were living quite close to us in Liscard.'

Baker had been sent Lord's address, indicating that he likely wrote to his wife earlier that summer about his own misgivings over what he had heard aboard the *Mount Temple* and the British inquiry's focus on the *Californian*, which had become evident in May.

As to the belief that Lord and Rostron had both been on the *Conway* with him, Baker was simply mistaken – Rostron had indeed been there at the same time as Baker, but the latter must have been confusing Stanley Lord with a Henry Lord, with three of that exact name being *Conway* cadets, along with others of the surname Lord at different times. Cadets, incidentally, were instructed to refer to eachother by surname only.

The *Empress of Britain* was indeed in Halifax at the same time as the *Mount Temple*. Captained by James Anderson Murray, she arrived there on Friday April 26, complete with a tale of encountering an iceberg while going slowly in fog the previous Wednesday, April 24. The *New York Times* turned this into 'swerved just in time to avoid a serious collision,' but in fact engines had been reversed. Many of the 1,460 passengers had been on deck at the time (10.30am) and were 'panicky' since 'all were aware of the *Titanic*'s fate,' but were assured there was no danger. Even so, the iceberg became a 'giant,' and it was even claimed the ship had struck 'a glancing blow,' which resulted in no damage.

Baker wrote to Lord in his August letter: 'You will of course have heard all about our collision,' but he was not referring to any iceberg escapade. Instead, on July 27, the *Empress of Britain* had collided with the steamer *Helvetia* when about 300 miles from Quebec in the St Lawrence river.

The speedy *Empress*, with a thousand passengers aboard, had been going 12kt in a fogbank that Saturday afternoon (her top speed was 18½) when she heard a foghorn on the starboard bow, followed a minute later by another, closer, blast. The *Empress* had been blowing her own whistle every minute and a half.

Murray ordered engines full speed astern. 'We were going full speed astern for a minute and a half, and then this vessel loomed right up ahead of us,' he told the subsequent inquiry, which opened on August 1, 1912. 'We crashed right into her … she was broad across the bow.'

The *Helvetia* was gashed in the aft-end of the engine room. 'Seeing that the [other] ship was badly injured, I put our ship at slow ahead and kept her in the gap,' said Murray. Jacob's ladders were thrown over the wrecked bows of the *Empress* for the crew of the *Helvetia*. They were also hauled up by ladder, and forty in all, the full crew, escaped.

'After we were sure that we have got absolutely everybody off, into our ship, we then backed off, and the *Helvetia* sank very quickly.' The incident had taken 45 minutes and Baker, who had helped the crew aboard, snapped a dramatic picture of the impaled victim.

Captain J.C. Connell, Master of the *Helvetia*, then had to watch his new ship, 2,719 tons and built in Newcastle just the previous year, disappear into the St Lawrence. The *Empress* returned to Quebec, where she was dry-docked with her bows smashed or missing to a depth of eight feet from the stem post. It was there that Baker penned his letter to Lord.

Captain James Anderson Murray of the Canadian Pacific liner *Empress of Britain*.

Dramatic photograph taken by William Henry Baker of the *Helvetia* impaled by the bow of the *Empress of Britain*. The former has damaged upper works and one of her lifeboats smashed.

Damage to the bows of the *Empress of Britain* following her collision with the *Helvetia*. Picture taken in Montreal by *Mount Temple* temporary officer William Henry Baker.

He did not waste time writing on the collision, dramatic though it was, demonstrating that Baker was no self-publicist either. Instead he had a major revelation to impart – that he had been told 'by the officers and others' on the *Mount Temple* that the *Titanic* distress signals had been seen.

'They told me that they not only saw her deck lights but several green lights between them & what they thought was the *Titanic*.' The crew was 'on deck, watching her lights, & what they said were the green lights burnt in the boats.' This is corroboration of the tales told in St John, New Brunswick, before Baker had even arrived in Halifax.

Baker makes it clear the *Titanic* was seen, saying the 'finale' came some time after sighting her. And this end was audible, immediately conveying proximity while recalling the claims of passenger Mlynarczyk about being able to hear as well as see.

The officers, said Baker, had said their ship was not more than 14 miles away when the ship turned. 'These men were fearfully indignant,' and 'greatly incensed' at the Captain's inactivity – again an echo of both Zurch and Keurvorst, both of whom mentioned or 'emphasised' unhappiness among the officers at the time, that they had 'besought' (beseeched) Moore to action, with even the rumour of their temporarily taking command from him.

The mention of lifeboats seen (via the green flares Boxhall testified about and rescuer Rostron saw) also recalls Mlynarczyk's remark that 'the ocean in that vicinity was full of lifeboats.' And it brings to mind Moore's addressing, in newspaper interviews, the very idea that he might have launched his own lifeboats, but specifying reasons against it.

Baker had just offered a whole new panoply of possible witnesses. Who were these 'officers and others'? And what sort of man was whistleblower William Henry Baker?

HEARSAY & HEROISM

EVENTS were moving quickly for Captain Stanley Lord, who was not one to lie down under unfair aspersions on his character. He wrote to Captain Arthur Rostron, asking him the pertinent question whether he could identify either of the steamers he saw from the *Carpathia* in the early morning, neither of which, Rostron testified, was the *Californian*. He got this reply:

Royal Mail Steamship *Carpathia*
New York
Septr. 5th '12.

Dear Lord,

I was very glad to hear from you & hope things are looking brighter for you.

I'm sorry I cannot give you any detailed description of the two steamers seen by me. All I know – one, [a] four master one-funnel steamer dodging about, I suppose amongst the ice, to Nd., the other – [a] two master & one funnel coming from W to E straight on his course.

I did not see colour of funnels or notice anything which might distinguish either. You can imagine I was quite busy enough.

Can't you get your position when stopped & get approx. courses you steered, with speed – to where we met?

I'll do what I can, but you know I can only say what I know & what I saw & did. My word it isn't much, & I'm sorry too.

If you can suggest anything I should be happy to help you, but you see I know so little, [and] have said all I really do know too.

Anyway, Lord – you have my sympathies. I understand more than I can say, especially about the calling business.

I may state <u>for your private information</u> – I have had quite long talks with Captn. Bartlett about you.

With best regards,
Yours sincerely,
A.H. Rostron.

Charles A. Bartlett was the influential White Star Line marine superintendent at Liverpool, and later Captain of the *Titanic*'s sister ship, HMHS *Britannic*, when she was sunk by a mine in the Kea channel during the Great War. Bartlett later wrote to Lord: 'I still believe you were unjustly treated and would gladly help you at any time if it is in my power to prove it.'

But Captain Lord was currently interested in pursuing anything Rostron could remember, since the rescuer of the *Titanic* survivors was someone who was actually on the scene on the catastrophe in April 1912. He wrote back in response to Captain Rostron's reply, this time enclosing a copy of the startling correspondence he had received from officer Baker of the *Mount Temple*. A further reply eventually arrived:

RMS *Carpathia*
Gulf of Lyons
Novr. 6th '12

My dear Lord,

Many thanks for yours of 12th Oct., which I received in New York, but was really too busy to reply from there.

Honestly – I wish I could do something to help you. If you can suggest anything, I would do my best. Of course I gave you all information in my previous letter.

I am very much interested in Baker's letter and I certainly would get legal advice about publishing it.

I couldn't imagine you to have been the mystery ship. I wonder if the four master single funnel ship was the *Mount Temple*?

Could you find out if he was dodging about somewhere about 5.30 or 6am? I certainly saw 'the' steamer turning & dodging about that time & if a two ~~funnel~~ master one-funnel steamer passed them about 6 to 6.30am coming from the westward.

Lord, I certainly think Mersey was both unkind & unfair in his treatment of you & his remarks were anything but proper from a judge.

I'm surprised to know you are an old *Conway*: I'm afraid I don't remember either you or Baker. I was there '85, 86.

By the way, do you come from Bolton? I knew a Lord who went to the High School about '82-'83 in Mason's time.

If you are a member of the Guild, see Moors, the Secretary. Put the whole case before him & I certainly would clear myself if I were you – even at the expense of *Mount Temple* man – who doesn't seem to have behaved very nicely.

I certainly sympathise with you & hope to hear better news soon.

In meantime,

Believe me,

Yours sincerely,

A.H. Rostron

Later in the year, Lord also received a letter from the senior surviving officer of the *Titanic*, Charles Herbert Lightoller, to whom he had also sent a copy of the Baker missive:

On board RMS *Majestic*.
December 16th 1912

Dear Capt. Lord,

We have so little time at home that my letters have to wait till I get to sea. I have read your enclosure with great interest – it certainly does seem extraordinary. All the same those *Mount Temple* chaps might have volunteered the information when it would have been of some use to you …

With regard to the steamer seen – I saw a light about two points on the port bow & could not say whether it was one or two mast head lights or [a] stern light – but it seemed there about 5 or 6 miles away. I did not pay much attention to it beyond calling the pass.rs' attention to it – for their assurance.

I really do hope you will be able to clear the matter up. As to the BT [Board of Trade], their attitude towards you is as inexplicable as in many other things – I don't hold any brief for them.

Wishing you success.

Believe me,

sincerely yours,

C.H. Lightoller

Titanic second officer Charles Herbert Lightoller, second left, on his arrival in Liverpool in
May 1912 after disembarking the *Adriatic*. This *Daily Sketch* photograph shows him beside an
advertisement for Canadian Pacific steamship services to Canada.

Lightoller refers above to the mystery ship, having been asked by Lord, and emphasises once
again how close she came, and how he calmed passengers by indicating to them that rescue was
imminent. The identity of that vessel is all the more important to establish, given that her very
appearance may have impeded the filling of lifeboats and led ultimately to greater loss of life
than should otherwise have been the case. It was false assurance.

But Lightoller had another point. Not one of the *Mount Temple* officers on the voyage in
question had come forward to support what the letter said. It is also clear that a few had instead
signed a telegram in their Captain's support when the furore first broke.

But Captain Lord was forging ahead, taking Rostron's advice about his professional
association before it had even been offered. On August 27, he laid the *Mount Temple* claims
before the Board of Trade in an official communication through the Mercantile Marine Services
Association (MMSA), of which he was a member, the missive signed by its secretary, Charles
Grylls.

The Board's immediate internal reaction to this extraordinary development, the accusation of
another ship, is visible in the file to this day. There appears to be a trace of alarm in the official
scrawl that declares: 'This must be kept 'secret' for the present.' The handwriting is that of
Walter J. Howell, no less a figure than the head of the Board of Trade Marine Department.

It appears, meanwhile, that Captain Lord had by now met with Baker, who had imparted
fresh detail. The MMSA letter to the Board, in extract, declared:

> From information given to us in confidence, there appears to be strong grounds for stating that
> the steamer's lights seen on the *Titanic* before she foundered, and by the survivors in the boats,
> were those of the s.s. *Mount Temple* and not the *Californian*.
>
> The only witnesses called from the *Mount Temple* were the Captain and the Marconi
> operator. Had the Officers of that vessel been called, we are informed that they would have
> given remarkable evidence as to having seen the distress signals, the lights of the boats of the
> *Titanic*, and the ship herself.
>
> Knowing by wireless the *Titanic*'s predicament, the Officers were exceedingly anxious to
> go to her assistance, and their feeling against the Master of the ship because he would not do
> so at once was very strong, so much so that it is stated they refused to sit at the head of the
> dining table with him.
>
> In view of the serious nature of these allegations, and in justice to Captain Lord of the
> *Californian*, who has suffered the loss of his position as a result of Lord Mersey's strictures and
> the public opinion against him, we feel this matter should be cleared up if possible, and as the

Mount Temple is due in London about the end of the week, we would suggest that statements should be taken from Chief Officer Sergeant; 2nd Officer Heild; 4th Officer Thomson; Chief Engineer Gillette, and Mr Roberts, Surgeon, or other witnesses of the *Mount Temple*.

I shall be glad to know whether, having regard to the importance of the matter, the Board of Trade will consider the advisability of taking sworn statements from the Officers of the *Mount Temple* upon her arrival.

I am told that one of the Officers was so outspoken in his condemnation of the inaction of the Captain that he has been transferred to an appointment in the Owner's service in Canada. I give this information for what it is worth, and in strict confidence.

I am, yours faithfully, etc.

It appears likely that Lord brought Baker to meet secretary Grylls, as the latter – a 46-year-od former journalist and author – would certainly have wanted to check his facts before embarking on the serious step of taking the august Board of Trade to task.

Only Baker could know (and only by talking to his fellow *Mount Temple* officers) that the man whose departure made necessary his own transfer from the *Empress of Britain*, had been 'outspoken in his condemnation' of the Captain. That man was former third officer A.H. Notley.

Again the concern and near-rebellious state of the officers is underlined, even if loose language suggests that Master and mates would all usually have crowded the head of the dining table while leaving the rest of it free. More seriously, the allegations are of the full set – *Titanic*'s rockets seen, the lights in her lifeboats seen (all of the lifeboats had lights, although only one burned green flares) and the ship herself seen.

Baker is being held in strategic reserve and is not named, although Captain Lord shortly afterwards commented in correspondence with his local MP: 'I took the liberty of showing your letter to Mr Baker. He says he is quite willing to give evidence at any time.'

Of course Baker's evidence could only ever be hearsay – he was not aboard the *Mount Temple* on the night in question – and the hope was that the Board of Trade would obtain its own direct corroboration.

The names suggested are illustrative (Baker said his original information came from 'the officers and others') but may be a guide as to some of the persons from whom information was obtained by him. Thomson, however, was not on either crossing, and neither was Roberts, the new surgeon.

But realisation that the original ship's surgeon had moved on, and therefore might be more independent, led to an effort to communicate with him. A similar initiative was launched with Notley.

William Arthur Bailey was the doctor who had made all the *Titanic* preparations, according to Baker's letter, which in the same breath mentioned crew 'watching her lights,' suggesting that Baker had not only spoken of the matter with Bailey on the homeward trip, but that the doctor himself may have witnessed what was happening on the sea.

In due course Baker wrote Dr Bailey a letter (as did Captain Lord):

Town Green,
near Ormskirk
Lancashire
Sept 15th 1912

Dear Doc

Just a few lines to see how you are getting along as I hear that you are in the P. & O. I called the other day on your brother to get your address, but he was out at the time but got it later from him. I can tell you I was very glad to hear you had got in a good ship & away from that old 'bounder' Moore; but I know you would be sorry to leave the others. I hear at the office that Gillett [Chief Engineer] was getting married this trip, so I called upon him, but he was away. I should so like to have seen you, for I wanted to have a chat with you re that *Titanic* affair. I may say that Captain Lord of the *Californian* is an <u>old friend</u> of <u>mine</u> & I know that from what you fellows told me re the affair that a great act of injustice has been done to him, and if only you fellow's [sic] had been called upon at the time to give evidence the whole story would have come out and thus old 'swine' Moore would have been place [sic] in the position that my friend Captain Lord is now in, which, as you know, Moore fully deserves.

Now Old Man, I know that it is not right to ask the other fellows in the ship to tell Capt Lord what happened on that night when you saw her lights, for they would be afraid of getting the sack, but as you are out of the company, & independent of them, a full description of what you saw & heard & did, on the night you received the S.O.S. call, would greatly benefit Capt Lord & would practically reinstate him again with his owners, who had had to ask him to resign simply on account of public <u>opinion only</u>.

I enclose you a cutting from the *Journal of Commerce* which will show you what the public think of the *Californian* being made the scapegoat.

I know you will do this for my sake Old Man as it means a lot to my friend, for it will only require the slightest reasons made to them to give them an excuse of reinstating a man that they are loath to think ill of, and which [sic] they had ~~to sack~~ through public opinion & Lord Mersey's report to ask to resign. Capt Lord is writing you himself, and if you will give him the information I ask here you will be doing a great act of kindness, not only to him but myself also as he is my friend.

W.H. Baker

This letter was written eleven days after the Board of Trade had replied dismissively to Secretary Grylls and the MMSA, having failed to seek statements from anyone on the *Mount Temple* in her intervening landfall.

Sir Robert Ellis Cunliffe, solicitor to the Board of Trade had been asked internally for comments on the MMSA submission, and quickly noted that the accusations were expressed in 'confidential' terms, which was probably just a legal precaution on Grylls' part.

The bureaucracy's law adviser agreed with the somewhat self-serving opinion of Sir Walter Howell that 'the Board could scarcely take action in so grave a matter on information given in strict confidence,' and it was the obvious duty of any persons in a position to throw light on the issue to communicate directly with the Board.

That much was said in reply. But Cunliffe also advised the Board, for its own consideration only, and prior to the response being sent: 'It is doubtful whether any purpose would be served by giving any further hint of the possibility of action on our part if we did receive direct evidence. It is very difficult to see what we could possibly do at this stage.'

On the face of it, in the reply to Grylls, Lord and Baker, officialdom was pretending to seek what it expressly did not want. If officers of the *Mount Temple* had not come forward directly, the Board of Trade made sure to keep well away from them.

Meanwhile the Board of Trade's solicitor was earnestly combing the files and transcripts in a defensive operation, the thrust of which would be that the addition of the *Mount Temple* would not subtract a failure to respond to rockets on the part of the *Californian*, although it was perfectly appreciated by everyone that the distinct insinuation of the British inquiry report was that Captain Lord's vessel had been the mystery ship, seen within five miles of *Titanic*.

In the course of a detailed analysis (document M31921 at the UK national archives), Cunliffe addressed 'rumours that people on board' the *Mount Temple* 'seemed to think that at some time she saw lights.' But then he entered in brackets his own opinion – '(probably the flares from the boats in the water)' – which should immediately have made the Canadian Pacific vessel a prime case for investigation.

Now as I have stated before whatever may be said

against the Captain of the "MOUNT TEMPLE" by those on

board, and there are rumours that people on board seemed

to think that at some time she saw lights (probably the
and that she did not do all she could to get to the Titanic
flares from the boats in the water) as I am not able to

Above: The Board of Trade's solicitor, R. Ellis Cunliffe, opined in an internal note that lights seen by the *Mount Temple* were 'probably' flares from *Titanic* lifeboats.

Left: Sir Robert Ellis Cunliffe, solicitor to the Board of Trade, saw the reputational danger of entertaining any claims about the *Mount Temple*. Nonetheless he was prepared to assume she could have seen the flares of lifeboats in the water.

The Board of Trade solicitor conceded the opinions of those on board *Mount Temple* that their ship 'did not do all she could to get to the *Titanic*,' but it was unclear on what he was basing his opinions – unless the Board had press clippings of what was variously alleged in North America in addition to the letter it had received.

He concluded that whether Moore omitted to do something he ought to have done 'may be a matter for further enquiry,' but added that he did not see how it could help Captain Lord, which was to ignore completely the wider point. Cunliffe also hopelessly misunderstood the evidence and thought it was being contended that the *Mount Temple* was on the east side of the ice barrier, being the steamer nearby to the *Californian* when the latter lay stopped, whereas Captain Moore's vessel was much further south (just as the *Titanic* was much further south) and to the west side of the icefield when seen the next morning.

Despite the admission that the claims might be 'a matter for further enquiry,' the Board was determined to do nothing. Cunliffe was of the impression that wireless operator Durrant had testified in America (he had not), and found it hard to believe that both Moore and Durrant would have given evidence in London that would have amounted to 'a tissue of lies' if the contrary allegations were correct.

Cunliffe commented in his analysis that if there were any allegations which persons on board *Mount Temple* desired to make against the Captain, 'or any evidence which they thought ought to be ('have been' crossed out) before the Court in England, they clearly ought to have volunteered to have come forward as witnesses on the subject.'

But this ignores two salient points. The first is that those passengers making the allegations were now resident in the United States or Canada, and impecunious after their crossing; furthermore, Lord Mersey in his inquiry had specifically ruled out the taking of evidence on commission from emigrant *Titanic* survivors in their new land, indicating they would not be heard unless they bodily presented themselves in Britain (and perhaps not even then, as they would have to be called by the Attorney General, leading the case for the Board of Trade, who had unique powers in the presentation of witnesses.)

Secondly, any crew members in Britain – and many had deserted or departed in Canada – were naturally dependent for their livelihoods on the vessel, and the idea that they would jeopardise their positions by taking crusading action to the steps of the court in London was pious in the extreme. It is hard to believe the solicitor was so naïve in relation to what considerations occupy the minds of men of low station in life, but if crewmen were cynical or despairing of being understood – much less taken seriously – by officialdom, he had just proven their point.

A sensitive Board would have been proactive on the matter, and sought to have taken statements from *Mount Temple* crew on landfall, if establishing the truth was actually its first priority. The presence of investigators at the docks would have given comfort and reassurance to any men with tales to tell. As it was, the Board of Trade had received serious allegations from a serious body, the Mercantile Marine Services Association, and was instead performing gymnastics in an effort to avoid all of the implications.

On careful reading and re-reading of the MMSA letter, it can be surmised what the Board of Trade privately concluded after its receipt. It would have looked to Cunliffe and Howell from the letter's phrasing that while the MMSA had 'information,' it was also seeking corroboration of this material from the officers of the *Mount Temple*. Therefore the MMSA likely only had claims from a couple of ordinary crewmen, and did not have anything from navigating officers aboard. In this scenario, any low-level assertions could assuredly be resisted by authority.

Yet it might also be assuming too much to expect that the MMSA had actual *Mount Temple* evidence, and its 'information' could have been hearsay from what had appeared in the papers, although only the Quitzrau material had been covered in Britain, and then briefly. Suspecting a possible bluff or fishing expedition, Cunliffe somehow managed to place the onus on the Leyland Line (operators of *Californian*). They 'should have produced evidence' if they had any, he wrote, and 'could produce this now.'

This internal legal briefing demonstrates clearly that the Board of Trade was thus viewing the entire case through the prism of the court's condemnation of the *Californian*, which it was determined to shield at all costs.

The letter that replied to the MMSA gambled that anonymous informants would not have the resolve and fortitude to present themselves directly before the Board, and it sweetly told Grylls: 'Perhaps you would suggest this to them.' But it also added, in the very same paragraph, and in a sterner tone: 'If any persons considered themselves in a position to throw light on the circumstances attending the unfortunate disaster, it was their obvious duty to communicate with the Board of Trade before the conclusion of the inquiry.' Anyone who came forward could thus expect to have this thrown in their face, and their honour suspected.

Captain Lord, in his own case, badly needed someone to come forward to back up Baker, who quite appreciated the position. Both thus wrote to Dr Bailey, and meanwhile the vital third officer, A.H. Notley, was soon expected home. Persons making claims in North America were assuredly out of reach, but the larger prize – as they had alerted the Board of Trade – lay with the navigating officers.

For the moment however, Lord was only left with Baker. A pleasant man, who had signalled his willingness to give evidence, he had been able to convince the secretary of the MMSA of his veracity and bona fides. But what character assessment of him may be formed by the modern reader?

In a letter to his MP in October, Lord had mentioned that Baker was available to be contacted at his family address in Ormskirk, but that he would be leaving on another voyage later that month. In the manifest of this sailing (from Southampton, aboard the White Star liner *Oceanic*) on October 30, 1912, can be seen Baker's name and address, and his identification as a ship's officer. He was travelling as a passenger, bound to join another vessel in New York – and immediately preceding his name in the manifest is that of Courtenay Bennett, the British Consul General in that city, along with his wife and daughter.

Bennett played a role in taking depositions from crew survivors of the *Titanic* in a rearguard action mounted by his Government in response to the American decision to enquire into the circumstances of the wreck, and was knighted the next year. He would have made an interesting partner if Baker had managed to engage him in conversation, and Bennett might have learned something too.

The manifest shows Baker as 42, with a light complexion, fair hair and blue eyes. He had a small circle tattoo on his left wrist, which may have been a *Conway* boy rite from many years before. A father of five, he had been decorated in the routine way for Boer War service and had assisted in the rescue of *Helvetia* passengers, but something much more dramatic was to come …

A year later, while the steamer *Volturno* of London was in the North Atlantic, a fire broke out in the forward part of the ship. It was October 9, 1913, and the blaze could not be subdued, leading to the *Volturno* transmitting an SOS as she became wreathed in smoke.

Left: Courtenay Bennett, the HMG Consul in New York at the time of the *Titanic* sinking in 1912.

Below: The *Volturno* ablaze in mid-ocean in 1913, with the Leyland liner *Asian* in the background. Picture taken by former *Mount Temple* replacement officer William Henry Baker.

William Henry Baker, marked with an 'x,' far right, in a photograph taken of mercantile marine officers decorated for bravery by the King. The *Liverpool Courier*, October 2, 1915.

Eleven vessels responded to the distress, including the British ships *Carmania, Narragansett, Rappahannock, Devonian, Minneapolis* and *Asian*. William Henry Baker was serving under Captain Alfred Trant as second officer of the *Devonian*, of the Leyland Line. The other vessels that responded comprised the *Czar* of Libau, the *Seydlitz* and *Grosser Kurfürst* of Bremen, the *Kroonland* of New York, and *La Touraine* of Le Havre.

THE KING HONOURS RNR OFFICER – SEQUEL TO THE *VOLTURNO* DISASTER

A sequel was enacted to the terrible *Volturno* disaster at Buckingham Palace this week, when King George conferred the honour on Lieut. W.H. Baker, R.N.R., of pinning on his breast the Board of Trade Life-Saving Medal for his gallant act in assisting at rescuing 41 women and children from the steamer *Volturno*, which was on fire in the North Atlantic.

The steamer, which was outward bound from Holland for the United States, caught fire in mid-Atlantic after a series of explosions. She was carrying a large number of passengers of the emigrant class, and mostly foreigners. Although every endeavour was employed, and many daring deeds were done, with a view of dominating the fire, it was all to no purpose, and the fire spread fore and aft the ship.

The state of panic into which the poor passengers were thrown can well be imagined. A gale of wind with the high sea added to the difficulties of the critical situation. Wireless messages were sent out over the ocean for help, and these were picked up by several steamers, all of which hastened to the scene of disaster.

Amongst others that arrived on the scene was the Leyland liner *Devonian*, and, although other vessels had previously arrived, a boat from the *Devonian* was the first to be engaged in the rescue work. This boat was in charge of the second officer, Mr W.H. Baker, who with great skill and perseverance in the handling of his boat succeeded in making two trips between the burning ship and the *Devonian*, in which he was successful in taking off 41 women and children and safely getting them on board his own ship.

Considering the great difficulties that had to be contended with in handling a small boat in a turbulent sea, with the respective vessels rolling heavily in the trough of the sea, it was a brave and gallant act that Lieut. Baker and his boat's crew could well be proud of, and the honour conferred on Lieut. Baker was certainly not lightly won.

For this service Lieut. Baker has already been presented in New York with a silver life-saving medal, a silver-mounted barometer and illuminated address. He was also the recipient of a handsome pair of binoculars from the British Government, and a silver tea service from the owners of the *Devonian*.

The Liverpool Shipwreck and Humane Society also conferred their silver medal on Lieut. Baker. His last and greatest honour from the King's hands, pinned on his country's uniform, is one that will ever be remembered and highly prized by Lieut. Baker, and if need be, will always be an incentive to carry out every duty.

(*Liverpool Echo*, Saturday October 2, 1915)

Baker's descendants retain these awards. The Naval binoculars, made by Troughton & Simms of 138 Fleet Street, carry this inscription:

Presented by the British Government to William H. Baker, Second Mate of the Steamship *Devonian* of Liverpool, in acknowledgement of his humanity and kindness to the shipwrecked crew and passengers of the steamship *Volturno* of London, which was burned in the North Atlantic Ocean on 9th October 1913.

His Board of Trade Life-Saving Medal, deeply ironic in view of its treatment of matters pointed out to them at his instigation, is cited to be for 'various acts of bravery.' A separate inscribed silver plate reads:

Above: W. H. Baker, possibly taken aboard his wartime command *Tacsonia*

Left: Liverpool Echo clipping relating Baker's decoration by the King for heroic conduct during the burning of the *Volturno* in 1913.

Presented by the Liverpool Shipwreck and Humane Society to 2nd Officer W.H. Baker of the S.S. *Devonian* for gallant service in the lifeboat at the rescue of 56 passengers of the S.S. *Volturno* on fire in mid-Atlantic 10th October 1913. [The date given does not correspond with the one on the presentation box of binoculars.]

The New York barometer recognises 'his gallant service in the lifeboat at the rescue of 56 passengers of the S.S *Volturno*, on fire in the mid Atlantic on 10th October 1913. By the time of the presentation by the King, war had broken out. Baker, as a Royal Naval Reserve officer, found himself called up and tasked with helping to ensure, through armed trawler patrols, the security of the port of Liverpool.

His granddaughter retains an original telegram from the Admiralty to the Senior Naval Officer at Liverpool, asking him to 'report whether Lieutenant W.H. Baker RNR, trawler Tacsonia, can attend presentation of Board of Trade medals at Buckingham Palace ... ' etc.

Baker's own account of the rescue work was carried in the Liverpool *Echo* of October 14, 1913:

Second officer Baker, who was in charge of the first boat to rescue passengers from the *Volturno*, related a graphic story to a representative of the *Echo*.

'Early on the morning following our arrival on the scene of the disaster,' said second officer Baker, 'I determined to make an attempt to reach the burning vessel. 'Neck or nothing, let us go,' I said to the men, and a crew of eight men agreed to put out on a boisterous sea, and amidst obviously perilous conditions.

'When we were near to the vessel we could see that there would be a rush to escape. We called out to those in charge to keep back the men, who were pressing forwards, and to let us have the women and the children first.'

Four [*Volturno*] officers then used their fists to drive the men back, and some of them went down like ninepins. For a time the women were afraid to jump. They were terrified. Children were then thrown in by their parents.

Later on the women began to drop into the boat from a height of twenty or thirty feet, but the distance varied from the fact that a heavy sea was running and the lifeboat rocked constantly. Baker and his heroic crew made two journeys in all, and they were able to save forty-one women and children, together with the father of five of the children.

This man, Mr. Baker explained, had helped to get his wife and family into the boat and when they had disappeared down the side, he went back to the rest of the men on the deck. 'My man, my man!' shouted the woman, pathetically. 'Is that your husband?' asked the officer.

'I had seen what he had done, and it was because he deserved a reward for his splendid conduct, first in helping the people in, and then stepping back, apparently to meet his fate, that I insisted he alone of the men should come off then.'

When Baker's example was seen there was an immediate attempt on the part of the other liners to send their boats, and at one time there was a flotilla of these alongside the *Volturno*. The work was carried on with the most considerable danger. 'Sparks were flying, the heat of the sides of the vessel was intense and the smoke was blinding.'

From time to time, some relict of the fire, such as a disjointed derrick or a piece of the funnel, would tumble into the water, and might easily have injured rescuers and rescued alike. Some of the children actually did alight on their head, and one little one, whose legs struck the bulwarks was saved by the gallantry of one of the sailors.

'On the *Volturno*,' added second officer Baker, 'we could see the smoke coming up between the beams of the deck, and the men were almost standing in the flames. During the night, the scene was horrible. Shrieking was continuous, and several of the women held up their babies and outlined them in the glare, and begged of us to come and rescue them ...'

Later in the war Baker found himself in Halifax, N.S., where convoys were marshalled in the Bedford basin before being escorted across the Atlantic. Baker, a highly talented photographer, took pictures of the aftermath of the Halifax explosion of December 6, 1917, when the explosive-packed *Mont Blanc*, ultimately bound for war-torn Europe, collided with the *Imo* (formerly the White Star Line's *Runic*) triggering the biggest man-made blast before Hiroshima. Whole swathes of the city were reduced to matchwood. Killed in the blast was Baker's former Master in the *Empress of Britain*, James A. Murray, the port's senior assistant convoy officer. Lt Commander Murray died when his tug *Hilford* was flung from the harbour over two wharves to be smashed amid a lumber pile on pier 9.

Baker was also an accomplished watercolourist and cartoonist, and his sense of service and devotion to duty ultimately extended to his joining the Home Guard in 1940 at the age of seventy. He also gave a son to that war – David Marion Baker, known as 'Dick,' who was killed while Commander of the HMS *Patia*, an armed catapult ship that carried a Fleet Air Arm fighter. Attempting to swim back to the ship to retrieve the vessel's log, he was killed by enemy aircraft fire after the ship had been bombed in April 1941 off Northumberland. He was awarded a posthumous medal.

Like father, like son: D.M.B. Baker had already accumulated the Royal Decoration, as well as the Liverpool Shipwreck and Humane Society Medal, a Shipwreck and Mariners' Royal Benevolent Society Medal, and the Board of Trade Bronze Medal. He was aged 44 when he died, on April 27, 1941, one of 40 men who were lost in the sinking, just as 103 passengers and 30 officers and crew had died in peacetime aboard the *Volturno*.

Commander Baker's obituary noted that he had chosen the Merchant Navy for his career, 'as his father did before him,' and had also served in the Leyland Line. On the outbreak of the Great War he joined the Royal Navy, and in peacetime moved to the Elder Fyffe Line, becoming one of their chief officers.

Recalled to the Royal Navy on the outbreak of the present war, he soon rose to the rank of Commander, and for some time past he had been commodore of convoys, being at length given the command on an auxiliary cruiser. He had had the distinction of being mentioned in dispatches for his fine work with convoys. He had also had the honour, whilst in the Merchant Navy, of being decorated by the King with what is regarded as the Victoria Cross of that Service for gallantry in saving life at sea – a decoration also awarded to his father for his gallantry on the occasion of the disaster to the liner *Volturno* many years ago.

William Henry Baker was greatly affected by the death of his son, having lost his wife in 1938, but he soldiered on. Late in life, having spent more than half a century at sea and risen to command, he developed a nasty case of gangrene in his right leg.

The death certificate shows the 85-year-old retired Master Mariner passed away on Friday December 2, 1955, at Merton Road in Bootle, Liverpool, the home of one of his children. He died of congestive heart failure and chronic hardening of the arteries.

Acknowledged as a man of 'various acts of bravery' by the Board of Trade, it had also been courageous and typically selfless of W.H. Baker to come to the aid of Captain Lord of the *Californian* in 1912 when the latter had been cast adrift.

It is clear that Baker, who signalled his willingness to give evidence, could not have been inventing his story to Lord, which was subsequently conveyed to Charles Grylls and from him to the Board of Trade. It can only have been true that Baker was indeed told these allegations on the *Mount Temple* by 'officers and others.'

The only remaining question is whether those matters, which he conscientiously passed on, were themselves an accurate account of what had transpired on Captain Moore's ship that fateful night.

Counsel for Captain Moore: No questions, but I note that Mr Baker's ocean fare in October 1912 was paid for by F. Leyland & Co, on his way to join their ship, s.s. *Antillian*. He would remain with this company for the rest of his career. It occurs as a possibility that he was being rewarded by the Leyland company for something that was of use to them. No doubt he had by this stage burnt his boats with the Canadian Pacific.

William Henry Baker later in his career

MEN IN A DILEMMA

THE WAITING W.H. Baker duly received a reply from William Arthur Bailey, the ship's surgeon of the *Mount Temple* on the *Titanic* trip:

P. & O. S.S. *PERSIA*
Marseilles,
Sept. 19th 1912

My dear Baker,

I was much surprised to receive your letter & glad to know you are well.

As your letter is practically full of appeal on behalf of Captain Lord, what value would an unprofessional & worthless expression of details as to what occurred on the *Mount Temple* be in the face of what has been found.

It is clearly Captain Lord's best plan to seek his evidence from Notley at Montreal & the officers who were on the ship at the time who saw certain things & freely discussed matters together; why come to ask me who doesn't know the blunt from the sharp end of a ship?

I was sorry to leave the fellows, very much indeed, & hope Noel will be very happy in the future, but this is surely a promotion & I am fortunate to have been able to secure such a good billet. Up to the present everything has been very pleasant, & although the work is much harder & more responsible, I have tried my best to fill it properly.

I expected a group photo of me of the Specials you took at Halifax, but haven't heard from you as I hoped & wished.

Hoping you are going very strong & in the best of good health.

Wishing you the best of all possible good luck.

Yours very sincerely

W.A. Bailey

Bailey's letter expresses familiarity and friendship with Baker, even though they spent just one crossing together. His second paragraph, while excusing himself from involvement, concedes that there are 'details as to what occurred on the *Mount Temple*' available to be disclosed, except that it is already obvious that he will not be the man to disclose them.

The ship's surgeon indicates that there is evidence to be obtained from Notley, the third officer who left the ship in Canada and did not return to Britain with Captain Moore. That departure becomes linked to whatever it was that went on.

Furthermore Bailey also points to the 'officers who were on the ship at the time,' and becomes the latest in a string of persons who suggest that the officers of the *Mount Temple* are crucial witnesses to the whole affair. And now the letter spells out, albeit in general terms, that they 'saw certain things.'

Captain Moore, however, denies seeing anything of relevance all night, and testified to that effect.

There is a whiff of mutinous feeling in the accompanying phrase that these officers – and Bailey makes no exclusions from the four officers serving under Moore – 'freely discussed matters together.' Presumably it may also have been done at whatever dining table they took themselves to, after leaving Moore alone at meals by the MMSA allegation.

William Arthur Bailey, ship's surgeon of the *Mount Temple*, admitted in writing that other officers 'saw certain things.'

But Bailey divorces himself from the matter again, and drifts into small talk, responding to the report in Baker's letter that the chief engineer, Noel Gillet, was getting married. He clearly has no intention of jeopardising his 'good billet,' although he is now with the P&O Line and independent of Canadian Pacific.

The doctor also mentions group photographs, presumably of crew, taken by the camera-adept Baker at Halifax, which must have been taken in daylight, possibly when mariners were mixing in town. Baker wrote to Lord that he was taken out of the *Empress of Britain* at 'ten minutes' notice,' while the *Mount Temple* sailed twenty minutes after Moore and Durrant rejoined her, departing at 11.20pm. These photographs are now lost.

On the same day, Dr Bailey wrote a similar letter to Captain Lord, who had equally been trying to enlist his assistance:

P. & O. S.S. *PERSIA*
Marseilles,
Sept. 19ᵗʰ '12

Captain Lord
Dear Sir,
    I beg to acknowledge receipt of your letter of the 15ᵗʰ, just received.
    Not being a navigating officer, no information I could give would, in the circumstances, be of the slightest use to you, when all the evidences as to what occurred on the *Mount Temple* on the morning of the *Titanic* catastrophe are close to you in the officers of that ship, and now in the service of the C.P.R.
    These might, if obtained, be valuable to your cause. I request this letter to be privileged.
    I am
        Yours truly,
        W.A. Bailey.

This note is economical, and much more formal in tone. Bailey leaves open the possibility that he could, in theory, supply information, but suggests that he would be a worthless witness as he had no navigational qualifications. As an excuse, it lacks enough fibre to be even called threadbare, and ignores the passenger evidence that was extensively heard in the American inquiry – although not, it should be pointed out, at the inquiry convened in Britain, which ignored passengers completely, apart from the Managing Director of the White Star Line, and

The P & O liner *Persia*, aboard which Dr William Arthur Bailey found 'a good berth' following his *Titanic* voyage with Captain Moore

a First Class aristocratic couple who sought to be heard as they believed society gossips were sullying their reputation, a good name that Lord Mersey vigorously upheld in his final report, while also making it clear that shipowner J. Bruce Ismay had nothing to reproach himself for.

Bailey again points to the officers of the *Mount Temple*, although adding superfluously that they are in the service of the CPR Line. It was for that very reason that Lord and Bailey had written to Dr Bailey in the first place. Any evidences obtained, hints the surgeon, might be 'valuable to your cause.' Finally, in acknowledgment that something indeed transpired on the ship that night (the phrase 'what occurred on the *Mount Temple*' appears in both letters), he requests his deflective response to be privileged, or in other words, kept secret. It is thus, at best, a nod of encouragement that there is material to be mined.

What is also noticeable is that, while Bailey complains to Baker about not being sent a photo the latter might have promised him, he expressly does not take issue with Baker's description of Captain Moore to him in the initial approach. Baker called Moore a 'bounder' and a 'swine,' and suggested he 'fully deserves' the public opprobrium that had been heaped on Captain Lord, whose vessel had been subtly conveyed to the public as being the mystery ship.

Not only did Dr Bailey, who worked closely with Moore by the signs of the official log, not take issue with this character detraction of the Master of that ship by someone who had made only a single crossing with him – unlike Bailey, who had made several round-trip voyages – but neither did he dispute the obvious suggestion that it was the *Mount Temple* herself that was the mystery ship. At its most charitable interpretation, Dr Bailey simply ignored the point, if his silence on the matter was not to be taken as conceding it.

Yet he responded to the specific point made by Baker – that Bailey would be glad to get out of the ship, away from bounder Moore, but sorry to leave the others – by answering that he was indeed 'very sorry to leave the fellows,' meaning his peer group. He omits the Captain from those he was sorry to leave. The tacit agreement is obvious. Bailey is admitting, in a coded way, that he shares a very low opinion of the Master of his former ship. The indications, also, are that the Master was on one side and 'the fellows' were on the other.

Baker had asked Bailey to tell what 'you fellows' had witnessed, hoping for a chronology of what had happened on the night that 'you saw her lights.' This statement is clearly put to Bailey. The doctor does not write back and say 'I saw no lights,' or that the lights seen were not those of the *Titanic*. The subtext of Dr Bailey's letters to both William Henry Baker, with whom he is still friendly, and to Captain Lord, to whom he writes in more circumspect tones, is 'Yes, the *Titanic* lights were seen' and there is more to be uncovered. While extricating himself from the dilemma, he has at least written back to Captain Lord, whom he presumably has never met.

When one looks past the personal refusal, it can be seen that Dr William Arthur Bailey is trying, in however limited a way, to be helpful.

Finally, there is the open question of why Dr Bailey left the *Mount Temple* himself. Of course, restless seafarers regularly moved from ship to ship, but surgeons were more likely to stay in a 'good billet.' Bailey wrote to Baker that he was 'fortunate' to have found one on the *Persia*, even though the work was much harder.

DR. WILLIAM ARTHUR BAILEY (1876-1948)

Bailey was born in St Helens, Lancashire on July 10, 1876. He was aged 23 in the 1901 census, when appearing as a medical assistant in Wigan. Aged 35 in April 1912, he gives a Liverpool address in the *Mount Temple* crew agreement of 437 West Derby Rd.

Bailey's brother Matthias (named after their father) was seven years his senior, and preceded him into medicine, qualifying in 1896. In the 1901 census, Matthias Bailey is described as a ship's surgeon of the White Star Line.

William Arthur Bailey had himself qualified as a member of the Royal College of Surgeons in 1900, accomplishing his prized recognitions in quicker time than his elder brother, who was already a medical student by the 1891 census.

But the younger Bailey initially stayed ashore. He became Assistant Surgeon at the old Northern Dispensary in Liverpool, and was later the House Physician at the. Ladies' Charity & Lying-in Hospital in the city. Soon he was back at the Northern, this time as the House Surgeon.

William Arthur Bailey married Florence Lomax at Huyton parish church on his 31st birthday, July 10, 1907. He was a physician, residing at 69 Church St, St Helens, son of Matthias Bailey, cattle dealer. She was 25, residing at Fern Hill, Huyton, the daughter of the wealthy George Edward Lomax, colliery proprietor.

But Florence Bailey died just two years later, having turned 28. Bereft, at the end of 1909, Dr Bailey went to sea to get over the death of his wife. The life gradually suited him as it had his brother – who seems have been irked by William's imitative actions – and he found himself on the North Atlantic three years later.

After the *Persia* (sunk in World War One, with Lord Mersey's son aboard, who survived), Bailey stayed with the P&O Line in the *Malwa*, and in peacetime was to be found on other of the company's vessels making the Australian run.

He served on the *Morea* from 1919-21, and then switched to the *Mantua*. It was on the latter that he met the woman who was to become his second wife. She was 23, he 45 – virtually double her age.

Dorothy Alcock sailed from Melbourne to Britain on the *Mantua* in May 1922, along with her family. Her father was the brilliant engineer and inventor Alfred Upton Alcock, who was credited with bringing electric light to Melbourne and one of whose 'contraptions' is said to have enabled the development of the hovercraft.

The unlikely couple fell in love on the sailing, although how Alfred felt about his eldest daughter's liaison with a man just eleven years his junior is unclear. Dr Bailey, it is safe to vouchsafe, was unaware that Alcock, in addition to designing a new ship's telegraph system, had also spent four years in England attempting to perfect artillery range-finding for the War Office.

Dr William Arthur Bailey, widower, married Dorothy on December 1, 1922 at Moseley Parish Church in Kings Norton, Birmingham. Thereafter Bailey gave up the sea, and the couple were to be found living at the romantic-sounding Belle Walk in the suburb of Moseley.

But any parental misgivings were to be proved right, and the couple split within a few years, having no children. Bailey now moved to Cheltenham and later to Sheffield, while his wife lived in London.

After World War II, William Arthur Bailey returned to London while suffering from cancer of the bile duct, and there appears to have been a limited reconciliation with his spouse. Aged 71, a retired medical practitioner, he died on May 27, 1948 at University College Hospital in London.

The informant on the death certificate, possibly thousands of which Bailey had signed in his own career, was his widow, Dorothy Bailey, of Lovelace Gardens, Surbiton, Surrey. She was 49, and shared the house with her parents.

Bailey's demise made a single-line notice in the *British Medical Journal* of June 1948. His widow lived to be 96, and died on December 26, 1994 at Budleigh Salterton Hospital, Exeter. She was a retired librarian, but there was never anything in writing left behind about Bailey's involvement with the *Titanic* disaster.

What does survive, in a sheaf of documents compiled by the MMSA on Captain Lord's behalf, and now in the custody of the Merseyside Maritime Museum, is a letter sent by William Arthur's brother – Dr Matthias Bailey – to the former Captain of the *Californian* shortly before Christmas 1912:

[Dr.] Matthias Bailey
December 14, 1912

Dear Sir: I regret you called and found me 'not in.'

I may say I & my wife have not heard any tidings of my brother;
We do not even know if he is on the P and O *Persia* & cannot obtain any definite news of him. I regret when I saw you I did not, in confidence, inform you that there had been family trouble; & not being friendly we cannot get in communication with him.

I regret missing you when you called last time; my hours certainly are 'up to' 12 o'clock; but these certain few weeks (epidemic influenza etc) I may times leave meeting before; that is the reason, Anything I can do, let me know. If you intend calling again, drop me a line; – notify me – I will see you any time.

If I am not at home just then you can certainly wait a few minutes or so for my return. I may say, if you will allow me, you are not misjudged altogether. To my knowledge the sea faring community <u>Know</u> the true facts of the case.

I wish I could help you, and if I had been friendly with my brother I would have done my utmost to assist you in that direction.

I can say this: I have been told by an officer on the *Mount Temple*: distress signals were observed & preparations made, etc. I may be mistaken, but they were 10 miles away, you were 25.

Yours very truly,

M. Bailey

Counsel for Captain Moore: 'Before passing from Dr Bailey himself, I trust I may be allowed to point out that a William Bailey, surgeon, 32, travelled as a crew member aboard the P & O *Persia* to Melbourne as early as October 1909. It is therefore highly likely that he was simply renewing acquaintances with that vessel in September 1912, and not some sort of refugee from the *Mount Temple*, as the prosecution would like to portray it.'

The point is acknowledged. In turning to Dr Matthias Bailey, then, the estranged brother of the *Mount Temple* ship's surgeon, we can see that even in December 1912, Captain Lord, late of the *Californian*, was pursuing his enquiries.

Matthias Bailey's wife, whom he married in 1903 with his brother as best man, was named Elizabeth, née Smith. The source of the 'family trouble' is unknown, but may have been of relatively recent origin, it being only a few years, for instance, since William's wife had died and he had decided to go to sea.

It would seem, however, that the brothers, 'not being friendly,' were incommunicado for the whole of 1912. Accordingly, Dr William Arthur Bailey is not the source of Dr Matthias Bailey having an understanding that the seafaring community knows the true facts of the mystery ship case, as he describes it.

Matthias keeps his best wine 'til last. 'I can say this: I have been told by an officer on the *Mount Temple*: distress signals were observed … they were 10 miles away, you were 25.'

It is likely that W. H. Baker may have spoken to Matthias Bailey, but also probable that Lord mentioned the *Persia* (or showed the letter received) when he dropped by the house and spoke to Elizabeth Bailey. If Matthias had met *Mount Temple* replacement officer William Henry Baker, he would almost certainly have learned the latter's full purpose and that he was a friend of Captain Lord – as Baker expressly stated in his letter to the younger Bailey.

In such circumstances, knowing Baker was in turn closely associated with Captain Lord, it seems Matthias would have mentioned Baker by name if *he* was the officer of the *Mount Temple* from whom Matthias had learned further incriminating material.

A corollary of this – which might initially seem a paradox – is that if Matthias Bailey had been told such important claims by Baker, he would simply have no cause to mention it to Lord at all – because Lord obviously knew all that Baker had to say.

It is thus a very open question as to the identity of the 'officer on the *Mount Temple*' who told Matthias Bailey (a former ship's surgeon – apparently well known to the seafaring community) that distress signals were observed and that Captain Moore's ship was but ten miles away at the time

It is not clear whether Captain Lord in fact had any follow-up conversation with Matthias Bailey. What is known, from the account of his son, Stanley Tutton Lord, is that his father remained convinced all his life that the *Mount Temple* was the *Titanic*'s mystery ship.

Matthias was not available to tell what he knew for much longer. In early 1914 he died unexpectedly at Liverpool, aged just 44.

Counsel for Captain Moore: 'It is, one regrets to say, perfectly possible that no such '*Mount Temple* officer' existed, and that no name could thus be supplied. Matthias Bailey could have been sugaring the pill on his own inability to assist, a common enough syndrome of ingratiation.'

ARTHUR Howard Notley, who lived in London, not anywhere near Matthias Bailey, had in the meanwhile agreed to meet Captain Lord in Liverpool. The encounter apparently came about

Arthur Howard Notley, third officer of the *Mount Temple*.

through the offices of Baker, who must have written to Notley as he did to Bailey. Perhaps Lord also wrote separately, as before, but there is no reason to suppose that Notley, the officer of the *Mount Temple* who left the ship in Canada, ever had anything to do with either man previously.

Captain Lord's later stalwart champion, MMSA general secretary Leslie Harrison, would write in 1986 that Baker introduced Notley to Lord at a meeting in Wallasey, Liverpool. Harrison's book, *A Titanic Myth*, recounts:

> Over lunch one day, Lord and Notley had a long but inconclusive discussion about the whole affair. While Notley assured Lord that he would willingly give him any information that he asked for, he was not prepared to volunteer a statement to the Board of Trade in case it prejudiced his prospects within the Canadian Pacific Railway Company.
>   In the light of his own tragic experience, Lord could only confirm Notley's fears, and he accepted his decision without question.

What Notley related to Captain Lord is unknown. Lord may have respected his decision, but it is regrettable that Notley was not asked, for instance, to provide a sealed deposition only to be opened in the event of his death. Captain Lord, who could have promised only to carry around what he was told in his head, might nonetheless have sought some honourable way of leaving the issue to posterity.

The nearest bequest was a sworn affidavit, made by Captain Lord on June 25, 1959, three years after Notley's death and three years before his own –

'Through Mr Baker, I met Mr Notley, the officer referred to in Mr Baker's letters who had been taken out of the *Mount Temple*. He confirmed that he would give his evidence if called on to do so, but could not volunteer information because of the adverse effect this might have upon his future employment.'

The only public mention of Notley in 1912 remains what was reported by North American east coast newspapers when reporters flocked to the *Mount Temple* at St John in the wake of the Quitzrau allegations; 'One of the sailors, who says he was on watch Sunday night, says that he heard Third Officer Notley tell the Captain of the distress signals, and that instead of the steamer heading directly to the wreck, she steamed away on her own course, so that the lights were soon lost ...

'Third Officer Notley, who was the officer of the watch when the wireless messages were received, could not be found.'

It will be remembered however that Charles Grylls of the Mercantile Marine Services Association wrote to the Board of Trade on August 27, 1912: 'I am told that one of the Officers [Notley] was so outspoken in his condemnation of the inaction of the Captain that he has been transferred to an appointment in the owner's service in Canada. I give this information for what it is worth, and in strict confidence.'

And Dr Bailey, replying to Baker, had written: 'It is clearly Captain Lord's best plan to seek his evidence from Notley at Montreal ... [who, with others] saw certain things ... .'

The witness, his tongue stilled by death, is nonetheless now called.

ARTHUR HOWARD NOTLEY (1876-1955)

The third officer of the *Mount Temple* was aged 35 in 1912, with an address at 15 Nightingale Lane, Hornsey, London. He was finally paid off from the ship on April 29 that year.

From the *Journal of Commerce and Shipping Telegraph*, Saturday, January 2, 1937:

> Captain A.H. Notley, R.D. R.N.R., marine superintendent at Antwerp, who has been appointed to succeed Captain Dobson, has been with the company 30 years.
>   Captain Notley began his sea career at the early age of 11, as an apprentice in the 1,611-ton barque *Stracathro*, owned by Mr David Bruce of Dundee. On the completion of his period of

Arthur Howard Notley at the time of his own command in the Canadian Pacific line.

apprenticeship, during which time he was engaged chiefly in the Australian trade, he joined the Aberdeen White Star Line.

While with this company he served as second mate and mate in both the *Cimba* and the *Romanoff*.

After a further period in sail, Captain Notley decided to enter steam, and joined the China and Manila Steamship Co., of Hong Kong. He served for about ten years with this firm, engaged in trading on the Chinese coast. Among the steamers he commanded were the *Ruby*, *Zafiro*, *Diamante* and *Perla*.

He left this company, and in 1907 joined the Canadian Pacific Co. as fourth officer of the *Montezuma*. After serving in the various grades, he was appointed to command of the *Minnedosa* in 1922.

Captain Notley's other commands with the company have included the *Melita*, *Montnairn*, *Marglen* and *Montrose*, while he has also served as staff captain in the *Empress of Britain*, the *Empress of Japan* and the *Empress of France*.

He was subsequently appointed assistant marine superintendent, in which capacity he served both at Liverpool and London, and in 1933 was appointed to his recent post as marine superintendent at Antwerp.

During the [Great] war, Captain Notley served in the Royal Navy Reserve, and was in command of the destroyer P 27 and the trawler *Scott*. During the whole of his war service he was engaged in minelaying, minesweeping and the escort service.

While he was serving in the trawler *Scott* the vessel struck a German mine, and only three of the crew were saved. For his war services Captain Notley received the Reserve Decoration.

Notley was born in Cork, Ireland, on October 31, 1876, the son of 41-year-old Adolphus Notley, a civilian clerk in the Royal Engineers whose career took him to different depots.

Adolphus's own father, Samuel, had been with the British Mission to Mexico in the 1820s. Notley's mother Ellen, for her part, had a father who rejoiced in the role of Page of the Backstairs to Queen Adelaide, consort to William IV.

'One of his [Arthur Howard Notley's] stories was of how he ran away from his boarding school, Dover College, and went prize fighting in Canada to earn enough money to enter a Merchant Navy training school,' relates his grandson, Tim Notley, now living in Barcelona. 'He must have been a brave and adventurous man, even assuming that he did exaggerate.

'His main concern, and advice to me, was the necessity to be able to stand up for myself physically. He was very strong, he showed and made me feel his large biceps. He had been a boxer and tried to teach me, but I was never very enthusiastic.

'Although a great defender of the weak, he could have severe altercations with officials. Once when carrying the family silver in a suitcase on a train, he decided to empty it out on a seat in the train (something only he would do) to check it, or something. The guard of the train on seeing this became suspicious (AHN could look very scruffy when out of uniform) and started asking questions – which started a heated altercation.

'I think AHN was envious of the comparative success of his elder brother, Sir Franke Notley, who was a senior captain on the P&O Line, and his exaggerated eccentricity was his way of dealing with the envy. But this is a purely personal opinion, probably miles from reality.'

One of the souvenirs from Notley's exciting time abroad is a protractor from the Russian cruiser *Makarov* which he obtained at Manila in 1900. 'Quite a few items went ashore at the time, something to do with Russian naval ratings not being paid adequately or at all.'

Arthur Howard Notley married violinist Hannah Grave in Barrow-in-Furness in 1907. He was 31, and his bride, known as Nancy, 28. The Graves were all slightly dark skinned 'and AHN used to say that they were washed up with the Spanish Armada.' That family originally had Irish roots, and his wife insisted instead that she was descended from the King of the Galway tinkers, or gypsies.

The Notleys had two sons, one of whom, Arthur Charles Salisbury Notley, would always be known within the family as 'Tinker.' The elder lad was John Franke, and both would go on to serve their country in the Second World War.

A.H. Notley became a Lieutenant in the Royal Navy Reserve in October 1909, and was called up when war broke out five years later. He would be officially listed as wounded in action on October 22, 1915.

The wound may have been sustained when, in command a small flotilla of minesweepers, his vessel struck an enemy mine. Family lore is that one of the Kelvin's balls next to the compass was blown off and struck him in the head. No-one else is supposed to have been injured or killed in this incident, which seems to pre-date the sinking of the *Scott*, although the stories may have become confabulated.

Notley suffered one other injury during the Great War, but it was self-inflicted. At home on leave, he brought back some Naval gunpowder to entertain his young sons with a big bang. 'He filled a brass ball-cock with the gunpowder, put it at the bottom of the garden, and then made a trail of gunpowder back to the house.

'He then tried to ignite the trail, unsuccessfully, getting nearer and nearer to the ball-cock each time. When very near he obtained his explosion. The ball-cock shattered into hundreds of little bits and made a lot of tiny cuts on his face, with the result that he was streaming with blood, luckily without damaging the eyes. He returned to the house beaming with triumph to a shocked family.'

After the war, Notley – who was bestowed a medal for helping to save life in the *Scott* incident – returned to service in the Canadian Pacific Line. He rejoined the *Empress of Britain*, a ship he had served on from early 1913 until the outbreak, and was later on the *Melita* (the Latin name for Malta) from April 1921.

It was while he was on the *Melita* that he assumed command for the first time in civilian life in unfortunate circumstances. Shortly after the vessel had left St John's, Newfoundland, Captain Harry Waite was taken ill with appendicitis. An operation was performed by the ship's surgeon, accompanied by two other doctors on board, but he never rallied. As the vessel reached the Lizard – practically home – Captain Waite succumbed to septicaemia and died.

Captain Arthur Haywood Clews eventually replaced Captain Waite, and Notley moved on to the *Marglen* and *Empress of Britain* again, before becoming Staff Captain on the *Empress of France* in 1924. Later that year Canadian Pacific finally confirmed him as Captain in his own right, and he took charge of the *Minnedosa*. At age 48, it was about usual, possibly a little early, for command of a major passenger ship of the line.

The following year, he briefly skippered the *Marloch*, came back to the helm of *Minnedosa*, and then had the *Marglen*. In 1926 he returned to the *Melita* as Commander, in fresh tragic circumstances brought about by the on-board death of another of her Masters.

CAPTAIN SHOT DEAD AT ANTWERP
Affray in Canadian Pacific Liner
Brussels, Oct. 21 [1925]

Captain A.H. Clews, commander of the Canadian Pacific Steamship Company's liner *Melita*, which is lying in the port of Antwerp, was shot dead this morning, and Assistant Chief Engineer David K. Gilmour and Junior Second Engineer John Holliday were wounded, by, it is alleged, Chief Officer T.A. Towers.

According to the information which has been given to the police, Chief Officer Towers returned to the ship from the shore about half past 2 this morning. Arming himself with his revolver, he entered the Captain's cabin and fired at Mr Clews, who received the bullet in his right eye and was killed instantly.

Towers, it is alleged, then proceeded to the cabin of Mr Holliday, whom he wounded with a second shot. Awakened by the shots, Mr Gilmour and an engineer rushed on deck and threw themselves on Towers. In the struggle Mr Gilmour received a bullet in the lungs. Towers was eventually overpowered and the two wounded officers taken to hospital.

The police, having been informed of the affair, boarded the vessel and arrested Towers. In the course of his interrogation by the police Towers is reported to have declared that the Captain, aided by other officers, had determined to wreck his career.

Thomas Augustine Towers, 56, was mad of course. Captain Clews, 49, who was married, was shot as he slept, the bullet actually piercing his left eye, as established at inquest.

Arthur H. Clews, the murdered Master of the CPR liner *Melita*.

Whatever trace of personal misgivings about succeeding to authority in a vessel where two prior commanders had died aboard, Captain Notley had to restore morale amongst the somewhat shaken officer cadre. It helped when, in November 1926, the 14,000 ton *Melita* happened to be the 10,000th ship to arrive at Antwerp that year. A special reception was held in the town hall, with Captain Notley and the crew being congratulated by the Burgomaster. He was presented with a gold medal and an illuminated address.

Notley next had a stint with the *Montnairn*, before in 1928 becoming Captain of the liner *Montrose*. This vessel collided with the *Rose Castle* in the St Lawrence – a similar accident to that of the *Empress of Britain* and the *Helvetia* in 1912. No-one was injured, but the incident made for an unwelcome mention in the press:

LINER IN COLLISION IN THE ST. LAWRENCE
Montreal, July 27 [1928]

With her stem piece twisted and buckled and the plates of the port bow torn off, the Canadian Pacific steamship *Montrose* docked here today after a collision in the early hours of the morning with the Dominion Coal Company's collier *Rose Castle*, near Sorel, on the St Lawrence river, 35 miles eastward of Montreal.

The *Montrose* was coming from Liverpool and the collier proceeding towards Sydney, Nova Scotia, when the collision occurred. The collier was badly damaged and was beached with the engine room flooded. The passengers on the *Montrose*, awakened by the crash, ran on to the deck, but there was no panic, and after ascertaining that the crew of the collier was safe, the *Montrose* proceeded slowly to Montreal.

(The *Times*, July 28, 1928, p. 11)

Notley reportedly lost his temper at the subsequent inquiry – even though not on duty at the time of the smash – and this display did not go down well. He was not blamed by the findings of the investigation, and retained command for another two voyages. In 1929 he transferred to Captaincy of the *Beaverford*, a new vessel, but a freighter, not a passenger liner, and of 10,000 tons displacement compared to the 16,500 of the *Montrose*. She would later go down with all hands after gallant resistance to the *Admiral Scheer* in 1940.

Notley finished his career as Staff Captain on the *Empress of Japan*, and it was obvious his navigating days were over. The shipping slump of the 1930s saw him take early retirement. But the next war resulted in him being returned to uniform, and he served as a marshalling Captain of the naval dockyard in Liverpool. He also saw his sons take arms – infantry officer John Franke was taken prisoner in Iraq in 1941 and held in a German Oflag for five years, but a worse fate was to befall 'Tinker.'

Second son Arthur C.S. Notley was killed on Christmas Day 1940 while Chief Officer of the *Jumna*, of 6,000 tons, sunk by the heavy cruiser *Admiral Hipper*, which encountered her sailing alone while the German warship was returning to Brest from attacks on an Atlantic convoy. Notley Jr was aged just 26, one of 64 crew and 44 passenger victims. None escaped.

A.H. Notley had lost his wife, aged 61, earlier that year. After the war, he moved to Northam in Devon, where he was cared for by an unmarried niece, Eileen Isobel Notley.
Arthur Howard Notley suffered a heart attack and died at age 78 on June 2, 1955.

Following his death, his niece distributed his belongings, many of which went to his surviving son, John F. Notley. Included was a small journal of writings. But John Franke had suffered a stroke and was 'not the same man as before.' The family member who delivered the mementos to him from AHN was 'shocked at his lack of interest and indifference.'

The son eventually went into a British Legion home. Before he did so, he disposed of all papers, including the small journal, whatever it contained. He brought only photographs with him as he transferred to what would be his last residence.

Arthur H. Notley and his son 'Tinker', who later died at sea aboard the *Jumna*.

If, however, the original report from St John is to be believed, then one of the sailors, who said he was on watch aboard the *Mount Temple* on Sunday night, heard officer Notley 'tell the Captain of the distress signals.'

This most likely means distress *rockets*. It may even, as a further possibility, mean Morse code lamp flashes from the *Titanic*. But it cannot mean mere wireless transmissions, because the Captain was already in full possession of that knowledge of distress, and had received it from another source.

Officers 'saw certain things,' conceded Dr Bailey, who was present that night. Bailey pointed explicitly to Notley, when writing to Captain Lord, citing him as the man most likely to contribute 'valuable' information.

Baker's earlier opinion was 'that it is not right to ask the other fellows in the ship to tell Capt Lord what happened on that night when you saw her lights, for they would be afraid of getting the sack.' And Notley never did go public, but he did meet with Captain Lord.

Notley also twice left the ship in Canada. The clear inference from these four scraps of information is that Notley at least witnessed the *Titanic*'s screeching skyrockets as she appealed vainly for assistance.

Counsel for Captain Moore: 'This has all been most colourful, but it adds not a whit. There is no evidence at all from officer Notley himself in relation to the *Titanic*, either in 1912 or thereafter. His descendants have heard nothing. Evidently the only reason he left the *Mount Temple* in Canada was because of the attractions of the shore appointment he took up. All else is speculation and unsupported assertion.'

ENIGMA OF THE OFFICERS

HERBERT Heald was the officer in charge on the bridge of the *Mount Temple* during the middle watch, from midnight to 4am, on April 15, 1912 – the precise timeframe in which the *Titanic* sank.

Aged 38 in 1912, Heald was 5ft 6½in tall, and had both forearms tattooed in sailor tradition. His operational command of the ship, while Moore slept, before the first distress message came through, was reported in the St. John newspapers and mediated further afield.

In his American evidence, Captain Moore said that on getting that message 'I immediately blew the whistle on the bridge ... and told the second officer [Heald] to put the ship on north 45° east.'

He informed Heald what was the matter, to get the chart out, and to come down at once. The Captain and officer then consulted in the chart room 'and found out where the *Titanic* was.' Of course there were subsequent claims that the officers had identified precisely where she was, not from transmitted latitude and longitude, but from visible rockets and later the lights of the ship herself.

'Second Officer Heald says that if he wanted to talk he could tell a lot, whatever that means, but it is not his business to talk and if anyone wants information to go to the Captain,' reported the *Boston Globe* on April 25, 1912.

Heald never did talk. It was 'not his business,' and his loyalty, as he saw it, was owed to Moore. He was a signatory (along with Chief Officer Sargent and wireless operator Durrant) to a cable sent by Moore to the US inquiry, which stated they were 50 miles away from *Titanic* and 'did not arrive at her position until 4.30am, when could not see the *Titanic*'s lights.' The latter statement appears qualified by the dawn, whereas the White Star vessel was two hours sunk by then, but the overall insistence was that the *Mount Temple* could offer no insights at all – and could not be the mystery ship that was by then being widely discussed.

HERBERT HEALD (1874-1942)

Heald was born in Chorley, Lancashire, on May 4, 1874, and died on March 17, 1942, at the age of 67.

By 1912 he was a married father of two: an eight-year-old boy named Sydney, and a two-year-old toddler daughter. She was named Lucy after his wife, Lucy Elizabeth Fletcher, whom he married at the end of 1902 at Trinity Methodist Church, Chorley.

Heald, who had grown up in a house in Friday Street, eventually settled at 14 Windsor Road in the town. After the *Mount Temple*, he served aboard the *David Lloyd George*, a vessel of 4,700 tons, as first officer. As the name suggests, she was a Welsh freighter, with most voyages begun and ended in Barry Dock. He also had a stint with the ss *Toromeo*, another cargo vessel.

In April 1919, seven years after the sinking, Heald served on the hauntingly-named *Titania*, which coincidentally was based in Southampton. Three years later his only son died at the age of 17 in an accident.

It appears Heald worked to the west coast of Africa for a time, although he also served on the British India Line's *Neuralia* to Bombay and Karachi, as well as the African east coast. In 1937, he and his younger brother William were brought home as passengers from a trip to Marseilles in the Bibby Line's *Staffordshire*. Heald was 62.

Above left: Herbert Heald, second officer of the *Mount Temple*, pictured later in his career. Heald was quoted in newspaper reports from St John as saying that if he 'wanted to talk, he could tell a lot.' He referred anyone seeking information to the Captain.

Above right: Herbert Heald in uniform around the time of the sinking. Captain Moore said this man was on watch when the distress signal was first received, but a sailor allegedly also on watch said third officer Notley informed the Captain of 'distress signals.'

His wife, Lucy Elizabeth died in February of the following year. Broken hearted, Heald would last only a few years thereafter.

Herbert Heald's obituary appeared in the *Chorley Guardian* of March 28, 1942: 'Mr Herbert Heald died at Ladyhough, Chorley, on Tuesday [March 17, 1942] in his 68th year. He was a retired master mariner, undergoing early training on the *Conway* after leaving school. In the last war he was commissioned in the RNR. His wife died four years ago, and one married daughter, Mrs. H. Stansfield, survives. Her husband, solicitor, is serving in the navy.'

Elizabeth Lomax, the granddaughter of Herbert Heald, was five years old when he died. 'I knew he had been on a ship that tried to go to the rescue of the *Titanic*, but nothing else,' she says.

Heald 'could tell a lot,' but never did, at least not publicly. If Heald was proud of what he had done that night, might he have talked more to his family about it?

Heald's signature to the Captain's cable is, on the face of it, contradictory. He was certifying Moore's insistence that there was nothing to report. But instead he was quoted in the newspapers as saying there was a lot to be told.

And he could simply not have told a lot if his ship merely travelled through unrelenting darkness. Like Notley, telling much would have involved much more.

Counsel for Captain Moore: 'Empty rhetoric. Everything about Heald suggests an ordinary life and an ordinary attempt to help in 1912, and nothing more. No questions for this witness.'

The prosecution tenders *Mount Temple* officer William Sydney Brown. Mr Brown, please –

WILLIAM SYDNEY BROWN (1881-1962)

The fourth officer of the *Mount Temple* was born in Skelton-in-Cleveland, Yorkshire, on November 19, 1881. He was thus 30 years old during the voyage in question, but still gave his address as 90 High St, Skelton – the family home.

Lloyd's register shows that Brown obtained his officer's certificate in 1905, followed up with a Master's cert the following year, and finally achieved an Extra Master qualification in 1909.

His first vessel as an officer was the *Ovingdon Grange* in 1906, followed by the *Warwickshire* three years later. The *Mount Temple* was only his third berth.

During the return to the *Titanic*, as Moore has it, that ship met ice. 'We double-lookouted, and put the fourth officer forward to report if he saw any ice coming along that was likely to injure us.'

Later Moore repeated of Brown: 'The fourth officer we put on the forecastle head, so, if the ice was low down, he perhaps could see it farther than we could on the bridge.'

Thus, if there were rockets to be seen – and the *Mount Temple* was heading towards the general area – it is presumably certain that Brown would have seen them. He was at the very stem of the ship – and even if looking down towards the sea, he could not have missed a flash in the night, and thereafter, any falling pyrotechnic stars.

Brown did not sign Moore's cable to the US inquiry. He did not testify in Britain or America, and neither was he quoted by name in any newspaper. He was also the most junior, and the most youthful – by five years – of the ship's officers, whose ages increased according to their responsibilities.

Captain Moore testified that in the later daylight of April 15, 1912, 'my fourth officer [Brown] took two observations, and of course, he is a navigator, and also, an Extra Master's

William Sydney Brown, fourth officer
aboard the *Mount Temple*.

William Sydney Brown, fourth officer aboard the *Mount Temple*, using a sextant.

certificate is held by him, which is a better certificate than mine. And he took those observations both times, and both of them tallied.'

It is noticeable that in his evidence in Britain, Moore mentioned none of his officers by name or even by rank. In his much longer American evidence, again no names are mentioned, but while mentioning his second officer and chief officer just once, he specifies the fourth officer on three occasions.

At perhaps a psychological level, this might suggest that Captain Moore had no fear about his fourth officer being put on the stand to verify the observations he took, and becoming thereby prey to other questions, although it might be a long-odds idea in the first place that Brown, or others, might be summoned to Washington. Moore made reference, as he testified, to the fact that his ship was then on its way from St John to Halifax.

William Sydney Brown's family had a long seafaring tradition, but his grandfather had jumped the wrong way on one important occasion, and lived to regret it. He was a shiphandler and nautical adviser to the famous firm of Palmers of Jarrow, which built nearly a thousand ships from its foundation in 1851 to ultimate closure in the 1930s slump.

Early in the firm's history, the elder Brown was given command of a new-fangled steamship to try out as her Master. He distinctly didn't like this new beast, and authoritatively advised the company the future belonged indisputably to sail. It was a horrible mistake, which cost the firm dear in resisting the advances of mechanical propulsion.

Family tradition has it that Brown himself stuck to his guns far longer. His own inherited firm had been very successful running tall ships out of Whitby, but the absolute conviction that there were no prospects in steam ultimately 'lost all the family money.'

William Sydney Brown stayed with the *Mount Temple* for the next year, and transferred in 1914 to the *Lake Michigan*. He saw out the Great War in the merchant marine, serving next in the *Montfort* and *Mattana*, in doing so somehow achieving a reputation for 'not getting torpedoed,' implying such a fate might have commonly befallen his pre-war cohort.

After the conflict he returned to Canadian Pacific, following a short stint as Chief Officer on the *Sardinian*. He was next to be found in the *Montcalm* and the *Bosworth*.

Thereafter Brown served as Chief Officer of the *Batsford*, *Montreal*, *Marglen* and *Melita*. These latter two are especially significant, because he served as number two to the Master of both ships, one Arthur Howard Notley, formerly his immediate superior on the *Mount Temple*.

It would be interesting to know what passed between the two senior officers about the *Titanic* affair, if anything, from the beginning of October 1925 to the end of June the following year. Neither had spoken publicly at the time, although Notley clearly had something to say when he agreed to meet Captain Lord, and both he and Brown had made progress in the Canadian Pacific thereafter, even allowing for the interruption of the war.

Brown's service record shows a break between the end of June 1926 and his joining the *Minnedosa* in April 1927. This is explained by his marriage to Dorothy Witham in Doncaster, South Yorkshire, towards the end of 1926. He was 45, his bride 33.

The couple had met on the *Marglen*, where she was working as a nurse and stewardess. A butcher's daughter, she would live to the ripe old age of 106, dying just before the turn of the millennium in December 1999.

They had two children – Elizabeth, born in September 1927, and Margaret, born in the summer of 1932. Both are living, but know little of their father because he was away at sea so much. Elizabeth says: 'He was a very private man. We have no records whatsoever. He wouldn't have talked about it [the *Titanic* episode].

'My father's career was obviously involved. He was a very professional man, and when it was over, that would have been it. He did not discuss his seafaring at all. It was not done in those days.' Even after Brown's death, his widow conveyed nothing to his daughters.

Brown continued his career through the Hungry Thirties, on the *Montclare*, *Montrose*, and *Duchess of York*. He finally gained captaincy at the age of 53, despite his extensive early navigational qualifications, and first became Master of the *Beaverbrae* in 1935.

An image of Captain W.S. Brown of the *Montclare*, from the frontispiece of a *Daily Telegraph* supplement on cruising holidays and ocean travel, dated March 6, 1939.

It was while back on the *Montclare* as her Master for three years that his photograph featured on the front page of a *Daily Telegraph* supplement on 'cruising holidays and ocean travel' in March 1939, one hand gripping an engine room telegraph.

Five months later, in August, twenty-seven years after the *Titanic*, came a strange resonance. Captain Brown received an SOS message from the *Beaverhill*, a sister Canadian Pacific liner, of 10,041 tons, bound from Quebec to London. She had struck an iceberg …

The collision happened off the eastern end of Belle Isle Strait in a fog. Bow plates crumpled in the crash, and a distress signal was received by the ice patrol cutter *Champlain*, the Cunard White Star liner *Ausonia*, and by Brown. All went to the *Beaverhill*'s assistance. But in the meantime it was determined that the victim was not making any water. Remarkably, the inner hull had not been breached. The *Beaverhill* within the hour reported that the damage was slight, and she would be continuing her voyage.

It must have brought back memories … and did elsewhere. The *New York Times* headlined: 'Ship Hits Iceberg Near *Titanic* Site,' unconcerned that the proximity was a mere 640 nautical miles.

A second war arrived, and in 1941 W. S. Brown commanded the *Duchess of Atholl*. Preserving his lucky streak, he had left her by the following year, when she was sunk off the west coast of Africa. Her Captain on that occasion was one Harry Allinson Moore – the son of Captain James Henry Moore of the *Mount Temple*.

Brown's final vessel was the *Empress of Canada*, which he left at the end of 1942. He was sixty, and would have a short stint of shore employment before he retired.

On April 17, 1962, two days after the 50th anniversary of the sinking of the *Titanic*, William Sydney Brown passed away at Clatterbridge Hospital, Bebington, on the Wirral. He was eighty, and died of pneumonia.

His remains were cremated a week later at Landican, and his ashes scattered in bed 15 of the memorial garden. Brown's death notice in the Liverpool newspapers described him as 'a dear husband, and father to Elizabeth & Maureen; of 6 King's Walk, West Kirby.'

Counsel for Captain Moore: 'No questions. This witness does not assist in any way.'

It is now proposed to take the Chief Engineer of the *Mount Temple* very briefly, before addressing what the Chief Officer can contribute. This will conclude the prosecution case, and counsel for Captain Moore shall lead whatever evidence he sees fit. Closing arguments will follow thereafter.

JOHN NOEL GILLET (1874-1954)

Mr Gillet, aged 37 on this voyage, was the Chief Engineer of the *Mount Temple*, with an address at Silverbeed Rd, Seacombe, where he was born, on Merseyside.

Mr Gillet is significant in that he maintained an engine room log, which not only recorded telegraph signals from the bridge – such as any order to go 'full speed astern' – but also the revolutions made, and therefore the speed of the vessel. From indications of the work done in the bowels of the vessel, a good approximation of distance travelled could be obtained.

Captain Moore said in his US evidence that, once he was sufficiently dressed, 'I went down to the chief engineer and told him that the *Titanic* was sending out messages for help … I also told him to inform the firemen that we wanted to get back as fast as we possibly could.'

While the Mercantile Marine Services Association begged the Board of Trade in August 1912 to take a statement from 'Gillette,' he was not a signatory to Captain Moore's cable, nor was he ever quoted in any forum.

In the direct allegation of William Henry Baker that when the *Mount Temple* returned to Gravesend in May 1912, her Captain and Marconi officer were 'sent for' – and we do not know

John Noel Gillet, Chief Engineer of the
Mount Temple.

John Noel Gillet, right, Chief Engineer
of the *Mount Temple*, carrying a
wrench on deck.

Marriage certificate for John Noel Gillet, Chief Engineer, in September 1912, giving his home address as the ss *Mount Temple*. William Henry Baker made efforts to contact Gillet over what had allegedly been seen from the ship on the night the *Titanic* went down.

by whom, whether the Board of Trade or the Canadian Pacific company – there is also a claim of two navigational logs being taken off the ship. But there is no mention of the engine room log, and if it survives its present whereabouts is unknown.

Mr Gillet's father, Daniel, died when he was three. The grandson of Noel Gillet, the former Governor of Castle Rushen jail on the Isle of Man, he and his brother Thomas both went to sea, the latter as a navigating officer.

In the 1891 census, Gillet is a 16-year-old marine engineer's apprentice, living in the chemist shop run by his widowed mother Elizabeth in Liscard, Cheshire. Thereafter he is a constant seafarer.

Baker mentions in his letter to Dr Bailey of September 1912 that he had heard 'that Gillett was getting married this trip, so I called upon him, but he was away.'

John Noel 'Gillett' indeed married in September 1912, his bride being Edith Mary Pike. The marriage took place in Bristol on the fifteenth of that month, and the certificate shows that it involved the 38-year-old Chief Engineer, whose residence is given as the 'SS *Mount Temple*.' His bride was fifteen years younger, the daughter of a coal merchant

This attempted meeting demonstrates Baker's determination in seeking out potential witnesses, or the men who were his *actual informants* during the homeward voyage to Britain. It is impossible to know into which category Gillet falls, but it may be, because of this personal journey, that he occupies both. Baker had taken the trouble to obtain his whereabouts.

Gillet's wife died in 1946, and he remarried two years later – at the ripe old age of 74. His 57-year-old bride, Gertrude Barmby, had a son by a former marriage. This marriage would last for six years before it was terminated by death.

John Noel Gillet succumbed to a clot in the lung, complicated by congestive cardiac failure, on July 2, 1954. He was 79, and passed away at home, 45 Shirehampton Road, Bristol. His stepson, Gerald, informed the authorities.

Gertrude, 'widow of John Noel Gillet, Chief Engineer (Merchant Navy),' died in November 1974. Mr Gillet appears to have left no trace of his involvement with the *Titanic* sinking.

It may be that the best way to introduce the next witness is to read from his obituary in the *Formby Times* from November 1946:

FORMBY'S OLD 'SEA DOG' BRAVED OCEAN THRILLS IN PEACE AND WAR
Commander Sargent Helped in the Capture of Dr. Crippen

One of Formby's most colourful residents, greatly beloved by the district's children, died last Friday. He was Commander A.H. Sargent, RNR, of The Elms, Kirklake Road, who died in Liverpool Royal Infirmary following a heart attack in Liverpool.

Alfred Henry Sargent, chief officer aboard the *Mount Temple* in April 1912.

Captain Alfred Sargent, left, with another prisoner-of-war in German propaganda newsreel boasting of the success of its maritime commerce raiders.

Eighty years old, Commander Sargent had many thrilling adventures. He was directly concerned in the arrest of the notorious Dr Crippen on board ship in the Atlantic. He served as an officer on board the first ship to be equipped with wireless. He was one of the few survivors of a disastrous shipwreck on the Goodwin Sands when many men were lost. He took part in a battle with a famous German commerce raider in 1916, and spent a great part of the first world war in German prisoner of war camps.

Comdr Sargent was born in Ireland in August 1866, his father being a well-known Irish shipowner. Comdr Sargent made his first voyage at the age of 15, when, in 1881, he went to sea on the barque *Lake Simcoe*. Until he received his Master's certificate he served continuously in sailing ships.

It was during his apprenticeship that he was shipwrecked on the Goodwin Sands while serving aboard the sailing ship *Berengaria*. Young Sargent was eventually rescued by the Harwich lifeboat, which found him unconscious, lashed to a spar, at dawn on Christmas morning, 1883.

His first steamship company was the Orient Line. Then, in 1903, he joined the Canadian Pacific Line, with which he served for the rest of his sea career. It was while he was chief officer of the ss *Montrose* that he played an instrumental part in the capture of Crippen and Ethel Le Neve.

Crippen and his confederate were wanted for murder, and were known to have left the country. All ports were on the alert for them, but in those days there were no passports or other identity papers needed for the voyage to Canada, and the search was therefore more difficult.

Crippen and Ethel Le Neve, the latter disguised as the murderer's son, joined the *Montrose* at Antwerp. They aroused the suspicion of the chief steward, who informed the Captain. The latter in turn told Commander Sargent to keep an eye on them.

As the *Montrose* crossed the Atlantic, Comdr Sargent became increasingly suspicious of the pair. He noticed that the boy's trousers were held up by a safety pin, and that the 'boy' had a habit of continually putting up his hand to tidy his hair. Eventually Comdr Sargent decided that the two were the wanted couple. He told the Captain, and then went to the radio cabin to inform Scotland Yard. That message was a historic event.

It was the first time wireless had been used to assist in the capture of a criminal.

When the *Montrose* was 24 hours out of Quebec, a pilot came aboard. That pilot was in reality Insp. Dew of Scotland Yard, who, in answer to the radio call, had crossed the Atlantic ahead of the *Montrose* in a faster ship and arrived a few hours earlier.

Crippen was asked to step into the Captain's cabin, and there, in the presence of Comdr Sargent, he was arrested by Detective Insp. Dew.

When the First World War broke out in 1914, Comdr Sargent was made Captain of the SS *Mount Temple*, and it was in the early days of that war that he helped to carry the Royal Naval Division across to the Continent in what proved to be an heroic, if abortive, attempt to hold Antwerp against the advancing Germans.

In November 1916, the *Mount Temple* was intercepted and sunk by the notorious German commerce raider *Möwe*, the *Graf Spee* of the First World War. Comdr Sargent was taken to Germany as a prisoner and spent the rest of that war in various prisoner of war camps.

After the First World War he resumed his nautical activities, sailing all the time on the North Atlantic run.

In 1926 he 'swallowed the anchor' – naval slang for retirement from the sea.

He settled in Formby about 25 years ago. Comdr Sargent was popular and admired throughout the district. He was a firm friend of all children, and loved to tell them exciting stories of his many adventures. They called him 'Gran'dad.'

Lately he has been living with his married daughter, Mrs R.W. Corkhill, whose husband is at the moment in the United States on a business trip.

What immediately becomes apparent, on reading the above, is that the old commander's stories do not include mention of the *Titanic*. This is despite the fact that it was far more famous than the admittedly exciting apprehension of the Hilldrop Crescent murderer by Inspector Walter Dew, by means of the magic of wireless and the speedy *Laurentic*.

Wireless is a motif in the above tribute. Sargent served aboard the first ship fitted with wireless. The message sent from his ship, *Montrose*, was 'a historic event.' But much more a historic event was the wireless message of distress sent by the *Titanic*, of which there is no mention. It seems Sargent left that vessel out of his stories of many adventures to the children of the district. Why so?

Sargent's great grandson, James Kay, says: 'I have asked all the members of my family and none knew anything about his being on the ship [*Mount Temple*] during this *Titanic* voyage. The fact that he never told any story or talked about it, I find very hard to believe.

'With such a terrible loss of life and suffering and being on a ship so close to the *Titanic*, why does no one know anything about it? It is a total mystery that I cannot understand or explain.'

ALFRED HENRY SARGENT (1866-1946)

Aged 45 when chief officer of the *Mount Temple*, Sargent was born in Passage West, Cork, on August 17, 1866. He was the youngest son of a family of twelve, made up of three brothers and nine sisters.

The son of Thomas Edward and Elizabeth Sargent, his father was a Cork shipowner, although the family was originally from Battle, near Hastings in Sussex. The senior Sargent used to peer through a telescope from his house on the coast at his ships going in and out to Cork – the very waters in which the *Titanic* would make her last port of call in 1912.

Sargent's grandfather had been a merchant marine Captain. His older brother, Thomas Edward Jr, became a Captain too, and was Master of the *Lake Simcoe*, managed by W. Thomson and Sons of Dundee, when Alfred Henry was taken on as an apprentice.

He served for two and a half years in this vessel, trading between France and Montreal in the wine and brandy business. At the end of that time, the ship was sold and Captain Thomas Sargent transferred his brother's indentures. The budding sailor then took to the *Berengaria* for a voyage to the East. On the return voyage disaster overtook the ship, which had almost arrived at her port of destination, when she wrecked on the Galloper Sands:

MARITIME DISASTER

The *Berengaria*, of Greenock, from Melbourne for Sunderland, laden with wheat, struck on the Galloper Sand at 8.30pm on Monday night, came off, and sank in deep water. The chief officer and 13 of the crew landed at Aldeburgh at 2am yesterday. Sixteen men were left behind, it is supposed in the rigging, &c. The Harwich steam tug has gone with the lifeboat *Springwell* in search of them. Five men landed at Southwold in the ship's boat yesterday morning.

The vessel lies in 14 fathoms, with yards above water. The *Berengaria*, an iron ship, of 1,394 gross tons, was built at Glasgow in 1874, and is owned by Messrs Hendry, Ferguson and Co., Greenock.

(The *Times*, Wednesday December 3, 1884, p.11)

The Master, second officer, and eight of the crew were drowned with the *Berengaria*. A pilot, who had been taken aboard prior to the wreck, stayed aboard and was also lost. This disaster, given that almost half the complement was lost, must have had a powerful effect on the 18-year-old Sargent, even if the more likely story of his own escape, as recorded in 1916, was that he slid down the davit ropes from the deck to where one of the ship's boats had been lowered, just 'before she was driven from the side of the ship.'

Nonetheless, he stayed in his chosen career, and obtained his second officer's ticket. He then went into steam, and served in several companies until securing his Master's certificate when he joined the Orient and Pacific Steam Navigation Company.

Sargent served in both the Australian and Pacific liners for about a dozen years, leaving when he had attained the rank of chief officer to join the Canadian Pacific company in 1904. By this point he had married Marion Leslie, two years younger, a Scot from Dunoon, Argyle, whose father had been a buccaneer blockade-runner, even engaging in 'blackbirding,' or illegal slave trading to the United States from Bermuda.

To celebrate his betrothal, he had an intertwined shamrock and thistle tattooed on his left forearm.

In 1906, Sargent was on the *Lake Erie*, and the following year went aboard the *Lake Champlain*, which was indeed the first vessel installed with wireless, but in 1901. Here he stayed until he joined the *Montrose* in time for the Crippen episode in 1910.

Sargent was thus aboard the *Lake Champlain* in 1909 when this happened:

STEAMER HITS AN ICEBERG

The *Late Champlain*, 1,000 Passengers, Puts Into Port with Hole in Bow

St. John's N.F., May 7. – The steamer *Lake Champlain*, bound from Liverpool for Montreal, put in here today leaking from a hole stove in her bow by heavy ice off Cape Race yesterday. There are about a thousand passengers on board.

The vessel made water so rapidly that it was considered unsafe to proceed for her destination, and it was decided to dock her for temporary repairs.

The *Lake Champlain* left Liverpool on April 28 for Montreal, in command of Capt. Webster. She is a steamer of 4,685 tons net, and is owned by the Canadian Pacific Railway Company. She was built in Glasgow in 1900.

It was about 6.30 o'clock last evening when the *Lake Champlain* struck a small iceberg on her port bow, during a dense fog. The passengers were all at dinner when the mishap occurred and ran to the deck. There they were told there was no danger and that the ship was leaking only slightly, so that all went below again and resumed their dinner.

(The *New York Times*, Saturday May 8, 1909, p. 4.)

This occurrence, and the passenger unease, must also have stayed fresh in Sargent's memory. It is not clear what speed the vessel was doing in the fog – presumably a cautious one – but the damage had still been extensive. To go at high speed in ice-infested waters when responding to another ship's distress call at night could be expected to worry the later chief officer of the *Mount Temple*.

Certainly the 1909 incident was recalled in evidence at the British *Titanic* inquiry, by a stewardess named Annie Robinson, who also happened to have been a crew member on the *Lake Champlain* on the occasion.

The CPR liner *Lake Champlain*.

A veteran of two iceberg incidents, Ms Robinson was aboard the *Devonian* (with officer William Henry Baker) one dark night in October 1914 when the vessel 'slowed down in a heavy fog. Mrs Robinson apparently became nervous, and the continual sounding of the whistle so worked upon her nerves that she feared another disaster.' She jumped overboard and was lost.

On June 9, 1911, barely a week after the launch of the *Titanic* at Belfast, Alfred Sargent joined the *Mount Temple* as chief officer. It was on his seventh voyage that news came through that the maiden voyager was sinking.

Captain Moore testified that in daylight he searched for a passage through the ice barrier. He had one crewman pulled to the top of the foremast in a bowline, 'and I had the Chief Officer at the mainmast head, and he could not see any line through the ice at all that I could go through.'

Reports from St John were later to the effect that the 'First Officer' states that he 'went aloft for three hours and never saw any signals of any kind.' But of course the signals had ceased by then. Sargent would nevertheless have had a commanding view of the scene, but he was never called to any inquiry.

But Sargent's log book was taken off at Gravesend on the return voyage, according to whistleblower Baker. 'The Captain and Marconi officer were sent for, also the two log books, Scrap and Chief Officer's. What they wanted with the scrap log I cannot understand, for there was only about a line and a half written of what occurred during the four hours, and quite half a page in the Chief's book! I saw that myself.'

Half a page in Sargent's log about the incident. The Official Log of the *Mount Temple*, written entirely in Captain Moore's hand, even though Captain Sargent replaced him for a few days, is blank about the *Titanic*. Either Baker did indeed see half a page about the emergency, written by Sargent, or he did not.

It was the chief officer's duty to maintain a log. Sargent actually gave evidence to this point in a far more mundane inquiry in October 1913, when the *Mount Temple* went aground in the St Lawrence while under pilotage leaving Montreal. He testified:

Alfred Henry Sargent, right, on the flying bridge of the *Mount Temple*. (Officer Robert Pugh, left)

Did you make any entries in the log book?

Sargent: Yes, I put the soundings in the log book. I simply copied the record.

Have you your log book here? – Yes.

I would like to have these entries, from the time the ship left the dock? – I can give it to you.

(The following is the entry appearing in the log book)

'S.S. *Mount Temple*. From Montreal to London.

September 24th, 1913. Moderate breeze. Fine, clear weather. 5.20am, engines standby. Pilot L.Z. Bouille on board. Made tugs fast; 'John Pratt' forward, 'H. Dupré' aft.

5.22, let go from pier. Engines as required on pilot's advice. 5.40, all clear of pier and proceeded. Let go after tug. 5.50, let go forward tug.

6.02, took the ground while swinging on starboard helm, passing 181 M buoy on starboard hard. 6.06, stopped engines and used as required. Tug 'Spray' was called and made fast aft.

At 9.30, ten more tugs made fast, and with ship's engines worked until 0.45pm without beneficial results.

After grounding, bilges were sounded immediately, and found O.K., but No. 1, 3, 4, and 5 tanks making water rapidly, and No. 2 tank slightly. Soundings were taken around ship. 27 feet 6 inches to 28 feet were found by after part of saloon deck on port side, and 28 feet by jiggermast on starboard side, remaining soundings being 30 feet and over.'

Sargent's notes are copious, and as one would expect. It must be that a year earlier he had made similar entries about the *Titanic* incident. Those notes were removed from the vessel and have not come to light.

The *Mount Temple* in the Canadian Vickers dry dock 'Duke of Connaught' in 1913 after going aground on the Longueuil shoal opposite Maisonneuve, Montreal.

Sargent also made it clear in his 1913 testimony that the 'scrap log,' or rough operational notes, was maintained on the *Mount Temple* by the third officer. A year earlier that would have been a certain Arthur Howard Notley.

He was asked:

> The time you have here, '6.02, took the ground,' is from the log? – Yes.
> Where did you get that time? – Personally I got it from the other log book – the third officer's log – the scrap log.
> Was that time actually taken on the bridge? – Yes, by the third officer's watch.

Sargent's great grandson says: 'Regarding Gravesend, I have asked members of the family and unfortunately nobody knows anything about what happened there. We did not even know anything about the *Titanic* connection, which to me is very strange.'

The chief officer had taken over as Master of the *Mount Temple* in 1916 when she was intercepted and sunk while bringing over 700 horses to the Western Front. The crew were taken aboard their destroyer, the SMS *Möwe*. As the ship sank, horses struggled to break free and escape.

'Alfred Henry Sargent many years later mentioned to my grandmother that the noise of the drowning horses had haunted him for many years.'

Why was he not haunted by the idea of 1,500 human beings dying in the freezing North Atlantic a few years earlier?

Captain Alfred Sargent, chief officer aboard the *Mount Temple* in April 1912.

Captain Alfred Henry Sargent and first officer Robert Pugh with horses shipped aboard the *Mount Temple* to the Western Front, *c.* 1916.

Sargent served out the rest of his career with the Canadian Pacific line from 1919 to 1926, having command of the *Holbrook*, *Bolingbroke*, *Bosworth*, *Brecon*, *Marloch*, *Bruton* and *Batsford*. He retired to Merseyside, where he made whistles out of wood for children, told them his prisoner of war stories, and allowed them to wind his ship's chronometer.

Alfred Henry Sargent collapsed on the street in Liverpool in October 1946. He was taken by ambulance to the Royal Infirmary, where he appeared recovered. His granddaughter Anne received a message to go to the Royal to collect him, but when she arrived discovered he had already discharged himself and was making his own way home.

On the way he again collapsed. This time he was admitted to the Royal Infirmary where he was found to have suffered a heart attack. He passed away a few days later and is buried in St Luke's Church in Formby.

Counsel for Captain Moore: 'Chief officer Sargent appended his name to a cable from his Captain refuting passenger Quitzrau's claims. That much is clear from 1912. He was not haunted by anything to do with the *Titanic* because he had nothing to regret or reproach himself for.'

The prosecution rests.

THE DEFENCE

Counsel for Captain Moore: The defence will be as brief and economical as possible, as befits a matter of short shrift. May we have John Oscar Durrant, please.

JOHN OSCAR DURRANT (1891-1951)

Mr Durrant was 21, living in Hughan Road, Stratford, London, in 1912. Born in West Ham, he was the son of a labourer, and later machine-minder named John, and his wife Ellen, six years older, both hailing from Suffolk.

For further background, the transcript is submitted of an article published in the *Great Eastern Railway Magazine* in 1921:

An Interesting Letter to the Editor

Ten Years as a Wireless Operator

WRITING from the P. & O. S.S. *Nellone*, Port Said, on August 31st, Mr. J.O. Durrant, who left many friends behind at the Stratford Works, thus describes his somewhat exciting experiences since leaving the company's service:

'Until I was twenty-one, I served as a junior clerk in the Running Shed, Loco Machine Shop, Loco Repairing Shop, Brass Finishing Shop, and Wagon Department Stores. I then learned wireless telegraphy at evening classes, and on October 7th 1911 left the G.E.R., the late Mr. Winmill giving me a reference, which I still keep with pride. Since then I have had a much-varied and interesting ten years at sea.

'Places of call include France, Belgium, Gibraltar, Malta, Greece, Egypt, Aden, India, Ceylon, Singapore, Dutch East Indies, Australia, New Zealand, Fiji, Raratonga, Tahiti, Honolulu, Madeira, Sierra Leone, South Africa, and several ports on the Atlantic and Pacific coasts of U.S.A. and Canada.

'I have been twelve times through the uninteresting Suez Canal, once through the wonderful Panama Canal, and have crossed the Equator twenty-six times. My ships, too, have been varied, ranging from the *Mauretania* of 32,000 tons and a luxurious ex-German of 19,500 tons, to a Glasgow tramp and a small wooden steamer of 1,400 tons. The latter caught fire in mid-Atlantic in very bad weather, and gave us ten anxious days until we put into Queenstown.

'I had only been at sea six months when the *Titanic* struck an iceberg forty-nine miles from our steamer, the *Mount Temple*, and I was the first to answer her S.O.S. Although we hastened through the ice-field to her position, we were too late for rescue work. Of about seven ships who received the distress call, I was the only operator to keep a detailed log, a fact I am proud of, considering my inexperience at that time. I received some praise at the inquiry, and promotion in consequence. The *G.E.R Magazine* had a short article referring to it. (This appeared in the July issue, 1912, under the title 'A *Titanic* Echo.' – Editor.)

'One interesting trip was from London to Victoria B.C. as a passenger, to join a new steamer. The journey included three thousand miles in the train across Canada. I thoroughly enjoyed it, and shall always remember the magnificence of the Rocky Mountains. I was genuinely sorry when we reached the Pacific coast.

Mount Temple wireless operator John Oscar Durrant on a vessel later in his career.

I was north of Fiji, bound to Honolulu, when war broke out, and we received the news by wireless from Auckland, a distance of 1,200 miles. Later my steamer became a troopship, carrying Aussies from Sydney to Europe. In August 1916 she became a hospital ship, and after three months in the Mediterranean, made 190 trips between Southampton and France. The 190th was her last; in utter darkness she was torpedoed. There were 605 wounded and sick aboard, all of whom had seen service in France. One hundred and twenty-three lives were lost, and the rest suffered intense agony during transhipment to the small boats. The steamer (*Warilda*) was the last hospital ship to be torpedoed, and I lost a comfortable home, after nearly six years aboard her.

Since the Armistice I have been mostly in P. and O. steamers running between London, Egypt and India. I've enjoyed sea-life, and my work is exceedingly interesting, but like many other seamen, I now wish to settle down in some quiet little place on shore.'

Durrant is writing nine years after the *Titanic* sinking. In that time, despite being years away from Captain Moore and any possible repercussions, he has not changed what he said to the *St John Globe* in April 1912: 'At the time I received the first message, I would judge the *Mount Temple* to be fifty miles from the *Titanic*'s position.'

Here he specifies 49 miles. That was his opinion, he was an independent operator aboard ship, a free agent as his globe-spanning career would indicate, and he owed no particular loyalty to anyone, certainly not someone who might be a coward and engaged in a self-serving cover-up, which would hardly be likely to withstand scrutiny.

Two years later, in the summer of 1923, Mr Durrant married Eva May Firman in Stow, Suffolk. He was 32, and Eva 34. His bride, known to her family as 'Curly,' had a railway connection similar to his own. The Firmans lived at Stow Upland railway station, where John George was a porter.

The couple set up home in Liverpool, but would not be blessed with any children. This article about John Durrant was published in *Sea Breezes* in February 1951 to mark his retirement:

He Served in Sixty Ships

After 39 years of service with the Marconi International Marine Communication Co. Ltd., during which he has never been absent from work through sickness, Mr John Oscar ('Jod') Durrant, storekeeper for the past three years at the Liverpool depôt, retired on January 13

Aged 60, Mr Durrant, a native of London, began his career at the age of 14 as a clerk with the old Great Eastern Railway. In October 1911 he left the railway company to join the Marconi Company as a junior wireless operator, his first ship being the famous *Mauretania*, in which he made one voyage.

It was while he was wireless operator of the steamer *Mount Temple*, in April 1912, that he received the distress call from the *Titanic*, 49 miles away. On arrival at the scene it was found that the *Carpathia* had rescued the survivors. At the subsequent inquiry into the disaster, held in London, he was commended.

Mr Durrant has, during his career with the company, served for 19 years as a radio officer in some 60 vessels, ranging from the *Mauretania* to an Aberdeen trawler. He has served for 17 years as an inspector at Oslo, Trieste, Bremen, Alexandria, Avonmouth, London, and finally, Liverpool. He came to Liverpool as inspector 12 years ago, and three years ago was appointed storekeeper.

During his career he has crossed the Equator 76 times, passed through the Suez Canal 44 times, the Panama Canal five times, and the Manchester Ship canal twice. During the First World War he was serving as wireless operator in the hospital ship *Warilda*, when, on August 3, 1918, with 603 wounded on board, she was torpedoed and sunk, 129 lives being lost.

Mr Durrant describes the advance in marine radio technique as amazing, and recalls that 'when I learnt about wireless, valves weren't heard of.' He warmly praises the Marconi Company for the good treatment he has received throughout his connection with the concern. He lives at Mossley Hill, Liverpool.

Mount Temple wireless operator John Oscar Durrant outside a ship's wireless shack with a fellow operator.

Again, Mr Durrant, who must be the source for such a wide-ranging article, asserts that the *Mount Temple* was indeed 49 miles away. It is now nearly 40 years since the sinking, but the most salient feature remains unchanged.

John Oscar Durrant did not have a long retirement; anything but. He died of stomach cancer in Mossley Hill, Liverpool on June 21, 1951.

After his demise, his widow sold the house at Benmore Road and moved home to Suffolk to live in Lowestoft with her sister, Ethel Olive Catchpole. There Eva May Durrant died from a heart attack on April 4, 1960. She was aged 71, and described as the 'Widow of John Oscar Durrant, Marine Wireless Inspector.'

His niece, Betty Sutherland, says John Oscar borrowed money from his father to study the Marconi wireless course that led to his life at sea. As to the *Titanic* voyage, 'we never talked about it, and I'm kicking myself that we didn't. My father told me that he was on the *Mount Temple* and that he stayed up all night listening to the SOS and other messages. Afterwards he gave evidence in court proceedings.

'It was quite some distance, I know, as they were trying to get to her and they couldn't. They were trying to get near all night. I got the impression they couldn't get there in time.'

The prosecution in cross-examination of John Oscar Durrant:

> 9451. Tell us the ship's time when you first got a message as to the *Titanic* being in distress?
> — 12.11am.
> 9457. Is your next entry 10 minutes after that? That would be 21 minutes after midnight?
> — Yes. I have got down here, '*Titanic* still calling CQD.'
> 9463. That is 12.21. Then five minutes after that, 12.26, is your next entry '*Titanic* still calling CQD'? Have you noted there about that time that you had turned your ship's course? — Yes.
> 9464. And started to their help? — Yes; that was about 15 minutes after we got the signal. It may have been sooner.

Of course it should have been sooner, and his log was maintained as he went along. At question 9523 in the British inquiry, when Durrant has just described how he logged at 1.27am the *Titanic* declaring 'engine room flooded,' he agrees that his ship has been steaming towards her for an hour. 'Yes, since 12.26, I have here.' He agrees in the next question that the start time is 12.26. Yet his ship was begged to come 'at once' a quarter of an hour earlier, and his attempt to soften the issue only draws attention to its glaring nature.

Now, on a much more minor matter, be it said that the British inquiry transcript is completely silent as to this gentleman's claim to have received 'praise' or to have been 'commended' for his testimony. There are no such recorded remarks at all, when even the trivia as to when to adjourn is taken down by the stenographers in London, the only place in which he gave evidence.

Mr Durrant says he was promoted. We know that he did not make the following voyage on the *Mount Temple* following his arrival on the return trip to Gravesend. He instead turns up next on an entirely different run, to Australia, and has been removed completely from the North Atlantic. That is not so much a promotion as perhaps an extraction, even if gilded a little.

Durrant says he spent nearly six years aboard the *Warilda* before she was sunk in the English Channel. That incident took place on August 3, 1918. Six years prior is 1912, the year in which the *Warilda* entered service on the Australian route.

It would appear that Durrant's 'interesting' 3,000-mile overland trip across Canada, after a similar-scale voyage from London, took place in 1912. He was going to British Columbia on the west coast to indeed join a 'new' steamer – a brand new steamer, *Warilda*. Durrant was sent to the Pacific, and the question is why that was done.

Captain Moore's counsel: Mr Durrant's log entry for when his ship turned is perhaps an addition by way of afterthought. His log was to record wireless information, not his own ship's navigation. As he says himself, it may have been sooner that they turned, but he only

HMHS *Warilda*.

happened to remark it at a time that was 12.26am, when he received another *Titanic* message, thus beginning an entry.

Apropos of the *Warilda*, the *New York Times* reported that the survivors had been transferred from lifeboats to destroyers, 'which arrived promptly on the scene of disaster in response to signals of distress.' Wireless operator Durrant must have sent those messages, after the ship had been attacked 'in the blackness of the night' (between 1.30 and 2am), when she took on an immediate serious list, that led one survivor to remark: 'There was always the fear that the vessel might disappear from under our feet at any moment.'

Durrant, thereafter, would keenly know the meaning of lost life in a shipwreck in darkness. Following the *Warilda* experience, he could not have denied and repressed his conscience if there was anything to be told about the *Mount Temple* and the sinking of the *Titanic*.

The defence now introduces what we will say is a crucial document that effectively absolves the *Mount Temple* of any possible idea that she could have been the *Titanic*'s mystery ship. It is a matter deserving of careful attention.

The document was discovered among the papers of Captain Lord of the *Californian* in August 1964, having previously been overlooked. It appears to have been a note prepared in 1912, probably weeks after his ship returned to Liverpool in May of that year, allowing for it to dawn on Captain Lord that his own vessel was being accused of being the mystery ship.

The two-page document is written in pencil and headed by the words 'April 15. _Almerian_,' and it appears to be a description of events on the vessel of that name – which was also a Leyland Line steamer, like the *Californian*. It describes the early hours of that date, just after the *Titanic* sinking.

The person describing events is apparently the Captain of the *Almerian*, a Master Mariner by the name of Richard Thomas (1876-1942).

Most of the writing is indisputably in Captain Lord's handwriting, but the first few paragraphs appear in a different hand. Lord formed very small sized words, but the first paragraph is much more expansive in writing style. Formations of particular words are different. Lord used to miss out the cross-stroke on T in the word 'the,' instead superimposing a stroke resembling a dash over only the last letter, so that it resembled 'lhē' ... the cross for the T coming two letters late.

The opening paragraphs in the document have bold cross strokes in the definite article that go fully across the first letter and the word. Thus it would seem that the document begins to

Above: An initial extract of what the *Almerian* saw and did on April 15, 1912. Believed written by Captain Richard Thomas and reproduced by permission of his descendants. Captain Stanley Lord later took up the writing of this narrative, which Thomas must have dictated.

Left: Captain Richard Thomas of the *Almerian*.

The words 'officer' and 'official,' written by Captain Thomas in a 1931 letter, sandwich an abbreviation for 'second officer' in a 1912 manuscript. The unusual formation of the first syllable is judged to mean that Thomas began to write an account of his ship's experiences on the night the *Titanic* sank. There are a number of other strong calligraphic similarities between the writing of Thomas generally and the opening script in the *Almerian* account.

The *Almerian*, commanded by Captain Richard Thomas was in the vicinity of the *Titanic* sinking and halted at the icefield.

be written by one author, before Captain Lord takes over the writing – with the original source now dictating.

The author has obtained handwriting samples of Captain Thomas from later in his career, and there are very close similarities in the words formed in his personal letters in comparison to the 1912 document. What this would mean is that Captain Thomas personally assisted Captain Lord. These two men thus met face to face – with the Master of the *Almerian* giving a direct version of events to his company colleague.

In any event, it is the material contained within the document which is important. It begins:

> At 3am (approx.) I was informed there was ice alongside. I at once ordered the ship to be stopped. There was a steamer then on the port quarter. I asked the 2 Offr, Mr Havard, if he had communicated with her. He said he had endeavoured to, but could not understand her signals, only OUNT.
>
> At daylight (about 4am) we could see ice extending as far to the NE + Southward as we could see. Field ice and ice bergs.

The *Almerian* was a two-master of barely 3,000 tons, half the size of the *Californian*, but with a funnel like hers, of blushing pink with a black top. She was not equipped with any wireless.

Captain Thomas's vessel left Mobile, Alabama, bound for Britain with a cargo of cotton, lumber and staves at 10am on April 3, 1912. She docked in Liverpool on April 25. She did not know about the *Titanic* disaster until her arrival in port.

On the morning of April 15, however, Captain Thomas found himself on the western side of an icefield. His story goes on – now taken up in Captain Lord's handwriting – as follows:

> I proceeded at various speeds in a northly direction on the western extremity of the icefield with the object of finding a way to clear water in the East. The vessel which at 3.0am was on the port quarter + stopped was also steering in a North.ly direction + as we thought endeavouring to find a passage through the icefield to the East.
>
> Later we saw apparently at the Eastern extremity of the icefield, about 6 or 6½ miles off, a large 4 masted steamer. With the aid of the telescope we saw she had derricks up at No. 1.
>
> We could not distinguish her funnel. Shortly we sighted smoke ahead, which in nearer approach turned out to be a Leyland liner. At this time the vessel which had been stopped at 3.0 am on our p. quarter, + since been steering to North ahead of us, suddenly headed NW. This surprised me at the time up to this point as I thought she was an Eastbound ship.
>
> As we approached + before we got up to the Leyland liner ? she commenced steaming through the ice in the direction of other 4 masted steamer we could see East of icefield.
>
> I cont.d in a north.ly direction, not having had communication with any vessel. To my astonishment, the (*Mount Temple*) which had been in sight the whole time headed to the East.d and approached, so that with the aid of the glasses I made out her name (*Mount Temple*). After reading her name, she again steamed NW.
>
> I cont. North until about 9.50 am, when I steamed slowly through the icefield, which I cleared at 10.30 am. I did not see any more of the vessels mentioned.

Captain Thomas has described signals between his ship and the vessel he noticed on his port quarter when he gave the order to stop the *Almerian* because they were encountering ice. It was 3am by the *Almerian*'s clock.

The other vessel, which was then noticed on the port quarter, was stopped; and both remained immobile such that the *Almerian* attempted to communicate in the only way she could, by Morse lamp. The flashes that came back could only be deciphered as 'Ount,' but it is clear that it was the *Mount Temple*.

Later, in the daylight, the *Almerian* picked her way to the north. The '*Ount' Temple*, which had been on her port quarter, was now steaming line ahead, 'to north ahead of us.'

This following of the *Mount Temple* by the *Almerian* precisely matches what Captain Moore recounted in his evidence about a two-masted steamer:

> I think he was under the impression that I was going to the eastward, that I was bound to the eastward, and I think when I turned back after we both stopped, when we found the ice too heavy, he followed me, because when I turned around, after finding the ice too heavy to the southward, after I went to the southward later on in the morning, when it got daylight, and I went down to where he was, thinking he perhaps had gotten into a thin spot, when I got there he had stopped, he had found the ice too heavy. I went a little farther, and I turned around because it was getting far too heavy put the ship through. But that would be about 5, or perhaps half past 5, in the morning, sir.
>
> ... I have not seen her since the morning I saw her, 9 o'clock in the morning, because she followed me right around this ice pack, you know, sir.'

The *Almerian* thereafter sees a four-master, which must be the rescue ship *Carpathia*, because she has her derricks up at No. 1 hold, consistent with raising lifeboats – and she took on 13 *Titanic* boats to New York. The derricks, or yard-arms, would normally be folded up to the mast when at sea, so the sighting of deployed derricks is most unusual.

Next the *Almerian* met a ship of her own line, coming down head-on, which was the *Californian*, commanded by Captain Lord. The *Almerian* says this ship swerved into the icefield while in sight ahead, which must have further perplexed and amazed those on board.

Captain Lord confirmed in evidence in 1912 that he met a pink-funnel steamer of his own type, yet does not identify her (just as Captain Thomas does not specifically cite the *Californian*). His evidence in London was:

> 7399. Then at 6.30 you steered a southerly course and passed the *Mount Temple* ... at about 7.30?
> Captain Lord — Yes.
> 7400. Was there another vessel near the *Mount Temple*? — There was. A two-masted steamer, pink funnel, black top, steering north ...

Now we come to the crucial part of this document, from the defence point of view. The bottom of the sheet contains positions for the *Almerian* at the relevant period, together with a longitude and latitude for the *Mount Temple*, this being the position which was given to the inquiries as her location when she was turned around at 12.30am.

The note for the *Almerian* says that at 3.05am on April 15, when she was stopped, she was in a position of 41 20 N, 50 24 W.

This position is 26 nautical miles short on the North-South axis, and 16 miles on the East-West axis, from where the *Titanic* was actually sinking.

The precise co-ordinates of the *Titanic* wreck on the seabed are known today. The White Star liner's debris field is a colossal 31 nautical miles as the crow flies from where the *Almerian* says she was at about 3am. If she then noticed the *Mount Temple* on her port quarter, it follows that Captain Moore's vessel was a similar distance from the sinking.

Even assuming the *Almerian* was facing east and putting the *Mount Temple* a mile to the north, the actual distance only declines by that mile. The distance to the SOS position, where the *Titanic* was not, is 26 nautical miles.

It is abundantly clear from the *Almerian* evidence, therefore, that the *Mount Temple* could not have been the *Titanic*'s mystery ship, seen at a distance of five miles.

The defence now turns to outline the character of the man before you, Captain James Henry Moore. Some recollections of his descendants will be tendered in evidence.

The Master of the *Mount Temple* was born in Birkenhead, Merseyside, on March 22, 1860. He was therefore 51 years old in April 1912.

Captain James Henry Moore in summer whites. Did this man suffer a failure of nerve on the night the *Titanic* went down with catastrophic loss of life?

He appears first in the 1861 census when his family is living at Meacock Street in the town, and is shown to be the son of an Irish dock labourer named William, born in 1820, and his English wife Elizabeth. James Henry is aged just a year old, the youngest of four sons, with brothers George, 9, Robert, 4, and Arthur, three.

Their father later became a baker, while mother Elizabeth worked as a maid at the mansion of the famed shipbuilder John Laird, who would become the first MP for Birkenhead.

Captain Moore's mother died in the early summer of 1877 at the age of 54, when he had just turned 17. The family was already beginning to fragment, and James Henry was confirmed in a life at sea while his widowed father would eventually end up in the Birkenhead workhouse.

Robert Moore, the seafarer's brother, became a baker like his father. He wed a woman named Annie Bellis, and James Henry Moore became smitten with her younger sister, Mary, a mistress at a boy's school. He married her in 1884, when he was aged 24.

A year later and Moore began his sea career on the North Atlantic, having sailed in the home trade prior to this. His first crossing was aboard the *Dominium*, and two years later he was an AB aboard the *Quebec*, of 2,600 tons, owned by the Mississippi and Dominion Steamship Co, and powered by an engine built by Laird of Birkenhead.

In 1888 Moore joined another ship of the same line, the 3,300-ton *Toronto*. That year she collided at night in the Mersey with the *Freidis*, a wooden barque of 632 tons, and sank her. All but one of the 14-man crew of the barque, including the Captain and ship's boy, were drowned – the only survivor being chief officer Leonhardt Larsen, who jumped aboard the *Toronto* at 11.37pm, when the head-on collision occurred.

The Master of the larger vessel, Francis Bouchette was held not to have navigated the *Toronto* with proper care, the vessel having steamed at high speed, and his certificate was suspended for six months.

Moore stayed with the *Toronto* until the end of 1890, when he transferred to the *Oregon*. He was at sea when his wife Mary, 33, filled out the 1891 census form at their house at Ince Avenue, Litherland, Ormskirk. Two sons had been born – Harry Allinson Moore, aged 5, who would later become a sea captain himself, and William Cecil, aged 2.

The *Cambroman*, first command of Captain James Henry Moore.

In 1894, Moore became an officer on the Dominion line's *Sarnia*, of 3,700 tons. He was aboard her that December when she lost her rudder in a storm when on a voyage from Halifax to Liverpool. She signalled to the *Anchoria*, of the Anchor Line, and was towed by hawser for two days before the cable parted 130 miles off the northern Irish coast. Nonetheless, she made port.

Spells on the *Oregon*, *Vancouver*, *Canada* and *New England* followed, before Moore became Master of his own vessel for the first time. He took over the *Cambroman* in September 1898, and within a few months his ship was at the centre of a celebrated international case which seemed to pre-figure that of the fugitive murderer Dr Crippen in 1910.

The advent of shipboard wireless was still two years away when a 'Mrs Pierce' and her daughter booked aboard Captain Moore's ship for the crossing from Montreal to Liverpool in July 1899. Thus Moore was surprised when met at the landing stage after his voyage by Scotland Yard detectives who took the passenger into custody on a charge of child abduction.

Divorced from her husband, but having lost custody, she was in fact a Mrs Derot from Baltimore, who fled with her nine-year-old daughter Gladys to New York, crossing the border into Canada. It became suspected that she had boarded the *Cambroman* at Montreal, and a grand jury in Baltimore returned indictments. The State Department in Washington then wired to London, requesting the woman's arrest pending extradition.

It is a coincidence that Moore's next ship was the first vessel to be fitted with wireless: the *Lake Champlain*, which he served aboard as Chief Officer. On her June 1901 voyage from Montreal, she established communication with Crookhaven shore station in Ireland, 'and numerous service and private telegrams were despatched notifying the steamer's safe arrival.'

The next station contacted was Rosslare, when 45 miles distant. 'For more than five hours there was a continuous stream of messages, upwards of 50 being sent.' Holyhead was then engaged by means of the ether, and Liverpool when 37 and three-quarter miles away, 'a message being received from the owners, congratulating Captain Stewart on his excellent passage and the very successful operation of the telegraph.' Newspaper reports added that 'on the Canadian side, great interest had been manifested in the experiment, and a number of scientific men visited the *Lake Champlain* to see the installation.'

Captain Moore went home, to his new family address at Birchdale Road, in Waterloo, Liverpool. He now had a further son, Reginald James, six, and a daughter, Doris Emmeline, four. A baby named Hilda had died in infancy.

The owners of the *Lake Champlain* were meanwhile trumpeting to the newspapers the 'most wonderful results' achieved by their wireless innovation, declaring in addition: 'We feel sure that it will greatly minimise the risk of casualty.' The Marconi system was speedily introduced to Moore's next ships, the *Lake Megantic* and the *Lake Erie*.

Captain Moore, top right, just before his retirement. In front, right, is a sister of renowned explorer Earnest Shackleton, who had crossed earlier. Others unidentified, although two sisters reportedly delivered seveal dogs as a gift to their brother.

He returned to command with the *Milwaukee* in November 1904. Moore was now a Captain with the Canadian Pacific Line, which had taken over the fleet of Elder Dempster, owner of the Lake-class, in 1903. His vessel was 7,300 tons.

In 1906 he took over the helm of the *Montrose*, but she went aground in the St Lawrence a year later. His Captaincy of the *Mount Temple* followed, from the end of 1908, and continued after the attempt to succour the *Titanic*, until the end of 1913.

Captain Moore transferred to the *Montcalm* in March 1914, and when war broke out in August saw that vessel fitted up as a dummy for the battleship HMS *Audacious*. This imposture did not last long however, as the real *Audacious*, of 23,000 tons and 26 guns, struck a German mine off Donegal in October 1914. She began to sink over many hours, and one of the vessels that responded to distress calls was the RMS *Olympic*, sister of the ill-fated *Titanic* of two years earlier. All 900 crew were successfully evacuated by a variety of helpmeets.

Moore's only significant action of the Great War was to take charge of the seized German steamer *Professor Woermann*, and to sail her from Africa to Britain. She was unarmed, and had been intercepted by the HMS *Carnarvon* off the coast of West Africa in September 1914. The 300 German reservists aboard would find themselves interned in Sierra Leone.

Captain Moore sailed the 6,000-ton vessel from Freetown to London in November, where she would eventually become a confiscation operated by the Union Castle Line, and renamed simply the *Professor*.

After the war, Moore returned briefly to the service of the CPR, and on one Atlantic voyage brought the famed explorer Ernest Shackleton to Canada for a planned North Pole expedition which fate dictated would never be mounted. In 1919 Moore retired, and the following year he moved permanently to Canada.

James Henry and Mary Moore moved to northern Saskatchewan. They stayed with son Reginald, who had moved there in 1910 before he returned to Europe to fight on the Western Front. Another son, William, was next door in British Columbia, where he would eventually marry a Cree native and have 'umpteen kids.

Left behind in Britain was another son, Harry Allinson Moore, who had married and was a sea captain like his father. Harry would find himself Master of the *Duchess of Atholl* when she

Captain Moore framed in the doorway with his wife Mary and their son Reginald, wearing army uniform, shortly before the latter shipped overseas for the Western front.

was torpedoed and sunk off West Africa in 1942, and he was awarded an OBE the next year for his conduct on that occasion.

But the Moores did bring to Canada their daughter Doris, who was a 'surprise' birth in Birkenhead in 1896, and was now in her early twenties. She would later marry a Japanese man in Toronto.

Captain Moore settled in the sparsely-populated Brightholme district, southeast of Shellbrook, with its population of 1,270. But his retirement would not be prolonged. In September 1922, feeling poorly, he was diagnosed with cancer of the spine, a malignancy which had also spread to his liver and his lung.

Captain James Henry Moore died the following month at the age of only 62. He now lies buried in the tiny graveyard of the wooden-shack church known as St Mary's, a building started by a donation of $500 from his wife, and named partly in tribute to her.

The headstone reads: 'In loving memory of James Henry Moore, who departed this life October 12, 1922. God called him home.' His wife lived to 91, and died after the second war. She is buried alongside in the meadow of the little Anglican church in Brightholme, but there is nothing to signify her presence.

The Moore descendants have no knowledge of any *Titanic* involvement. The only one with a fragment of lore is Midori Brown, the daughter of Moore's youngest child, Doris. She was born ten years after his death .

'He was somewhere not too far away, and they received the SOS from the *Titanic*,' she says. 'They (*Titanic*) were supposed to have told them where they were, and that's where they went. They weren't there. They had given the wrong co-ordinates. They had helped themselves to sink.

'I heard there were some flares seen. There were some who thought he should have gone faster, but he didn't have the biggest boat.'

The declaration about flares is made, but it has not the least value because Ms Brown is advanced in years and much hearsay and legend has agglomerated in that time. Midori, incidentally, means green in Japanese. She indeed has no direct experience of these matters.

She did once possess a drawing of Captain James Henry Moore, made by a passenger on the *Mount Temple*, and given to the Master as a symbol of gratitude, no doubt by someone as admiring as F.J. Swift and his son Horace had been in 1912. Those voyagers were in no doubt as to their Captain's courage, character and decency.

Midori's portrait of Captain Moore has disintegrated over the years. She can no more put it together today than the prosecution can present a convincing mosaic to persuade you that this fine mariner ever did less than his full duty.

The grave of Captain James Henry Moore in St Mary's church meadow at Brightholme in Saskatchewan.

CLOSING ARGUMENTS

THE prosecution must now deal with the *Almerian*, raised by counsel for the defence. Thereafter will come final submissions as to why Captain Moore should be convicted on a specimen charge of perjury.

The *Almerian* saw a vessel at 3am that is likely to have been the *Mount Temple*. But there is no further progress by either of these ships until daylight. Captain Moore says his ship began to meet ice at 3am, but – crucially – that he did not stop until 3.25am.

While there will have been differences between the clocks of both these ships, Captain Moore stated that when he stopped first (at 3.25am) he was 14 miles from the SOS position – but that he subsequently reached that vicinity at 4.30am.

Leaving aside certain matters (Moore's top speed, the fact that his ship was initially stopped for an unknowable duration, and the fact that he simply could not have reached the SOS position in the remaining time when proceeding slowly), what is important is that Moore makes clear that he eventually reached the western edge of what might be called the *Titanic* icefield – so that there was further steaming after his first stop, which occurred at 3.25am.

Therefore the *Almerian* was not met at an earlier icefield.

She was met at the *Titanic* icefield.

Captain Richard Thomas of the *Almerian*, who got there at 3.05am, noticed the *Mount Temple* already there. And it is Captain Thomas, an independent witness, who makes it clear that there was no further steaming by either ship. Both simply waited for the daylight, which came only an hour later.

There is thus a simple clash between Captain Thomas and Captain Moore on what time the *Mount Temple* got to the *Titanic* icefield. In reality, the *Almerian* must actually be called another witness for the prosecution.

Almerian saw the morning developments at the *Titanic* vicinity, and knew that the *Mount Temple* had been stopped at the icefield when she herself got there at about 3am. Crucially, she does not say that she saw the 'Ount' steamer arrive and stop.

It appears, therefore, that the *Mount Temple* was there the whole time, with *Almerian* being the late arrival. This is corroboration of the tales of some of Captain Moore's passengers.

Thus Captain Moore's story is false, because he cannot have made any onward progress since 3.05am by the *Almerian* clock. And it also follows then, by the *Almerian* account, that Moore could not have been 49 miles away from the SOS position, because this stop was always at the *Titanic* ice barrier, and in the immediate vicinity of the distress co-ordinates.

Moving on, the longitude and latitude positions given in the same document for the *Almerian* (and therefore for the *Mount Temple*) are, we the prosecution say, simply wrong. This is because the cited positions are much too far west. This veracity of this can be established from the rest of the *Almerian*'s account.

The *Almerian* was judging her location by dead reckoning, or a simple estimate based on course and speed. She was going east, and Moore, when going east, said his ship would have had the Gulf Stream – a current that pushes to the north and east, as was said at the British inquiry. *Titanic* fourth officer Boxhall, separately at the US inquiry, gave evidence that the effect was 'to the northward and eastward.'

Almerian positional estimates that night were likely too far to the south and west for another reason: Because if *Mount Temple*'s testified diagonal course to the SOS position from her own claimed turnaround point had been true, then the *Almerian* should not have seen her. Her course would have lain outside the *Almerian*'s visibility arc, had the *Almerian*'s own positional estimate been correct.

This discrepancy has been used to suggest that the *Almerian* was not there at all, because Captain Moore does not mention her. But the fact is that the *Almerian* saw the 'Ount' vessel, and Captain Lord saw the pink funnel of the *Almerian* the next morning, such that she was indeed there. Captain Moore cites a two-masted steamer, but gives a different funnel colour.

The *Almerian* account gives not only her position at 3.05am, but also at 10.30am when she 'cleared ice,' with a further latitude and longitude for noon on Monday, April 15, 1912.

These show that her location in darkness must be in error, as will be explained. That night position must be an estimate, because no longitude observations can be taken when there is no sun (nor any visible horizon for star sights, as with early evening and early day). A longitude fix would give the ship's position on the West-East axis.

Conversely, the following noon position will be absolutely accurate because all officers will have taken observations when the sun reached its zenith. Longitude is simply achieved by reference to the ship's chronometer and Greenwich time.

But first of all, consider this: The *Almerian* night position and the *Mount Temple* turnaround point (41 25 N; 51 14 W) cannot both be accurate, as counsel for Captain Moore has implied in his remarks.

To reach the *Almerian*'s 3.05am position (41 20 N, 50 24 W) would mean Moore steaming 38 nautical miles since 12.30, a practical timeframe of two and a half hours.

This gives a speed of 15.2 knots, which is beyond Moore's top speed, which he gave alternatively as 11 and 11½ knots. While the clocks of both ships will not exactly correspond, it should be remembered that the time difference between them could be the other way, meaning a gap between these signposts of even *less* than 2½ hours.

Accepting *Almerian*'s evidence means that Moore cannot have been 14 miles from the SOS position at 3.25am, and neither, by any stretch of the imagination, could he have been 49 miles away at 12.30am.

The same document revealing the 'Ount' story contains a notation that the *Almerian* cleared ice at 10.30am in 41 48 N, 50 24 W. The longitude here is exactly the same for that given at 3.05am, and only the latitude (distance north) is different. Because one minute of latitude is always equal to one nautical mile, Captain Thomas indicates that he has simply steamed 28 miles due north, which would make sense, because there was an icefield in his way to the east.

We know Thomas and the *Almerian* were moving along the western side of the icefield the next morning because he was seen by Captain Lord, coming along the western edge in the opposite direction. But Captain Thomas states in his account; 'At daylight (about 4am) we could see ice extending as far to the NE + Southward as we could see.'

An important aspect here is his mention of the icefield running '/ ' to the northeast. He therefore cannot simply have 'cleared ice' by steaming 28 miles due north, unless the field paradoxically doubled back on itself, like so – '\' – which seems inherently unlikely.

The two positions, at 3.05am and 10.30am, are therefore inconsistent – which calls into question the reliability of these positions in the first place.

They are inconsistent for another reason. Captain Thomas states in the document that he continued heading north until 'about 9.50am, when I steamed slowly through the icefield, which I cleared at 10.30am.'

He therefore steamed north and then east, creating a right angle of sorts. The steaming time to enter and clear the icefield is forty minutes. Captain Moore estimated it was five miles wide. The obvious indication, therefore, is that the *Almerian* was doing no more than 7½ knots. But it could be that the speed was even less, because Captain Thomas would obviously choose to cross at a point that might appear less wide than the field in general.

The point is that the 10.30am position and the 3.05am position are both given as longitude 50 24 W, which would mean progress only of a northern variety – which is totally contradicted by the 40 minutes of eastward progress which is also described for the *Almerian*.

But assuming the position given for 10.30am, we now look at the difference between it and the Noon position, which is likely to be unimpeachably accurate because of co-ordinated sun shots by the ship's officers, each of them using a sextant. The position comes out at 41 51 N, 50 W.

It means, however, that in ninety minutes, from 10.30am until noon, the *Almerian* has completed a distance of 18 nautical miles, which would mean a speed of 12 knots.

This is very unlikely, as she took several hours to complete 28 miles north between her night stop position and 10.30am. If this was over a period of nearly five hours (5-9.50am), or five and a half hours (5-10.30am), the previous speed cannot have been better than six knots

The *Almerian's* design top speed was 12kt, two knots less than her sister ship *Californian*, which never reached that maximum even when responding as fast as she could to the emergency in the same morning. But the *Almerian* had no wireless and knew nothing of the disaster. She was on a routine voyage.

If her noon position is correct, as it is very likely to be, then it means that her 10.30am and 3.05am citations are impossibly too far west (the longitude being the same for them both). Therefore the *Almerian* – and *Mount Temple* – must both have been much closer to the sinking during the night than is indicated on the face of the co-ordinates offered for 3.05am.

There is also the possibility that *Almerian* reverse-estimated her earlier positions from what she learned subsequently about the sinking. That morning she saw what she later grasped to have been the *Carpathia*, and believed her to be in the SOS position (*Titanic's* transmitted place – which was actually beyond the western rim of the ice barrier, where the *Almerian* was).

Almerian then piled error upon the *Titanic's* initial error. She estimated her own longitude to be even further west than the *Titanic's* distress longitude, because she thought that position coincided with where the *Carpathia* was seen. Everybody thought the *Titanic* would have her SOS right, instead of her actually sinking where she did, 13 miles further east. A large error in the document's 'backfill' longitude for the *Almerian* can now be understood.

Meanwhile, consider this separate and startling possibility – that the pink funnel steamer is actually Moore's 'black funnel' (or black, with a white band) steamer. Witnesses saw only a single two-master in the vicinity the next morning. Just the one – and it must be that some witnesses are describing her wrongly.

Almerian, which had a black top to her funnel, did exactly what Moore described – follow him in the morning, thinking he was eastbound. *Californian* officer Charles Victor Groves, who saw her only end-on the next morning, thought she had a black funnel – but only the top would have been visible to him as his ship came down on a closing course from the north. Groves described a vessel the size of the *Almerian*, but did not see her broadside. If he had done, he might have discerned that the rest of the funnel was actually pink.

Captain Lord described *Almerian* accurately, and made no mention of any other two-funnel steamer, such as the one Captain Moore mentioned. Captain Rostron of the rescue ship *Carpathia* saw the *Mount Temple* and *Almerian* in close proximity to each other, but could not distinguish funnel colour. He did not see three ships.

In mentioning only two other vessels, at a distance of seven to eight miles (Q. 25551 in the British inquiry), Rostron declared: 'It was light enough to see all round the horizon.'

At this time – which he specified as 5am – both these other vessels were at a higher latitude (further north) than Rostron's own. This evidence also clearly indicates, from reality, that the *Almerian's* suggested night position was too far south, emphasising again that this 3.05am position was in error.

Having waited at the icefield for daylight, which he says came an hour later at 'about 4am,' *Almerian* could not have travelled north by some 23-26 miles in just sixty minutes to gain either the wreck latitude or the distress latitude. Yet she was seen by Rostron at 5am in just such a vicinity.

Consider that there may have been no separate two-master steamer with a black funnel, with or without a white band (with some device in it), as described by Moore. The Captain of the *Mount Temple* is then pointing at the two-master (*Almerian*) but is being either deliberately obscure about her, or else can't recall her accurately.

In this scenario, Moore would be blaming the *Almerian* – even in a roundabout way, and for whatever reason, whether by accident or design. Yet if the *Almerian* was alongside the *Mount Temple* for part of the night – and privy to rocket scenes – then Moore's determination not to be solely implicated as 'the' unfeeling bystander becomes completely understandable.

But it may be that Moore, thinking about it, realises that if he identifies her, *Almerian*, then *she will identify him* ... He may immediately grasp that his ship sent the letters 'Ount' and all the rest of the *Mount Temple* name to the two-master that night.

So he can't admit she had a pink funnel and was an obvious Leyland liner. He has to disguise her identity, in order that she is not found, so that he can thereby camouflage himself.

What time did *Mount Temple* stop? Had she been stopped there long before the *Almerian* arrived? Why does the wireless log of the *Mount Temple* make no mention of the fact of the Canadian Pacific ship being stopped before 4.46am? Why does the Official Log provide no entry about the *Titanic* episode at all?

Durrant's entry for 4.46 is 'All quiet; we're stopped amongst pack ice.' Moore said he made a stop at 3.25am. Why does Durrant's PV not reflect that? But Durrant also has an entry for 2.36am that says: 'All quiet now. *Titanic* hasn't spoken since [1.33am, ship's time.].'

Why is it 'all quiet' at 2.36am? Is it because the *Mount Temple* is not rushing to assist? Does one 'all quiet' – at 4.46am – suggest that the 'all quiet now' at 2.36am means that the *Mount Temple* is also stopped at this time? On the face of it, those first three words are not needed at 2.36am if the *Mount Temple* is still rushing headlong for the scene – the meat is in the next statement: that the *Titanic* has not spoken since whatever time.

Durrant mentions no initial stop and no resumption, just a first 'all quiet' and then a further 'all quiet' when daylight comes and reveals their ongoing quietude, their immobility, in a vicinity full of pack ice ...

Adrian Havard is the grandson of the *Almerian* officer who told Captain Thomas about the 'Ount' signals. 'My recollection of what my father told me is as follows,' he says. 'He said that his father had told him that the *Almerian* had been stopped for the night because of ice in roughly the area of what turned out to be where the *Titanic* sank.

'During the night, he and some of the crew had seen lights in the sky that looked like the distress rockets then in use, but that no action was taken by the ship to investigate. On hearing about the sinking of the *Titanic*, he realised that the time he saw the lights in the sky would have been the same sort of time as the *Titanic*'s rockets being launched.'

The mystery ship was described by officer Boxhall as a three or four-masted steamer with 'beautiful lights.' In the United States he declared: 'The only description of the ship that I could give is that she was, or I judged her to be, a four-masted steamer.' Recalled to the stand, he said: 'She might have been a four-mast ship or might have been a three-mast ship, but she certainly was not a two-mast ship.' *Almerian* was a small two-mast ship.

In the final analysis, the mystery ship certainly saw *Titanic*'s rockets. If the *Almerian* saw those rockets, then the *Mount Temple* also saw them, because the latter was beside the former at 3.05am.

Moore had bolstered his lookouts, knew from the earliest by wireless of the emergency, and had headed in that direction – but insisted that he never saw any rockets or signals at all. This denial is simply not credible. But the denial is made because any admission to seeing rockets would naturally fling open the door to much more.

The prosecution would ask you to look particularly to the crew evidence, such as it is. Dr Bailey frankly admits that the crew 'saw certain things.' Second officer Heald could reportedly 'tell a lot.' Third officer Notley met with Captain Lord and must have made confidential disclosures. Replacement officer Baker, who was subsequently decorated for his bravery, declares: 'the officers and others told me what they had seen on the eventful night when the *Titanic* went down.' What they had seen, he reported, included 'her decklights.'

Lots of crew deserted. Some officers never breathed a word about their *Titanic* experience, even though a genuine but doomed attempt to render assistance would have made for a sobering fireside story. But a ship's cook, John Vincent Ehmig, verifiably on the ship's articles for that voyage, declared in print that his vessel was 'so near at the time of the accident, I am sure she could have saved nearly all of the passengers.'

The number of claimants about the *Mount Temple* is multiples of the case with the *Californian*, which was blamed as the mystery ship in 1912. No other ship mentioned as a possible candidate features anything like such a wide range of allegation-mongers. Something certainly happened on the *Mount Temple* that night – but only one man told a story about the danger caused by a baleful schooner.

If something did not happen, then all of these people who made allegations are suffering from a species of hysteria, which would be an interesting contagion for study, given that the outbreaks are widely dispersed – in the United States, both sides of Canada, England, even privately in Marseilles – and seem to affect not alone passengers but crew as well, and not just ordinary hands but officers also.

Moore's vessel can only have been the *Titanic*'s mystery ship if she was lying about her position. And the record shows that absolutely none of Captain Moore's navigational claims adds up consistently.

One *Titanic* passenger, Charles Stengel, saved in lifeboat number 1, told how 'we followed a light … which looked like in the winter, in the dead of winter, when the windows are frosted with a light coming through them. It was in a haze.'

Might this suggest that the mystery ship, coming to the rescue, had been blocked by ice? Boxhall said his ship had been heading to the west. The mystery ship was 'meeting us.' Then that steamer stopped and lay watching … until she eventually turned and went away, and did so in a 'westerly' direction, in the direction from whence she came, he agreed.

Yet the *Mount Temple* did not meet this three or four-mast steamer on her course! By her own account she herself was there soon after it all, at 4.30am. Not meeting any three or four

Essex Harries Havard, second officer, aboard the *Almerian* in 1912. He was
stated in a contemporary document to have communicated by Morse lamp
with a nearby steamer whose name he could only read as 'Ount.' A 1913
storm ripped away many of the poop fittings where Harvard is standing.

master, which must have set out towards him if they are different ships, Moore instead offered a two-master (which had been in view throughout) as potentially the mystery ship, when she patently could not have been on any grounds.

But a mystery ship attempting to routinely go east (i.e., not one responding to the SOS; one instead without wireless or an active listening post) would either stop where she was because of the impassable ice – which is the most likely occurrence, as *Almerian* and *Californian* demonstrate, and which Moore said was the 'usual thing' – or else she would probe to the south, in order to find the tail of the field, and hook around it.

Such a ship, in the latter instance, would come back up to her former latitude on the far side. Great circle navigation for eastbounders would impose that action upon her. Broadly speaking, she would steer towards the *Carpathia*. No ship did that because no such ship was seen coming up from the south by the *Carpathia*. Thus, the possibility that the mystery ship did not have wireless must be considered less than the likelihood that she did.

If she did have wireless, and learned of the emergency, then she must have used her wireless in response at some stage.

And if she possessed wireless but somehow knew not – perhaps because a sole operator was asleep – then she would have learned immediately of the disaster in the morning through the transmissions of calls to 'all shipping.' Even without seeing unusual activity (such as a passenger liner with derricks deployed), she would instantly have realised that she was in the immediate vicinity. Yet no previously unknown steamer ever responded.

These considerations show that the parameters for the mystery ship are actually very limited. *Almerian* does not mention any ship that passed her in scouting south. The probability must be, therefore, that the mystery ship is actually one of the known participants. An ever-excluding series of equations produces only one likely match.

The mystery ship did indeed go away, because she could not go east. But she did not go to the south. Nor did she go to the west, where she would have met the *Mount Temple* by the latter's evidence. That leaves only one direction – north – and yet the *Californian*, crossing the icefield later that morning, and then heading down the western side to *Mount Temple*, mentions no other steamer seen before she meets *Almerian*.

If there was a mystery ship whose name remains unknown, then she did very well indeed to escape the noose of the nexus of *Mount Temple*, *Almerian*, *Carpathia* and *Californian*. Those ships close the bag. Yet relatively big unidentified three- and four-masters, the type that would show beautiful lights at night, are in spectacularly short supply.

The prosecution points out that Captain Moore's vessel is the only one whose movements and profile fit those of the mystery ship. Furthermore, her morning navigation betrays shame in not going to the *Carpathia*'s side, while her failure to use wireless when she believed she was at the SOS position is otherwise inexplicable. There is also the fact that Captain Moore desperately tried to create alternative, unidentified, suspects.

 That the mystery ship was eventually near at hand is abundantly described in the official transcripts. *Titanic* officers, crew and passengers alike could see the light. Those dropped to the surface of the sea in low lifeboats could see it still, even after they were afloat. Captain Smith himself, then nearing retirement and by far the most experienced commander of the White Star Line, was in little doubt about her close proximity.

Witnesses, both passengers and crew, gave evidence of the Captain giving instructions to two *Titanic* lifeboats that they were to 'row straight for those ship lights over there, land the passengers aboard, and return as soon as possible.' The Master of the largest ship in the world believed rowboats could certainly make the distance and alert the apparently inattentive stranger, which was ignoring distress rockets. The other vessel could not have been a vast distance away, else struggling muscle could not have performed the feat demanded – nor could puny lifeboats have continued to see her once sent away.

The *Titanic* officers were all of the same opinion. Senior survivor Charles Herbert Lightoller was busy filling lifeboats and did not closely observe the light or lights, except to note that it was 'certainly not over 5 miles away,' corroborating Boxhall. To the American inquiry the second officer said the lights were: 'Four or 5 miles away. I would say 3 to 4 miles, roughly. I did not stop to look at them.'

The mystery ship, likely having wireless and therefore full knowledge, behaved in a very cautious and ultimately cowardly manner. Captain Moore was pathologically afraid of either ice, or his company's instructions, or both. He had seen Captains cashiered, and he himself had been admonished to be more careful in future. He also indeed had a vessel stuffed with emigrants, as he was afterwards keen to point out.

The prosecution asks you to convict Captain Moore of a specimen charge of perjury in his denial that his ship saw rockets.

THE defence will once again be brief. Captain Moore has no case to answer here. He voluntarily left the Dominion to answer every question in another country, the United States. He attended a second inquiry, in London, and answered every question there. His accusers, however, have not answered their own single overwhelming question: Why, if they had so many charges to make, no matter if many of them were contradictory, did not a single person attend in person to have their say?

History cannot be doing with sneaks and tittle-tattle. Captain Moore's attempt to assist the *Titanic* casualty is a fact that cannot be gainsaid. The 'swine' or 'bounder' canvassed here would surely not even make that attempt in the first place. The reality is that Captain Moore did make every effort, and it is an inescapable certainty that he did. That he should then be calumnised is little short of an outrage.

'It is pretty hard after all that to have mud slung at me,' he said in a newspaper interview, and his towering indignation can be glimpsed even now in press clippings. He, however, backed up his words with deeds – he attended. Others did not. Captain Moore is entitled to that benefit, against the nebulous doubters, who may have been encouraged or even embroidered by the yellow journalism of the day, and who may not have later even recognised what they were supposed to have said, but who nevertheless did not give those alleged opinions any physical form.

The principle of *habeas corpus* is one of the oldest known to justice. Captain Moore at least produced himself, in answer to one of its precepts. He was a witness who assisted two inquiries. It is absurd for him now to be made a defendant against spurious outsiders, who may have written vague letters from personal animus, or been beguiled by imagined riches in the new land to which they came, with the newspapers already speaking of the vast sums paid to wireless operators for their tales of the *Titanic*.

We are asked to conceive of the motives of these claimants as noble and pure, but of those of Captain Moore as venal and base. But the record shows that he came to the assistance, and then he came to the inquiries. He brought with him the Marconi man, independently employed by an outside company, a man who could have had the money of operators Bride and Cottam, of *Titanic* and *Carpathia*, if he had succumbed to the temptation to concoct a sensational story to rival theirs, which naturally needed no improvement. But operator Durrant did not succumb. He told the truth. And it is the pinnacle of significance that this man corroborated his Captain completely. He is the on-board, independent alibi of Captain James Henry Moore.

My learned friend has wasted much of his time in discussing times and claimed positions and suggested distances and speeds. All positions that night were estimates, the *Titanic* one badly wrong. But that was an innocent mistake, and impugning various pieces of data does not make anyone guilty – not when the night, the shifting sea, the current and the frailty of human calculation all conspire against the accuracy taken for granted today. Nearly right, as they were likely to be, does not mean damnably wrong and culpably so.

The burden of proof does not lie with the *Mount Temple*. In any criminal court, were you presented with two contradictory indications or a number of possible interpretations of objective facts, you would be instructed of your obligation to assume that which is favourable to the defendant. It is right and proper that it should be so, because what is left to us, even after death, if not our good name?

Look to what you know of the character of Captain Moore, a character that prompted the unsolicited letter from F. J. Swift and his son, one that declared the Master of the *Mount Temple* to be 'honest, straightforward and courageous.' Is this not the plain and simple truth, devoid of colour and extraordinary assertion, but seen time and time again in his lifetime of service?

Captain Moore, late in his life, did not shirk the call of duty. He took a prize ship home in wartime from the coast of West Africa. He was at the service of his country, just as he had been at the service of other ships.

Passing illustrations may be cited. The *Times* of November 29, 1910, on page six, reported from St John, New Brunswick – his destination in April 1912 – that the 'British schooner *Lone Star* [was discovered] waterlogged; crew taken off by the British steamer *Mount Temple* and landed here.'

The record thus shows that Captain Moore was solicitous to his fellow seafarers. In January 1912, as has been mentioned, he stood by the British steamer *Dart* off Cape Race, the *Mount Temple* reporting by wireless the position of the casualty when her own abilities were not equal to the task at hand.

Was Captain Moore a Good Samaritan in January 1912, only to 'pass by on the other side,' as the parable has it, three months later? No, a man cannot change his character in so short a time.

And if that character is good, mere suspicion cannot prevail against it. Much is made of the insistence that Captain Moore must have seen rockets. He tells you that he did not. But he is also supported by his chief officer, Alfred Henry Sargent, who was pulled aloft to the top of a mast to keep a lookout there, and who put his name to a cable stating formally that no such signals were seen.

Sargent said nothing subsequently to his family for one very good and simple reason – that there was nothing to be said. They had indeed seen nothing at all, only a nightscape that slowly gave way to a sunny, ice-laden morning and bad news. As Captain Moore said somewhere, they might as well not have been there at all.

And Sargent, too, was a man of character. A man who fought to save his ship in 1916, and who suffered privations as a prisoner of war. A man who was haunted by the strangulated whinnies of drowning horses, but who was entirely unperturbed by any remorse in relation to the *Titanic*, because he had nothing to reproach himself about.

It may very well be that William Henry Baker is a good and brave man too. His character does not actually come into it. He may have been so innocent of mind, indeed, as to fall prey to sailors' tall stories – imagine it, that a seafarer might have many an entertaining yarn! – and it is perhaps noteworthy that any new man on a ship is always likely to be made subject to a leg-pull. But when he swallows it, writes his letters and makes his visits, then the joke has gone too far, and there is none thereafter to offer a shred of substance of any of it.

What then, of the *Almerian*, and of a grandson saying she saw rockets? It is another tale, worn threadbare by the passing of a century. Because that man's father – who was the son of the grandfather, and therefore one generation closer to the truth – actually put a different story into writing.

John Heywood Havard wrote to the Mercantile Marine Services Association, whose general secretary was campaigning on Captain Lord's behalf, on July 24, 1980. His short note is as follows: 'My father, Essex Havard, was first mate of the above ship and told me many years ago that he believed it was possible that the *Almerian* was the mystery ship at the time of the sinking of the *Titanic*.

'He said that on that night they were in an ice field and thought they could see a ship not far distant. They fired some rockets, thinking that if the ship was in trouble they would answer with a distress flare. There was no reply.

'There were a lot of shooting stars that night, caused by the Aurora Borealis.' It is signed 'John Havard.' This makes it clear that it was the *Almerian* firing rockets, and that no rockets were seen as fired from any other ship.

Of course it clashes with what this man's son recalls, and what was found in Captain Lord's papers in 1964 relating to what he apparently gleaned in 1912. John Havard seems to have changed his story, or he has perhaps confused himself, but he was 62 at the time of writing the above – hardly in his dotage – and his father had died when the son was 34.

The fact that there was no reply suggests that no rockets were fired, but merely signals sent by Morse lamp, and that the unsatisfactory response is of the same nature as that described in the 'Ount' story. Thus these two ships were close, yes, but neither saw rockets and neither fired them. Captain Moore is thus entitled to the benefit of his corroborated statement that his ship saw no rockets, and these entirely contradictory claims must be dismissed by reason of their total unreliability, complete inconsistency, and likelihood to have become contaminated with subsequent information about the *Titanic* and her distress rockets.

The *Mount Temple* has been described as if she conforms to some formula for the *Titanic's* mystery ship. In fact, there is no formula – there were lights seen, and some thought it a fishing boat and some a steamer. Fourth Officer Boxhall offered us a three- or four-masted steamer. How did he know? They could not even tell whether the mystery ship was responding to their Morse lamp or not. Those lights were not so 'beautiful' as to be actually read. Yet Boxhall thinks he can discern extra masts, when only two masts on a steamer of any size would ordinarily be lit, and he has said he could see two masthead lights.

It is submitted that he simply could not know how many masts a ship, some five miles off, might possess. Even if he makes a surmise, he might very well be wrong. And Boxhall is the man who got his sums wrong to the extent of thirteen nautical miles. He is not infallible. His calculation error could indicate that he was confused and excitable. There is no-one to whom he confided his assessment at the time, and so there is no independent confirmation that this is what he actually thought when looking at her, before he had gone through trauma and been exposed to all sorts of claims and suppositions that might have coloured his view in retrospect.

There were 1,609 people on board the *Mount Temple* that night. The number from her complement who are gossiping might be the nine. But how does this compare with the 1,600 who have nothing to say, no allegations to make, no complaints to lodge on landfall? We must

John Heywood Havard, son of the second officer of the *Almerian*, who informed the Mercantile Marine Services Association in 1980 that his father had had tales to tell of the night the *Titanic* went down.

Captain Moore smiling in an undated photograph.

conclude that these people are grateful indeed to Captain Moore for his efforts on their behalf, and the failure to move this large number must simply mean that there were no grounds for any of them to be bestirred in any way. The suggestion that all and sundry were on deck, looking at these lights, is simply laughable in the face of what the silent figures show.

Look at the desertions and departures, where the same equation is on offer. A man who was jailed for abuse left the ship when he didn't like his punishment. Others left for their own reasons. But the vast majority stayed with Captain Moore. This is what makes talk of a mutiny so absurd – because Captain Moore was one man, easily deposed if the officers had any reasons to act. They did not depose him, and ergo the evidence is that there could have been no motive in that direction. These tall tales are cut down to size through a moment's consideration of the reality. His crew substantially stayed with him, and he stayed with the ship.

No, Captain Moore has nothing to confess. His spirited engagement with even the newspapers showed he had nothing to fear. He was a man prepared to confront a challenge and a crisis, and he demonstrated that quality in his own difficulty and detraction. We can rest assured that this is a man who did indeed do his best.

On Christopher Wren's plain stone marker in St Paul's Cathedral in London is the inscription 'Lector, si monumentum requiris, circumspice.' It means: 'Reader, if you seek a monument, look about you.' Captain Moore cannot answer rumour and allegation at this remove; he cannot disprove whisperers absolutely, of which we may suspect there will always be some. But you can instead study what remains, the surrounding structure of his career and what his long service can only say about his character.

In concluding, perhaps little better can be done than to paraphrase Robertson Dunlop's final appeal in relation to Captain Lord at the British *Titanic* inquiry in 1912: 'For all the reasons I have urged, I do ask you not to pass any censure upon this man, and I venture to think that if you do not censure him, then truth and justice and mercy will meet together in your report.'

***

APPENDICES

APPENDIX 1. OFFICIAL LOG

T.S.S. *Mount Temple* March-May 1912.

Official number 113496   Port of Registry Liverpool
Registered tonnage 8,790 Net 6,661
No. of cert 07162
Jas H. Moore, Master.
11 Neville Road, Waterloo, Liverpool.
Nature of the Voyage
St John NB, via Antwerp
14 May, 1912.
Stamped C.H. Davies,
Superintendent, M.M. office.

Left London at 9.30am on Friday, March 29, 1912.
Arrived Antwerp, Saturday March 30.
Left Antwerp at 1pm on Wednesday April 3, 1912.
Arrived St John, Friday April 19, 1912.
Left St John at 7am on Saturday April 27, 1912.
Arrived Halifax, Sunday April 28, 1912.
Left Halifax at 11.20pm on Monday April 29, 1912.
Arrived London 14 May 1912.

Mar 29th – London. 29/3/12. J. Pearce and G. Pearce, trimmers, failed to join. Dis A & Eng. 2 returned to shipping master, Dock St, from Gravesend.
Signed: Jas. H. Moore, Master. H. Shaw, Purser.

April 2nd – Antwerp. 2/4/12. J. Meinchad & H. Kritsch signed as trimmers, wages £5 per month commcg 1st. H. Torner signed articles as fireman, wages £5 10/ per month comcg the 1st.
Signed: Jas. H. Moore, Master. H. Shaw, Purser.

April 2nd – Antwerp. 2/4/12. The following men signed articles as Asst Stwds, wages £3 –15-0 per mth, comcg 30/3/12: J. Mees, L. Gogo, C. Naudts, J. Stevens, H. Belont, J. Stockmoery, P. Krause, and F. De Nys, comcg 1st, L. Broeckaert, F. Growet, L. Breuw, J.S. de Linde, I. Van de May, & A. van Ring.
Signed: Jas. H. Moore, Master. H. Shaw, Purser.

April 2nd – Antwerp. 2/4/12. J. Ehmig signed articles as Asst Cook, wages £3 15/ per mth, comcg 30/3/12.
Signed: Jas. H. Moore, Master. H. Shaw, Purser.

April 2nd – Antwerp. 2/4/12. G. Luxon, trimmer, promoted to Fireman, 29/3/12, wages £5 10/ per mth.

Signed: Jas. H. Moore, Master. H. Shaw, Purser.

April 2ⁿᵈ – Antwerp. 2/4/12. H. Torner, fireman, disrated to trimmer ¼/12, wages £5 per mth, he being unable to perform the duties of such.
Signed: Jas. H. Moore, Master. H. Shaw, Purser.

April 3ʳᵈ – Antwerp. ¾/12. Copy of above entry handed to H. Torner, his reply being 'All right.'
Signed: Jas. H. Moore, Master. H. Shaw, Purser.

April 7ᵗʰ – Latitude 49° 27' N, Longitude 15° 35' W. 7/4/12. G. Luxon, trimmer, was this day seen by surgeon, suffering from burns of second degree of left arm, caused by back-draught of fire. Placed off duty.
Signed: Jas. H. Moore, Master. H. Shaw, Purser. W.A. Bailey (mrcs, London) surgeon.

April 9ᵗʰ – Latitude 48° 4' N, Longitude 26° 30' W. 9/4/12. G. Luxon, trimmer, progressing favourably.
Signed: Jas. H. Moore, Master. H. Shaw, Purser. W.A. Bailey (mrcs) surgeon.

April 13ᵗʰ – Latitude 43° 2' N, Longitude 44° 13' W. 13/4/12. G. Luxon resumed work of a sutiable [sic] light nature.
Signed: Jas. H. Moore, Master. H. Shaw, Purser. W.A. Bailey (mrcs) surgeon.

April 14ᵗʰ – 3.50am. Latitude 43° 56½' N, Longitude 46° 43' W. 14/4/12. Surgeon was called to see Dozko Oziro, aged three months, and on examination found child to be quite dead. He had not been medically treated whilst on board and post mortem examination found that the child had died from early broncho-pneumonia.
Signed: Jas. H. Moore, Master; W.A. Bailey (mrcs), surgeon; H. Shaw, purser.

April 14ᵗʰ – Noon. Latitude 41° 38' N, Longitude 48° 20' W. 14/4/12. The body of Dozko Oziro committed to the deep.
Signed: Jas. H. Moore, Master; H. Shaw, purser, W.A. Bailey (mrcs) surgeon.

April 19ᵗʰ – St John, NB. 19/4/12. J. Flood, A. Stamberg & J. Maguire, cattlemen, deserted, leaving no effects behind.
Signed: Jas. H. Moore, Master; H. Shaw, purser.

April 20ᵗʰ – St John, NB. 20/4/12. S. Simpkins & T. O'Brien, F.men, for using profane language to a Customs official, & A. de Ruijter, Asst Pass. Ck, for being drunk, were lodged in St John jail.
Signed: Jas. H. Moore, Master; H. Shaw, purser.

April 22ⁿᵈ – St John, NB. 22/4/12. R. Klacker signed articles as Trimmer. 1/ per mth. J. Walters as Asst Steward, 1/- mth.
April 22ⁿᵈ – St John, NB. 22/4/12. B. Englischer, Asst Stwd, 2/. T. Meinschat and D. Driscoll, trimmers, deserted ship this day leaving no effects behind. S/M notified. Dis As deposited. Wages due 1/5/5, 1/8/7, 2/10/1.
Signed: Jas. H. Moore, Master; H. Shaw, purser.

April 22ⁿᵈ – St John, NB. 22/4/12. A.H. Notley, 3ʳᵈ Mate, paid off.
Signed: Jas. H. Moore, Master; H. Shaw, purser.
April 23ʳᵈ – St John, NB. 23/4/12. The following men were this day paid off. P. Krause & W. Bomberg, Asst Stwds; J. Ehmig, Asst Cook; J. Van Almen, 3ʳᵈ baker, L. Aerts, Asst Stwd & F.

Jones, Ship's Cook.
Signed: Jas. H. Moore, Master; H. Shaw, purser.

April 23rd – St John, NB. 2¾/12. The following men deserted ship this day, leaving no effects behind: G. Pfuhl & K.A. Andersen, ABs, J. Penna, Seaman. J. Johansen, AB; A.R. Janssen, seaman. Dis As deposited with s/Master. Wages due 2/6/4, ½/2, 3/14/6, 1/14/11.
Signed: Jas. H. Moore, Master; H. Shaw, purser.

April 24th – 6.30am, St John, NB. 24/4/12. L. Michael, Asst Stwd, fell down No. 6 hold, sustaining injuries to arms and back. Removed to General Hospital.
Signed Jas. H. Moore, Master; H. Shaw, purser; _____ surgeon.

April 24th – St John, NB. 24/4/12. C. Lightening & W. Bickman signed articles as Trimmers, wages £5 per month. J. Thorpe signed as Seaman, wages £5 per month. C. Lightening failed to join.
Signed: Jas. H. Moore, Master; H. Shaw, purser.

April 25th – St John, NB. 25/4/12. J.H. Moore, Master, signed clear of articles.
Signed: Jas. H. Moore, Master; H. Shaw, purser.

April 26th – L. Michael, Asst Stwd, paid off.
Signed Jas. H. Moore, Master; H. Shaw, purser.

April 26th – St John, NB. 26/4/12. A.H. Sargent, Chief Mate, superseded [sic] J.H. Moore as Master, all papers being turned over to him.
Signed: Jas. H. Moore, Master; H. Shaw, purser, A.H. Sargent, Master.
April 26th – St John, NB. 26/4/12. A.H. Notley signed articles as 2nd Mate. Wages £11 per month.
Signed: Jas. H. Moore, Master; H. Shaw, purser.

April 26th – St John, NB. 26/4/12. H. Heald, 2nd Mate, promoted to Mate. Wages £14 per mth. W.S. Brown, 4th Mate, promoted to 3rd Mate. Wages £9 per mth.
Signed: Jas. H. Moore, Master; H. Shaw, purser.

April 26th – St John, NB. 26/4/12. Upon fine being paid, S. Simpkins, T. O'Brien and A. de Ruijter ret.d to ship.
Signed: Jas. H. Moore, Master; H. Shaw, purser.

April 26th – St John, NB. 26/4/12. J. Walters, Asst Stwd, promoted to Trimmer. Wages £5 per mth.
Signed: Jas. H. Moore, Master; H. Shaw, purser.

April 26th – St John, NB. 26/4/12. A. Charles, Greaser, and S. Simpkins, Fireman, deserted ship, leaving no effects behind. Dis. As returned to S/Master. Wages due 3/9/2, 3/1¾.
Signed: Jas. H. Moore, Master; H. Shaw, purser.

April 27th – St John, NB. 27/4/12. W.S. Thomas, Asst Stwd, promoted to Seaman. Wages £5 per mth.
Signed: Jas. H. Moore, Master; H. Shaw, purser.

April 27th – St John, NB. 27/4/12. D. Maertens, Asst Stwd, promoted to Seaman, wages £5 per mth, with H. Stock, Fireman, promoted to Greaser, wages £5 15/ per mth. P. Hill, Trimmer, promoted to Fireman, wages £5 10/ per mth. W. Bickman, Trimmer, promoted to Fireman, wages £5 10/ per mth. L. Gogo and J. Colli, Asst Stwds, promoted to Trimmers, wgs £5 4/ per month.

Signed: Jas. H. Moore, Master; H. Shaw, purser.

April 29th – Halifax. 29/4/12. J. Carroll signed articles as Seaman, wages £5 4/ per mth comcg 24/4/12. A.H. Notley, 2nd Mate, signed clear of articles. W.H. Baker signed articles as 4th Mate, wages £8 per mth.
Signed: Jas. H. Moore, Master; H. Shaw, purser.

April 29th – 11pm. Halifax. 29/4/12. On J.H. Moore, Master, rejoining ship, A.H. Sargent & H. Heald, restored former positions as Mate and 2nd Mate.
Signed: Jas. H. Moore, Master; H. Shaw, purser.

April 29th – Halifax. 29/4/12. F. Mees, Asst Stwd, deserted ship, leaving no effects behind. Wages due 2/13/6.
Signed: Jas. H. Moore, Master; H. Shaw, purser.

April 29th – Halifax. 29/4/12. O.A. Le Meix, Asst Stwd, promoted to Trimmer, wages £5 per mth, cmcg 27th in the place of L. Gogo, who was promoted from Asst Stwd to Trimmer, and he being unable to carry out the duties of such returned duties as Asst Stwd. 27/4/12.
Signed: Jas. H. Moore, Master; H. Shaw, purser.

April 29th – Halifax. 29/4/12. For loss of services, T. O'Brien, Fireman, and A. de Ruijter, Asst Cook, forfeit wages from April 20th – 25th, six days each, viz. £1-2-0 & 15/ respectively. Deducted and retained by Master.
Signed: Jas. H. Moore, Master; H. Shaw, purser.

'The above entry, dated the 29th April 1912, is the last entry made or contained in this logbook.' Stamp 14 May 1912. Signed W.H. Williams, Superintendent, Mercantile Marine Office, Dock Street, London.

OTHER entries, contained elsewhere within the log –

April 14, 1912. Latitude 43° 56½' N, Longitude 46° 43' W. Death of Dozko Oziro, three months, son of Luc Oziro, labourer.
    A Russian Galician from Tydowkowice. Died of bronchopneumonia. Certified by J.H. Moore, Master; H. Shaw, purser; W.A. Bailey, surgeon. [Stamped by the shipping master of St John, NB.]
    'I certify that I have enquired into the circumstances which attended the death of the above named infant passenger, and that I am satisfied that the entry herein correctly sets forth the same and that no further inquiry is necessary.' M. G. McKeon, Superintendent of Mercantile Marine Office, Dock St, London. 15 May 1912.

Boat Drill practised	Life-Saving appliances examined	Fit and ready?	
April 7th	7/4/1912	Yes	Jas. H. Moore, Master.
May 12ᵗ	12/5/1912	Yes	A.H. Sargent, Mate

APPENDIX 2. THE *MOUNT TEMPLE* PV
PROCÈS-VERBAL BOOK, STEAMSHIP '*MOUNT TEMPLE*.'

New York Time.   Sunday April 14, 1912.

AM
6.35 Ex (Exchange) T.R.s (time rushes) *Californian* – West – Nil.
6.50 Ex T.R.s *Parisian* – West – Nil.
7.45 *Titanic* working.
9.53 Ex T.R.s *Amerika* – East – Nil
10.10 Ex T.R.s *Baltic* – East – Nil

PM
4.15 Standing by – Several ships busy.
4.18 Sigs M.Z.N. [*Parisian*] – Nil
4.37 Ex T.R.s *Carpathia* – East – Nil.
4.38 Ex T.R.s *Antillian* – East – Nil.

8.30 M.G.Y. [*Titanic*] and M.C.E. [Cape Race] working.
9.55 (Equivalent to 11.41pm *Mount Temple* time, difference 1 hour 46 minutes from New York time). Sigs M.P.A. [*Carpathia*] Nil.
10.25 (12.11 ship's time) *Titanic* sending C.Q.D. Says requires assistance. Gives position – Cannot hear me. Advise my Captain – His position, 41.46 N., 50.14 W. {Nobody else answers
10.35 (12.21) M.G.Y. [*Titanic*] gets M.P.A. [*Carpathia*] and says 'Struck iceberg; come to our assistance at once.'
10.40 (12.26) M.G.Y. [*Titanic*] still calling C. Q. D.
10.40 Our Captain reverses ~~engines~~ ship and steams for *Titanic*. [Added in brackets alongside: We are about 50 miles off.]
10.48 (12.34) *Frankfurt* gives M.G.Y. [*Titanic*] his position (39.47 N, 52.10 W)
10.55 (12.41) *Titanic* calling S.O.S.
10.57 (12.43) *Titanic* calling *Olympic*.
10.59 (12.45) *Titanic* working *Carpathia*.
11.00 (12.46) *Titanic* calling *Virginian* and C.Q.D.
11.10 (12.56) *Titanic* calling C.Q.D.
11.20 (1.06) *Titanic* gets *Olympic* and says 'Captain says get your boats ready. Going down fast at the head.'
11.25 (1.11) *Frankfurt* says 'Our Captain will go for you.'
11.27 (1.13) *Titanic* calling C.Q.D. and *Baltic*.
11.30 (1.16) *Titanic* calling C.Q.D.
11.35 (1.21) *Olympic* sends M.S.G. to *Titanic*. *Titanic* replies 'We are putting the women off in the boats.'
11.41 (1.27) *Titanic* says C.Q.D., Engine room flooded.
11.43 (1.29) *Titanic* tells *Olympic* 'Sea calm.'
11.45 (1.31) *Frankfurt* asks: 'Are there any boats around you already?' No reply.
11.47 (1.33) *Olympic* sends M.S.G. to *Titanic*. *Titanic* acknowledges it and sends 'Rd.' (Received).
11.55 (1.41) *Frankfurt* and *Birma* calling *Titanic*. No reply.

Monday, April 15, 1912.

AM
12.10 (1.56) *Olympic*, *Frankfurt* and *Baltic* calling *Titanic*. No reply.

12.25 (2.11) *Birma* tells *Frankfurt* he is 70 miles from *Titanic*.

12.50 (2.36) All quiet now. *Titanic* hasn't spoken since 11.47pm.

1.25 (3.11) *Carpathia* sends: 'If you are there, we are firing rockets.'

1.40 (3.26) *Carpathia* calling *Titanic*.

1.58 (3.44) *Birma* thinks he hears *Titanic*, so sends 'Steaming full speed to you; shall arrive with you 6 in the morning. Hope you are safe. We are only 50 miles now.'

2.00 (3.46) *Carpathia* calls *Titanic*.

3.00 (4.46) All quiet; we're stopped amongst pack ice.

3.05 (4.51) *Birma* and *Frankfurt* working.

3.20 (5.06) *Birma* and *Frankfurt* working. We back out of ice and cruise around. Big bergs about.

3.25 (5.11) *Californian* calls C.Q. I answer him and advise him of *Titanic* and send him *Titanic*'s position.

3.40 (5.26) *Californian* working *Frankfurt*. *Frankfurt* sends him the same.

4.00 (5.46) *Californian* working *Virginian*.

4.25 (6.11) *Californian* working *Birma*.

5.20 (7.06) Sigs. *Californian*; wants my position; send it. We're very close.

6.00 (7.46) Much jamming.

6.45 (8.31) *Carpathia* reports rescued 20 boatloads.

7.15 (9.01) More jamming.

7.30 (9.16) *Baltic* sends M.S.G. to *Californian*: 'Stand by immediately. You have been instructed to do so frequently. Balfour, Inspector.'

7.40 (9.26) *Carpathia* calls C.Q. and says: 'No need to stand by him; nothing more can be done.' Advise my Captain, who has been cruising around the ice field with no result. Ship reversed.

9.15 (11.01) *Carpathia* and *Olympic* still busy. Standing by rest of day. *Carpathia* and *Olympic* very busy all day. Much jamming going on.

APPENDIX 3. THE *MOUNT TEMPLE* CREW AGREEMENT

Name	Age	Born	Address	Last ship	Occupation
Jas H. Moore	51	Birkenhead	11 Neville Rd, Waterloo, Lpl	Same	Master
A.H. Sargent	45	Cork	23 College Rd,	do	1st Mate
H. Heald	38	Chorley	Stonelea, Chorley	do	2nd Mate Prom 1 – 26/4
A.H. Notley	35	Cork	15 Nightingale Lane, Hornsey.	do	3rd Mate Left 22/4/12
W.S. Brown	30	Skelton	90 High St, Skelton	do	4th Mate Prom 3rd 26/4
Frank Livett	34	London	20 Ennis Rd, Finsbury Pk	?	Carpenter
James Parsons	47	Torquay	61 Sebastopol St, Swansea	do	Boatswain
H. Marner	24	London	62 Culloden St, Poplar	'	AB
A. Nylander	28	Russia	On board	do	AB
L. Pickelman	27	Bavaria	40 Swete St, Plaistowdo		AB
G. Pfuhl	34	Germany	62 Culloden St, Poplar		AB
J.P. Johansen	24	Denmark	Dow's boarding house Glengall Rd, E	'	AB Deserted 23/4

Name	Age	Origin	Address	Previous Ship	Rating
A. Norgrove	28	Wellington NZ	41 Southwell, Grove Rd, Leytonstone	'	Seaman
A. McLeod	25	Stornoway	80 Glengall Rd, L.	do	Seaman
J. Martin	23	London	147 Cornwall Rd Notting Hill	do	AB
F. Gibson	22	do	41 Southwell Grove Rd, Leytonstone	'	AB
A.P. da Costa	32	Portugal	Sailors Home, L.	*Thirlby*	AB
C. Gutschmidt	22	Germany	62 Culloden St, Poplar	Same	Seaman
D.R. Jansson	24	Sweden	do	do do	Seaman Deserted 2¾
L.R. Reidersson	27	do	Scan Home, L.	do	AB Deserted 2¾
James W. Blake	25	London	13 Great Bath St Clerkenwell	HMS *Pembroke*	Seaman
James Downey	24	do	47 Burcham St, Poplar	*Avondale C.*	Seaman
J.W. Penna	24	Adelaide	Scan Home, L.	*Wanderer*	Seaman Deserted 23/4
John H. Budworth	17	London	9 Bedford Row, Holborn	'	Deck boy
J. Durrant	21	do	35 Hughan Rd, Stratford (London)	*Victoria*	Marconi operator did not appr to rec wages
R. Telaelir	37	Germany	Nieder-Lomnitz Gy	*Montreal*	Trimmer did not appr
J. Thorpe	22	London	8 Banestead Rd, Meenhead	*Cruizer*	Seaman
A.H. Sargent	45	Cork	23 College Rd, Lpool	Continues	Master
A.H. Notley	35	Cork	15 Nightingale Lane, Hornsey	do	2nd Mate
W.H. Baker	40	Reading	23 Grasmere Drive, Liscard	*Emp of Britain*	4th Mate
Jas H. Moore	51	B'head	Waterloo, Lpl	Continues	Master
A.H. Sargent	45	Cork	Lpool	Continues	1st Mate
James Carroll	33	Lpool	4 Ellenboro St, Lpool	*Astarle*	AB
John Noel Gillett	37	Seacombe	Silverbeed Rd, Scmbe	Same	1st Engineer
Robert G. Cragg	34	Bootle	144a Brownhill Rd, Catford	'	2nd Engineer
J. Brown	31	Lpool	185 Prescott Rd, Lpool	do	3rd Engineer
A.C. (Alfred) Hill	39	London	11 Priory Hill, Dover	do	4th Engineer
Herbert A. Paxton	21		58 Clovelly Rd, Soton	do	5th Engineer
Arthur Hugh Reed	21	do	55 Atherley Rd Hill,	do First	6th Engineer
J. Smith	29	London	39 Lincoln St, Leytonstone	Same	Engnrs' Storekeeper
W. Cartin	49	L'pool	80 Glengall Rd, M'wall	do	Donkeyman
T. Williams	40	London	33 Trooper Rd Custom H,	do	Greaser
R. Hopkins	31	do	1 Dock Ctges, Poplar	do	do
W. Charles	24	do	30 Whiteman St, Custom h.	'	do Deserted 26/4
S. Simpkins	29	do	81 Woodstock St, CanningTn	'	Fireman Deserted 26/4
F. Duggan	30	do	39 Partree St, P'lar.	do	Fireman
G. Bell	28	do	54 S water R., Bow.	do	Fireman
W. Reeves	21	do	39 Burchan St, P'lar.	do	Fireman

The *Mount Temple's* crew agreement for the voyage coinciding with the *Titanic* disaster.

H. Stock	31	do	14 Havana St, M'wall	do	Fman promoted Greaser
Timothy O'Brien	31	do	52 Corporation St, W Ham	'	Fireman
Charles Sambrook	32	do	11 Endive St, Stepney	*Galway Castle*	Fireman
W. Evans	31	do	59 Ordnance Rd, Canning Tn	*Minnewaska*	Fireman
T. Allison	30	do	11 Woodstock St, do.	*Highland Laddie*	Fireman
C. Robertson	28	do	33 Dongola Rd, Plaistow	*Montrose*	Fireman
D. Sullivan	34	do	20 Kelland Rd, do.	*Abchurch*	Fireman
~~J Pearce~~	~~36~~	~~do~~	~~5 Rowat Rd, Blackwall~~	~~Same~~	~~Trimmer~~ Failed to join
G. Theobald	36	do	30 Victoria Bds, Clerkenwell	'	Trimmer
~~G. Pearce~~	~~31~~	~~do~~	~~5 Brunswick Pce, B'Wall~~	'	~~Trimmer.~~ Failed to join
C. Brady	23	Carrickfergus	4 Eagling Rd, Bow	'	Trimmer

Name	Age	Origin	Address	Ship	Role
George W. Luxon	24	London	37 Wellington St, Bromley	*Durham Castle*	Trimmer promoted to Fireman 29/3/12
Daniel Driscoll	20		1 Bloomsbury St, Poplar	*Galway Castle*	Trimmer Deserted 22/4 St John
John Wm Spooner	21	do	71 Willis St, do	*Montezuma*	Trimmer
P.W. Hill	23	do	69 do	*Dunluce Castle*	Trimmer prom. Fireman 27/4
T. Meinschad	24	Austrian	Germ. House Perg	*Montrose*	Trimmer Deserted 22/4 St John
H. Krietsch	33	German	14 Fosse du Bourg, Hamburg	Foreign	Trimmer
H. Tormer	24	Swedish	S.H. Yarbies	do	Fireman degraded to Trimmer 1/4 Form M
Chas Laitinen	26	Sw'land	Keteringfor, Finland	*Moama*	Trimmer Failed to Join StJ
W. Beckman	39	Chelsea	16 High Gate St, Canning Tn	*Kaimate*	Trimmer pro F'man
Harold J. Shaw	24	Liverpool	12 Risington Rd Egremont Ches.	Same	Purser
William Arthur Bailey	38	Liverpool	437 West Derby Rd Liverpool	do	Surgeon
Geo. Hy. Scott	37	Bristol	67 Woodland Rd, Bristol	do	Chief Steward
Thomas H. Bird	35	Reading	3 Polygon, Clifton	do	2nd Steward
Percy Thos Stacey	29	S. Shields	96 E. Ferry Rd, L.	do	Bar & Storekeeper
J. Symanski	46	Galicia	Antwerp	do	Stewardess
Ernest Pretty	18	Charlton	17 Wellington Rd, Charlton	*Lady Cordwright*	Captain's Steward
W. Kelly	20	London	37 Claremont St, Nth Woolwich	1st Ship	Officers' Steward
S. Atkins	20	Greenwich	6 Laurel Blgs, Kent	Same	Asst Steward
H. Peske	20	Litherland	243 Crosby Rd, Seaforth	*Montrose*	Asst Steward
P. Wilson	26	London	12 Offley Rd, Brixton	Same	Engineer's Steward
Frank Vidler	15	do	10 Bataan St, Plaistow	*Spheroid*	Asst Engrs' Stward
Frans Venesoen	42	Belgium	Antwerp	Same	Chief Steerage Steward
H.B. v Langwilt	36	Belgium	Rotterdam	do	2nd Stge Stwd & Interpeter
J.C. Irwin	24	London	173 Gloucester Rd, Peckham	do	Asst Steward
A. Ellis	35	Walmer	29 Granville Gar. Shepherd's Bush	do	Asst Steward
Jozef Colli	23	Belgium	Antwerp	do	Asst Steward promoted
Lodewijk Michiel	21				
Ferd. Marx	27	Germany	do	do	Asst Steward
T. Bull	42	Belgium	do	do	do
D. Maertens	20	Holland	Antwerp	Same	Asst Steward promoted to Seaman 27/4
A. Peeters	30	Belgium	do	do	Asst Steward

S. Bray	18	London	16a Winnifred St, Nth Woolwich	do	do
J. Van Loon	23	Belgium	Antwerp	do	do
Louis Kockx	35	do	do	do	do
Koes Sorus	33	do	do	do	do
L. Aerts	23	Belgium	Antwerp	same ship	Asst Steward Left MC 23/4 St John
Fr. Peerens	26	do	do	do	
Os. La Meir	20	do	do	do	
D. Van Dyck	28	do	do	do	Prom to
B. Englischer	26	Poland	44 Clifton S. Oxford Circus		First Asst Stwd Deserted 26/4 StJ
Fredk Geo. Sanders	40		Croydon 7 Stanley Villas Wallington do		Asst Stwd
Frank Gasson	21	Dorking	1 Atholdene Rd, Earlsfield	do	do
G. Versbreper	32	Holland	Antwerp	*Montrose*	do
J.P. Dunn	19	Nottingham	12 Gilling St, Ladywell	*Bronian*	do
C.H.S. Smith	27	Madras	19 East Terrace, Gravesend	First	do
E. Defrates	25	Broadstairs	48 Millman St, Bloomsbury	*Dorset*	do
W.S. Thomas	20	London	7 Wotton Rd, Deptford	*Cairnrona*	do prom Seaman 27/4
H.H. Stone	24	Essex	2 Woodstock Rd, Forest Gate	*Durham*	do
J. Downs	25	London	110 Glengall Rd	*Montfort*	do
W.E. Parsons	38	Weymouth	109 Palmerston Rd, Wood Green	*Montrose*	do
E. McIlroy	23	London	54 Beckway St, Walworh	*Canada Cape*	do
J.S. Walter	20	do	108 Berry St, Edmonton	First	do
Woolf Bomberg	26	London	20 Tenter Bldgs St Mark's S.	*Caledonia*	Asst Steward Left MC 22/4 St John
Vernon H. Sewell	26	Enfield	Elm Villas, S. Chingford	First	do
Chas Pickard	33	Peckham	30 Ruskin Ave. Manor Park	*Jas Williamson*	do
S. Allan	26	London	2 Brighton House Camberwell Green	First	do
E. Withall	28	do	122 Royson Rd, do	do	do
H. Rendell	20	do	6 Durham Rd, Canning Town	Same	do
F. Lowry	26	do	18 Athol St, Poplar	Ausonia	do
G. Burleigh	28	Aberdeen	37 Baron Road Canning Town	*City of Aberdeen*	do
P.P. Burbon	31	London	9 Parrock St, Gravesend	First	do
J. Krawinkel	28	Belgium	Antwerp	Same	do
Jas J. Larsen	30	Denmark	17 Torrington Square, Holborn	*Heredia*	do
H. McGregor	44	Glasgow	99 Clifton Rd, Canning Tn	Same	Chief Cook
F. Jones	30	London	10 Pelly Rd. Plaistow	*Dunluce*	C. Ship's cook Left MC 23/4 St John
B. Bedford	17	do	70 Kempton Rd, E. Ham	*Minira*	Scullion
J.C. Raithby Grimsby	28		15 Ennismoor Rd, Liverpool	Same	Pass. Cook

J. Bailey	32	Manchester	53 Thorpebank Rd, Shepherds Bush	*Avondale C.*	do
P. Durlet	40	Belgium	Antwerp	Same	Asst. Pass. Cook
A. de Ruijter	35	Holland	do	do	do
W. Crossman	30	Somerset	Ravenhurst Collingwood	do	Chief Baker
G. Eykelberg	40	Holland	Antwerp	do	2nd Baker
Jan Van Almen	33	Belgium	Antwerp	Same	3rd Baker Left MC 23/4 St John
Benjamin Thomas	42	London	4 Monteith Rd, Bow	do	Asst Baker
G. Strickland	30	Gravesend	33 Athol St, Poplar	*Ionic*	Asst Stwd
A. Gaurines	48	London	14 Tomlin Terrace, Limehouse		Chief Butcher
F. Potter	21	do	36 Clevedon St, Mile End	First	Asst do
J. Hardstone	24	Catford	158 Rushey Green, Catford	*Mooltan*	do
Frans Mees	20	Belgian	17 Impasse des Roses, Antwerp		Asst Stwd Deserted 29/4 H.fax
Louis Gogo	25	do	24 Quai du Rhin, Antwerp	*Montrose*	Asst Stwd
Ch. Naudts	25	do	Impasse Antoines Haut Chemin	Same	do
J. Stevens	25	do	32 Place de l'ancien canal	do	do
H. Van Beroud		Dutch	271 Rue Zetternam	*Montrose*	do
T. Stolemoney	36	Belgian	147 L. Rue Van Bloes	do	do
Paul Krause	27	German	21 March'au Lie	*Samara*	Asst Stwd Left MC 24/4 St John
F. De Nys	24	Belgian	107 Rue Basse	*Montrose*	do
Leon Broeckaert	35		Haume n. Antwerp	*Montfort*	do
F. Grollet	22	do	Malines, Belgium	Foreign	do
L. Brews	20	do	do	do	do
J.S. van de Linde	26	Dutch	Amsterdam	*Montrose*	do
O. van de Mey	44	Belgian	6 Rue de Arives	*Montezuma*	do
A. van Ring	33	Dutch	30 Quai du Rhin	*Montrose*	do
John Ehmig	29	Austrian	21 Rue d'Amsterdam	Foreign	Asst Cook Left MC 23/4/ St J
Frans Wouters	25	Belgium	163 Hoff Street, Antwerp	*Lake Michigan*	Asst Stwd
J. Flood	37	Burton-on-Tweed	263 S. Martin St, Montreal.	*Montezuma*	Cattleman Deserted 19/4 St John
A. Stambery	31	London	44 Lansdowne Rd, Clapham	Same	C.man Deserted 19/4 St John
J. Maguire	44	Glasgow	75 Crown St, Glasgow	Same	C.man Deserted 19/4 St John

Shipping Office, St John, N.B.

Vessel Arrived 19th April
Articles deposited 20th 1912
    Returned 26th

Rate of exchange for right drafts on London $466 = £100

I hereby [sic] that the within named J. Hood, A. Stambery, J. Maguire, G. Phufl, Y.P. Johansen,

K.A. Andersen, J.W. Penna, D. Driscoll, J. Meinschad and B. Englischer have been left behind at this port on the alleged ground of their having deserted, that I believe the allegations to be true, and that proper entries in the official log book of such desertions have been produced to me.

I further certify that the within named L. Michael has been left behind under medical certificate in the General Public Hospital at this port, ill and unable to proceed in the vessel, having been injured in the service of the ship, and I have sanctioned his being so left.

The Master has deposited with me form CC 6, together with Dis. A and balance of wages due. Effects delivered to seaman. I further certify that I have sanctioned the discharge of the within named A.H. Notley, L. Aerts, W. Bomberg, F. Jones, Jan Van Almen, Paul Krause and John Elvinig* J. Hood, A . Stambery on the grounds of mutual consent, balance of wages due being paid in my presence.

I further certify that the within named A.H. Sargent has been promoted from Mate to Master in place of J.H. Moore. I further certify that the within named A.H. Notley, R. Klacker, J. Thorpe, Chas Laitinen, W. Beckman and F. Wouters have been engaged at this port on the terms of the ship's written agreement, which was explained to them before signing in my presence and which I am satisfied they fully understood.

I further certify that they within named H. Heald as been promoted to Mate from the 26th of April and his wages increased to £14. 0. 0. per month and the within named W.S. Brown has been promoted to 3rd Mate from 26th of April and his wages advanced to £9. 0. 0. per month.

B.S. Purdy
Shipping Master

[* John Elvinig refers to John Ehmig; L. Michael to Lodewijk Michiel.]

Shipping Master's Office, Halifax, N.S.   April 29, 1912.

This agreement was deposited on the APR 29 1912 and is this day returned.

I hereby certify that A.H. Notley has been discharged at this port by mutual consent and has signed his release in my presence. I further certify that W.H. Baker and A.H. Sargent have been engaged at this port in the terms of this agreement. I also certify that J.H. Moore has become Master and A.H. Sargent has been transferred to 1st Mate.

Signed: H.H. Drake.

DESERTED   (14)

G. Pfuhl	34	Germany	62 Culloden St, Poplar '		AB Deserted 23/4
J.P. Johansen	24	Denmark	Dow's boarding house Glengall Rd, E. '		AB Deserted 23/4
D.R. Jansson	24	Sweden	do	do	Seaman Deserted 23/4
L.R. Reidersson	27	do	Scan Home, L.	do	AB Deserted 23/4
J.W. Penna	24	Adelaide	Scan Home, L.	*Wanderer*	Seaman Deserted 23/4

W. Charles	24	London	30 Whiteman St, Custom h. '	do	Deserted 26/4
S. Simpkins	29	do	81 Woodstock St, Canning Tn '	'	Fireman Deserted 26/4
D. Driscoll	20		1 Bloomsbury St, Poplar	*Galway Castle*	Trimmer Deserted 22/4 St John
T. Meinschad	24	Austrian	Germ. House Perg	*Montrose*	Trimmer Deserted 22/4 St John
B. Englischer	26	Poland	44 Clifton S. Oxford Circus	First	Asst Stwd Deserted 22/4 St J
Frans Mees	20	Belgian	17 Impasse des Roses, Antwerp		Asst Stwd Deserted 29/4 Hlfax
J. Flood	37	Burton-on-Tweed	263 S. Martin St, Montreal	*Montezuma*	Cattleman Deserted 19/4 St John
A. Stambery	31	London.	44 Lansdowne Rd, Clapham	Same	C.man Deserted 19/4 St John
J. Maguire	44	Glasgow	75 Crown St, Glasgow	Same	C.man Deserted 19/4 St John

The *Mount Temple* photographed from the decks of the *Möwe* after being stopped by her in mid-ocean in December 1916. The Canadian Pacific liner's defensive stern gun is clearly visible. Within a short time the *Mount Temple* will be at the bottom of the North Atlantic.

Sketch of the 'highwayman' *Möwe* by the *Illustrated London News*, showing her concealed armament

Extract from the war diary of the German commerce raider SMS *Möwe* identifying her victim as the *Mount Temple*, bound from Montreal to Brest and London.

Captain of the vessel that sank the *Mount Temple*, Count Dohna Schlodien of the SMS *Möwe*.

LEFT BY CONSENT (7)   (MC = mutual consent)

A.H. Notley	35	Cork	15 Nightingale Lane, Hornsey		2nd Mate Left MC 29/4 Hfx
L. Aerts	23	Belgium	Antwerp	same ship	Asst Steward MC 2¾ St John
W. Bomberg	26	London	20 Tenter Bldgs St Mark's S	*Caledonia*	Asst Steward MC 22/4 St John
F. Jones	30	London	10 Pelly Rd. Plaistow	*Dunluce*	C. Ship's cook MC 2¾ St John
Jan Van Almen	33	Belgium Antwerp	Same	2nd Baker	MC 23/4 St John
Paul Krause	27	German	21 March'au Lie *Samara*	Asst Stwd	MC 24/4 St John
John Ehmig	29	Austrian	21 Rue d'Amsterdam	Foreign	Asst Cook MC 23/4/ St John

APPENDIX 4. THE SINKING OF THE *MOUNT TEMPLE*

The *Mount Temple*, commanded by Captain Alfred Henry Sargent, left Quebec on November 28, 1916 *en route* to Brest with a cargo of wheat, flour, corn, lumber, bacon, cheese and canned goods.

She was also carrying over 700 horses consigned to the French Government. And she had aboard 22 crates of dinosaur fossils, excavated in Alberta, intended for the British Museum. Just over a week later she encountered the German commerce raider, or 'highwayman,' SMS *Möwe* (*Seagull*), Captained by Count Dohna zu Schlodien.

Sargent, unaware of the firepower of the armament deployed against him, 'made a plucky attempt to save his ship.'

He ordered *Mount Temple*'s single gun to be readied to open fire from the stern at the enemy pursuer. As this was being done, *Möwe* fired at a range of a quarter of a mile, killing two members of the *Mount Temple* crew instantly – chief steward William Oddy (signed aboard as William Gilbert), and a Swedish AB named John Janssen. Seaman George Baker died later.

At this point, Sargent surrendered and took the way off his ship. He ordered the boats prepared, and the *Möwe* was soon alongside, ordering all crew to abandon and row over. A party of Kriegsmarine officers took a boat in the opposite direction and placed time-delay explosives about the *Mount Temple*.

The ship sank on Wednesday December 6, 1916 in 46 44 N, 34 05 W. This position is 600 nautical miles NNW of the Azores and 725nm from the *Titanic* wreck.

The remaining 108 men of the *Mount Temple* were taken prisoner of war.

Their former vessel lies in 14,500ft of water.

The war diary of the *Möwe* for December 6, declares:
1.45pm: Smoke sighted; course changed to head for its origin.
3.36pm: Approached a big British cargo vessel to within 600 meters. It carries a gun on the stern. Since a man aims the gun towards the *Möwe*, the order is given to fire at it. The steamer is hit in the funnel and the boat deck.

As a result of our fire, the gun on the steamer is abandoned at once. The starboard engine room of the steamer is immediately abandoned by the crew, the ship still making headway. The rudder is hard a-starboard, which makes the despatch of a boarding party very hazardous.

The boarding party reports. The name of the British freighter is *Mount Temple*, en route from Montreal via Brest to London. Two people on board are dead: William Gilbert, chief steward, and John Janson [sic], able seaman.

Furthermore, two are badly injured: Simon, the Canadian horse keeper, and Geo. Baker, a British AB. The former had to have his right foot amputated on board the *Möwe*. The latter died during the night as a result of injuries sustained. His mortal remains are committed to the sea the next morning. The ceremony is attended by a German delegation and all the British.

The gun (7.5 cm) could not be transferred because of its great weight (ca. 1 ton) and the heavy swell. The lock, viewfinder and a cartridge are taken on board. Around 4.30pm smoke is detected, probably from another steamer, headed towards the *Möwe*.

The *Mount Temple* complement is taken over, and the ship itself scuttled with explosive charges at 6.10pm. The newcomer is pursued at once. Obviously, it has great speed and has gained such a lead that seizure is impossible. *Möwe* returns to the sinking site of the *Mount Temple* and passes it 3 nautical miles to the northward. No trace of the ship is seen.

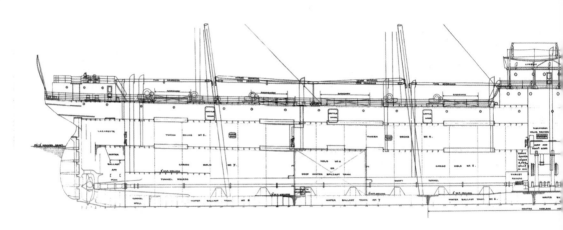

Cutaway plan of SS *Mount Temple*.

RRANGEMENT

MPLE.' — № 709.

- I FOOT.

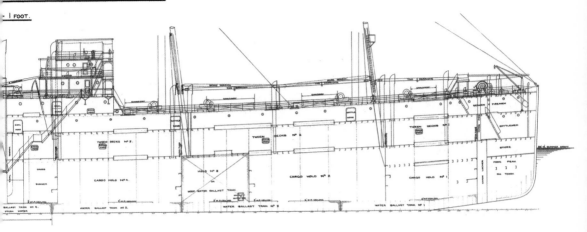

ACKNOWLEDGEMENTS

The author wishes to acknowledge the material assistance of James Kay, Captain Jack Sanderson, who also provided the benefit of his long experience, Paul Slish of Buffalo, New York, who proof-read the manuscript, liaised with the descendants of Willem Keurvorst and contacted the family of Stanislaw Mlynarczyk and Herbert Heald on my behalf, Geoff Whitfield, who undertook some research in Liverpool, Barbara Currie for providing photographs in her exclusive copyright taken by former *Mount Temple* replacement officer W.H. Baker, Rob Kamps for his efforts in Antwerp and for assisting in the research of Dr F.C. Quitzrau, John Alcock, Ruth Ball, the Berkeley Library TCD, Ray Birnie, Margaret and Iain Felton, Lisabeth Fette, Hanneke Blindenbach, Arnon Ehmig, Elizabeth Lomax, John Hartley, Jane Hemming, Holger Hempel, Hilda Klughart, Midori Brown, the Havard family, Derek Grout, Merseyside Maritime Museum, Donald and Doreen McCallum; Jane McPhee, Lee & Audrey Wark Tim Notley, Christopher Notley, Tony Woolfall, National Maritime Museum, Greenwich, *Bundesarchiv-Militärarchiv,* Koblenz; Marine Museum, Wilhelmshaven; Southampton City Archives, Brad Keurvorst, Barbara Batt, Stan Krolczyk, John Reed, Friederike Von Starck, Thomas Weiss and Valerie Wissinger, and Lee and Audrey Wark.

Any omissions are regretted, and my thanks are due to a significant number of others who were of ancillary assistance.

FURTHER READING

The transcripts of both official inquiries are available for study. 'The Loss of the SS *Titanic*, Report, Evidence &c,' can be ordered in a 972-page tome from the Public Record Office: PRO Publications, Ruskin Avenue, Kew, Surrey, TW9 4DU, United Kingdom (ISBN: 1 873 162 707).

The 1,162-page American report, today entitled '*Titanic* Disaster 1912 Hearings' is available from Documents on Demand (1800-227-2477, or from outside North America 1-301-951-4631), email: cisdod@lexis-nexis.com. DoD is an arm of the Congressional Information Service, Inc., 4520 East-West Highway, Bethesda, Maryland 20814-3389 USA.

Both transcripts are available in a CD-ROM produced by the PRO at Kew entitled '*Titanic*: The True Story' (see: http://www.pro.gov.uk). They have also been uploaded to the internet via the Titanic Inquiry Project at http://www.titanicinquiry.org

Books specific to the controversy over the *Titanic*'s mystery ship include:

Harrison, Leslie, *A Titanic Myth* (William Kimber & Co, 1986)
Molony, Senan, Titanic *and the Mystery Ship* (Tempus, 2006)
Padfield, Peter, *The* Titanic *and the* Californian (Hodder & Stoughton, 1965)
Reade, Leslie, *The Ship That Stood Still* (Patrick Stephens Ltd, 1993)
Other books of interest include:
Beesley, Lawrence, *The Loss of the SS* Titanic (William Heinemann, 1912)
Bisset, Sir James, *Tramps and Ladies* (Angus & Robertson, 1959)
Boothby, Cmdr H.B. *Spunyarn* (Foulis, 1935)
Gracie, Col. Archibald, *The Truth About the* Titanic (Mitchell Kennerley, 1913)
Lightoller, Charles, Titanic *and Other Ships* (Nicholson and Watson, 1935)
Rostron, Sir Arthur, *Home From The* Sea (Macmillan, 1931)

PICTURE CREDITS

INDEX

A contemporary Canadian Pacific card, advertising the Atlantic crossing.